THE HOME THAT WAS OUR COUNTRY

A Memoir of Syria

Alia Malek

NATION BOOKS
New York

Published by Nation Books, an imprint of Perseus Books, LLC, a subsidiary of Hachette
Book Group, Inc.
116 East 16th Street, 8th Floor
New York, NY 10003

Nation Books is a co-publishing venture of the Nation Institute and Perseus Books.

Books published by Nation Books are available at special discounts for bulk purchases
in the United States by corporations, institutions, and other organizations. For more
information, please contact the Special Markets Department at Perseus Books, 2300
Chestnut Street, Suite 200, Philadelphia, PA 19103, or call (800) 810-4145, ext. 5000,
or e-mail special.markets@perseusbooks.com.

Designed by Linda Mark

Library of Congress Cataloging-in-Publication Data

Names: Malek, Alia, 1974– author.
Title: The home that was our country : a memoir of Syria / Alia Malek.
Description: New York, NY : Nation Books, an imprint of Perseus Books, LLC,
    a subsidiary of Hachette Book Group, Inc., 2017.
Identifiers: LCCN 2016037114 (print) | LCCN 2016050029 (ebook) |
    ISBN 9781568585321 (hardcover) | ISBN 9781568585338 (ebook)
Subjects: LCSH: Malek, Alia, 1974– —Family. | Damascus (Syria)—Biography. |
    Damascus (Syria)—History. | Syria—History.
Classification: LCC DS99.D3 M346 2017 (print) | LCC DS99.D3 (ebook) | DDC
    956.91/440423092 [B]—dc23
LC record available at https://lccn.loc.gov/2016037114

10 9 8 7 6 5 4 3 2

For my parents,
for Maha,
for Teta

Author's grandmother, ca. 1955

What crime did I commit for you to annihilate me, my brother?
I will never release the binds of this embrace.
And I will never let you go.

—*"He Embraces His Murderer," Mahmoud Darwish*

ماذَا جَنَيْتُ لِتَغْتَالَنِي يَا أَخِي.

لَنْ أَحُلَّ وِثَاقَ العِنَاقِ

ولَنْ أَترُكَكْ

— **"يعانق قاتله" للشاعر محمود درويش**

CONTENTS

TRANSLITERATION NOTE

THE CHALLENGE OF TRANSLITERATING FROM ARABIC INTO ENGLISH is that there are many systems used by authors and scholars to represent the Arabic sounds and short/long vowels that can only be approximated in the Roman alphabet. Strict adherence to this or any other system of transliteration, however, can often obfuscate a word or concept readers may already have come across, especially with Syrian towns and names constantly appearing in the news over the course of the current conflict.

Many readers may be unaware that there are various spoken dialects of Arabic that differ from Modern Standard Arabic (MSA). Thus my goal was to stay as true as possible to both Syrian dialect when spoken and to correct MSA when called for—without compromising readability for non-Arabic-speaking readers. For that reason, I have made a few choices. First, I have opted not to use most diacritics, which might end up confusing more readers than they would help, but I did represent the back-of-the-throat ع as a (') and the ء, or glottal stop, as ('). And second, where there are Arabic words, proper nouns, or English approximations of Arabic concepts that readers will likely recognize—for example Tahrir, Alawite, Shiite, Ain—I've opted to use them.

A Note on Names

Almost all names have been changed in this book to safeguard as much as possible people's privacy and safety—this includes both given and family names. Pseudonyms are consistent with era, language, and meaning of original name. Should a real Abdeljawwad al-Mir exist anywhere, it is purely by coincidence.

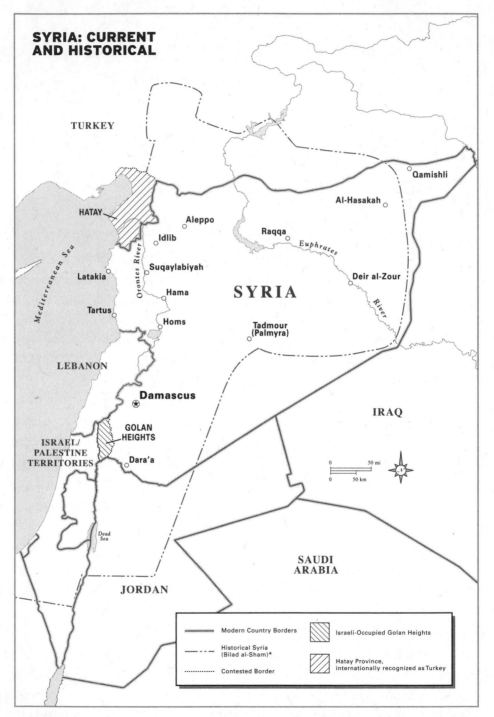

SYRIA: CURRENT
AND HISTORICAL

TURKEY

HATAY

Aleppo

Idlib

Al-Hasakah

Qamishli

Raqqa

Euphrates

Mediterranean Sea

Orontes River

Latakia

Suqaylabiyah

Deir al-Zour

Hama

SYRIA

River

Tartus

Homs

Tadmour
(Palmyra)

LEBANON

Damascus

IRAQ

GOLAN
HEIGHTS

ISRAEL/
PALESTINE
TERRITORIES

Dara'a

0   50 mi

0   50 km

N

Dead
Sea

SAUDI
ARABIA

JORDAN

	Modern Country Borders		Israeli-Occupied Golan Heights
— · —	Historical Syria (Bilad al-Sham)*		Hatay Province, internationally recognized as Turkey
·········	Contested Border		

*Bilad al-Sham does not refer to a fixed geographic entity with sharp border distinctions as
shown on the map. This rendering is merely to assist the reader visualize what is elucidated
in the text.

PROLOGUE: LEAVING

Damascus, May 2013

B Y THE TIME I LEFT SYRIA IN MAY 2013, MANY IN MY FAMILY WERE happy to see me go.

For them, the day hadn't come soon enough.

The country was already more than two years into the blackness that would consume it. Its disintegration would see hundreds of thousands killed; millions displaced from their homes both inside and outside Syria's borders; villages, towns, and cities in rubble; unknown numbers disappeared; and the futures of several generations stolen.

When authoritarian regimes in Tunisia, Egypt, and Libya were overthrown in 2011, all eyes turned to Syria as if it would be next. But despite both peaceful and armed opposition, the regime that had ruled Syria for over forty years remained entrenched. Syrian president Bashar al-Assad—who had inherited power from his father, Hafez al-Assad—blamed a foreign conspiracy at work against Syria. The regime dismissed any reports that would belie its account of events as fabrications, venomously accusing the media of perpetuating lies. Western journalists had already disappeared and died in Syria to much international attention. Syrian journalists—professionals and those initiated in citizen reporting—were dying as well, just more silently and in greater numbers.

So as far as many in my family were concerned, my being both a dual national American and a journalist added up to nothing but trouble, and the sooner I left, the better.

While most foreign journalists were denied legal access to Syria, I had been able to enter and move about Damascus with relative ease. Though I was born abroad, both my parents are Syrian, and, more importantly, had registered my birth with the government, in anticipation of our planned return to Syria, where they had intended to raise their family. That meant that I had a Syrian national identity card and the access it can provide.

Ever since moving to Damascus in April 2011, I had been constantly answering inquiries as to what I was doing there. Although people regularly pry in Syria—most often about your relatives, your marital status or prospects, or your income and property—the question as to why I was in Damascus *now* was more than mere prosaic meddling. It was potentially dangerous.

Unlike in many other cities, there is no anonymity in Damascus. There is no disappearing into it. Four different security bodies, known collectively as the *mukhabarat*, with at least twenty-two branches in the capital alone, have for decades carried out the regime's surveillance of its people. (It is estimated that the *mukhabarat* have 65,000 full-time employees—or 1 for every 153 adult citizens—along with hundreds of thousands of part-time or unofficial employees.) They are a much less refined version of the Stasi, with very little of the East German agency's precision or accuracy. What they lack in sophistication, though, they more than make up for with gusto.

The best way to explain this is with a joke I first heard back in Syria in the 1990s. It goes like this: the world's intelligence services gather at an elite training site. Present are the CIA, the KGB, Israel's Mossad, and the Syrian *mukhabarat*. They are brought to the edge of the forest and told they must each go in, track a certain fox, and bring him back. Both the CIA and the KGB get it done in an hour. The Mossad completes the task even faster. The last to go are the Syrian *mukhabarat*. They disappear for hours into the woods. When they return, they are holding a severely beaten-up rabbit. The other agents laugh at them or are perplexed. "That's not a fox," they say. The Syrians, in their leather jackets, are coolly smoking; one of them is holding the rabbit up by his neck. Their leader responds, "He confessed. He admitted that he is a fox."

After generations of being watched over and eavesdropped on, Syrians have internalized the *mukhabarat*; even in their absence they are present.

Well before 2011, in Syria, just talking about the regime could land a person in prison, where many are quickly forgotten except by those who love them. Even Syrians abroad would sometimes unconsciously drop their voices to a hush when they criticized the regime.

Up to 2011, Syrians generally understood the difference between what information would get someone in trouble and what just accumulated in dusty files. But in the new disquiet and growing chaos, no one was sure what would be damning and to which fate. My presence was just too random. Many suspected I must be working as a *jassousseh*, a spy.

§⌁§

I HAD COME to Syria, in part, to finish the restoration that my parents had started of my maternal grandmother Salma's house, which now belonged to my mother. But I was also there because Syria had shadowed my life from birth, though I had never fully been a part of it. I wanted to be there at a moment when the entire region was in the throes of change. For an optimist, Syria was on the precipice of something better. For the pessimist, it teetered dangerously on the abyss.

I was an optimist. Syria had been to me many things until that point, from that ever-present phantom in the diaspora to a destiny it seemed I had mercifully dodged as a teenager to a frequently visited and loved homeland, one that seemed to be shackled by a ruthless regime and the geopolitical fault lines that cradled it. Now I wondered what I could be for Syria. A lawyer and a journalist, I was open to whatever role I might play in recasting the nation as it transitioned (I hoped) from decades of stifling and corrupt dictatorship into something better for all its peoples. In what would come *after*, could I teach or train lawyers or journalists? Could I advocate? Could I report?

Though I had written a few pieces for the *New York Times*, *The Nation*, and the *Christian Science Monitor* in the two years since I had moved to Damascus, they were without a byline. As far as most people in Damascus knew, I wasn't practicing journalism in Syria. Nonetheless, it made no sense to anyone that I would stay in Damascus when, as an American, I could go at any moment, a luxury and a privilege so many Syrians desperately wanted for themselves, and which I had by accident already, thanks to my parents' emigration. I tried transparency, explaining that I was thinking of writing a book about my grandmother, which I had indeed been considering for years. But in a place where nonfiction is usually only written about important men, this was an unlikely story. Similarly, explaining that I could get paid for the idea of a book, before it had been written or a single copy had been sold, was so fantastical that it invited only more suspicion.

It didn't help that as a lawyer, I had been to Palestine and Israel several times (which my family knew, even if the regime didn't). Although my work had always been on behalf of the very people—the Palestinians—whom the regime claimed to have championed more than any Arab country, that didn't change the fact that I was technically in violation of Syrian law. Anyone who has been in Israel is forbidden to come to Syria.

Then there was the reality that I was an unmarried woman who wasn't living by the rules for unmarried women, which are much harsher than those for their married counterparts. Most people in Syria assumed I lived with my parents in Baltimore and were surprised to learn I lived on my own in another city—even though I was in my late thirties. When I gently reminded them that I was a lawyer and a journalist and that I worked, they nodded politely as if to spare me further embarrassment. An unmarried woman living on her own hinted at sexual impropriety. Many Syrian women are college-educated and professionals, but that had not changed the expectation that they would be wives and mothers first, and chaste until the wedding.

Some of my family members wanted me to leave Syria simply because they loved me. In addition to fearing I might catch the regime's eye—which seemed to be tolerating my presence thus far—people had begun that year to take advantage of the regime's focus on its opponents to kidnap and ransom wealthy Syrians. Because I was an American, people might presume that money would follow me. Other relatives feared for their own safety. The regime had survived for so many years because it viewed guilt as collective or by association, and people were often punished for the sins of their kin. Even people who might be inclined to speak up tended to keep their mouths shut and their heads down so as not to endanger those they loved. Then there were the family members who imagined they could use me to curry favor with the regime, and started dangerous rumors that I was an American spy. It was never clear whether they did it just for the theatrics of distancing themselves from me or to actually get me to go.

There was nothing new for me about leaving Syria; separation has always been the defining condition of my relationship to the country. I first left Syria before I was even born, when my mother, pregnant with me, traveled to join my father in the United States for what was meant to be a temporary stay.

But in 2013, my optimism began to seem naïve. I realized that time might be running out, that the relative safety of central Damascus could evaporate from one day to the next, and that leaving this time might be more permanent than ever before. Already, people and places were rapidly disappearing from the face of the country. Though I wanted to stay as long as possible, in April 2013, my father was diagnosed with a life-threatening illness, and the prognosis was grim. I decided to take a job in the United States and be with my family as he faced his illness. My father instructed me to tell no one he was sick; thus I could only say "*Insh'allah,*" God willing, when relatives tried to cheer me in my final days, saying they'd soon see me and my parents again in Syria, once things got better. So those who wanted to see me leave, for my own safety or theirs, believed I had at last given in to reason, to their pleas, or to their own intimidation.

৪◊৪

ON ONE OF my final afternoons in Damascus, I stood on the front balcony of my grandmother's house, running my fingertips farewell over the leaves of a bitter orange tree, whose upper branches reached our second-story flat.

I did not know if I'd ever be able to return, and if so, when that would be, and what I would or wouldn't find if I did. But unlike so many Syrians who had already fled the country, often on a day they hadn't known would be their last in their homes, I was leaving somewhat on my terms. I was able to say goodbye, and I did, to everything, alive and dead, sentient or not.

Because Friday is the day of rest in Syria, there was hardly any traffic noise. People were at home; moving by car had become cumbersome, with all the checkpoints halting the flow. Only mortar and gunfire rumbled in the distance. It was also Orthodox Good Friday, and many of the city's Christians would wait until later that night to decide whether to attend Mass.

My grandmother Salma's apartment in the Tahaan Building was now restored, almost exactly as it had been in her day, and I lived in it alone, though always accompanied by her ghost and those of the others who had passed through it. From the balcony, I looked up and down the block. The trees, many of them citrus, were lush with leaves; delicious loquats were hanging in little clusters from branches tauntingly close. As in many parts of Damascus, I could smell the jasmine.

Our street, together with three others, made up the neighborhood known as Ain al-Kirish. On the south it was bound by the centuries-old, maze-like quarter known as Sarouja. The newer buildings, like the Tahaan, were erected in the 1940s and 1950s, a modern expression of a country emerging from decades of French domination and finally headed into the future.

There were many versions of how the neighborhood got its name. An *ain* is the source of a spring of water. My grandmother, according to my aunt, had said the original name had been Ain al-Shirsh, "Source of (plant) Roots," because of a spring in the area that allowed so many orchards to fill the quarter. With time, the groves were razed, houses were built, and the pronunciation changed to Ain al-Kirish.

According to the neighborhood's *mukhtar* (the official responsible for registering residents' births, marriages, and deaths), who also said there had been a spring in the area, the name derives from when there was a fee of one Syrian penny—a *qirsh*—to enter the area for its water, so it was the Spring of a Penny. In his telling, too, time had changed the pronunciation. Yet another version says that the water of that spring had bicarbonate in it, and as such, felt good in the belly, which is what *kirsh* actually means, thus the Spring of the Belly.

But *ain* can also mean "eye," and until I inquired, I had always assumed, incorrectly, that Ain al-Kirish meant "Eye of the Belly," which I quite liked. I found it poetic, because I thought this was some flowery Arabic way of saying "belly button" (which in Arabic is actually *surra*). Though I had been severed from it long ago, my attachment to this place had always felt umbilical.

After all, this was the house that in 1949 my grandmother had come to from Hama—a small city more than one hundred miles north of Damascus—after marrying my grandfather, Ameen, who was from Homs. The newlyweds had first lived together in this house when Syria was newly free, and the Tahaan had also been newly built. My mother was born in a hospital down the street and raised here. They had remained until 1970, when my grandparents moved their family to a larger house, renting the Tahaan home to a discharged and wounded veteran. This was the same year that Hafez al-Assad—father of the current ruler Bashar al-Assad—came to power, a military man himself.

Salma had intended the house for her eldest daughter, my mother, Lamya, once she married and had a family of her own. But the new tenant refused to leave, and he was protected by the law, as it favored renters over landlords, especially if they had been in the military. My mother was only able to retake the house after a new law in 2004 provided a process to resolve these sorts of disputes, as so many Syrians were locked in similar situations. Under the new law, landlords could evict their tenants if they paid them 40 percent of the property's value. It would take my mother six years to oust her mother's tenant. Salma did not live to see the house finally back in the family's possession.

My parents wanted the house in Damascus because, nearing their own years of retirement, they missed home, and their desire to return to Syria had begun to outweigh their need for sure footing in the United States. They were established in Baltimore, and could begin to dream again of Syria. With their own house in Damascus, coming for extended visits would not be prohibitively expensive or uncomfortable. After taking the house back, they had decided to restore it—though, with the exception of updates to the bathrooms and kitchen, they did not really change it.

None of us knew now if they would ever see it again or spend any time in it, as no one knew anymore who would possess the country (or the house) in the future.

As I began to lose myself in these thoughts, I looked across at the neighbors watching me from their balconies. Our shared street was narrow, and we could easily talk to each other over the divide. We saw each other there every day—when we had our morning coffee, still in our bathrobes; when we wrung and hung the laundry at midday; when we smoked an afternoon cigarette; when we watered the plants at sunset; and when we cracked sunflower seeds with friends and family and chatted into the night. After the violence started, we'd often rush out onto our balconies to figure out, together, what had just happened and, really, to be a little less alone in our fear. Christian and Muslim, we'd always wished one another a healthy year during our respective holidays, shared our best home cooking, and ululated for the neighborhood's new brides and grooms when they left their parents' homes.

As I smiled and waved at the family across the street that afternoon, a gust of wind came through, and we all heard a crash. We looked around until one of the neighbors' children pointed to a higher balcony next door to me. A birdcage had fallen onto the roof of a one-story shop below, and a colorful parakeet was hopping around, dazed.

The bird's owner came running out onto his balcony. "*Salaam*," he greeted all of us, and we hurriedly told him what had happened, gesturing to the bird on the loose. Someone yelled down to the young boys kicking a ball on the street, telling them to scale the shop's roof and catch the bird before it could escape.

Instead, the boys startled the bird and it flew to my balcony. Everyone yelled at me to grab it, but it fluttered and perched out of my reach.

The owner laughed and told us not to worry; this bird wanted to come back to its cage, he assured us.

We all tried to coax it back, me especially, as I was still nearest to the bird, but then it flapped frantically and suddenly flew away in a flash of green and yellow.

"Freedom!" laughed the owner.

"At least for him," someone answered.

We looked around nervously and hoped that no one who might inform on us had heard our transgression.

"Poor thing," a woman covered for us all. "A cat will get him."

Thinking it better to avoid any further metaphorical conversation, I retreated from the balcony into the house to continue packing.

I had not had time to furnish the house completely; most of it was still empty. My footsteps echoed loudly. Only the master bedroom and my office were complete; my father and I had picked out the furniture together when he had come to visit in November 2011, before he knew he was ill, though the disease had been progressing for years. During that trip, he was still hoping against hope that Syria wasn't about to leave him.

In the bedroom, he had kept pajamas, and in the bathroom, as I began removing my own toiletries, I saw the razor and shaving cream he had tucked away for his return. Staring at these small items, I thought of all the little and big things Syrians all over the country had left behind, thinking they were coming back. And as happens in war and displacement, I wondered who would use them again first—their owners, if they lived? Or those who would squat or borrow houses and things that weren't theirs but, at least for the time being, appeared to be abandoned.

I, too, decided to leave things in Salma's house, as if to reassure her that I would return. Most importantly, I left a framed picture on my nightstand of me as a child, laughing with her and my sister in a moment of silliness, just months before her terrible fate would befall her.

PART 1

Generations

Author's great-grandfather, c. 1921.

Author's great-grandmother, middle of back row, surrounded
by her children, c. 1928. She would have one more child.
Author's grandmother is in front row, center.

1

ORIGINS

Suqaylabiyah, 1889 – Hama, 1949

E VERY FAMILY HAS ITS LORE, AND SOMETIMES IT EVEN BRUSHES UP against that of a nation. This is the case for the al-Mirs, my family on my maternal grandmother Salma's side. The man who looms larger than life in our family tales is Salma's father and my great-grandfather, Sheikh Abdeljawwad al-Mir.

Abdeljawwad was born an Ottoman subject in 1889, and he died in 1970, a citizen of a Syria that Hafez al-Assad would seize control of just weeks after his death. Abdeljawwad's life thus spanned both the messy and genocidal end of empires—near and far—and the messy and genocidal rise of the new local, regional, and world orders that would dominate the twentieth century.

He was tall and handsome, with a robust chest and blue eyes. He spoke with a commanding voice (because he was always giving commands), wore his *tarboush* (Arabic for fez) well into the 1960s, and always carried worry beads in his right hand. He came from a small village and vastly increased his family's wealth through land and crops, making himself into a kind of feudal lord even as a new century dawned. A Christian with the honorific of "sheikh," he had *shakhsiyeh*, a trait my grandmother would forever be drawn to. It means, literally, "personality," but also connotes presence and charisma.

She would remain in awe of him throughout her life, even as he scripted the unhappiness of her adult years.

Those who knew Abdeljawwad attributed many traits to him, first and foremost his extreme generosity. Indeed, his name, from *abd-al-joud*, means the "slave of generosity." His dining table was always decadently spread for guests, and when he was the guest, he showered his hosts with bounty he'd bring from the countryside. He was also notably shrewd, entrepreneurial, and pragmatic, and therefore, he became quite rich. Only the most obsequiously polite omit that he was also well known for being a *niswanji*, womanizer. This was such an accepted fact that even in the stories the family tells about itself, his inclination for seduction is spoken of quite dispassionately.

Abdeljawwad apparently so excelled at it that at age eighty-one, he whispered amorous sentiments to the young nurses—many of whom were nuns—who tended to him in a hospital as he lay dying. But let's start with how his life began.

☙❧

ABDELJAWWAD'S PEOPLE WERE said to be Ghassanids, a pre-Islamic Arab tribe from modern-day Yemen that had migrated to Syria by the fourth century CE. According to some accounts, when the Ghassanids left the southern Arabian Peninsula they were already Christian; others say they embraced the religion after arriving in Syria, where Christian communities already existed.

My direct ancestors then settled in the Ghab Plain, which lies between two mountain ranges—one that runs parallel to Syria's Mediterranean coast, and another one inland to the east. Abdeljawwad was born in the Ghab Plain's village of Suqaylabiyah in 1889. It was located in a territory that had for centuries been known as Bilad al-Sham (the Lands of Sham), which stretched from the Taurus Mountains in the north to the Sinai Desert in the south, and from the Mediterranean Sea in the west to the Euphrates River in the northeast and the Arabian Desert in the southeast. These natural borders held in their embrace a territory that had long had its own coherence. Today, this would put Bilad al-Sham in parts of modern-day Syria, Lebanon, Israel, Palestine, Jordan, and Turkey. Then and now, "Sham" has generally been imperfectly translated as "Syria." To distinguish what is meant by Bilad al-Sham from modern-day Syria and its reduced borders, scholars sometimes translate it as "Greater Syria." (And I will, too, but this use of the term should not be confused with the political concept popularized in the 1930s and 1940s in response to European colonial divisions of historical Bilad al-Sham.)

The Ottoman Empire had captured the region in 1516. Forged in the late thirteenth century, the Ottoman Empire ruled over a multinational, multilingual, and multireligious empire that at its peak controlled much of southeastern Europe, western Asia (including the Eastern Mediterranean), the Caucasus, North Africa, and the Horn of Africa. Islam was central to the empire's structure, and the ruling Osman family framed its legitimacy in terms of being the protector of Islam. However, other faith groups were integrated members of the empire, though their conditions varied over the course of its six-hundred-year existence.

The Ottomans were by no means Syrians' first imperial rulers. Greater Syria is ancient, and it was home to some of the world's earliest civilizations. The kingdom of Ebla (in modern-day Idlib) was founded in 3500 BCE and flourished for two thousand years. Since the third millennium BCE, many empires, dynasties, and caliphates had ruled Greater Syria. They read like a greatest hits of the ancient, classical, medieval, and Islamic eras: the Akkadians, Sumerians, Egyptians, Hittites, Mitanni, Assyrians, Babylonians, Canaanites, Phoenicians, Arameans, Persians, Greeks, Romans, Byzantines, Muslims (Umayyad, Abbasid, Mamluks), Crusaders, and Mongols.

My great-grandfather's birthplace, Suqaylabiyah, had once been an Aramaic town but prospered later as a military post for the great Seleucid city of Apamea (Afamia today). The Seleucids, a Hellenic empire, ruled from 312 to 63 BCE, though Apamea continued to exist until the thirteenth century before it was abandoned, leaving behind magnificent ruins. Suqaylabiyah was deserted earlier when an earthquake destroyed it in 1157. Its inhabitants fled to the surrounding mountains and lived there for the next seven hundred years. They came back down to their old village when the Ottomans gave them incentives to return in the mid-1800s—the Ottomans found it easier to govern (and tax) their subjects when they lived in less mountainous regions.

Suqaylabiyah was located in the *sanjak* (Ottoman administrative division) of Hama, which took its name from the district's main town. Hama had the usual range of government offices, and by the early twentieth century it had begun to be connected by railroad to Damascus, Beirut, Aleppo, and distant Constantinople. Hama was an agricultural district known for its produce, wheat, olives, and grapes. It also had a textile industry, famous for its silks and hand looms.

Suqaylabiyah was thirty miles from Hama, and its inhabitants were almost all Arabic-speaking Antiochian Orthodox Christians. My great-great-grandfather, Abdeljawwad's father, is credited on a stone inscription with restoring the new church there in 1890, the year after his son (and last child) was born. When my great-great-grandfather died, Abdeljawwad was only four. He would forever blame his father's death on smoking, and as a result, he would forbid his own children to smoke. Many of them and their spouses would, in fact, smoke, especially my grandmother Salma, who was a true addict. All of them, however, were careful never to be seen doing it.

Abdeljawwad's mother, the widow Marta, raised him, and it was from her that he learned his famed generosity. She would earn her own place later in Suqaylabiyah's history for her actions in World War I: she, too, had *shakhsiyeh*. Before the fortunate birth of Abdeljawwad, she had only had daughters—three of them—making him a *waheed*, an only son. That earned him a very important exemption meant to protect his life: he could not be conscripted. Even if it was the daughters who comforted and cared for their parents, it fell to the sons to provide for them. Abdeljawwad was precious to Marta, and once his father died, she needed him to grow from boy to man fast, so he could fulfill this role.

But having been widowed so young, in the meantime Marta had to defer to her first daughter's husband, who was the ranking man in the family. When her first daughter died, after having borne him six children, he married her sister: after all, he needed a woman to raise them. So unfortunately for Marta, the same man became her son-in-law twice over, which gave him considerable power over her life. With the second daughter, he had another six children. His large broods were both half-siblings and cousins. Marta's daughters' inheritances from her dead husband were now essentially in the hands of one man. He also managed whatever lands her husband had left behind—at least until Abdeljawwad was grown.

The most important decision her son would make, as he became an adult, was who he would take as his wife. Marta was determined to find him a girl of her own liking. Then, her son went and did what he did.

When Abdeljawwad was nineteen, he fell in love with Sara, a very pretty fourteen-year-old girl from the village. She was also quite taken by Abdeljawwad. They had seen each other at the village well, where many a romance had been sparked by a glance or a smile. One afternoon, while Sara was kneading dough for bread outside the steps to her parents' house, Abdeljawwad came by with his horse and took her. They rode straight to the priest, who readily married them.

Did he kidnap her, or did they elope? That question quickly became moot, as they immediately began having children—and they would continue having them for the next sixteen years. In the end, eight would survive to adulthood, and of these, six—*masha'allah!*—were boys. My grandmother Salma, born in 1924, was the fifth child and the first daughter to live (two of her elder sisters perished as infants).

Sara was tender and kind, and she was remembered fondly by her grandchildren (thirty-four in all), each of whom she would welcome with excitement and love. As each one was born, she would make room for his or her photo next to those of her own children in a small wooden cabinet in her bedroom. There, she also kept an icon of the Virgin Mary with a lit oil candle in offering. As both wife and mother, she was dutiful and deferential.

But for Marta, the marriage was a disaster. Not only was this done without her consent, but she had been deprived of attending her son's wedding. Worse still, Sara was related to Marta's influential son-in-law (her father was his first cousin). Marta resented that he might have encouraged the union. She was so unhappy with the marriage that some in the family believed that she herself began to nudge her son to seek the comforts of other women. Sara had stolen Abdeljawwad from her; Marta would return the favor and take him away from Sara.

If Marta meant to hurt her unwanted daughter-in-law by encouraging her son's amorous behavior, it worked. Abdeljawwad became not only a prolific adulterer but a brazen one as well, seducing women Sara knew, even showering some of them with jewels they would wear in her presence. His wife, who rarely asked for anything for herself, was deeply wounded by his repeated betrayals; when she confronted him about it, he'd dismiss her, sometimes reacting violently. In those instances, he would grab her by her long hair, wind it around his fist, and remind her that she had no say.

Throughout his life, Abdeljawwad would always do as he wanted. The rapidly changing times called for boldness, and his boldness (and his belief in himself) meant that not only did he survive them, he thrived in them.

☙❧

ABDELJAWWAD WAS NEARLY thirty years old in the seismic year of 1918, when World War I finally ended and many of the world's empires collapsed. After flourishing for six centuries, and ruling Greater Syria for four, the Ottoman Empire, too, crumbled.

But in 1918, Ottoman rule was all Abdeljawwad or any inhabitant of Greater Syria had ever known. And he had done quite well under it. By then, my great-grandfather already had three sons, and he was prominent in his village. He had taken the family wealth and multiplied it. The lands he had inherited from his father were being used to cultivate wheat. Abdeljawwad acquired more land by both purchase and debt and expanded his operations to include cotton. He also distilled *arak* (an anise-based liqueur), which he sold far beyond Suqaylabiyah.

In the mid-nineteenth century, thanks to changes in the Ottoman land laws, the wealthy were able to buy more land while *fellaheen* (the rural poor) worked it in a near serf-like capacity. This inequitable distribution made the large landowners richer at the expense of the laborers and laid the groundwork for discontent that would later become a critical part of Syrian politics. In the Ghab, in addition to poor Christians, many of those workers were poor Alawites, a minority sect, marginally Shiite, who were considered the lowest rung of society.

The Ottomans' success in ruling Greater Syria was due in considerable part to their integrating its people across classes. Historians have particularly focused on the elites at the top of the socioeconomic hierarchy, called the "notables." These were generally wealthy Sunni (the majority sect) families, several of whom could trace their ancestry to Islam's prophet. They tended to come from the cities, including Aleppo and Damascus, though as the empire expanded outside of urban areas, their rural counterparts also became integrated. Although Abdeljawwad didn't come from a Sunni family, he made himself in the notables' image.

Suqaylabiyah was a Christian village, so Abdeljawwad didn't have to compete with Sunnis for a position of leadership. Moreover, though it was built on ancient foundations, Suqaylabiyah was nonetheless relatively new and still small, and Abdeljawwad was able to become its biggest fish. This is how he came to be known as a "sheikh." Like other men of this stature, he saw himself as being responsible not just for his family and his village, but also for the laborers who toiled in his fields. This hardly meant that he was interested in fundamentally altering any paradigm where he had laborers toiling in fields for him, however.

This patronage system in Syrian society would outlive the Ottoman era. People looked to the notables for everything from counsel to mediation, money, and protection. While no doubt many extended their benefaction out of genuine feeling or a sort of noblesse oblige, to remain relevant a notable also had to deliver for his client constituents. Given Greater Syria's diversity, this meant their charges were all the people in their ambit of power, regardless of sect or ethnicity. Abdeljawwad embraced those responsibilities and was tested young, when, in 1914, the Ottoman Empire joined World War I on the side of the Germans, setting in motion its own demise. At the time, he was just twenty-five years old.

As old as it was, the Ottoman Empire did not come apart neatly. Its borders had already been contracting for over a century—though, as is often the case with borders, these excisions were hardly surgical. It had once connected East and West, encompassing nearly thirty ethnic and religious groups and at least forty different languages and dialects. At its largest, the empire had roughly the same number of Muslims as it did non-Muslims.

Since the mid-eighteenth century, the Ottoman Empire had been hemorrhaging territory and power, with European countries hungrily eyeing what remained of its lands. Elements within the empire had been seeking to reverse its declining fortunes, though with wildly differing visions as to how, and from the late nineteenth century until its end, the Ottoman Empire was also beset by internal power struggles. This led to its disastrous participation in World War I and to its slaughter of its own Armenian, Assyrian, and Greek subjects.

For Syrians (as well as for Lebanese and Palestinians), the miseries associated with the duration of the war have been lumped under the term *seferberlik*, which in Turkish generally means "war mobilization." In Arabic, it refers to the suffering caused in the war years, and its agonies became the stuff of literature and even contemporary theater and film. As much as 15 to 20 percent of the population of Greater Syria perished from war, famine, and disease. The primary feature of *seferberlik* was military conscription—which was, in essence, a death sentence. The men taken served for free or very little, without training, and many didn't come back.

The *History of Suqaylabiyah*, by Adib Qundraq (a local), collects the oral histories of the few from the village who survived military service. They tell of long marches without food or water, saving their urine in their tobacco tins to drink when they could bear the thirst no more. A man named Tanous recounts how, when he could no longer walk, his Turkish commander beat him until he became unconscious and left him to die. When he awoke, he walked back to Suqaylabiyah, where he stayed in hiding. There was no mercy for deserters. In the book, Qandraq illustrates the severity of the consequences with an anecdote from his own family's history: His grandfather's brother, a deserter, once refused to help his wife with household chores, so she stepped out into the street and screamed that there was a deserter in her house. A neighbor quickly came and shushed her, reminding her that no domestic dispute could be worth losing her husband.

Another man from the village, Salim, who didn't desert but fought in the war, told Qandraq, "We fought in a battle, against whom, we didn't know. They gave us weapons and showed us how to shoot. But we were hungry. It happened then a non-Turkish battalion came to where we were stationed, . . . and we found out they were Germans. I told myself they are Christians like us, so I crossed myself. They responded by giving us food, fruit, biscuits, and stuff that I didn't know what it was." He also told Qandraq that soldiers with bad coughs were burned alive, lest they spread tuberculosis. Wounded soldiers were thrown into a pit or well or simply left in the elements to die.

Recounting one particular incident, even many decades later, Salim began to weep: "One time my companion and I were ordered to throw [a] wounded soldier into the well. But he started to scream and beg us not to do it, so we lay him next to the well. But the Turkish commander came toward us with his gun telling us to hurry up in throwing the man or it will be our fate too. Before throwing him in, we told him, 'Death will be more merciful than this life.' After that I knelt and begged God to forgive this crime that I didn't have a choice in committing."

Seferberlik did not spare those who were left behind, either. There was a terrible famine in Greater Syria, the result of locusts and drought, Ottoman confiscation of available grain to support the war effort, and an Allied blockade of the Eastern Mediterranean. Adulterated flour was common, and the lower nutritional levels, combined with a breakdown of municipal services, caused epidemics of dysentery, typhus, smallpox, diphtheria, malaria, and cholera. In addition to disease, famine led to emigration, prostitution, crime, suicide, and even cannibalism in some areas. Gangs of deserters from the Ottoman Army raided villages, essentially killing local trade. Hundreds of thousands of refugees poured into cities, and an estimated 500,000 people died.

An only son, Abdeljawwad was spared conscription; by then he had become the man of his father's house. However, famine came to his village, right to his very doorstep, and his mother, Marta, my great-great-grandmother, became a part of local legend. Her deeds were memorialized in *The History of Suqaylabiyah* and in another book by Anthonios Anis Khoury, a Syrian journalist and village émigré in Argentina.

As the story goes, one dawn Marta awoke to find a dead man at the foot of the gates of their house—he had come seeking food, but no one had heard him knock in the middle of the night, or perhaps he had been too weak. He died there of hunger, alone. When she realized the next morning that he had come to her house in need, she was said to be so upset that "she wailed and beat her face." She summoned men to remove the gates from their hinges, so that after that day there would be no barrier to prevent anyone in need from reaching her. In the place of the gates, Marta built two *tanour*, ovens made of mounds of bricks and dirt. She always left the fires lit underneath them, baking bread constantly so that all those in need in the village would have something to eat.

Although *seferberlik* in the popular imagination doesn't include the slaughter of Armenians north of Greater Syria (in modern-day Turkey), that ethnic cleansing happened in the same years and also became a part of Syrian destiny, especially when its survivors—who had lived through unspeakable trauma—sought refuge in Syrian cities, towns, and villages. They, too, came to my great-grandfather and great-great-grandmother's doorstep.

The empire, having decided that Armenians, as well as Assyrians and Greeks, were a fifth column, tried to exterminate them. From 1914 to 1918, historians estimate that as many as 1.3 million Armenian subjects, 275,000 Assyrians, and 350,000 Greeks were murdered. Inhabitants of Armenian villages—men, women, children, and the elderly—were massacred, butchered, burned, or drowned in the Black Sea. Concentration camps were set up. The vast majority of the population was deported to Aleppo, Greater Syria's most important city in the north, literally at the end of the line of the railroad. From Aleppo, the Ottomans forced the corralled Armenians to march into the Syrian Desert, ostensibly to another deportation center, but the death march was in fact the point. They were not provided cover from the sun, or given food or water. Sometimes they had to march in circles until they collapsed. Most died in the desert, the dust of their bones still discernable today among the grains of sand.

In August 1915, the *New York Times*, quoting another account, reported that "the roads and the Euphrates are strewn with corpses of exiles, and those who survive are doomed to certain death since they will find neither house, work, nor food in the desert. It is a plan to exterminate the whole Armenian people."

Around 1914, a woman showed up at Marta and Abdeljawwad's house—the one with no gate—with her small children. She spoke no Arabic. She had walked to Suqaylabiyah after seeing her husband and parents butchered in front of her in Anatolia. Marta and Abdeljawwad took them in and hid them. The Ottomans sought out Armenians who had fled the death marches, and those whom they caught were sent back. Syrians who hid them could be punished, some even sent with the Armenians to the desert.

Mercifully, no one was caught. The woman would become an intimate part of our extended family for generations, even as Abdeljawwad moved the family to Hama and then as my grandmother moved to Damascus. My mother's generation would come to call her "Teta Marie" (grandmother Marie).

Many Armenians—an estimated 100,000—found refuge in Greater Syria, mostly in Aleppo (70,000), where they resurrected what they could of their former home. While on a trip to that city eighty miles from Suqaylabiyah, Abdeljawwad met a seven-year-old boy, Nazarian, who had been orphaned by the genocide. He brought the boy and a few Armenian families back to Suqaylabiyah; they lived in Abdeljawwad's house, and he gave them work picking grapes for the *arak* he distilled. Years later, Nazarian also recounted his story in the *History of Suqaylabiyah*, describing my great-grandfather as "the handsome gentleman" who "protected him in a fatherly way and gave him what he needed, clothes, food, and money." Abdeljawwad asked the other Armenian families to give him extra care because he was an orphan.

And so we absorbed into our family one of the region's most violent cleavages, as did Syrians collectively. Its trauma and scars became a part of us; the generations before me looked it in the face each time they sat with Teta Marie. Her wounds joined those already inflicted on the lands, bodies, and psyches of the people of Greater Syria. The memory of the unspeakable violence and death of *seferberlik* was present every day in the fact that whoever was alive was also a survivor of its agonies. But there was no pause to process this, to reconcile with it: life went on and everyone lived with what had been done.

But as is often the case with trauma, even if the scars were not visible, they were there, and it haunted Syrians individually and collectively and shaped their health, their actions, and their decisions, consciously and unconsciously.

Those who were slaughtered—the Armenians, Assyrians, and Greeks—were all Christian. With their deaths and expulsion, most of the empire's remaining Christian subjects were now those living in Greater Syria, most of them, like Abdeljawwad, Antiochian Orthodox. The church's seat was at Antioch in Greater Syria's northwest, approximately sixty miles from Aleppo. Catholic and Maronite communities, which were also prevalent, looked to the Vatican.

Though they must have felt a hint of insecurity, these Christians didn't likely think they'd be next to the slaughter. At the time, those communities exterminated by the Ottomans were seen as having been made tools of British, French, and Russian imperial policy. Also, they were perceived as being potential separatists, based on their distinct ethno-national identities. Christians in Greater Syria were instead—like the majority, their Muslim (and back then Jewish) brethren—all Arabic speakers, with no other empire or country to claim them. Greater Syria's people (inasmuch as they thought about it) saw themselves as being part of the Ottoman Empire.

The elites in Syrian cities and towns knew Ottoman Turkish, which was taught in Ottoman-built schools. However, the empire only built elementary schools in villages with more than five hundred houses, and schools the next level up where there were more than one thousand houses. So Abdeljawwad hadn't learned Ottoman Turkish, because Suqaylabiyah was too small, although he had been taught the very basics privately. (The first school in the village was built several years later—in great part thanks to Abdeljawwad.)

While to be Ottoman was not synonymous with being Turkish or Muslim, Sunni Islam was at the empire's core, which undoubtedly complicated things for anyone who was not a Sunni. This was likely the case not just for Christians but also Ottoman Jews, Shiites, Druze, and Alawites. Being a minority is complex in any country, even one that is full of minority communities. But despite any resentment or dissatisfaction Abdeljawwad might have felt, the reality remains that he also became a rich Ottoman and was fully active in the civic life of the town, and he would only become much more so in the coming years.

It's tempting to imagine the impending collapse of the empire giving way to a specifically Syrian nationalism, bursting at the seams to happen. Or that the peoples of Greater Syria would organically welcome the revolt against the Ottomans begun by other Arabic-speaking Ottoman subjects from the bordering province in the Arabian Peninsula, out of some sort of pan-Arab nationalism. That uprising, abetted by the British, is the story that the film *Lawrence of Arabia* purports to tell. Indeed, this kind of nationalist narrative has long been told and wielded in the service of different agendas—from justifying the European presence in the territories that were "liberated" from Ottoman rule to creating an appealing founding mythology for the new nation-states that would eventually emerge to uniting the disparate interests of these societies under a pan-Arab banner. This is also the version of history that has come to be taught in Syrian schools.

For a long time, this was also my understanding of what had happened—that Syrians had thrown off the unnatural yoke of Turkish rule and readily embraced the rule of brethren Arabs. So when *Lawrence of Arabia* was re-released in 1989 (my freshman year of high school, and one hundred years after Abdeljawwad's birth), and it played at Baltimore's famous art-deco Senator Theater, I watched it in rapture, thrilled to have such a well-scored, cinematographically stunning depiction of "my history." That the Arab protagonist, the handsome Egyptian actor Omar Sharif, was a distant relative of Abdeljawwad's youngest son's wife, somehow made it all the more plausible. (Sharif's father had emigrated from Bilad al-Sham to Egypt; formerly Christian, he had converted to Islam to marry the iconic Egyptian actress Faten Hamama.)

In a broad-strokes telling of time, the blurring together of years is argu-ably not so bad; after all, both Syrian and Arab nationalism would eventu-ally emerge within the coming years (though these nationalisms evolved and changed). And those who had once unquestioningly thought of themselves as Ottoman would in fact embrace, and in many cases prefer, the future. But a closer look reveals that the truth was much more nuanced than that, and there is meaning and relevance in those complexities. As recent scholarship has shown, most of Greater Syria at the time saw itself as Ottoman, and its fate as tied to the fortunes of the empire. (It is important to note here that there were exceptions, such as the Maronites of Mt. Lebanon, who aspired to their own Christian nation and would look to France as a patron, although within that community as well there were dissenting views.) Even as the population grew weary of the war and what it demanded of them, many celebrated Ot-toman victories and hoped the empire would prevail against the Allies—and against any kind of European colonization of their lands. Soldiers and civil servants from Greater Syria served the Ottomans until the bitter end, which is why, when it came, it was anything but surgical or antiseptic.

࣓

THE DEFEAT OF the Ottoman Empire and its aftermath would leave the inhabitants of Greater Syria in freefall, vulnerable to the plans and desires of everyone but themselves. Strip away the neat nationalist veneer, and what becomes clear is that it was a time of great uncertainty and anxiety.

When the Allies occupied the Ottoman capital, Constantinople, they began partitioning the territorial spoils according to agreements they had already negotiated among themselves during the war (agreements, of course, that had never asked the people of these lands what they wanted). The most notorious of these was the Sykes-Picot Agreement, secretly negotiated in 1916, which split Ottoman loot between France and the United Kingdom. Under its terms, France would take what would eventually become Syria and Lebanon, and the United Kingdom grabbed Palestine (which included Jordan) and Iraq. In the separate Balfour Declaration (1917), the United Kingdom had also encouraged the Zionists to seek a Jewish homeland in Palestine.

At the same time, the Allies had backed the revolt against the Ottomans of Hussein bin Ali, Sharif of Mecca, in the empire's Hejaz province (modern-day Saudi Arabia). To convince Hussein to revolt in the first place, the British offered him military support (enter T. E. Lawrence) and promised him a united federated Arab kingdom spanning loosely from Aleppo to Aden, Yemen. Hussein's son Faisal would be ruler of a "kingdom of Syria" that the British would help him create. Thus the British promised to Faisal territories they would also promise others.

Contrary to the *Lawrence of Arabia* version of this story, plenty of Syrians (a term by now in widespread use in Arabic by the inhabitants of Bilad al-Sham / Greater Syria to refer to themselves) eyed Faisal's arrival with Allied troops skeptically. It goes without saying that no population is monolithic, but many Greater Syrians still saw themselves for the most part as Ottomans. Many—particularly in the north—were still hoping to rejoin whatever would eventually rise from the ashes of the Ottoman Empire. After all, Greater Syria had been part of a large empire, with its vast economy and markets unified by a common currency, cosmopolitan cities, and organized bureaucracy.

Moreover, many viewed Faisal not only as an outsider, but as a puppet subject to European oversight and control. Indeed, more than hated, Faisal was mocked, despite his efforts to bribe both the rich and the poor of Damascus (he even retained poets to compose paeans to him and his government).

But whether Syrians would embrace Faisal's vision of the Arab nationalist narrative or remain skeptical eventually became irrelevant. France clearly had Syria in its sights as a backstop to its own loss of power. The French also harbored nostalgia for a romantic Crusader past, which they believed entitled them to Syria. (During France's Second Empire, the nation's unofficial national anthem, once Napoleon III banned the Marseillaise, was "Partant pour la Syrie," a song about a Crusader knight leaving for Syria.) So it was that the Syrians—with European forces already on their lands, eager to collect Ottoman spoils—officially threw in their lot with Faisal, who supposedly had the ear of the Allies (though they ultimately were not listening).

Syrians—having been ruled by an empire—had long been relieved of deciding for themselves what sort of government suited them and of navigating the basis for belonging in a place of many religions, sects, ethnicities, and languages. Now they had to prioritize an external threat before putting their own internal affairs in order. To the encroaching Europeans, they repeatedly said in official communications that they wanted no French or British presence or rule over them; they wanted "self-determination," a term in vogue thanks to US president Woodrow Wilson. That the Europeans only paid lip service to these concepts cemented for many in Greater Syria an assessment of their would-be rulers as duplicitous. The autonomy the Syrians called for encompassed a Syria within its natural borders, essentially what had always been Bilad al-Sham, and they vehemently refused the Zionist ambitions in Palestine.

Retaining Greater Syria's territorial integrity was critical. The Europeans had already begun divvying up the land, and the new borders had already yielded negative consequences; imposing different currencies in the different areas, for example, wreaked havoc on the economies of places that had long been bound to each other in fluid trade and commerce.

Greater Syrians expressed their desires in many forums, including at the Paris Peace Conference in 1919. There, the Allies agreed to form the League of Nations while also agreeing (apparently without irony) to award themselves the territories of the vanquished as "mandates." If the victors of World War I were going to force foreign oversight, Syrians appealed that it be the

United States in their case, as that country did not appear to be as hungry as the others to dominate their land. They rejected any French presence. The Europeans completely ignored local desires, however, and with French intentions to rule Syria abundantly clear, many Syrians revolted. The French threat mobilized a broad spectrum of Syrians—many of whom had different visions for the future—choosing to fight for a common goal: to oust the French colonizers. Among them was my great-grandfather Abdeljawwad.

Though he is not in the major history books, Abdeljawwad's deeds at this time appear in the histories of Suqaylabiyah, and his presence animates many of the tales told in my family. Times, rulers—they may have been changing, but sheikhs like him were still responsible for the people who looked to them for protection and their very livelihoods.

The most notable of the early uprisings against the French spread from the rural mountainous regions of the northwest, heavily populated by Alawites, and from urban Aleppo in the north. Saleh al-Ali led the Alawites, a minority group that followed a heterodox sect of Islam and had long been persecuted by different rulers. Ibrahim Hananu led the revolt in the north and would prove to be a true thorn in the sides of the French. They were very different men.

Suqaylabiyah's location brought Abdeljawwad into contact with both Ali and Hananu, and he was quick to aid them. He funneled money to both, and he fed Ali's troops when they were in nearby Tel al-'Ashraneh. He also gave Ali a sword and a horse as tokens of friendship and appreciation. The unity and solidarity recounted in these stories delighted me when I first heard them. A Christian, an Alawite, and a Kurdish Syrian—all doing their part for a new Syria free of the French. As I started to delve deeper into the histories surrounding these men, however, I began to see that time had smoothed out the rougher edges of the truth, though scholars have meticulously been reconstructing them.

Hananu, for example, received support from Mustafa Kemal Atatürk in the north. Under Atatürk's leadership, the Turks were fighting back against the Europeans and their proxies and helping Syrians in their struggle against the French. More than just taking Turkish support, Hananu was fighting the French with hopes of rejoining Atatürk. Hananu came from the city Aleppo, whose economic, social, and cultural ties to Anatolia (an Ottoman state that would remain in modern Turkey) were long established. He had been an Ottoman municipal officer and had studied in Constantinople, and he had little regard for Faisal's Arab kingdom project, which to him was completely artificial and collaborationist. Ali was an Alawite leader from the mountains, without Hananu's cosmopolitan exposure. His legacy and motivations are less in focus, though when an independent Syria would finally emerge in 1946, his deeds were exalted as part of nationalist celebrations.

In learning more, I discovered that fighters under both Ali and Hananu had attacked my great-grandfather's village. Some Alawite bandits used the chaos to come down from the mountains and pilfer the village; others scapegoated Syrian Christians as stand-ins for the French, whose colonialist rhetoric made much of France's Crusader past and Christian credentials. Troops under Hananu—many of whom were Turkish or had strong ties to the insurgency in Anatolia—in fact carried out an attack on the village that killed many inhabitants. After Abdeljawwad notified Ali and Hananu of these deeds, both leaders forbade their troops from bothering the village again. Indeed, Hananu had a field commander executed for killing its residents. He believed that the Turks had instructed the field commander to carry out the attack on Suqaylabiyah and other villages to tarnish the image of the Syrian rebels among Syrian Christians.

Why? Because while Atatürk was fighting on several fronts against the Allies (and their proxies), the French, who were fighting him from the south, offered him a deal he couldn't refuse: they would relent on the front between them and establish a border with Syria that ceded more territory to Turkey, if he would agree to withdraw support for the Syrian revolt. (The French, of course, had no popular legitimacy or authority to negotiate borders—they were on Syrian soil solely by force of arms.) As it became clear that the new Turkey would not include the new Syria, Hananu's goals shifted toward the creation of an independent nation-state of Syria.

Perhaps in the stories we tell ourselves about the making of a nation, we cannot afford complexity or duality in our heroes, but the more I looked into the motivations and actions of my great-grandfather and the men he supported, the more I saw that reality is flexible. People could be patriots as well as having a bit of the opportunistic criminal in them. What they were willing to fight for could change or evolve. So how was I to interpret all the money Abdeljawwad gave to the revolts? Was it patriotism? Pragmatism? Revolt tax? Payoff? After speaking to the scholars of this era, I think it was a little bit of all these things. Abdeljawwad was one of the village's important men—he had to protect its residents just as much as he had to follow his heart or political leanings.

Yet, despite some early successes, the French were hardly dissuaded. In late July 1920, France issued an ultimatum to the government in Damascus under Faisal—who was ostensibly still in charge—to submit to French rule or face attack. Faisal promptly surrendered, knowing the French would easily overrun the country. Syrians, however, resisted. In Damascus, people of all classes denounced *both* Faisal and the French. The insurrection spread from the streets to Faisal's palace, and the Syrians attacked Faisal's troops. They seized weapons from the citadel, and at least a hundred Damascenes died in the clashes. The next day, a similar uprising broke out in Aleppo.

Local newspapers denounced France's colonial ambitions. One broadsheet declared in a two-page boldfaced spread: "Tell the Pope, the clericalists, the capitalists, and the politicians who aim at conquest that young Syria will never submit to old France!"

Even though it was a suicide mission, Faisal's defense minister, a Damascene, raised a small army of volunteer men and women to confront the French. Many were unarmed, but on July 24, 1920, they met the European power on the battlefield at Maysalun west of Damascus. Within hours, the brave defense minister was killed, the Syrians vanquished. The French entered Damascus victorious.

Once in control, the French set out to undermine any Syrian solidarity built on resisting France by splitting up Greater Syria (excluding the parts that were now British mandates) into semiautonomous territories under ultimate French control. In brief, they attempted to divide and conquer Greater Syria by exploiting geographical differences and by promoting territorial divisions according to sectarian identities. (Indeed, in Bilad al-Sham, sectarian identity had not previously been seen as a relevant basis for creating administrative divisions; this French insistence on viewing the region in such a manner ultimately gave it currency.) Aleppo and Damascus became states. Areas where the Alawites lived in the northwest and where Druze lived in the south became states named for their sects. (The Druze are another of the minorities that make up the region. Their religious practices are kept secret, even from most of the members of their tightknit community, but they are understood as an offshoot of Ismaili Islam.) Both the Alawite and Druze communities are Arabic speaking, but the French were able to prey on the divisions that preceded them. This was particularly true in the case of the Alawites, who had long been persecuted and disdained in Syrian society.

The French also carved out Greater Lebanon, whose people—with the exception of Maronite-dominated Mt. Lebanon—demanded to stay part of Syria (they were ignored). Out of the Aleppan state, the French gave the district of Alexandretta (what Syrians called Iskenderun) semiautonomous status, because it had a Turkish minority and because the new Turkish negotiators pushed for it. Syrians (across Greater Syria), however, did not give up. Even after Maysalun, the Orthodox Church, for example, to which Abdeljawwad belonged, continued to raise gold for the rebels. My great-grandfather remained a generous donor to the cause. But soon, both Ali and Hananu were on the run.

To protect his children, Hananu hid them from the French with Abdeljawwad. The French were so blinded by their sectarian way of viewing Greater Syria that they assumed Christians would side with them. They never thought to look for Hananu's children among Christian families. The French captured Hananu in 1922 and put him on trial—a very public trial, to make a point. They summoned Abdeljawwad to testify against him, still not realizing he had hidden Hananu's children. As my family tells it, my great-grandfather told the French he would do as they please, but on the stand, he testified on behalf of the rebel leader. Thanks to the fact that the trial was public, Hananu was acquitted. (And that was the end of public trials on the part of the French.)

The former rebel leader transitioned into politics. He continued to encourage rebellion, but most Aleppines demurred. Ali, after having been sentenced to death *in absentia*, was granted a pardon in 1922, but he abstained from all political activity thereafter.

Abdeljawwad, meanwhile, fed up with bandit attacks against Suqaylabiyah, decided to move his family to Hama. By then, he had four sons, and in 1924, my grandmother Salma would be born. She was the first child to be born in Hama, and Sara's first daughter to survive infancy.

෧෬෧

HAMA WAS A medium-sized town, enriched by the agricultural yields of the surrounding countryside. Sitting on the Orontes River, it was known for its *noria*, waterwheels developed in the Byzantine era to lift water from the river and then pour it into the aqueducts that irrigated the nearby farms. Hama was also known for its tough people and conservative and honorable families.

In Hama, Abdeljawwad would come into more frequent contact with the French, and he learned how to deal with them while continuing to subvert their rule. The family celebrates his shrewd ability to play them in a number of stories, including one from 1925, when Syrians again rose up against the French in the Great Syrian Revolt. The uprising would antagonize the French for two years before they put it down. It began in the Druze Mountains and quickly spread despite French attempts to divide and conquer the Syrian people, particularly through their minorities. And a major episode would take place in Hama, where Abdeljawwad had moved his family.

With much of the population behind them, the rebels captured Hama from the French. In response, the French bombarded Hama (and its essentially civilian population) from the skies. Numerous shops and homes were destroyed, and French reinforcements had already been called in to rout out the rebels. Fearing further destruction, influential Sunni families from Hama met with the French and agreed to convince the rebels to evacuate the city if the French would stop the shelling. The negotiation was successful.

At the same time, one year after my grandmother was born, Sara gave birth to another baby, whom Abdeljawwad had intended to baptize Hanna (Arabic for John); instead, in an effort to appease the French with flattery, he named him Sarrail, after Maurice-Paul-Emmanuel Sarrail, the French high commissioner in Syria. (It was pronounced the same way as *sarai*, Arabic for palace; in Ottoman usage, it referred to an important government building.) As soon as he reached the age of majority, my great uncle would officially change his name to the similar-sounding Arabic name "Sari," ridding himself permanently of the price he had paid for his father's cunning.

By the time the family moved to Hama, Abdeljawwad's wealth was only growing, as was his ever-expanding family. Sara would continue having children until 1929. But the couple was already moving apart. In Hama, Abdeljawwad had increasing access to people of power, education, and wealth, and he wanted to move in their circles. He complained that Sara had remained a simple village woman, while at the same time he expected her to instill in their children the proper religious and village customs—which she did.

In Hama, my great-grandparents lived in a traditional house, an enclosed rectangular compound that from the outside did not reveal its secrets. The thick walls guarded their privacy and kept them cool in summer and warm in winter. Inside the structure was a large roofless courtyard open to the sky. Filled with pomegranate and fig trees and flowering bushes, at its very center was a well. The rooms were built around the courtyard, and the ones on the second floor had internal terraces overlooking it.

At opposite ends of the courtyard were two sets of stairs that each went up one story to separate large rooms, called 'aliyehs. These rooms extended out of the main rectangular compound walls onto the street until they met those of the house across the way, appearing to be suspended above a passerby's head. From the outside, they looked like an enclosed bridge (think Bridge of Sighs in Venice, but in much more cramped spaces). The children often played under them, as they protected them from the sun and the rain.

In Abdeljawwad's house, one of these was reserved for him and Sara. Only their room had beds; the children slept on mattresses on the floor in the other 'aliyeh, which was divided into two rooms by a wall. The older boys slept on one side, while the younger children slept on the other; the older boys' side was also used to receive guests in the morning. Sara often slept with the younger children on the floor. But in the summer heat, this would all change: they would sleep on the internal terrace overlooking the courtyard, piling their mattresses on top of a straw carpet rug. They'd cover themselves with a namouseeyeh to protect themselves from the mosquitos; more opaque than a mosquito net, it also offered some privacy.

The house also had two large semi-underground storage rooms. The first was for the grains (rice, bulgur, and freekeh, or roasted dried bulgur), lentils, dried beans, semneh (clarified butter used for cooking), and the mouneh— the dried, pickled, and preserved summer fruits and produce. Sara's store of mouneh was so large that it fulfilled all the needs of the house from one summer to the next. In the other storage room, they kept the chopped wood necessary for heating and cooking and the dried grapevines that they used as kindling. From there, a door overlooked a connected courtyard, where they kept the chickens and sheep. This courtyard was surrounded by a cellar where arak was stored in large barrels. After distilling and bottling it, they would sell it locally or in villages in what was now called Lebanon. There was a room in this secondary compound where they would host overnight guests from the village.

Back in the main house, the kitchen took up an entire quadrant. It had three ovens and one kerosene heater. The family would bathe once a week in the room next to the kitchen, close enough that they could easily boil the water needed to wash and carry the heavy pots over. But they spent most of their time in a room above the courtyard that, when the house was awake, had a continuously lit charcoal heater in its center. On this heater a pot of coffee was always ready, for the constant visitors who came and went. In the evening, they would pass the time here listening to stories, a Syrian tradition, or play records on the phonograph. The children would save their weekly allowance to buy new records as they came out, but they wouldn't have a radio until World War II. Once the movie theater opened in Hama, they'd occasionally go on a Sunday, but only if Abdeljawwad gave them permission.

The nicest room in the house was the one reserved for guests—Abdeljaw-wad loved to entertain, and his house was ever full of people eager to feast at his table. A guest's happiness was so fundamental to him that when, during a luncheon party in 1930, he was quietly informed that his mother had just died in an adjacent room, he hushed the women who had been attending her and forbade them from wailing, insisting that they serve lunch as if nothing had happened. He had adored Marta, and she him. But he kept the matter a secret to avoid disturbing the guests' pleasure while under his roof.

For all these feasts, Sara—who proved to be a talented cook—prepared the copious amounts of food required. She had the help of young women who worked with her in the kitchen, many of whom her husband was rumored to have bedded. Sara's life wasn't all work, though. Her friends, too, would come over to visit. According to the *istiqbal* custom, each woman designated one day of the month to receive the others. Over homemade refreshments they discussed the matters related to their lives—husbands, children, and home—and of course gossiped.

Abdeljawwad liked taking trips to Beirut and Damascus and meeting new people along the way. He liked feeling part of a larger world. Women from the cities were different from Sara, who never wore makeup and always kept her long hair tied in a low bun at the nape of her neck. The dresses she had made for herself were always simple, made of light wool crepe in winter, a lighter cotton in summer. The cut never varied: the V-neck bodice would either button down the front to her waist or off to the side if it was double breasted, and the skirts were A-lined with pockets.

He may have become dissatisfied with her lack of airs, but she had become disenchanted with her philandering husband. Under her breath in later years, she'd curse him. Sometimes, she'd even allow herself an audible outburst. As their children grew, Abdeljawwad decided to give up many of the vices he didn't want them to learn—such as gambling, and eventually, politics. His one truly beloved addiction—women—however, he would not give up, and all those trips to the other cities facilitated it.

Nevertheless, for their moral education, my great-grandfather made sure to take his children back to the village to remember the customs, especially during the holidays, and the visits were always eventful. When Abdeljawwad would pass through the village square on his way from Hama to his mother Marta's house, people stood up in respect, and the next day they'd visit him with gifts of eggs, butter, and milk. Of the holidays, Easter was more important in the Eastern calendar than Christmas and was particularly magical for the children. In the village, the celebration lasted a whole week, but the highlight was Easter Monday, when, after Mass, the village staged a procession of horsemen.

My grandmother Salma—who never cared much for religion—preferred the local poets who came to see her father during his trips to the village. They would engage in *zajal*, an emotional duel of poetry, where the verses were semi-sung to musical accompaniment (usually just percussion, such as tambourines or Arabic hand-held drums). The bards would go at it for hours, on topics from the political to the erotic; competitors each had to create a verse out of the previous poet's final words, fitting a complex metrical form. The more *arak* the participants drank, the bolder the contest got.

Abdeljawwad also wanted his children to be properly schooled. He himself could read and do numbers, but he had always regretted that he hadn't been educated in the village. As a result, he helped build the first public school in Suqaylabiyah in 1922. To do so, he had to lobby the French, even as he contributed generously to the revolts against them. He sent his own sons to private boarding schools around Syria and then even to Tripoli (modern-day Lebanon). His daughters were schooled in Hama at a Catholic-run school. Some of the children excelled; others, including my grandmother, did not. Salma disliked the Catholic nuns and often played pranks on them, incurring frequent disciplinary measures. Finally her father allowed her to finish her schooling with the Orthodox, who were less strict and also ran an orphanage. The orphans were educated alongside the other children, and Salma felt comfortable among them. But as rebellious as she had been at school, she knew better than to flout her father's rule at home. His word was final, and punishment was swift when he was not obeyed—as he had proven with her eldest brother.

Abdeljawwad had sent his firstborn son to France to study agricultural engineering. He lavished some of his other sons with educations abroad as well, both in Europe and the United States. While the eldest son gained that valuable training in France, Abdeljawwad decided on a girl for him from a nice family, thinking they would marry upon his return. Instead, the young man fell in love with a woman from Homs who was working as a schoolteacher in Suqaylabiyah. His father forbade him to marry her: her brothers had a reputation for being troublemakers, and she wasn't rich. More importantly, Abdeljawwad had already chosen his son's bride. So, like his father before him, the young man eloped. Without hesitation, Abdeljawwad disowned his son. Salma was fifteen, and the incident impressed her. The newlyweds couldn't live in Hama and set up life in Damascus in 1939.

In that year, France would cede the district of Alexandretta—in breach of the terms of the League of Nations' Mandate for Syria and the Lebanon of 1923—to Turkey. Because it was a predominantly Arabic-speaking, Syrian region, Syrians would never recognize the deal. Then World War II broke out, and France put Syria under martial law (another nasty habit that would linger in the new Syria). When France fell to Germany the following year, the French administration in Syria and Lebanon declared allegiance to Vichy. Again there were shortages and terrible inflation.

Nevertheless, my grandmother always remained nostalgic for her childhood in Hama. The house was always full of guests and feasting. The family would spend holidays back in the village, where they rode horses and participated in the local Christian pageantry. There were vacations in Lebanon and shopping trips with her father in Damascus, where she'd try to politely ignore that he bought things for his mistresses as well as for her. She loved both of her parents, even as it pained her how her father treated her mother. Sometimes in later years, she would hint at Sara's lack of sophistication, almost as a justification for how her father treated her. Salma couldn't see Abdeljawwad as anything less than the perfect man.

So it was that she fell in love with a man much like him—so much like him that her father forbade her to marry him. Abdeljawwad believed the man could never be a faithful husband. Though heartbroken, Salma would not follow in her eldest brother's footsteps and elope. She would not disobey Abdeljawwad, but she wouldn't rush into an engagement with anyone else, either, though there were other suitors, many of whom Abdeljawwad rejected for a variety of reasons—such as not liking the man's vocation, his relatives, or the city he lived in.

On trips to Damascus to visit her disowned brother, however, Salma met a friend of his, a sweet man named Ameen, a technocrat in the Diwan al-Muhasabat (like the French Cour des Comptes, or Court of Audit, an agency that audits public institutions). He wasn't fiery and exciting like the other man, but her father approved of him. Ameen—and his position—would be a good addition to the family and a potentially useful tentacle to power in turbulent times.

In 1941, the Free French promised Syrians sovereign independence, and with British help, took control of Syria from the pro-Vichy forces. But even as World War II drew to an end, France tried to renege on its promises. Only in 1946, and with British intervention, did the French finally leave, kicking and screaming and demanding many concessions in return. After twenty-six years during which the mandate powers were supposed to guide their charges from Ottoman savagery to European modernity, the French had sliced apart Greater Syria, and they left new Syria with borders that made little sense. They had spent much on security and administration, creating the intelligence agencies out of which the Syrian *mukhabarat* would one day develop, while spending very little on transportation, infrastructure, and education in Syria. Some railways and utilities had been built, but France had granted French companies monopolies over them. And France had funded churches and schools for Catholics while neglecting Sunni communities.

France had also played favorites among the minorities, seeding sectarian fault lines. For example, when the French founded the military academy in Homs, they filled it with Alawite recruits, who had generally been excluded from positions of power in Syrian society. By the time the Alawite state rejoined the rest of Syria, separatist sentiments were present, if not widespread. One of the Alawites who would publicly object to being reabsorbed into Syria was the father of future president Hafez al-Assad.

Looking to a joint future, elected president Shukri al-Quwatli invited Saleh al-Ali, the Alawite leader who had helped lead the earliest revolts against the French, to be a guest of honor at Evacuation Day celebrations (for the day the last French soldier evacuated the country, also called Independence Day). It had taken a long time, but Syrians were at last in charge of their own destinies, and even if the French had crippled its development from the start, the country could now move on.

My grandmother also moved on. Salma may have loved the other man, but she also wanted out of Hama, and she wanted to be in charge of her own destiny—within the limits of what was acceptable for a woman. She married Ameen in Damascus in 1949, and they moved into an apartment in the newly built Tahaan Building, in a central neighborhood called Ain al-Kirish.

2

SHEIKHA

Damascus, 1949–1970

WHEN SALMA MOVED TO DAMASCUS IN 1949, HER NEW LIFE, LIKE the country, was more potential and possibility than broken promises. Under Ottoman rule, the capital hadn't been as cosmopolitan as Aleppo, two hundred miles to the north. But now that it was the seat of the national government in a newly independent Syria, it was rapidly expanding. Compared to Hama (pop. 80,000), Damascus was the big city (pop. 400,000). The trams moving through Damascus, laid by the Ottomans in 1907, gave it an air of modernity, as did the wider boulevards, which could accommodate large American sedans, the newly constructed apartment buildings, the bureaucrats in their three-piece suits and horn-rimmed glasses, and the urbane women, who shared the streets with men, going to work, university, or market.

Of course, the nucleus of Damascus—the Old City—the center from which it had expanded through the millennia, was still a remnant of another time, or rather, many other times. Damascus had been continuously inhabited ever since the third millennium BCE, and civilizations past were layered on top of each other or stood side by side. It was inevitable that a city would rise where Damascus stands, given its location in the fertile Ghouta oasis fed by the Barada River at the edge of the Syrian Desert. Because it was at the crossroads of Africa and Asia, East and West, and an important stop on the

Silk Road and on the pilgrimage to Mecca from the Ottoman center, it was also bound to flourish. While in the tight quarters of the Old City it might be hard to imagine Damascus's oasis origins, one didn't have to go far to find them. When Salma arrived in 1949, the Barada River still coursed through the capital, and it was surrounded by orchards, many of which were right in the center of the city.

Even though Salma came from Hama, a town many Damascenes would consider provincial, she herself was quite elegant. Unlike her mother, Salma paid attention to her appearance, having always preferred her father's more glamorous world. She had a striking beauty—olive skin and dark hair, with very green eyes, not the kind that could sometimes look blue or gray. Indeed, green was her favorite color, and she preferred jewelry with green stones.

The only makeup she wore was classic red lipstick, and she kept her wavy black hair long well into the 1960s. Before clothes were *prêt-à-porter*, she had hers made at the seamstress, and she wore only skirt suits or dresses. She first bought pants when she visited us in the United States years later. She stood at 5'7" and always wore stockings and heels. If she had an ideal, it was the Italian actress Gianna Maria Canale. In Syria, Canale was known for the film *Theodora, Slave Empress*, in which she played the former slave who married Justinian I, emperor of Byzantium. Canale's eyes were also green.

Salma was self-assured; her father was a rich man in Hama and influential in the countryside. Hama might have been small compared to Damascus, but she would forever take pride in the reputation of Hama's people for being tough and conservative, in the sense that the families were tightly knit and upheld the traditions and old ways. It gave her a swagger and earned her the description "sister of men"; though she did in fact have plenty of brothers, it was more a way of saying that she was like a man. And she did see herself in her father's and brothers' image.

Yet for all the excitement and promise that came with independence, in many ways it was illusory for both the country and Salma. On Syria's borders, the new states of Turkey and Israel had eaten away at Greater Syria's territory. To the former, the French had given away Alexandretta, and Atatürk had moved fast to "Turkish-ize" the province that Turkey now called Hatay. Israel had declared itself in Palestine, and refugees newly dispossessed of their homes and lands had poured into Syria in 1948. The country's frontier with Israel, the Golan Heights, was a militarized one. This made for hostile relationships with the neighbors.

The new Syria was also caught in the middle of several different power struggles. Both the United States and the Soviet Union saw in the Arab world a potential theater for their Cold War struggle. The regional powers—Jordan, Iraq, Egypt, and Saudi Arabia—all wanted dominance in the Middle East, and each sought to bring Syria within its sphere of influence. As is the case with external interference, all attempted to gain footing, influence, and power in Syria by exploiting whatever divisions they could create or deepen in its society. The Syrian state was still new and had yet to fully resolve several questions, such as the inequities of labor and land ownership, the basis for belonging, and the role of religion in public life. The long fight to be free from the French—a cause that unified society—had deferred these necessary conversations.

When Salma arrived in Damascus, the old elites, not surprisingly, dominated the earliest nationalist governments. They had won those early elections not because they necessarily had a political ideology that spoke to the majority of Syrians, but because they already held leading positions in Syrian society and could exercise the patronage that afforded them. Parties and specific political ideologies were, however, emerging, particularly among the younger generations, who were now more educated than their parents or grandparents had been, and who felt less tied to the Ottoman past and more willing to imagine something completely new. They offered competing visions of what Syria should be and where it belonged in the world.

Among these groups there were four that stood out: the Qawmiyun (Syrian Social Nationalist Party), which envisioned a multiethnic and multireligious state spanning present-day Syria, Lebanon, Iraq, Kuwait, Jordan, Palestine, Cyprus, Sinai, southeastern Turkey, and southwestern Iran, based on a belief that the people within those boundaries shared a common history; the communists, inspired by the Soviet Union; the Syrian Muslim Brotherhood, who espoused a religiously oriented platform that favored political pluralism and religious tolerance; and the Ba'ath, who embraced a kind of pan-Arab socialism.

Many of the new groups threatened the privileges of the old notables and the power structure that supported them. But which vision would have won out in a free exchange of ideas is hard to know, because with so much external interference, the scales tipped for reasons other than the appeal of these ideologies or democratic will. These early lessons in realpolitik convinced enough politicians who sought power that at least in the short term, they needed to sacrifice democracy and cooperate with the army if they were to get their (often idealistic) programs in place—they naïvely thought they would ultimately be in control under such an arrangement. These miscalculations would set the course for the future in Syria.

Salma, too, was handicapped, not by geopolitical proxy wars and struggles, but simply because she was a woman. She would have fared better had she actually been born a man or in another time. For starters, her adoration for her father was unrequited. Abdeljawwad had already made clear that his two daughters would not inherit from him. Their children would not carry his surname, and he had remained bitter at how his father's wealth had passed on to the control of his sisters' shared husband. Even in new Syria, family matters were still governed by the rules of a person's religious sect. Unlike Islam, Christianity did not safeguard a daughter's right to an inheritance, though Islam only guaranteed that a woman got half of what her brothers' shares might be. Nonetheless, it was a relative protection, and it was always in a father's discretion to leave his daughter more than what was required.

Shortly after Salma's marriage and move to Damascus, Abdeljawwad had begun to build a new home in Hama, a modern multistory building, with an apartment on each floor. While the ground floor and garden were for him and Sara, the five floors above each belonged to one of his sons (minus the one he had disowned). To Salma, being cut off simply because she was a woman was deeply painful, and the pain would only deepen over time. It was as if in becoming Ameen's wife, she had disappeared from the family's legacy.

But it wasn't just in her family that her sex disadvantaged her. Had she been a man, she would have been able to work outside the house, create her own livelihood, and have something that was just hers. True, she had hated school, but she had a mind for business and a yearning to be part of the world. She would have also had more power to marry according to her heart. Instead, a woman's role was as wife and mother, and her sphere was the home—a home to be shared with a husband, immediately after leaving her father's house.

In Damascus, Salma decided that at the very least, she would fashion that home as *she* wanted, into the world she craved, and she'd put herself at the helm. All this was only possible because Ameen wasn't the kind of man to impose his will on her or restrict her. Perversely, his gentleness would be the reason she'd never love him.

⊱❈⊰

THE NEIGHBORHOOD SALMA and Ameen moved into was once a place of lush groves fed by a fertile spring; families would come to picnic in the area and to escape the heat of the city's tightly inhabited quarters. It became a residential area in 1936, when developers began to carve a rectangular plot out of the green expanse that bordered Sarouja, Damascus's "Little Istanbul."

Sarouja was one of the first parts of Damascus to be built outside the ancient walls on the northwestern side. Developed in the thirteenth century during the rule of the Mamluks, to this day it is still a maze of winding streets that never anticipated cars. Lined with traditional houses like the one Salma had left behind in Hama, none of them are uniform in size or appearance. Bay windows or added rooms jut a story above onto the street, their shadows offering shade to those walking underneath. Where one family has spread across two sides of the street, the homes are joined by a room suspended above pedestrians' heads. Such underpasses offer vines and jasmine a place to grow, though they also take to the walls or arcades wherever possible. The light of the sun poking through their leaves makes for patterns on the cobblestone streets.

On the north, Sarouja's labyrinth suddenly gives way to Ain al-Kirish, which in contrast is defined by its four straight parallel streets running east to west. Two straight (though not entirely parallel) streets also bisect them north to south, creating three blocks per street. When my grandparents moved in, the neighborhood was bound (as it is today) on the west by 29 May Street and on the north by Baghdad Street, important boulevards to this day. The former is more commercial, with shops, restaurants, and eventually a cinema, the latter more residential. On the east, the four streets dead-ended into orchards and more old houses. They would be cleared in 1970 to make way for Revolution Street, another main traffic artery, which is today Ain al-Kirish's eastern boundary. Two people could walk side by side down the sidewalks, and two cars could comfortably share the street.

The newer buildings of Ain al-Kirish are multifamily apartment buildings covered in sprayed concrete painted white, generally rising three stories above the ground and set back four feet from the sidewalk. Buildings on the same side of the street are separated by about twenty feet. Many trees remain between the buildings and lining the sidewalks; there are all kinds of citrus, as well as loquat, magnolia, and olive. My grandparents settled on the third street from the northern boundary, closer to Sarouja and all the way east, where the streets melted into orchards and traditional houses. They were far from the increasing bustle of 29 May and Baghdad streets. Almost no one had a car, and so the neighborhood's children could own the block with their bicycles and soccer balls.

The Tahaan Building had just been completed in 1949. My grandparents were the first occupants of the apartment they had purchased. Like most buildings in Damascus, it had balconies on all sides; the largest faced the street. Comings and goings were never anonymous in Ain al-Kirish—at any given moment, someone was wringing laundry or watering plants or smoking a cigarette on a balcony. From these extensions of people's homes, it was easy to have a conversation with a person in an adjacent building. Many relationships were built over the moments when neighbors found themselves outside at the same time. Increasingly, as more buildings were built in Ain al-Kirish, residents wishing for a human-free vista would have to look up at the sky to find it. Although each building was already like a honeycomb, the entire street, where everyone knew everyone else, felt like a beehive.

The neighborhood was both residential and commercial. There were two bakeries, which meant that the air in the early morning smelled like fresh bread, while in the afternoon, when the date-filled pastries were made, it became sweeter. With no stoves in people's houses (until the 1970s), dishes that needed to be baked (*kibbeh*, for example, ground lamb with bulgur and seasonings) were sent raw to the bakeries to finish them. Salma had a kerosene heater for items that could be prepared on a stovetop, which is how many Syrian delicacies are cooked.

Along the streets were a few fruit and vegetable vendors, a butcher, a stationery shop, a pharmacy, and a roaster (of all kinds of nuts, both sweet and savory). A person could find just about everything one might need nearby, and what wasn't in a "brick-and-mortar" shop, the street vendors would be selling. With a donkey pulling a cart carrying the goods, they'd announce their presence by shouting out whatever they were hawking.

"Cucumbers! Like baby fingers!" (The perfect size for pickling.)

"Watermelon! We'll slice it open to show you just how red!"

The worst vendor was easily the overzealous kerosene seller, who used an obnoxious horn to announce his arrival on the street. With a barrel strapped across his donkey's back, he'd guide it slowly down the street until a maid or family member could run out with a family's aluminum canister to fill up.

Ain al-Kirish was well suited for Ameen and Salma—it was barely a ten-minute walk to Ameen's job at the Court of Audit in Seven Fountains

Plaza. And after they had children—my mother, Lamya, in 1950; my aunt, Suha, in 1953; and my uncle, Sa'ad, in 1959—it also became convenient to their school. Salma refused to put them in any institution run by nuns, priests, or brothers, so they attended a school not a five-minute walk away, the Laïque-Lycée Française-Arabe, from first grade until graduation. *Laïque* is French for "secular," and the children who attended the school came from Muslim, Christian, and Jewish families.

The Tahaan has four floors, one underground and three above. There is no elevator, only stairs. Arriving on each floor, standing on the last step you come to a rectangular hallway, fourteen feet deep and eight feet wide. One apartment lies to the left and another to the right, each with three doors: one for the men, one for the women, and one for the help and deliveries. Even if Salma and Ameen didn't come from families that separated the sexes socially, the separate doors allowed them to accommodate guests who might be conservative in these matters.

Salma and Ameen had bought an apartment on the second floor (where the first one is at ground level). Standing on its landing, their house was on the left. It was shaped exactly like an upside-down "L" with balconies all along its periphery and ten-foot ceilings throughout. Each apartment was a mirror of the one across the hall, and they were all identical to the ones above and below them.

In Salma and Ameen's house, the men's entrance led into the formal salon, which overlooked the street, and the women's entrance opened into the dining room. Though a door separated the rooms, it could be opened when entertaining. A continuous floor ran between them made of white marble square tiles crisscrossed by black marble bands, each joint punctuated with a white square. Adjacent to the salon was another room, which was in theory the children's room, but was often offered to overnight guests. The room next to the dining room was the informal family room. The last remaining room was the master bedroom, which anchored the stem of the upside-down "L." These other rooms all had white and multicolored terrazzo tiles, arranged in such a way as to decorate the floors with carpets of stone. There was also the kitchen, one full bathroom, and another washroom that had an Arabic toilet (no seat, just squat). Within the kitchen, the ceiling was lowered so as to accommodate two small rooms, accessible by ladder; one was to store the house's *mouneh*, and the other, if needed, for domestic help.

Like other buildings on their street and across Damascus, the inhabitants of the Tahaan were a microcosm of the people who made up new and old Syrian society. Several bore the wounds of displacement and war. Though mostly Damascene, they also included Syrians coming to the capital from other cities, towns, and villages (like Salma). There were Turks, Kurds, Arabs—and now Palestinians—all of different classes, some Christian and others Muslim.

But there was never a question of whether they'd be able to coexist in spite of those differences—that was a given, especially in polite and hospitable Syrian society. The more pressing question in multifamily buildings like the Tahaan was whether they could coexist as neighbors, or their personalities would clash in all the same ways they can for neighbors across the world.

There was no better or immediately discernable barometer of this kind of coexistence than the stairwells of these buildings. Damascus, which is dry much of the year, is dusty, and it didn't take more than a week's worth of grime to dim the sheen of the granite floors. Keeping the stairwell clean required collective action. To wash these common areas, hot, soapy water was dumped on the top floor and then pushed down the stairs and out into the street. Before the squeegee, this was done with a broom made of very coarse straw.

Visitors could discern how much harmony existed among the residents of a building as soon as they entered. If the stairs and landing were clean, then clearly there was accord on at least that floor. If different floors in the same building displayed different levels of cleanliness, then there was likely discord between floors. Of course, lazier neighbors could free-ride where another was more obsessive. Under Salma's self-appointed watch, the stairs in the Tahaan were always clean, and everyone contributed.

৪৩

IN THE TWENTY years that Salma and Ameen would live in the Tahaan, the residents would come and go as life brought marriage, divorce, death, eviction, exile, and emigration. Unlike the solitary family unit that was the traditional Arabic household, a multifamily building brought people into intimate contact with strangers, many of whom became like family.

Different neighbors had their favorites, and not all the friendships were equal, though everyone traded visits on their respective holidays. There were other buildings where some distant incident was still talked about, and could poison any communal feelings for decades after the original sin took place (like an upstairs neighbor picking too much fruit from the top branches of a tree belonging to a neighbor below). But in Salma's years at the Tahaan, happily, its residents weren't divided by the kinds of spats that can arise simply from sharing a space.

But when they first moved in, Salma's upstairs neighbors did become an immediate thorn in her side; given their circumstances, however, she tried to be patient. They were newly arrived Palestinians, and their lives had clearly been upended. Their household was ever in disarray. The many children had lost their mother; their father had remarried, and a stepmother was raising them—though really the parenting fell to the eldest sister. Of course, they had fared better than many of their countrymen who were living in tents and squalor on the borders of their own country, forced out and refused return by recently created Israel. Salma felt the upstairs family was traumatized; they seemed to be in a constant state of agitation (and as a result, they were agitating). The sound of their footsteps as they ran, and their thuds as they landed from jumps or falls, were constantly above her head. The children also liked to throw things from the balconies, and these things often landed on Salma's balconies. Polite admonishments fell on deaf—or incapable—ears.

One day, the kids made the mistake of dumping water onto Salma's balcony as her father was visiting from Hama, and it landed squarely on Sheikh Abdeljawwad's fez-covered head. In a fit of rage, Abdeljawwad promised Salma to lend her the money she needed to buy the flat above. Thanks to this arrangement, not only did Salma have rental income to supplement her husband's annoyingly honest government salary, but she also was able to decide what neighbor would rule the ceilings above her. (She would later secure a permit to build a small apartment above that flat, on the roof, which she would rent out as well. All three properties that she came to own in the Tahaan were in her name alone.)

As soon as Salma could get the Palestinians to move, she brought in her beloved and blessedly childless first cousin once removed, Madhat (his mother was first cousin to Salma, one of the many children born of Abdeljawwad's brother-in-law twice over). An officer in the Syrian Army, he was tall and handsome, with the looks of Tito, the Yugoslav revolutionary and then president, who was popular in Syria. The military suited him, as he was fussy about cleanliness and order, in both his house and his looks. When he wasn't in uniform, he'd wear a white suit, a style that was quite fashionable at the time. He had a contagious laugh and a good sense of humor, and the ladies in the building welcomed his arrival. Madhat would remain single for a long time, dangling hope in front of many. But he pined for another man's wife, whom he never knew, let alone spoke to—he would only watch her from the balcony of another cousin's home.

Madhat came from a village close to Krac des Chevaliers (the Crusader castle built in the 1100s). When his parents visited Damascus, they would stay with him, and gradually his younger siblings moved in with him to finish school, with their parents staying for longer stretches each time. His father was, like Madhat, tall and well-built. However, he never shed his traditional clothing. He wore his mustache long and twisted up at the ends. He adored his wife, Madhat's mother, who never did any housework; it was instead their daughters—with whom they were very strict—who cooked and cleaned. The other women in the family referred to her as *al-dalaleh*, the spoiled one.

Across from Madhat on the top floor was an improbably married couple. Baheej was a retired colonel in the army, from the sleepy town of Safita in the hills above the Mediterranean. He was looking for an entry into Damascene society when he met Lili, who was in her late twenties and didn't want to stay single. Baheej was short with a rounded stomach and a pleasant face, a pipe permanently between his lips. He had fought in the war against Israel, and he often regaled the building's children with the same story over and over about one battle. Lili liked to drop French words—*bonjour, bonsoir, merci*—into her conversation in Arabic. As unlikely a couple as they were, they managed to produce a son, Antoun, who was beloved by my mother and aunt; he was very funny and particularly talented at doctoring report cards.

Madhat had nicknamed Lili *Qwackooka*, and, rather unfairly, she was the butt of many a joke, beyond just her pretensions in French. For a rigid society, which wielded what was proper as a way to deter anyone from even thinking about being different, let alone breaching strict mores, she was a bit odd. Her sister had moved to the United States, and after visiting her there, Lili had returned to Damascus and emulated what she had seen. She would shock her neighbors by running errands on their street in her housedress, her hair in rollers, covered only in a hairnet. Conservative Syrian women didn't leave the house scantily clad, and no Syrian woman would go out ungroomed. Many of the jokes mocked how she made foods that could be easily purchased ready-made, or how she found new life for common household items. Today that would earn her comparisons to Martha Stewart, but at the time, the other women laughed that she was cheap.

But even if Madhat would entertain Salma with stories about his neighbor across the way, Lili was fond of him. When he was home alone, with no one to prepare meals for him, she would bring him some of her own cooking. Rather than send over platters—Syrians tend to exaggerate with their portions, especially when cooking for others—she'd instead pack the food onto coffee saucers. While this behavior contributed to her reputation for thrift, the gripe with her really came down to the cleaning of the stairs. She was very vigilant about only allowing the bare minimum of water to be drawn from her faucet, as residents paid for it. Though that was her right, the cost was negligible. But Salma figured out a way to outfox Lili in this matter. Together with Salma's downstairs neighbor, Refaat, they would strategically knock on Lili's door when she was out, and her more generous and older husband would allow the pretty young women to run the sink unfettered.

Refaat was Salma's favorite. Both women had moved to the building at the same time, and both were newlyweds. Refaat was from a Turkish family, and although she spoke Arabic, her mother and aunt, who frequently visited, spoke only Turkish. Her husband, Raef—tall and very handsome—was a rising officer in the Syrian Army. Refaat's firstborn was a boy, Ragheed, and she and her husband then became Um and Abu Ragheed in the building. (My grandmother would only become Um Sa'ad when her long-awaited son was finally born in 1959, when my mother was already nine years old.) As my mother and aunt grew up, they observed that Um and Abu Ragheed seemed to be a loving and happy couple, which stood in contrast with how they saw their parents, Salma and Ameen.

Salma and Um Ragheed's friendship grew over midmorning coffee, which they often shared after their husbands had left for work. Salma would call to her from her balcony, or Um Ragheed would shout up from below. A symbol of their closeness still stands at the Tahaan: when Salma's second daughter, Suha, was born, Salma planted a bitter orange tree in Um Ragheed's patio to mark the event. Years later, it would reach Salma's front balcony.

More importantly, the two women were there for each other in difficult times. When Suha was seven years old, a boy playing on the street hit her in her eye with a pebble from his slingshot, causing terrible damage and sending Salma into hysterics. The only treatment, urgently needed, was in Beirut. Unfortunately, the border between Syria and Lebanon was closed because of a political flare-up. Abu Ragheed used his high-level connections to help get Suha to the hospital, and they were able to save her sight. Suha, however, who was the only child to inherit her mother's green eyes, lost that beautiful hue in her left eye. Three years later, when Um Ragheed's life took a ruinous turn, Salma would not abandon her friend, even as others shunned her.

Across from Um Ragheed on the ground floor lived a large family—though their name meant "Picklers," they were actually in the linens business. They had eight well-behaved children, and the whole family was notably three things: kind, short, and chubby. They were also quite pious, and the mother and her adult daughters covered their faces in public. When the eldest son got married, he brought his bride to live in the house. No one ever knew how all those people fit into one apartment.

Misfortune struck when the Picklers' eldest daughter was divorced by her husband and, per Syrian tradition, forced to return to live with her parents in the Tahaan. She had already given birth to a baby boy, and the women in the building loved him. Though interpretations of Islamic law vary, the mother usually has custody only until age seven, when it is then automatically awarded to the father. So it was that each happy birthday celebration in the building was overshadowed by the reality that he was one year closer to that age. As the day approached, the building's women began to mourn with her, and when the boy was taken away, on his seventh birthday, their hearts broke with hers.

Below the Picklers and Um Ragheed were the two families who lived in the basement, which held cheaper apartments. One family was ethnically Turkish and spoke Turkish at home. The mother was a fairly talented seamstress, and Salma would have her children's clothes made by her. (Shoes were bought from Bata; one white pair for summer and one brown pair for winter.) Across from the seamstress was a Syrian family, a widow with her two daughters and two sons, one of whom would go on to become a well-respected Arabic-language teacher.

As for the other side of Salma and Ameen's floor, that changed in their first decade in the Tahaan. Initially, a widow lived there, and she filled her main balcony with potted trees, bushes, and flowers. When the apartment was put up for sale, Ameen's younger sister and her husband bought it and moved in with their three sons. The boys were close in age to Lamya and Suha, who welcomed their cousins' arrival. Salma had forbidden them from playing outside on the street; now they had ready playmates who couldn't have lived any closer and whom they could recruit to play at all hours.

Like Ameen, his sister Adèle was kind. Both of them loved to paint, and her sons could draw very well, as could Suha (who would later become an artist). Both of them also found themselves married to difficult people, though in very different ways. Adèle was nearly twenty years younger than her husband, Nikola; by the time they moved to the Tahaan, he was already heavily dependent on her, as he was losing his sight from the "black water" (cataracts). Her every move was coordinated around him; only when Adèle would leave the house to run her errands would she have a few moments to herself. Every day she would help Nikola across the hall to her brother's house, where he stayed while she went to fetch what was needed from the stores below. Sometimes he would insist on coming with her, but when he did, it always slowed Adèle down, as Nikola micromanaged everything, including the selection of the fruits and vegetables. When Adèle needed to cook or do the housework, he'd spend those hours listening to all the radio channels available to them, and because he could no longer read, he'd have his sons read to him. (Only a few years earlier, it was his sons who would sit rapt as Nikola told them stories of Sinbad and Tarzan.) The middle son, Rami, was the most patient and would read to his father for hours.

Salma's eldest, my mother, Lamya, very much liked Nikola. His origins and life fascinated her, and she thought he was like an encyclopedia. Nikola was from Antakya, which was in the Syrian territory that France had handed over to Turkey. When residents were given the choice to move to what was left of Syria, he had taken advantage of the opportunity to do so, as did approximately 50,000 others, including Armenians, who feared living in the Turkish state. Nikola had migrated south and ended up in Aleppo, but his mother had stayed behind in Antakya.

As a young man, Nikola had been sent to Russia to become a priest. While he was studying theology there, the Russian Revolution happened, and the ideas it represented changed him. He returned to Syria a communist. (Ironically, his last name meant "priest.") Back in Syria he had begun to work as a high school history teacher, but with his impending blindness, he had given it up. As Syria drifted further into the Soviet orbit, he found work as an interpreter for experts that came from the USSR to advise the Syrian Ministry of Agriculture.

Salma recognized in Nikola a sort of rigidity that she respected; like him, she was a strict parent. Their spouses, the siblings Ameen and Adèle, would have been more permissive, had either Salma or Nikola allowed it. But occasionally Nikola even outdid Salma, and she would intervene on his sons' behalf—for example, when he wouldn't let his youngest, most rebellious son back in the house to sleep after missing curfew, Salma took him in and forced his father to forgive him the next day.

Salma's daughters liked their paternal aunt, who was an excellent cook and could make many things from scratch, such as her cherry liqueur at Christmas. They were always impressed by her dedication to her sons and her husband. Adèle's tenderness was in stark contrast to Salma's lack of effusive exhibits of love. Though by all accounts Adèle was lovely, Salma had never been as nice to Adèle as she could have been. Salma always put her own family first, meaning her parents and siblings in Hama. Even as she established a new life in Damascus, they were never far away—and not just metaphysically speaking. Her house became everyone's pied-à-terre in the capital.

When Salma's family came from Hama, whether for business or pleasure, Salma would do everything she could to welcome them, even though it ate away at her that she was considered less a part of the family because she was not a son. They would be given her daughters' room, and my mother and aunt would drag their pillows and blankets to their parents' room, where they would remain throughout the visit. At one point, Salma's two younger brothers moved in with them while studying in Damascus. When one of them got married, the new bride came to live with them as well, until their house was ready. She was a beautiful blonde American who reminded everyone of Grace Kelly—Salma's daughters happily made way for her, awed by how glamorous she was. Eventually, rather than trekking back and forth across the house each time someone came to visit, the girls just ended up moving their beds into the master bedroom, where the entire family now slept. Suha, as the younger sister, would have to climb over Lamya to get to her bed.

Salma's devotion to her father was so complete that the only time she would put away her beloved cigarettes was when he came to visit. Sheikh Abdeljawwad's driver would begin honking the horn of his 1949 navy Chevrolet in warning as soon as he turned onto their street, and all the children would be put to work to frantically fan away the last remaining tendrils of smoke.

෯

EVEN AS SALMA became a mother to her own children, her Hama family always came first. No matter that she had a subordinate status compared to her brothers in her father's eyes: she much preferred the type of men her father and brothers were to her husband. Her children were reminded of this often, because she would frequently recite to no one in particular a verse from a poem written by a woman to her brothers. Salma had a deep love of poetry, which holds a cherished position in Syrian culture—memorization of poetry was an integral part of Arabic-language instruction. The lines Salma would say came from an elegy by the seventh-century poetess al-Khansa': "Every morning when I awaken, the first rays of the sun remind me of him / And every evening when the sun sets I mourn for him." Though Salma's brothers were still all alive and well, something about these laments spoke to her. I don't think it was that she was remarkably prescient, although more than one brother would die before his time, one violently murdered. Rather, I think she feared the depths of her love, and it helped to let al-Khansa' speak for her.

Ameen was mild mannered and modest, and also prudent, exactly as his last name, Hakim, would suggest. (According to family tales, the family name had originally been Salibi—meaning "Crusader." The story goes that at some point in the nineteenth century, the Ottomans had given them the choice to convert to Islam, change their name, or die. They changed it.) Ameen was also famously incorruptible. He made his salary and never sought to supplement it with the kind of kickbacks that enriched other bureaucrats, a nasty habit that would only metastasize in Syria's later years. He gave Salma the space to be who she wanted to be—which in great part meant remaining Abdeljawwad's daughter, and sister to her adored brothers. Ameen didn't try to interfere in her relationships with them—though she would confess to her closest friends that she wished in fact that he would. Salma wanted Ameen to tell her father that it wasn't right that she'd be cut out of the wealth. She wanted a strong man in her corner to advocate for her.

Because he didn't, and because he wasn't aggressive or flashy in his spending, he was often the target of her anger. She didn't hide it from her children or the maids or anyone else who might be inside the house. My grandparents inevitably fought at the beginning of each month when Ameen would get paid, and Salma would deride the amount. He never responded in an angry tone; he rarely raised his voice at her at all. He just waited for her to cool down, and tried to facilitate that by pleading with her: "*Ya* Salma, *ya* Salma." If Salma's mother, Sara, was around, she, too, would try to calm her down. Sara very much liked the kind of man Ameen was—honest and loyal, traits she hadn't known in her own husband.

For his children, Ameen was a wonderful father. My mother and aunt loved Fridays, their day off from school. With their father, they'd go to the Atlas bookstore, whose owner was one of Ameen's childhood best friends. While the men would sit and chat on the first floor, Lamya and Suha would wander to the second floor where the children's books were kept. Upstairs they'd also find picture books with illustrations of fish, wild animals, and flowers. Nearly every week Ameen would buy them a book to share, and eventually the girls had all the Arabic fairy tales, beautifully illustrated, in their collection at home. As they got older, they moved on to Dickens and Shakespeare. After visiting Atlas, Ameen would take them by tramway or horse-drawn carriage to visit their uncle, Abdeljawwad's disowned son, who was his friend.

Salma herself also admired certain traits in Ameen. He was impressively smart and fluent in French and English, though he had never lived outside of Syria. He knew much Arabic poetry by heart, and he used it to illustrate his conversation, something Syrians of his generation often did. But Salma remained in love with the forbidden man—the one she had not been allowed to marry—or at least she thought she did. Her daughters overheard her lamenting to her friends, sighing over a love not lived, and complaining that her devotion to her father had not counted for anything when it came to her pleas to marry the sort of man she believed she needed. As the girls grew, she would hint to them of that pain.

Salma poured her frustrated passion into her cigarettes. As if waiting for it even as she slept, she would bring the first one of the day to her lips as soon as she woke up. Rising from bed, she'd pull her *robe de chambre* over her nightgown and reach into its pockets, pack and lighter at the ready. She'd have that first smoke with a cup of bitter black Arabic coffee mixed with ground cardamom, which Ameen would make for her. This was how her children would find her when they woke up to get ready for school. Once they were dressed, she'd brush their hair, and they'd leave with Ameen to walk to school. Along the way he'd stop at the grocers to tell them what Salma had told him to have sent to the house so that she could prepare lunch, the day's main meal.

When the men left for work or errands and the children for school, the building belonged to the women of the Tahaan. With everyone out of the house, Salma would oversee its daily cleaning. Nearly every morning, Marianne, the daughter of Teta Marie—the Armenian woman taken in by my great-grandparents, with whom Salma had grown up—would stop by after placing her orders at the grocers and waiting for them to be delivered. Marianne had moved to Damascus when she married the cook for the French principal of the Laïque (the secular school Salma's children attended). It made Salma very happy to have someone from her childhood so close by. Um Ragheed from downstairs and other women often joined them. Once Salma's groceries arrived, she would start preparing lunch or oversee its preparation. If an extra hand was needed—to pluck the parsley from its stems or roll the grape leaves—Marianne would stay to help. Without fail, she would stay much longer than planned, and then she would dash off before the children arrived from school for lunch.

If Salma's father or older brother, Nazir, were visiting from Hama, they'd pick up Lamya and Suha in their car, much to their delight—Nazir had a long green-and-white Chrysler sedan. Neither my mother nor my aunt can recall Salma ever waiting for them herself at the school's entrance when the children would spill out onto the street. Ameen, who, like all government employees, finished his workday at three in the afternoon, would arrive after the children had returned to school. (In summer when the children were off, they would wait until their father finished work so they could eat together.) He'd share lunch with Salma, though she smoked through most of it and only lightly picked at the food, as delicious as it was. Like nearly everyone else in the city, they would then take a siesta. When the children would return around four o'clock, they would have hours of homework. Salma would help them when she could and always heard their recitation. Dinner was never a large affair (it isn't in Syria), and most evenings Madhat would come down and recruit Ameen for a walk or to visit friends.

Though as a grandmother Salma would play with her grandchildren, even pretending to be a cat or a dog, as a mother she was very rigid. She never kissed or hugged her children. There were no birthday cakes, and she refused to put up a tree at Christmas. They spent the holidays in Hama, and her children would have to wait until they arrived at Abdeljawwad's compound to see decorations and participate in festivities. Most of their toys had been sent to them by their Aunt Béatrice, Ameen and Adèle's sister, who had married in Boston—she sent toy beauty kits, a doctor's bag, and a kitchen set. They had also invented a board game that they played with their cousins, Adèle's sons, across the hallway.

Salma justified her strictness by telling them that she was instead saving money so they would each have a house of their own by the time they were married. Anytime their grandfather Abdeljawwad would give them money for the holidays, Salma would take it and save it in their names.

"You'll thank me when you're older," she'd say.

She forbade them to play in the street, especially after the boy hit Suha in her eye, but with their cousins across the hall, their neighbor above them (Antoun of the mismatched parents), and Marianne's daughters, Nadya and Margot, who would visit, they created a world of fun in their bedrooms, on the balconies, and on the stairs between the floors. They played cops and robbers or dragged all their books to the stairs and pretended to have a bookstore. Using the walls in the stairwell as a screen, they would create shadow animation, projected with a lamp. But they had to keep quiet on the days when Salma was suffering from one of her terrible migraines. The pain was so crippling that sometimes she would hit her head against the wall to try to make it stop. At least twice a week, she would take to bed and insist on darkness. She couldn't talk to her children, and they did their best not to disturb her. When it was really bad, a friend of hers would take the children out.

When the migraines came, Ameen would try to help by massaging her shoulders and neck, to no avail. Many times, Ameen or Lamya would call the pharmacist down the road, and he'd dispatch his assistant to come over to give her a painkiller injection. He'd ride over on his bicycle, and although he had a deformed hand, he would skillfully administer the shot. When Salma's brother returned from his medical training in the United States, he introduced her to another drug that helped her control them to some extent.

But when Salma was well, she was hostess and ringmaster to a lively world—one that she cultivated and curated all from her home in the Tahaan.

⚜

SALMA WOULD TELL Lamya and Suha stories about her grandmother Marta, who had torn down the gates to her home and in their place built ovens to feed the hungry. She wanted them to feel that they had a legacy, that they were strong—that women could be strong. Salma also admired the air of importance that surrounded her father, Abdeljawwad, particularly his ability to use his influence to resolve problems for others. She had wanted her husband to be like that, and when he wasn't (in that way), she decided she would be instead. Like Abdeljawwad, she opened her house to many, and the spectrum of the people who made up Syria passed through it.

In the evening, she would receive her callers wearing heels, a cigarette between her fingers and her green eyes sparkling with interest. She was attracted to different sorts of people. Some were great at conversation, able to entertain with a joke or anecdote or to move a room with recitations of verse. Others had power, and Salma had learned from her father to cultivate relationships with such people, even if it was only through their wives, sisters, and daughters. Among the regulars was a beautiful woman her age named Rose whom she had met before she had married Ameen. Rose's first husband was an older man who was an established judge in Hama, and Rose had been devoted to him. When he died, she caught the eye of a man named Ahmad who would become the love of her life. Rose referred to him as her *emir*—prince. He was a member of parliament, and at one point, minister of the interior.

It was Rose who introduced Salma to Iman, who was also from Hama. Two of Iman's brothers lived in Damascus, one an officer in the army, the other a judge. She also frequented Salma's salon. Rose's husbands and Iman's brothers were all influential men who could be called upon when help was needed, and help—especially in a country where the systems that should have enforced egalitarian principles still greatly favored traditional hierarchies—was often needed. By no means was this help a euphemism for corruption. Rather, these connections meant that disempowered people could be heard, and if they had a case that needed intervention, they would get it.

Rose and Iman were not that much alike, but they both had burdens to bear. Rose had caused a stir in her native Aleppo when she had eloped with the judge at the age of sixteen. Not only had she married a much older man, she had crossed the religious barrier. She was a Christian; he was a Muslim, as was her second husband. Iman was hardly as glamorous as Rose, and had no scandals in her past—she followed Islam's calls for modesty, wore no makeup, and never painted her nails. She tied a scarf around her head—not like today's hijab, but more in the style of Jaqueline Kennedy Onassis. Iman was utterly encumbered, however, by her mother, Um Abd, who was driving her slowly insane. Um Abd was so obsessive-compulsive and germophobic that she was almost an invalid. Iman had become her caretaker, and eventually the lady of the house. Unable to marry and have her own life because of her mother, Iman would come to Salma to vent, complain, and cry when her mother was visiting relatives back in Hama. My grandmother would try to make her laugh, and when that didn't work, she would urge patience, saying that Allah had chosen her for this.

On days when Iman needed a reprieve and her mother was in Damascus, she would bring her mother with her to Salma's house. Um Abd fascinated my mother and aunt. She refused to touch anything other than the Quran, and Iman had to cut her food and feed it to her. She was very pious, and prayed five times a day, but her ablutions were so excessive that her chafed hands were permanently red. Um Abd's faith was resolute, and she believed it could heal. When anyone in Salma's house was sick, she would summon the *Taaset al-Ra'beh*, the Goblet of Horror (a staple in Syrian homes). This was a deep, wide-mouthed copper cup engraved with zodiac signs or algebraic formulas on the inside. The idea was that when a person was suffering heart-racing anxiety or fear—because of an accident or bad news, for example—drinking ordinary water from this cup would be calming. Iman's mother would increase its potency and applications by first praying over it with verses from the Quran before my mother or her sister or brother would be made to drink the water.

Transplants from Hama, as well as those coming to the capital from its surrounding villages for different purposes, were often sent by Salma's father, with promises that she could help them. Eventually they'd knock on her door without his recommendation, as she became increasingly connected in her own right. Some came with business propositions, looking for a small investment of capital. She was always eager to hear these requests, as she desired to be more than a mother and wife, and she was constantly looking for ways to supplement Ameen's income. (The most successful of these enterprises was an olive oil business, when she backed a farmer in the countryside who sold directly to Damascus households.)

Others, however, knocked on her door in need, as they had done—and still did—with her father, Abdeljawwad. She always did her best to help, and in this task Ameen was her ready and willing ally. Some asked to borrow money as they stood at her door. After giving them tea inside the house and hearing their pleas, she would retrieve the needed amount from her armoire. Others had much more complicated problems. Injustices had been committed against them, and they had nowhere else to turn. Often, they were pitted against someone more powerful who was unyielding. She always began with Ameen, asking his counsel and his help as she went about trying to resolve the variety of woes. Salma became such an effective solver of problems that soon people from beyond Hama were showing up in Ain al-Kirish at all hours. These visitors were so frequent, and so frequently from the countryside, that Salma invested in plastic chairs that could easily be rinsed off from the dirt and critters they brought with them.

Many who asked her to intervene were women. The problems that involved girls close in age to her daughters were the ones that stuck with my mother and aunt the most. One such case involved a sixteen-year-old named Nevart. Her mother and her mother's sister-in-law came to Salma in a state of panic. Salma didn't know them, but they had come to her because they had heard she could help. As she often did, she invited them in. Salma offered them tea and tried to calm them down. They were Assyrians from the Hassaka in northeastern Syria. Though predominantly Kurdish, the area also was home to significant numbers of Assyrians and Armenians. The Assyrians are an ancient people who speak Aramaic and who became early adherents to Christianity. They continue to preserve their religious rites and language. Although Nevart is an Armenian name, in the Hassaka there was some mixing in the two communities.

In tears, the women explained that Nevart had married her Arabic tutor, an older Muslim man who had taken her one hundred miles away to his native Deir al-Zour. Her mother and aunt were adamant that she had been kidnapped; the man's relatives were claiming that she had gone willingly and refused to return the girl to her kin. The women had heard that Salma "knew people," and Nevart's mother began to beg Salma to help them, bending down to kiss Salma's feet. Salma quickly brushed off the humiliating gesture, helped her back to her seat, and promised to see what could be done. Salma began with her connections to people in the army and the legal system, including those in the Tahaan. They quickly tracked Nevart down, and she was given the choice to leave her husband or stay with him. She chose her family, and once she was safely back with them, they quickly married her off to absolve the dishonor.

A young girl who had been sent by her parents to Damascus for high school and university—a distant relative from Hama—spent nearly every weekend at Salma's house and quietly observed my grandmother from 1956 to 1966. Moved by her willingness to help anyone who knocked, she once asked Salma why she did it, and Salma answered, "It is in me, I cannot change." Strangely, even though those whom she perceived as weak could never capture her heart, her heart was with the weak.

Her skills as a problem solver were also of use in her own home. Like most middle-class families in Damascus, Salma sometimes had live-in domestic help. Poorer families from outside the capital would seek employment for their young daughters in the homes of those in the city. It wasn't particularly a luxury. (Many came from the impoverished of the Alawite sect. Parents would go door to door to offer their daughters in exchange for their year's salary paid upfront.) Of the girls who worked for them in Ain al-Kirish, Salma's favorite was Sabah. Olive skinned like Salma, she had shown up at Salma's door with her father, who wanted to see her employed. They came from Talkalakh. Sabah was short, with black shiny hair, and as she became more of a woman, even my mother and aunt, who were only a few years younger than her, recognized that she was quite sexy.

Salma taught Sabah how to read and gave her bonuses and gifts on the holidays to buy her own *siygheh* (gold jewelry), so she would have something that belonged to her when she got married; a woman's *siygheh* was meant to protect her, so she could always have access to her own wealth independent from her husband. As per the usual arrangement, Sabah's father had already collected her entire yearly salary in advance. Salma also taught Sabah how to be a *sitt bayt* (a real lady of the house). She would take Sabah to have her hair done at the salon, and she dressed her in custom-made clothing. In the *souk*, or marketplace, people thought Sabah was Salma's daughter.

The problem was, it wasn't just Lamya and Suha who thought Sabah was attractive. A young man who lived in a house one street over did as well. The back of his house and Salma's house faced each other, and he would see Sabah on Salma's kitchen's balcony twenty feet away. Sabah liked him as well. Apparently, they had built a rapport on stares and flirtations across their buildings' backyards and in chance encounters on the street. They would also meet in the theater when Sabah took Lamya and Suha to see a movie. One night when Salma and her family were out, either the suitor or Sabah came up with the idea for him to come over. When Salma, Ameen, and the children returned home earlier than expected, they found their naked neighbor scurrying out of Sabah's bed.

Salma interrogated both of them. She learned that Sabah had lost her virginity, which meant losing her honor as well. In her village, this might have cost Sabah her life. Salma was furious, but she cared for Sabah. So she told the young man, "Marry her now." If he would not, she would call the police. He balked and tried to leave. Salma forbade him to go and called for his parents. They adamantly refused any union: their son was firmly middle-class, and Sabah was a maid. But Salma wasn't done; she called her friends in the army. The young man was an enlisted soldier, and he had a code to follow. When she told them what had happened, they agreed to jail him until he relented. He lasted a night in jail, and the two young people were married soon thereafter. (Sabah and her husband would visit Salma until the end of her days, and her husband would thank her each time they visited for making him marry Sabah.)

One guest to the house at the Tahaan in particular was highly anticipated: Um Obeid, the seer from Hama. She came with the same sad mission to Damascus each month—to visit her firstborn son, Obeid, who was institutionalized in an insane asylum in the city. A woman of little means, she would sleep at Salma's, on a spare mattress Lamya and Suha would drag to the family room floor. Her mystical abilities were partly responsible for her impoverishment. In conservative Hama, which was becoming increasingly religious, what she did was considered *haram*, forbidden. And yet she had the true gift: she could read fortunes. After drinking a demitasse of Arabic coffee, people across the Arab world turn their cups over onto their saucers. The thick remnants that settle to the bottom as a person drinks the coffee coat the porcelain and concave curves of the cup, leaving behind patterns that to the believer reveal what fate has in store. Not many can decipher the meaning—though, as a form of entertainment, someone will often take a stab at it. Um Obeid, it was said, was a *mukhawiyeh*—a sister of the genie.

Even as little girls, Lamya and Suha would drink coffee just to have their fortunes read. It was Um Obeid who told my mother when she was still a child that she would live far from Syria one day, many mountains and seas away—well before emigration would become a common Syrian affliction. Inside Salma's house, Um Obeid kept her white scarf on her head in case any men should come in. On the street, she covered her face as well. She wore no jewelry, having sold her gold bracelets to support her family years before. But when friends, or friends of friends, in Damascus knew that Salma was hosting Um Obeid, they would come especially to see her. For pressing needs, she relied on much more than coffee grounds—after listening to someone's problem, she would almost go into a trance, turning her head as if someone were next to her, and start speaking to no one anyone else could see. She would deliberate with herself and with other voices before explaining to the waiting supplicants what their fortunes would be.

While dilettantes would always see the regular fates in the coffee—money, or love, or a child—Um Obeid's revelations were much more precise. Once, a woman dragged her son, a man of marrying age, to Salma's house. The anxious mother asked Um Obeid, whom she had never before met, if her son would get married soon. After taking his coffee cup, putting it down, and turning to consult the voices, she said to him, "You keep telling people you have no one, but take out from your wallet the picture of the woman in the polka dot dress." When he did, even the skeptical were quieted. But if she saw something bad in the cup or in her trance, she would never reveal it. Instead she would say, "I can't see anything, my power is not working."

It was her power which had undone her son Obeid. He had gone mad when the woman he loved was forbidden by her pious family to marry him— the reason being his mother's *haram* practice. When her other son fell in love, his would-be in-laws were more forgiving. They, too, were pious; however, they would allow the marriage, if—and only if—Um Obeid gave up her gift, even though it was a source of much-needed extra income for her family. She was so ridden with guilt over Obeid that she agreed to forswear telling people what she saw.

During Um Obeid's next visit, her son came with her to see Salma. My grandmother took him to task for condemning his mother to yet more poverty. "Why so much bother for a woman who would ask such a heavy sacrifice from your mother?" she demanded to know.

With his nasal voice that to this day both my mother and my aunt can imitate, he answered, "*Ya Um Sa'ad, al hub sultan.*" Oh mother of Sa'ad, love rules.

ॐ

AS FOR WHO ruled Syria—that changed so frequently that it all began to take on a familiar rhythm. In just Salma and Ameen's first year of marriage, the government would be overthrown three times.

With independence, Syrians were no longer unified by the pressing need to get rid of the French. And while the notable class still wielded significant power, they now had to contend with challenges from ideologically driven political parties and an increasingly powerful and political military. Relations between these three groups (though hardly monolithic internally) would set the course for Syria politically.

The politics of the established notable class were essentially governed by self-interest, not by an ideology like, say, communism. Their electoral victories were due in great part to their ability to exert influence over their tenants or employees to vote according to their will, which was easier as long as balloting was not secret. Voting blocks were often regional, representing the Aleppo and Damascus elites who faced off against each other, the People's Party and the National Party, respectively. Many in Aleppo saw their interests more closely aligned with cities in Iraq—since Ottoman days they had been doing business together, thanks in part to the trains that ran between their cities. The idea of union or federation with the Hashemites, who ruled Jordan and Iraq (until 1958 when the monarchy in the latter was overthrown), appealed to them.

That's not to say that the elites were necessarily unscrupulous—many were guided by a sense of what they saw as moral or just, motivated by a sense of paternalism, but all within a social structure they weren't necessarily interested in changing. They had, after all, benefited under it (like my great-grandfather Abdeljawwad—though by Syrian independence he had receded from the world of politics, he did continue to cultivate access to power, but ultimately for his business affairs).

Now that the French were gone, there was room to question the inequities within Syrian society and to prescribe ways for transforming it, which inevitably meant unseating the notables. The resulting movements and their leaders based their politics on ideology—whether that was socialism, nationalism, Islamism, or some combination. They weren't particularly democratic—they were arguably interested in elections insofar as the elections could deliver them to power (theoretically evening the playing field with the notable class).

Alongside these political players was the military. During the mandate, the French had intentionally recruited for the new Syrian Army men with fewer opportunities, such as from the rural poor. They also sought minority men, assuming that they might be less prone to any kind of nationalism, which the French had perceived as a threat to their colonization project. As such, the notable class was not heavily represented in the officer class. But then France wasn't creating a force for Syria to defend itself from external threats; rather, it was creating a force to assist France in maintaining internal order.

Similarly, the first Syrian president, Shukri al-Quwatli, who came from the traditional elite, had reduced the military's numbers as a way to curtail any potential challenge to his authority from these newly empowered classes. The military resented Quwatli for it, and their anger only grew when, in 1948, Israel easily defeated Syrian forces. The Syrian military became a scapegoat for the humiliation Syrians felt as a nation that was vanquished. However, like the elites or the new political parties, not all officers thought with one mind; among them, many were loyal to different ideological factions. Sometimes, that even meant being more loyal to military strongmen outside of Syria—who would rise to power in other countries, such as Egypt and Iraq—than to a class they were never part of inside Syria.

With the old elites able to dominate and manipulate institutions that should have been democratic, the ideologues became willing to work with the military in hopes of bringing about their envisioned changes. As might have been expected, eventually the men with guns could (and would) dump the philosophers. Thus, Syrians were introduced to the coup d'état, the attempted coup d'état, and the counter coup. While each coup that took place had different goals based on the philosophies of whoever was backing it, they all tended to follow a similar process.

In the 1950s and 1960s in Syria, it was the radio that delivered all the news. So that whenever the current government was being overthrown, one group of soldiers would be sent to the leader's home, while another simultaneously surrounded the radio station. Once the old new ruler was arrested (sometimes in his pajamas), the radio would cackle "Communiqué number 1!" Its main message was always something to the effect of, "Today the army has restored the honor of the country!" These were always followed by several other communiqués. They usually included number 2 (an announcement of who was now in charge and a denouncement of the former leaders for undermining the country), number 3 (that there was martial law, a curfew, and a prohibition on the carrying of arms), and number 4 (that all services would soon be restored and that government employees should report to work). For the children, coups meant school would be closed for days.

Many would tune their radios to the BBC, Voice of America, and Israeli radio to get something closer to the truth of what was happening. While this was particularly necessary during moments when official Syrian radio would be more compromised than usual, many Damascenes listened to several stations each morning before dressing (the way Americans listen for the weather) to triangulate what sort of day it was going to be.

There would be then the rapid executions, the march into exile, and the shuffle as different politicians were in and then out (again). Salma's good friend Rose saw her husband the parliamentarian arrested and released enough times from prison that he started to keep a suitcase ready.

Of the would-be new sultans, Salma was partial to Colonel Adib Shishakly, who came to power in the last of the coups of 1949. He was from Hama, her hometown, and for her, he had *shakhsiyeh*. Of all the many reasons I wish my grandmother had lived longer than she did, her political insights are not among them. Like many a voter today, she let her instincts about a leader's character guide how she felt about them, rather than any intellectually honest assessment of his deeds. (She admired strongmen like Napoleon and Sa'ad Zaghloul, the Egyptian revolutionary, after whom she had named her son.)

Shishakly did cut a strong and distinguished figure, and he stayed in power for over four years, which was, at that point, the longest stretch so far for a Syrian leader. He modernized the military and brought into the government some of the ideological politicians who had been building grassroots movements in the countryside and cities, deriving their legitimacy based on their ideas and not because they had inherited power from their notable families.

One such person was the socialist leader Akram al-Hawrani, whom Shishakly had known since his childhood in Hama, and who was effectively organizing the rural poor across sectarian lines. Initially, they were close; they also were both against unification with Iraq, as the notables from Aleppo were advocating. During Shishakly's rule, Hawrani united his party with the Ba'ath to form the Arab Socialist Ba'ath Party. In its later iterations, the Ba'ath would give the world both Saddam Hussein and Hafez al-Assad. However, none of that could have been foretold by its origins.

The Ba'ath Party was founded by two Syrians, Michel Aflaq and Salah al-Din Bitar. From the same part of Damascus my father comes from, the Midan, they had both been students in Paris in the late 1920s and early 1930s and both were schoolteachers. They named their party Ba'ath from the Arabic word for "resurrection" or "renaissance," and they envisioned a new society that transcended sectarian loyalties and the borders that foreign powers had imposed on the region. They, too, wanted to transform Syria's social structure, and they resented the notables for only thinking about their own interests and not those of the nation.

But things soured with Shishakly, as the colonel eventually dissolved all political parties and banned a number of newspapers. Hawrani, Aflaq, and Bitar all went into exile in Lebanon. (Yet this experience was not enough to disavow party thinkers of the idea that they should use the military as a shortcut to power.) They would return only after Shishakly himself left Syria (under threat of a coup); his exile took him as far away as Brazil (where he would be murdered by a Syrian).

When Shishakly left, parliamentary rule was restored, and optimistically, some historians refer to 1954 through 1958 as the democratic years. Indeed, in this era's reforms, the secret ballot was finally introduced. However, with Syria caught between regional powers vying for influence, as well as between the United States and the Soviet Union in their Cold War, there was much external meddling from various international actors backing one faction or another within Syria.

This period coincided with the arrival onto the scene—not just in Syria but in the Arab world—of the man with ultimate *shakhsiyeh*. A coup against the monarchy in Egypt had brought to power Colonel Gamal Abdel Nasser, a dashing and talented orator who promised to restore the honor of the Arabs. By this he meant essentially ending foreign interference in Arab countries and liberating Palestine. He was the first Egyptian ruler to successfully negotiate an end to British troops in Egypt, and he had faced down Britain, France, and Israel over the Suez Canal.

Salma swooned. Her neighbor downstairs in the Tahaan, Abu Ragheed, was a pro-Nasser colonel in the Syrian Army. With Um Ragheed, Salma's best friend in the building, she listened to Nasser's speeches on the radio. Nasser gave voice to Arab anger over what had happened to the Palestinians and to the way foreign countries had interfered in Arab countries. He also preached domestically a politics of nationalization and deprivatization—policies that, if enacted in Syria, would directly affect the wealth of landowners and factory owners like Salma's father, Abdeljawwad.

The Arab world swooned right alongside Salma, even though Nasser was antidemocratic, pursued economic policies of questionable benefit, unfairly scapegoated communities in the Arab world (such as Arab Jews), and would destroy much of the cosmopolitanism of Egypt. In Syria, specifically, political and military leaders began discussing the possibility of a union with the larger and seemingly strong Egypt as a solution to all the external meddling. Then, in February 1958, possibility became reality when the two countries formed the United Arab Republic (UAR), which was conceived of as a structure that could grow as other Arab nations joined. Syria ceased to exist as an independent state.

Salma's support for Nasser, like her support for Shishakly, made little sense personally. As the two countries brought their bureaucracies together, many Syrians were ousted from their positions to make way for Egyptians. Salma's husband, Ameen, survived only because he was actually that good at his job. Though Salma dominated her household, Lamya disagreed with her. Even at that young age, Lamya found it humiliating that Syria had been swallowed up and subsumed by Egypt. Her only fond memory of the short-lived union between Syria and Egypt was that Ameen's frequent trips to Cairo meant he'd bring crates of mangos back with him.

Nasser also made good on his promises to implement sweeping land reforms, and Abdeljawwad lost a vast amount of property. Indeed, Abdeljawwad came to despise Nasser more than any other foe. Eventually, Nasser's policies and his empowering of Egyptians at the expense of Syrians created a backlash from Syrian business and army circles, and in September 1961, a coup brought the UAR to an end. The new leadership in Damascus—sometimes referred to as the secessionist regime—now sought to repair relations with anti-Nasserist Arab countries such as Jordan and Saudi Arabia, which backed the government, as well as global powers such as the United States and Great Britain. From Egypt, Nasser denounced the secessionists, using his radio broadcasts as a platform—one speech decrying the coup lasted three hours. Meanwhile, Egyptian intelligence continued to infiltrate Syria and worked actively to undermine its government.

Although the notables had again reasserted themselves in the 1961 secessionist coup, their rule would soon be dealt a final blow. Inspired by the Iraqi Ba'athists' successful military coup in Baghdad in March 1963, military officers from Ba'athist and Nasserist factions carried out yet another coup in Syria. Although the civilian side of the Ba'ath Party consented to the coup, the officers were really in charge now. These Ba'athists quickly went about purging government employees and replacing them with their relatives, friends, and people who came from the same village or tribe, which coincided frequently with sect. People from the rural areas now came to Damascus to assume positions in the new government, regardless of whether they were qualified.

Although Nasserists had been major participants in the March 1963 coup, by late April, the Ba'athists were increasingly sidelining them, and even purging Nasserists and political independents. In July 1963, the Nasserist officers, who believed the union between Syria and Egypt should be re-established, launched an attempted coup against the new government under the leadership of Jassem Alwan, a colonel in the Syrian Army, and with the help of Egyptian intelligence. Alwan's deputy was my family's neighbor in the Tahaan, Abu Ragheed.

The Nasserists attacked Army Headquarters and the radio station, and hundreds of people were killed in the ensuing battle, including several civilian bystanders. But the coup failed, and many participating officers were arrested and immediately executed. Abu Ragheed, however, with Alwan, was able to flee and went into hiding in the countryside outside Damascus.

The residents of the Tahaan heard the news on the radio and went into a collective shock. They had just seen him, and nothing had seemed askance, they told each other. What would happen to his wife and children? Salma rushed to her neighbor and friend to keep vigil. Eventually, Abu Ragheed was caught and tried by military, and he pleaded guilty. He was sentenced to death, though soon after the sentence was reduced to life imprisonment.

It was a dark time for Um Ragheed; many shunned her, for fear of their own safety, but the Tahaan stood by her, Salma in particular. When Um Ragheed would go to visit her husband in prison, Salma made sure to send homemade food with her. After a year, an amnesty agreement was reached—the family was granted asylum in Egypt, and they quickly left. Um Ragheed, a dear friend who had been there since Salma had moved in, was suddenly gone.

The Ba'athist officers had succeeded in consolidating power in their ranks and moved quickly to put down popular dissent. The most organized of the dissenters were the Islamists, which in Syria meant the Muslim Brotherhood. Ideologically, Ba'athism and Islamism were at odds. If the Muslim Brotherhood believed that Islam was both religion and state, the Ba'athists believed that religion belonged to God, while the country belonged to all (in theory). Thus, in the spring of 1964, prayer leaders delivered inflammatory anti-Ba'ath speeches, and people took to the streets to demonstrate. The protests in Salma's hometown, Hama, took a violent turn, as more radical elements ignored the Brotherhood's call not to take up arms against the regime. The Ba'athists quickly put down the burgeoning uprising, even bombarding a mosque to which armed Islamists had retreated. They also survived demonstrations by the merchant and landowning classes, who bristled at the party's policies of nationalization and deprivatization.

By 1966, the military Ba'athists had dumped the old Ba'athist guard in another coup. The ousted leader at the time still had the backing of Aflaq, the party's founder and philosopher, and so Aflaq also went into exile, finally settling in Baghdad and endorsing the Ba'athist regimes in Iraq. That coup led to a permanent schism between the Iraqi and Syrian Ba'ath movements. Syria's rulers were now clearly the military, dominated by officers with rural and small-town backgrounds who had long resented the notable class. They were headed by Salah Jadid, an Alawite officer who set about to change the balance of power, and Syrians from less privileged backgrounds began gaining influence and responsibility. Unfortunately, many of those who were put in charge were not qualified for their jobs.

In the military, for example, many officers had been removed from their posts in favor of reservists who were being rewarded for their loyalty. The timing couldn't have been worse: war shortly broke out with Israel in 1967. Again, Syrian forces were at a self-inflicted disadvantage, and Israel destroyed the Syrian Air Force in a day, while most of its planes were still on the ground.

During the war, Salma sent all three of her children to her parents' house in Hama, believing that they would be safer away from the capital. She stayed with Ameen, who couldn't leave his job. My mother was seventeen now and actively journaling. She wrote how stunned she was at how quickly the Egyptian forces—which they had been led to believe were mighty—had been vanquished. Places that she had visited while on vacation just the year before—Ramallah, Jerusalem, and Bethlehem—were now off-limits.

My mother was already angry with the Ba'athist rulers who had nationalized her school, the Laïque, which she loved. Gone were the French administrators, replaced with Ba'athist loyalists. They had drastically changed the curriculum; where before students took math and science in both French and Arabic, now they were only permitted to study these subjects in Arabic. They were no longer permitted to study French history and geography, which was viewed as antipatriotic. The new administrators got rid of their music and science lab classes. Lamya detested the fact that, to equalize the education available in private and public schools, the new government had decided to eviscerate private education rather than improve public schooling. As a final insult, the Ba'athists had renamed her school the Freedom Academy (although in common parlance people still referred to as the Laïque). Now, when Syrian and Egyptian radio played nothing but nationalist songs and fabricated news about their heroism, she knew better. Bunkered at Abdel-jawwad's house in Hama, they again tuned in to the BBC and Israeli radio for more accurate information. And to Voice of America to hear the pop songs, especially Paul Anka.

At the time of the 1967 war, the powerful Syrian defense minister was a man named Hafez al-Assad. Although he and Salah Jadid had been close, they were quickly moving apart over who was to blame for yet another humiliating defeat at the hands of the Israelis. They also had different politics: Jadid favored more Marxist policies, whereas Assad was more of a pragmatist. Assad began replacing Jadid loyalists with his own supporters, gearing up for his final move three years later.

৪৹৪

THE DARKNESS OF these two decades, which were the backdrop to Salma's first years of marriage and the start of her new family and life in Damascus, made the comforts of song and poetry that much more important to her. And poetry was how Hassan Hamada came into her life. A singer whose stage name was Karawan (for the curlew bird), a well-known radio star who sang poetry set to music, was a frequent guest at Salma's. Hassan penned many of the poems that Karawan sang—and it was Karawan who introduced Hassan to Salma.

In the summer of 1970, Salma was ready to leave the Tahaan. She wanted to move to a newer building, and the Ain al-Kirish neighborhood was less convenient than it had been when she was first married and her family was young. Ameen was close to retirement, their son was enrolled in a school in a different neighborhood, and their daughters were now in university.

The building's makeup had also changed. Um Ragheed's apartment had remained empty for a long time and then was briefly rented to her relatives. Salma had sold the rooftop apartment that she had built years before, making a profit and putting it toward a new house. She immediately regretted the sale, however. While the couple, Abu and Um Ali, were kind, and Abu

Ali was in the army (which was always useful), their children quickly proved to be unruly and even delinquently inclined. As a family, they were also not keen on participating in the firm regime of stairwell cleanliness that Salma had installed. Although she was able to extract their cooperation, she'd be the last who could.

When Madhat, Salma's adored cousin who had been in the other apartment upstairs, had moved out in 1965, she had decided to sell that apartment as well. That time, she chose more carefully, selling to a newlywed couple who she felt would become good neighbors. The wife, Fatima, was from the coast, nearly two hundred miles from Damascus. She was only eighteen when she moved in—just a few years older than Lamya—and her husband was eighteen years her senior. Salma made sure to look after her, inviting her down whenever there were guests in her salon to hear the singing and poetry, calling up to her to share a cup of coffee, and helping her enroll her children in the nearby Laïque despite caps to prevent overcrowding. Salma also turned out to be quite right about Fatima; she raised well-behaved children, and the stairs were pristine.

In 1970, with Lamya already twenty, Salma imagined she would be getting married soon, and Salma was determined to provide each of her children with a house by the time they wed. So instead of selling the apartment, she decided to look for a tenant. Knowing this, Karawan brought Hassan to Salma.

Hassan was from Dara'a, a small city in southwestern Syria very near to the Jordanian border. He had been orphaned and impoverished at a young age, and the military had been one of the few options available to him to make a life for himself. He enlisted after having worked as a teacher in small villages in the south of Syria. But his calling had always been writing. During his military service, a comrade who was cleaning out his gun had accidentally shot Hassan in the kidney, earning him an honorable discharge with the rank of first lieutenant and the freedom to fully pursue his art. Even while he was still in the army, his work had appeared in magazines and in the theater. He was gaining some renown for his poetry, which was innovative because he wrote in the Syrian dialect, not classical Arabic.

When Salma met Hassan he was married and had a four-year-old son; he was also struggling financially. Salma liked Hassan's conversation and his poetry, and she wanted to help him in his burgeoning career. So she agreed to rent him her apartment in the Tahaan. On August 15, 1970, they signed a one-year renewable lease and he paid—as was the law—the full year's rent, which was 2,500 Syrian pounds (equivalent to $625 then). This was sup-posed to be a stop-gap measure while he looked for a more affordable place to live. To help him further, Salma left him much of the furniture that she didn't immediately need. She also left the kitchen fully stocked with plates, utensils, glasses, and pots and pans.

She took his wife Hilal and introduced her one by one to the women who still lived in the building, including the Picklers, Fatima, Lili, and Adèle. Happily, Fatima had a son the same age as Hilal's, and the Pickler boy (who had gone to his father's at age seven) often came around. Before leaving for her new home, Salma asked Hassan one thing—that he look after the bitter orange tree she had planted for Suha's birth.

Salma moved her family to a furnished apartment while she waited for the house she had bought to be vacated. Her eventual home was located in the Qasour, a neighborhood that had been developed years after Ain al-Kirish and reflected a different sensibility. With wider avenues and buildings set farther back from the street, it felt much more open. Salma would be able to sit on her balcony without immediately seeing anyone or hearing any con-versation across the way.

Just as her children were growing up, her parents were aging. Shortly after she signed the lease with Hassan, Abdeljawwad fell ill, and her brother, the doctor, brought him from Hama to Damascus to attend to him full time in the French Hospital. Once larger than life, Abdeljawwad could no longer get out of bed. His speech was slurred, and he was deteriorating by the day.

Nonetheless, he still had time for the ladies, and his hospital room was always full of well-wishers. Salma went to see him every day; tending to him became her focus. During one visit, when she was there with Ameen and Suha, Abdeljawwad told her, "I oppressed you. You didn't get what you de-served; you were the best one with me." He offered her a blank check to an account in Lebanon, where banking was still private.

She ripped it up. "I'm not like your other children," she told him.

It was a noble act, but it was not rewarded. When he died, if she expected her brothers to act on his change of heart, she was wrong: they did not.

Only days before her father passed away on October 3, the man whose pol-icies had cost Abdeljawwad so much of his wealth—Gamal Abdel Nasser—also died. The family would say it was almost as if Abdeljawwad, knowing Nasser was dead, could finally happily leave this earth. (Salma's mother, Sara, would die within a year of Abdeljawwad; she collapsed while seated at the kitchen work table, cooking yet another meal for one of her adult grandchildren on a visit to Hama.)

In the same month of Abdeljawwad's death, on October 30, 1970, Hafez al-Assad staged the last coup in Syria, which he would maintain was not a coup but simply a "corrective movement." (However, the Ba'ath party's founder, Aflaq, did not return to Syria from Iraq. Indeed, Assad would sentence him to death *in abstentia* in 1971.) Cousin Madhat, a brigadier general who survived all the coups, finally got married that year.

With her children much older now, Salma warned them about getting too involved in politics in Syria: "You know I like to talk and be free in my speech. Think as you like, whatever you want, but don't be in a party. It's enough to love your country and work toward its benefit."

The following summer, when Hassan's lease on the Tahaan apartment expired, he wanted to stay, and the lease automatically renewed. For Salma, he could remain until she needed the house back. To help Hassan save even more money for his eventual move, she decreased the rent.

Assad's term as president came and went, and he remained in power. Likewise, Hassan stayed on in the Tahaan. In the end, neither man would leave. Hassan, for his part, sold Salma's furniture for cash.

3

ADRIFT

Damascus, 1972–1979

I N EARLY SUMMER 1972, THERE WAS A KNOCK ON THE DOOR OF
Salma's new house. Lamya, now twenty-two years old, answered. An
elderly couple stood before her, catching their breath, having just climbed
three flights of steep stairs. The woman spoke, introducing herself. Her name
was Alia.

She explained that they had dropped by to see her husband's brother who
lived next door, but no one had answered. She asked if Lamya would kindly
let her brother-in-law know when he returned that they had been in the
neighborhood and had stopped by.

It was a hot day, and the same several flights of stairs awaited them, even
if the descent would be easier. Naturally, Lamya invited the elderly couple
in. They declined, but Alia did ask for a glass of water, which Lamya happily
provided, before continuing on their way.

It was just a fleeting meeting, but Lamya had made a positive first impression. As the mother of sons of marrying age, Alia had to keep her eyes open
for prospects, and so she inquired with her brother-in-law and his wife about
their young neighbor. She was pleased to learn that Lamya was much liked
and from a good family—a promising potential spouse.

Alia wanted her unmarried sons to marry Syrian women; her two eldest sons had both completed their engineering doctorates in West Germany and had married German women, who remained utterly foreign to her. Alia didn't want to lose any more future grandchildren to a language she could never understand. With the fourth of her five sons doing his medical training in the United States, the possibility was real. A Syrian wife would help lure him back home. He'd soon be returning for the first time since leaving two and a half years before. She wouldn't waste the opportunity.

With a bit of orchestration, Alia saw to it that her son, Sharif, met Lamya at a casual gathering at his uncle's house.

Sharif liked that Lamya was at university, training to be a pharmacist, and that she spoke French and English. She was also beautiful, sweet, and had blue eyes—less common in Syria and often coveted. Lamya was charmed by him as well. Not only was he tall, dark, and handsome, but he was also ambitious and supportive of her continuing her education. A Syrian doctor who lived in America and smoked a pipe—she saw a mix of East and West that she felt reflected her own spirit.

Though he came from a family of more modest means, they clearly valued education. Like his brothers, Sharif was forging his own path far away, based on his smarts alone. That seemed more important to Lamya than being born into money. Her cousins from Salma's brothers, who had inherited Abdeljawwad's wealth, had often flaunted it while they were growing up—much to Lamya's distaste.

Both of Sharif's parents came from families that had started their lives anew in Damascus after 1860 when they'd fled the violence with the Druze in their village, Raashiya al-Wadi, in what was now Lebanon. Many of their family members had been killed. They had made their way to the Midan, a neighborhood of conservative Muslim families where Christians were safe. As was often the case, especially for the women of Alia's generation, much of a family's resources would go toward educating the boys, who would be the providers. A son, by virtue of his education, might move into the professional classes and marry accordingly.

A boy's sister, however, would likely marry in keeping with her father's station. Alia's brother George, for example, had a doctorate from Georgetown University in Washington, DC, had been the Syrian ambassador to the United Nations, and, before retiring shortly after Hafez al-Assad came to power, had even taken a turn presiding over the UN Security Council. Alia and her sister were instead married to skilled but uneducated men from virtuous families. Alia's husband, Fahed, was a carpenter. (Yet, when it came to her own and only daughter, Alia had agreed she should quit school in the eighth grade and begin to earn the family much-needed money.)

In a whirlwind courtship, Lamya and Sharif met each other's friends and took day-trips, spending time at the hilltop resort at Bloudan and the convent and monasteries at Saidnaya. With Sharif's impending departure, they decided to go for it and get engaged.

Sharif went ring shopping while Lamya went dress shopping (engagements called for parties). He bought her a simple band and at the same time bought his mother a solitaire and band. Alia had never had a diamond ring; with six children to feed and his own mother to care for, Fahed hadn't spoiled her. At times she had even been forced to sell her own gold *siygheh* to help support the family.

Lamya and Salma traveled to Beirut, where ready-made clothing from Europe could be easily purchased. There Lamya bought a flowy floor-length dress that had been made in America (with a tag identifying it as union made). It was in Salma's favorite color, emerald green. Crafted from muslin, it had a romantic feel, its ornamentation a series of sheer delicate ruffles at the wrists, along the V-neckline, down one side, and at the bottom of the skirt.

On August 13, 1972, Salma and Ameen hosted the celebration at their house. The happy couple's friends and family all joined them. Ameen's sister, Adèle; her husband, Nikola; and their son Rami came from the Tahaan. Lamya had also invited Hilal, the young wife of Salma's tenant, Hassan. Hassan had started working on a TV serial, but he didn't have a television set to watch the weekly episodes. Salma would have him, his wife, and their little son, Shadi, over to her house each week so they'd never miss an installment. She would always have a light dinner waiting.

Lamya wasn't particularly charmed by Hassan; she felt he had a wandering eye, and she had felt it on her at times. But her engagement party coincided with Hassan being away in West Germany, and Lamya had insisted Hilal join them. When she came, Lamya was delighted. Hilal had borrowed a black dress from her sister (made for her own engagement party), had had her hair done, and was wearing makeup. Tall and radiant, she was hard to miss and looked so happy to be out.

Before the catered meal and the music and dancing, an Orthodox priest said a prayer, and Sharif and Lamya exchanged engagement rings. Shortly thereafter, Sharif returned to the United States to continue his medical residency.

ॐ

THE COUPLE WROTE to each other. He told her about his life in Baltimore, how late he worked, what he hoped for, and where in the hospital on his breaks he read her letters. She told him what was happening back home, what she thought of world affairs, and how her studies were coming along. They had much planned out: they would wed after she graduated, in the summer of 1973; she would further her studies in the United States; and after they both finished their training and saved some money, they would move back to Syria together.

But then, in March 1973, after a long Sunday lunch that she had spent all morning preparing, Alia collapsed dead of a sudden heart attack.

Worried about how devastated he would be, no one informed Sharif of his mother's death, and his family forbade Lamya from saying anything to him, whether by phone or by post. He was only twenty-eight years old, the furthest-flung of her six children, and very much alone in America. After he had moved there, Alia would send him large tins of food she had prepared to remind him of home and of her. The last of them—olives, walnut-stuffed and oil-cured eggplant, and apricot preserves—arrived in Baltimore a week after his mother died and still before he knew. On that same day, another Syrian doctor in Baltimore, tasked by Sharif's family to tell him of Alia's death, phoned him to ask if he could visit. Sharif was enthusiastic—he told his friend of the Syrian treats prepared by his mother's hand that had just been delivered and promised they would feast on them together that night.

In his apartment, Sharif had yet to unpack the delicacies when his friend delivered the news. He was dazed by the realization that his mother had been alive when the package had been sent, and dead before it had arrived. Though his friend saw the tears in Sharif's eyes, he barely spoke, saying only, "I should have been there."

By the time Sharif received the news, his mother had already been buried. There was no point in going to Syria. Instead, he simply went to work the next day. Lamya, however, attended Alia's funeral, and even though she was only Sharif's fiancée, she wore black for the traditional forty days. And, of course, she postponed the wedding. Decorum called for at least a six-month delay between Alia's death and her family celebrating anything happy.

But Sharif's siblings in Damascus complained. They felt she should have done more. They wanted the wedding to be delayed for at least a year, which would have left Lamya in limbo—unable to join Sharif in the United States and also unable to begin work in Syria. (Because university education was gratis, doctors and pharmacists had to complete a two-year commitment to an underserved area before they could take a regular job; she would not have enough time to finish that service.) His brothers and sister in Syria began to write to Sharif with their disapproval. Lamya's skirts were too short, they said—it was the era of the *mini-jupe*—and she often went out with her university friends, a mixed group of both men and women.

Sharif's older brother, who still lived in Damascus, visited Lamya to set her straight. Lest she think Sharif would marry her right away, he let her know that plans were in the works to send their youngest brother before her to America to finish his graduate studies and to live with Sharif. He also barked at her that his brother did nothing without consulting him first. She didn't see how life with such in-laws could ever be peaceful. As much as she liked Sharif, in November 1973, exasperated, Lamya took off the ring he gave her.

She didn't feel much relief. Instead, she mourned him and what could have been. She had already spent more than a year planning and envisioning a very different life, a shared life in a very different place, when she found herself adjusting to what seemed like a much less fulfilling reality in Syria.

⚙

BY THE TIME Lamya had broken off the engagement, Hafez al-Assad had been in power for three years, longer than most governments in Syria had usually lasted. His longevity was in part due to his expanding the *mukhabarat*, consolidating their heads under state institutions, and putting his brother Rifaat in charge—all to protect himself from further military coups. If Syria had become a one-party country after the 1963 coup, it was now a one-man party, especially once Assad had neutralized opponents within the party against him. Much of Syria's population was by then disgruntled with Ba'athism.

The Ba'athists (and the neo-Ba'athists, in particular, whom Assad had overthrown with his "corrective movement") had succeeded in transforming certain aspects of Syrian society. The old socioeconomic order—which had favored Sunnis from the cities—had been upended. The elite now consisted of young men of peasant origin, many from religious minorities, though not exclusively, who hailed from the most deprived parts of the country, such as Latakia on the coast, or Deir al-Zour or Dara'a (where Hassan came from).

In certain circles in Damascus, resentful Syrians referred to Assad with the alliteration *al qard min Qardaha*, "the monkey from Qardaha," Assad's home village in the hills above Latakia. (The emphasis on the "Q" phoneme, which is often dropped in Syrian dialect, is a distinctive feature of regions where many Syrian Alawites come from.) As much as Assad's authoritarian ways were resented, so were his Alawite roots. Anger against the oppressive regime was also driven by a class-based indignation that Syrian society's lowest rungs were now in charge. Because Assad was Alawite, those objections also took on a sectarian tinge, which would help to thwart a sense of solidarity across class lines in favor of sectarian identities. However, class was often more determinative of a person's everyday reality and opportunity.

Corruption, cronyism, and patronage were widespread among this new elite, both in the military and in the large bureaucracy, which Syrians had to engage if they were to get anything done (from buying property, to opening a business, to getting the necessary national ID card). Very little happened that didn't require greasing the palms of a government official, employee, or lackey. The exploitation of power by even the most low-ranking bureaucrat underlined the lack of commitment the new rulers had to Ba'athist ideals. The ideology had become merely a justification for behaviors that enriched specific individuals and their related communities.

People's anger toward these new rulers went beyond just their corruption and hypocrisy. In his years in power so far, Assad had overseen a fourfold increase in public spending and encouraged rural migration to the cities, including Damascus, which in turn had caused inflation. While this was one of the ways that Assad had consolidated his political power in the capital, many of the city's residents regarded the newcomers with suspicion and resentment. The land reforms had harmed the large businessmen and property-owning (once notable) families, and they had severely hurt the small traders and merchants by restricting private capital and trade.

When Assad had come to power with his "corrective movement," he had promised to ease many of the neo-Ba'athists' severe socioeconomic policies and moderate their anti-Islamist stance. These grievances, after all, had been at the heart of the violence in Hama in 1964. However, by 1973 the economic policies had long taken effect, and Assad's efforts to liberalize the economy—which was the basis for much of the resentment—were not yielding many results.

The Muslim Brotherhood, which had long been ideologically opposed to the Ba'athists because of their supposed secular nature, was also dissatisfied. Assad had made a few gestures toward them—he raised 2,000 religious functionaries in rank and increased their salaries; he appointed a religious scholar to head the ministry that oversaw religious and charitable trusts; and he enabled the construction of mosques while cultivating a public image of being a committed Muslim who wanted to preserve the Islamic identity of the country. But in 1973, these efforts were not enough. After 1964, and particularly under the neo-Ba'athists, the shift of power from traditional Sunni elites to the rural poor and increasingly to Alawites only accelerated. Prejudices against the Alawites had remained—because they were poor, because they had allied with the French, because they were a big part of the Ba'ath. Also, they weren't "real" Muslims, as far as the more orthodox were concerned.

In my mother's last semester of university, Assad published a draft of his new constitution, setting off a furor among the Islamists. While the draft implicitly mentioned Islam by declaring Shari'a as a main source of legislation, Assad did not include the special status it had had under the 1950 Constitution, which stated that the religion of the head of state should be Islam. Seizing on the opportunity to mobilize pious Sunnis to their side, Islamists in Hama denounced the regime as godless and began coordinating protests and condemnation. In response, Assad added an article stipulating that the religion of the president must be Islam. For good measure, he had a Lebanese Shiite cleric (Musa al-Sadr) pen a *fatwa* that Alawites were Shiite and therefore Muslims, while recruiting the support of a few Sunni religious scholars to his side (in exchange for access to power).

Although it may have just been political strategizing to placate those resisting his rule, Assad—of the supposedly secular Ba'ath—thus formalized in the Syrian constitution the inequality between Syrian citizens of Muslim faith and those who were not Muslim. Not that anyone in my family wanted to be president, but now, as it was reaffirmed in the new constitution, neither could any other Syrian Christian.

After Lamya's class graduated in July 1973, many were still struggling to find work, or any kind of sure footing in Syria. Increasingly, talented Syrians left Syria to start their professional lives. Many went to the oil-rich Gulf countries, as did low-skilled workers. Inevitably, these Syrians were introduced to different interpretations of Islam, including Saudi Wahhabism, a version of Salafism. In Saudi Arabia, Syrians had to comply with edicts that governed facets of public life that they were unaccustomed to. For example, Wahhabism forbade any public expressions of religions other than Islam, whereas in Syria, different religious groups not only had their own places of worship but saw their holidays included in official calendars. Wahhabism also prohibited the sale of alcohol, demanded strict gender segregation in public, and sneered at equality for its female citizens. Once Syrians were of retirement age, or left or lost their jobs, they had to leave the Gulf; thus many of these ideas would accompany returning Syrians home.

And then, within months of Lamya's graduation, in October 1973, Syria and Israel were again at war. This time, Israeli forces struck Damascus, and Lamya knew several of the people who were killed. A mother and son died as they walked on the street; her uncle's neighbors—an entire family—died in their home.

Right when Lamya and her cohort not only were supposed to start to work but would also begin to marry (or at least think about it), they were anxiously focused on what might come next for them individually, as a group, and as a nation.

⊱⊰

IN MARCH 1974, Sharif came back to Syria to attend the memorial service marking one year since his mother's death. Ever since he had learned of her passing and funeral, after the fact, he had decided he would attend this service. His brothers from West Germany also came to Damascus to pay their mother the respect she deserved and to say goodbye—having waited a year to do so.

Toward the end of his trip to Syria, he called Lamya and asked if he could visit her and her parents. Of course, she told him.

At her parents' house in the Qasour, they had a perfectly cordial visit, where she didn't explain her reasons for breaking off the engagement, and he didn't ask why. When she tried to give him back the engagement ring, he told her to keep it. At the door, he kissed her goodbye. She didn't think she would ever see him again.

Her friends, who had watched Sharif's siblings bully Lamya, urged her to talk to him and give him a chance to respond. Days later, she finally called him and suggested they meet, just the two of them. They sat together at the Piccadilly restaurant in the posh neighborhood of Abu Rummaneh, and she told him as he listened quietly.

Finally he said, "But we will be far away."

Lamya saw that his siblings' pettiness clearly had little to do with Sharif's life, which was already much out of reach in Baltimore. She also began to understand that by the time they would return to Syria, where they planned to live, their bond would be long cemented. She began to regret that she had broken off their engagement.

The restaurant's owner knew and liked Lamya, as his place was popular with her group of friends. Seeing her sitting with her onetime fiancé, he sent to their table the seer, a man able to read coffee cups and peer into their future. After examining their overturned demitasses, he told them that there was good news and many voyages in the coming months.

He was right. My parents decided not to wait any longer and to get married before Sharif's departure to the United States, which was only days away. Their wedding was so hastily arranged that Lamya borrowed a dress—a chic affair with a floppy white hat, which she wore with her own silver lamé platform heels.

The small reception took place at Piccadilly, of course, and the owner offered the five-tier cake as a gift. (A few years later, he was imprisoned for a time when a relative of the president wanted to force him into a partnership. Under these common arrangements, an entrepreneur of a successful endeavor would have to share his profit with the Assad family or a member of his inner circle, even though the latter wouldn't provide capital or ideas or income. These "partners" also often indulged in the goods or services a business provided without ever feeling the need to pay.)

After their hurried honeymoon in Beirut, Sharif returned to the United States, and Lamya waited at her parents' house in Damascus for a summons from the American embassy in Beirut. (There was none in Syria because relations between the United States and Syria had been severed due to the 1967 and 1973 wars. However, in the summer of 1974, Syria and Egypt finally signed a disengagement agreement, after which President Nixon visited Syria.) April, May, and June passed, and Lamya was still sleeping in the bedroom she shared with her sister, Suha.

During these months in which she was newly wed (and also now pregnant with me), Lamya filled the time with all the preparations for moving to the United States. Salma, as she often did, took charge. Ameen watched in silence and took orders when called upon. Clothes were made for Lamya that would be appropriate in America, a trousseau was assembled, and wedding gifts were sorted into what was possible to take and what would have to remain behind. When word came that her papers were finally ready, the needed arrangements became more frantic. Tickets were booked, travel plans made, and Salma began hosting in waves the many friends and relatives who came to say goodbye. Each evening there were trays of sweets, coffee, and tea brought out. The many visitors were a welcome distraction for Salma from Lamya's impending absence.

But as sad as Salma was to see her eldest daughter travel so far away from her, she liked Sharif. He was a doctor and from a respected family, and his uncle had been a good and affable neighbor. I think she must have also recognized something of herself in him. Lamya, according to everyone, was much more like Ameen, who was kind and soft-spoken. Sharif, like Salma, was also hungry for success and possessed the same unshakable belief in himself. Unlike Sharif, Salma was limited by her sex, though her hunger to have a place in the world other than as someone's wife or mother never abated, even as she entered her fifties.

Indeed, since leaving Ain al-Kirish, Salma believed she had found a way to realize her ambitions; she had become the sole agent of Avon in Syria. Unlike in the United States, Avon wasn't sold door-to-door in Syria; rather, the products were stocked in perfumeries, and Salma got them to buyers in Damascus, Aleppo, Tartous, Hama, and many other cities and towns across Syria. Ameen had retired, and he spent his spare time translating intellectual English and French books and articles into Arabic, but he also used his linguistic skills to handle all the paperwork necessary for Salma to run her business.

In the coming years, Salma would also open a clothing store, with a partner, in a commercial property she had bought. She was the first *sitt bayt* (lady of the house) in her circle to do anything of the sort. As a girl, Suha used to feel a bit embarrassed about it, believing it beneath her mother's station, but in later years she understood her mother's motivation. The experience was short-lived, but Salma thoroughly enjoyed it.

She had honed her talent for cultivating access to powerbrokers after all the years of facilitating affairs for people who needed the help (or mercy) of the powerful but lacked access to them. Under the new regime, it was a necessary skill for anyone who wanted to do business, and now she used it to be able to do this one thing—Avon—that made her so happy.

If there was something masculine in how Salma behaved—mediating like a sheikh, smoking her cigarettes, and making conversation in a husky voice, she also had her feminine side. She didn't import Avon's makeup as she didn't have much use for it—except for her red Dior lipstick—but she loved the beautiful names that Avon had given its perfumes, like *Charisma*, *Moonwind*, *Topaze*, and *Nearness*.

ജ&ൠ

ALTHOUGH EVERYONE KNEW it was coming, the day in July 1974 that Lamya would leave Damascus for America arrived faster than anyone wanted. Just ten months before, she had broken off her engagement to my father. Now she was married, pregnant, and leaving; there hadn't been enough time to fully process the all-too-real changes.

On her last morning, she awoke with a mix of excitement and sadness. She went to a hair salon and had her thick, tight curls blown out, and then she donned her new clothes. For her trip to America, she chose American colors—red bell-bottoms and a navy shirt with red and white stripes woven in. She would fly first to London, then to Copenhagen, where she would stay overnight in a hotel before flying to New York City's Kennedy Airport and then Washington National.

By midmorning, her closest friends had all gathered at her parents' house to see her off. Just as many of them had visited the old house in Ain al-Kirish, they had also become frequent guests in the new house in the Qasour. They had studied pharmacy together at the University of Damascus, putting in long hours in lecture, lab, and study sessions. Although they had graduated the year before, several of them were still looking for jobs, and those who were not from Damascus, who had come to study at its university, had stayed in the capital. For the moment, it was almost as if the days of university hadn't quite ended.

As excited as her friends were for her, it hurt to lose her, and though these were Lamya's own final moments in Syria, her leaving marked an ending not just for her, but also for all of those who would be left behind. Lamya had been the first in their tightly knit circle to wed, and now she was the first to leave—and not just to go to Lebanon or Europe or the Gulf, but to a place even farther away. Even though my mother's departure was only supposed to be temporary, everyone knew that few who left Syria would come back. Merit-based opportunities were more likely to be found elsewhere.

Lamya knew she'd miss her friends, but most of all, she regretted leaving her siblings. Her younger brother, Sa'ad, was only fifteen years old and would change quickly and dramatically while she was away. All her life she had shared a room with her sister, Suha, and each was close with the other's friends. Suha had been crying intermittently for weeks now.

But Lamya believed that she and Sharif would return to live in Syria, which made saying goodbye that day easier to bear. Besides, she was excited for what awaited her—her husband, a new baby, and an American education. She was eager to live in what she imagined was a free society. At university, teachers were hired and scholarships were awarded according to party membership. Criticism or dissent of the government were stifled or punished, and what Lamya saw as a cult of veneration of Assad was already becoming prevalent.

She couldn't wait to leave all that behind.

As the car was loaded with her luggage, she asked her friends to keep visiting the house, and not to leave her family alone, especially Suha. And when it was really time to go, they all posed for one last photo, my mother's swollen eyes hidden behind her large sunglasses.

Only a small group went to the airport. And only there did it start to feel real.

As Salma embraced Lamya for the last time, she told her daughter to take care of herself and to be a good wife. She also assured her that if things didn't work out, that she'd always have a home to come back to.

When Lamya boarded, Suha accompanied her, a bending of the security rules permitted her alone because of connections Salma had cultivated. Suha stayed with her sister—her friend and even idol in many ways—until the very last possible moment. All their memories and stories had been forged together; now they would live their own independent lives and make new ones. Suha could only weep and left the plane in tears.

Without her, Lamya's parents and siblings returned to the house and its silence. Salma avoided going into the bedroom Lamya had shared with Suha, and Suha averted her eyes from what had been Lamya's bed.

THREE MONTHS AFTER they were married, my parents saw each other again for the first time at Washington National Airport. Now they would not be parting ways only days later; nor would their relationship any longer consist of brief episodes separated by long intervals and letters. Both had to adjust to this new reality, even if much of their energies had been dedicated to dreaming and planning it.

As they drove into Baltimore, Lamya was taken by charming Mount Vernon Place and its centerpiece Washington Monument, a towering column beautifully lit in the darkness. Obviously older than the modern buildings she had just seen as they drove through Baltimore's downtown, the square was more how she imagined Europe than America. Of course, she had never been to Europe before the previous night.

Hopkins House, where my father had just rented a large one-bedroom apartment on the twelfth floor, seemed more American. It was a new building, eighteen floors tall, with an elevator, swimming pool, and a doorman at its entrance. Sharif had sparsely furnished it, waiting for his bride to finish the project. What Lamya loved was the long balcony that looked out on the tree-filled grounds of Johns Hopkins University.

The next morning Sharif went to work at the University of Maryland, where he was doing his specialist training. Lamya set out unpacking and doing what she imagined a wife should do, rearranging. There were foods in the kitchen cabinets that she didn't understand, particularly cereal. And when she found a jar of a beige paste in the refrigerator, after much consternation, she threw it out, convinced that whatever it was, it must be spoiled. (It was peanut butter.)

They settled into a pattern. While Sharif was at work, Lamya kept herself busy reading, studying English, and learning to cook. In the evening they would take drives in the city to acquaint her with Baltimore or they'd do the grocery shopping together. The first time Lamya went to the nearby Giant, she was awestruck. It was so completely different from Syria, where fruits and vegetables, dairy products, baked goods, meat, and household items were all sold separately at smaller shops. Some days, Lamya would walk there on her own, even if they didn't need anything at home; it was the only place she knew how to get to alone. There, she was often surprised to find older women who talked to her even though they didn't know her. They seemed lonely and just wanted to chat.

It was during those encounters or in their building's elevator and lobby that Lamya learned about American small talk. She also quickly discovered that while her English was good on paper, understanding what was being said to her and replying to others was a challenge. The American accent was also so different from that of the Frenchwoman who had been the English teacher at her school in Damascus. Lamya began to keep the TV on the whole day even as she did other things. What she watched or what she heard was often hard to follow, but with time, it helped. On the weekends, the young couple would go out to dinner, visit Hochschild-Kohn's, a department store, or take day trips to Washington, DC, or Annapolis.

After their engagement, Lamya and Sharif had planned for her to enroll at the university right away, and she imagined that she would make friends there. But with her pregnancy, those plans were deferred, and anyone she met, she met through Sharif. His community was the other Arab and foreign doctors—mostly from the developing world—in Baltimore.

Lamya missed Syria. Sharif did as well, but he had been away since the last days of 1969 and had grown used to the longing. She yearned for her family and friends, and missed how easy it was in Damascus to step out of the house and into the middle of everything. There she felt connected to the street and to the people on it, even those she never spoke to but who were nonetheless part of her everyday routines, such as her commute to school or her errands in the market. In Baltimore, it was nearly impossible to find the spices or foods from home. There was no Internet then, or satellite TV. Friends sent cassette tapes with the latest music from home, and my parents prized them, playing them well into the 1980s. (As children we ruined many of them, replacing the tracks with our high-pitched voices once we learned how to press "record" on our stereo.)

Phoning Syria was not only expensive, it was complicated. It required placing the call with an international operator, who would phone back once a line was available, and lines to a developing country like Syria were often scarce. Sometimes it happened in a couple of hours, other times the next day. With the time difference—seven hours—it was often the middle of the night in either Baltimore or Damascus once a line became available. But no matter the hour, Lamya took the call just to hear Salma's voice. Of course, the understanding that the operator on the Syria side was most likely listening to what was being said (on behalf of the regime) always circumscribed conversation. No one discussed anything political or risky in any way. Letters were what forestalled the drift. Lamya used the prestamped blue Aerograms to write to everyone back in Syria, and she was always happy when responses arrived with news of home.

That fall in America, Ramadan came and went with barely a whisper, whereas in Syria, as soon as the sun set and the fast could be broken, a loud canon was fired that could be heard across the city. Lamya craved the sweets made only during Ramadan and the time at home with family, watching the TV shows and serials made just for the holiday. A few months later, as Christmas approached, which was also her due date, the opposite was true. Christmas day was an official holiday in Syria, and of course the Syrian Christians celebrated it. But it was never as important as Easter, and it wasn't marked by the consumerism and consumption frenzy that my parents saw preceding it in the United States. Even though Christmas was a much bigger event in the United States than it was in Syria, my parents felt its religious meaning much more in Syria.

Unaware of any nearby Orthodox churches with Mass in Arabic, they stayed in on Christmas Day and waited for their baby to arrive. They hosted my mother's cousin, Rami, who was visiting from New Jersey. Rami was a doctor now and also completing his medical training in the United States. Not only were Rami and Lamya cousins on her dad's side, but they had also been neighbors growing up, when their families had lived across the hall from each other in the Tahaan.

It wasn't until late at night on December 28 that Lamya's water broke. Sharif and Rami rushed her to the hospital at the University of Maryland. My parents didn't know if they were having a boy or a girl—ultrasounds were not yet common. Lamya wanted a son, but Sharif had his heart set on a daughter, so he could name her for his beloved late mother. Sixteen hours later, he got his way when I was born.

They gave me an Arabic name, as they would my three siblings who would come after. We may have all been born American (years before my parents became citizens), but we expected to return to Syria, and our names were meant to help us belong there. Instead, in pre-multicultural America, where we would all come of age as their plans were derailed, our names only marked us as different.

Of course, for years my parents continued to see themselves and us as different. As outsiders to the limited racial paradigm that characterized America then—white versus black—they hadn't ever imagined that they would belong in the United States. In the 1970s, American hostility to Arabs, though already creeping upward, was relatively nascent. The years when it would fully blossom were yet to come, and no one thought of that when my father notified the family in Syria that a daughter had been born and her name was Alia.

News of a boy would have been greeted with much more excitement by other family members, but Sharif couldn't have been happier; he wanted to hear his mother's name among the living. When the New Year arrived two nights later, Sharif and Lamya rung it in at midnight in her hospital room, and on the first day of 1975, they took me home.

$$\text{\small ※}$$

A YEAR AFTER she left Damascus, Lamya returned home on a ticket her parents sent her, the first of her almost yearly (in those early years) trips home. Salma and Ameen wanted to meet their first grandchild. I was six months old and, by all accounts, an affable and flirtatious baby.

Sharif had just finished his medical fellowship and had remained in Baltimore to peacefully study for his medical boards and look for work. He also could no longer return, as all his deferments with the Syrian military had run out. It would be years before he visited Syria again. Lamya's trips were always alone with the children.

On that first trip back, Lamya spent the summer at her parents' house seeing her friends and family and introducing them to me. Sharif's father, the widowed carpenter, came every day to visit. He already had nine grandchildren, but they all lived far away in West Germany and Abu Dhabi; he barely knew them. I was the only one in Syria.

Now that Lamya had her own family, it was time to arrange a house for her eventual return to Damascus. In Syria, there were no private banks and therefore no mortgage loans; houses were a full cash purchase, and parents were often an integral part of acquiring a home. With Sharif's potential earnings in America, they might be able to purchase a home in Damascus eventually, though that would delay how soon Lamya would return. Besides, Salma already had the perfect house in mind, and it could be ready soon— the house in Ain al-Kirish. What better place than the home Salma had moved to when she herself was a new bride with a new family? Now Salma hoped that Lamya would raise her own children in it.

Although Hassan had yet to find the right house for his family, Salma hadn't needed the house back yet, so she had let him stay on, year after year. That changed once Salma met me.

That summer, Salma told Hassan he'd have to start looking for a new house, because she needed hers back now. She was surprised when instead he told her he was quite happy in the Tahaan and saw no reason to leave.

Unfortunately for my grandmother, the law was on his side, as long as he was paying rent, which he was. The way the law saw it, Salma owned another house, so she didn't need this one. To get around the ownership issue, Salma decided that year to have the house's title transferred to Lamya. It was not only the first step to reclaiming the Ain al-Kirish house, but also—and more importantly—a step in having me close by.

After Lamya returned to Baltimore, having spent two months in Damascus, Salma wrote to both her daughter and her son-in-law. She told my father:

> *I already used to think of all of you constantly, but now even more than before, most likely because of the beloved Alia. She left us in Damascus with our hearts attached to her. I listen to her recorded voice whenever I can, and all of us feel the burn of your absence and its duress. Your aunt and uncle, who also got attached to Alia, call and ask about her all the time.*
>
> *Don't yell at her if she does something bad because she belongs to me now, not just you.*

To my mother, she wrote:

> *I was in a difficult situation after saying goodbye to you and Alia. Since then your memory is always in my mind, especially when Alia clung to my neck when you tried to take her away from me at the airport.*

She then addressed me directly:

> *Alia I love you, you the light of my eye. How cute were you when Lamya was sleeping and I'd pass by you and you'd signal me, taking care not to wake your mother, to "Come get me and take me?" When I tell this story, everyone laughs and says how smart you are!*

SUMMER AFTER SUMMER, Lamya would return to Damascus, only to find that little progress had been made in the courts in evicting Hassan. Another law was also in play. Written in 1970 (the same year Hafez al-Assad took over Syria and Hassan took over Salma's house), it made evicting a military veteran impossible. Because of Hassan's injury, it was as if he was owed a debt by his nation and its people. Salma's only hope was that Hassan would agree to leave of his own accord.

Salma dispatched Ameen to plead with him, appealing to reason, morality, and mercy. As a sort of pension for Ameen's civil service, he was entitled to participate in a program whereby he could make installment payments toward acquiring a flat in one of the new buildings that would be completed in the coming years. Eager to get the apartment back, Salma and Ameen offered to sign Hassan up in Ameen's place. Hassan agreed, and Ameen made the first few payments. Shortly thereafter, however, Hassan pulled out of the arrangement and cashed out the share that Ameen's money had bought him.

This matter troubled Salma to no end. She had started to suspect that there was a disconnect between Hassan's public persona and his private life. During some of those visits to Salma's house, Hilal had complained, even cried, about how Hassan treated her and her son, alluding to abusive behavior. Salma was repulsed at what she heard but also angry with herself for having been duped and having put her family in this situation.

Finally, she authorized Ameen to offer Hassan money to leave the house. Unmoved, Hassan laughed in his face and is said to have told him, "This house is not your house, nor your daughter's house. It is my house." As beautiful as Hassan's words could be in his poetry, my family learned they could also be ugly, and the memory of these words stung for decades, which is why they are so well remembered.

There was also little love lost between Hassan and Lamya. Once, when Hassan had received a letter from abroad, Hilal had intercepted it. Unable to read English, she had brought it to Lamya and asked her to translate it. Lamya hesitated, but she read it for her when Hilal pleaded. It was what she had feared—a letter from a woman who was clearly a lover. When Hilal confronted Hassan with it, he also demanded to know who had helped her read it.

But for my mother—that someone could take what wasn't his, that an individual's rights depended on who they were—was symptomatic of what she saw happening in Syria. After nearly a year away in Baltimore, she would come back each summer to find new statues of Assad, new buildings named for him, and yet new slogans glorifying him as the "father of the country."

Things had changed at the Tahaan as well. While Abu and Um Ali (the owners of the small top-floor apartment) were well liked, no one really wanted their children around. They were constantly fighting with others in Ain al-Kirish, coming to blows over squabbles, sometimes even brandishing a gun. Um Ali was also less interested in the cleanliness of the stairs (or of the balcony of her neighbor below, Fatima) than the other women, and none of them had been able to persuade her to cooperate the way Salma had always done.

And what had happened to Adèle in the Tahaan had always haunted Lamya. By 1976, Ameen's sister had seen all three of her sons leave Syria for the United States and France. They left because of a lack of opportunities, out of distaste with the regime, and to avoid serving in the regime's army, as all males were required to do unless they were the only son. Adèle had also lost her ailing husband that year, which caused her to sink into an extreme depression. Before a year had passed after Nikola's death, she took her own life. Her death, by self-immolation, shocked everyone who knew her. Salma felt terrible remorse for not showing her sister-in-law the same kindness she had shown strangers in need.

For my mother, what transpired at the Tahaan and in the lives of its residents seemed like another consequence of the place Syria was becoming. Families were spread across the globe because there was no way to dissent from what the regime demanded of people and no way to choose your own path based on your own merit. If people disregarded anyone's welfare but their own, it was in part because the state made Syrians feel that everyone was on his or her own; people were being pitted against one another. With a corrupt and violent regime ruling them, it seemed to her that many Syrians began to feel that right and wrong were irrelevant concepts—besides, might made right. Was it any wonder then that people took advantage of a kind of lawlessness if it made their lives easier, like inexpensively keeping a roof over their families' heads? With each return to Damascus, Lamya had more misgivings about raising her children in Syria.

Yet, as dominated as Syria was at that time by men, especially one man, my experience of it in those early years, always returning with my mother, was dominated by women, especially Salma. And so despite having been named for my father's mother, my birthright always felt much more matrilineal. Salma's house—because she really was its core and its sovereign—was a world of its own. It was always full of motion and of people, with my grandmother directing its ebbs and flows. She still suffered from crippling migraines, and when they struck, everyone gave her the quiet she demanded. And when she was renewed, the house came back to life with her.

Even though those recollections were so distant, I clung to them as I grew, knowing they had been real and happy, because they were all I would have of Syria after 1980, when tragedy would strike. My memories of our visits were sketched mostly in sensations: The smell of diesel, jasmine, and roasting coffee beans. Dry Damascus heat on my skin. The calls to purchase, from cart-pushing hawkers selling everything from boiling corn on the cob to tanks of cooking gas. The calls to pray, to pause. Afternoon siesta and loose cotton nightshirts that would flutter for a coveted second, caught in the path of a rotating fan as it cut away at the heavy air of August. Embraces in the fleshy and hairless arms of all the women who loved me because I was Lamya's daughter and Salma's granddaughter.

4

PACK YOUR BAGS AND GO

Damascus, Summer 1980

B Y 1980, I WAS ALMOST SIX YEARS OLD, AND—DISTRESSINGLY FOR some—still unbaptized. In the Antiochian Orthodox tradition, a baptized soul is supposedly liberated from sin and helped by the heavens in the struggle against the temptations that we all face in life. Hence, infants are usually christened forty days after their birth, before much sin can be committed.

My parents were almost 2,000 days late, though it wasn't as if I had exhibited a greater proclivity for sinning than other six-year-olds. But they kept putting off baptizing me and my siblings until our always-imminent-yet-never-materializing move back to Syria. After all, churches in Damascus were much closer to the Holy Land than those in Baltimore, and my father believed that those baptismal protections would stick better if cast in territory that was actually biblical. Of course, christenings were also an event to be celebrated with family, and ours was in Syria.

Deciding they had really delayed much too long, as soon as I finished kindergarten in June 1980, my mother packed us up for yet another extended stay in Syria, again without my father. By this time, our family included my sister, Manal, who was almost three, and my one-year-old brother, Zayn. Lamya was pregnant with what I was promised would be the last sibling to be inflicted upon me. But that baby was not due until mid-October.

As we were already going to be having a group baptism, there was a thought to waiting one more summer. But given what would happen over the course of the next few months, just getting it done turned out to be a very good decision.

For the time being, the apartment in the Tahaan was lost to us. What Hassan had said to Ameen was true—it was, for all intents and purposes, Hassan's house. Only if he moved out would my mother be able to reclaim it, and he clearly had no intention of leaving. So in addition to protecting our souls from sin, Lamya had an even more important task before her that summer: she was going to start looking for a house to buy for our eventual return to Damascus.

My parents had just bought a house in Baltimore the year before (with a mortgage), but that was because the idea of paying rent, of throwing away money, was anathema to my father. The goal was still *le retour*, as Lamya called it. Each time she had gone back to Syria, my father had given her money to deposit in the central bank. With no private banks, a house had to be paid for in full. And my father was desperate to return to Syria. He was working over a hundred hours a week between his job and moonlighting, supporting a family of five-going-on-six, and was fed up with the disdain with which some American-born doctors seemed to regard the foreigner with an Arabic accent who was willing to work twice as hard as they were.

Before my mother left the United States that June, he told her—deliberately and in English—"I beg you to take me home."

My aunt Suha was also getting married that summer to her longtime love, Kamal. Right after their wedding, they would leave for France, where Suha's groom would begin training as a psychiatrist. My aunt, a delicate, romantic soul and a talented artist who loved Picasso and Matisse, could not wait to start a life with Kamal, and she was giddy that they would spend a few years in Paris, with all its museums and galleries. Lamya would be her maid of honor for the ceremony. I, more importantly, would be a flower girl, as would my younger sister, Manal.

In Baltimore, Lamya missed the support that grandparents and other relatives could provide for a mother trying to raise three children; in Syria, caring for us was easier. But for all her husband's unwavering faith that life in Syria would be better than in America, her reservations about life under the Assad regime only grew with each trip home.

In the meantime, Salma, ever savvy, had made nice with the new powerbrokers to facilitate her Avon business. Without them, she would never have been allowed to exceed the quota on imports necessary to get the business off the ground. Her connection to the regime was a female relative of Assad's wife; his in-laws, the Makhlouf family, parlayed their relations to become fabulously wealthy and powerful (even more so under Hafez's son Bashar). In return for her assistance, the woman helped herself to much of Salma's inventory. I'm not so sure in the end there was really much benefit for my grandmother. Regardless, even if it was the only way to do business in Syria, Lamya found it repulsive. She had begun to think that life in America, with all its isolation, would be better for her children.

Lamya had been born only two years after the onset of the Arab-Israeli conflict and the Cold War. She had grown up in a Syria that was constantly in a state of near war with its much more powerful neighbor, Israel, and that was a pawn and a proxy in the US-Soviet struggle for global hegemony. The region's instability and violence had been a part of everyday reality her entire life. Like others of her generation and those who would come after, that was their normal. And yet, as the Assad regime became more entrenched, things had felt different. Everyone knew that dissidents—of varying political leanings—disappeared. Yet barely anyone said anything, lest the same thing happen to them.

Salma's sister-in-law, my great aunt Clara (the American who looked like Grace Kelly), illustrates this best with her own testimonial. As happens in Damascus, Clara had a "balcony friend," a woman with whom she traded smiles and waves. They never spoke to each other, as there was a garden between them. But while Clara was on her balcony hanging clean diapers up to dry, the dark-haired Syrian woman would be ironing the white shirts of her three college-aged boys. Soon Clara noticed fewer and fewer shirts being ironed, until there were none. It was then that she heard that one by one, her neighbor's sons had been taken by the *mukhabarat*. Clara kept thinking that maybe she should do something—at least extend some kindness—but she was afraid to reach out and to appear sympathetic to those who had crossed the regime. Because someone might be watching, Clara never crossed the garden. The woman's sons never returned.

SINCE 1974 WHEN Lamya had gone to Baltimore, opponents of the regime had coalesced to support the Islamist Muslim Brotherhood, the most organized and implacable of the regime's antagonists. Thanks to a potent combination of resentments—particularly over social and economic policies—the Brotherhood had a much larger base of support than ever before. The regime had overturned the traditional social order, favoring rural Alawites over urban Sunnis, and instituted socialist policies opposed by the former elites. Strategically then, the Brotherhood had worked steadily to widen their appeal by defending such pro-capitalist and anti-statist values as private property ownership, freedom of trade, and private investment.

Beyond just railing against the secular (in name) nature of the regime, the Brotherhood also purposely stoked sectarianism, appealing to Sunnis (the majority in Syria) to resist rule by a religious and "heretical" minority. That sectarianism spread not just in the civilian population but among the country's military as well. By the end of the 1970s, the most significant opposition to the regime was coming from outside Damascus, from Aleppo and Hama, which saw mass anti-regime protests. Salma had not been back to Hama since her mother, Sara, had died in 1971. But it remained the place where she grounded her identity.

Since 1963, the Ba'athists had reduced the political and economic influence of these two cities' elites, though they had long been powerful players in both spheres. Their political isolation made them more susceptible to the economic policies of the regime, and indeed, there was increased unemployment in both Aleppo and Hama. Hama, which was home to many of the landowning notables, people like my great-grandfather Abdeljawwad, had been particularly affected by the land reforms. Many lost their property and saw it redistributed to the peasants, and much of the cotton production was shifted away from Hama to other parts of Syria. With both cities already religiously conservative, particularly Hama, they had many reasons to resent the regime.

The confrontations between the regime and the Brotherhood were becoming more and more frequent. The summer before, on June 16, 1979, Sunni gunmen—let in by a Sunni officer—had slaughtered Alawite cadets in the dining hall at the Aleppo Artillery School. In response, the regime had arrested the imam of Aleppo's grand mosque as well as 6,000 people right before a major religious holiday. Islamist protests and strikes carried out by the merchant class ensued in a steady crescendo until March 1980, a few months before we arrived for our summer in Damascus. At one angry protest, demonstrators killed eighteen Alawites; meanwhile, the government arrested or killed several hundred in Aleppo. The regime then occupied the city for a year, and it is estimated that in that time, security forces killed 1,000 to 2,000 people—some were killed randomly, while others were summarily executed. At least another 8,000 people were arrested.

In Hama, the rich landed families, which had suffered financial losses under the Ba'athist land reforms, began providing money and arms to Brotherhood protesters in Hama. While opposition there became increasingly radicalized, in Aleppo the regime neutralized opponents. It did so by partially meeting the traditional elite's demands, including dismissing the despised Ba'athist military governor of Aleppo (who didn't come from the city), replacing him with an Aleppine lawyer, and appointing other Aleppine professionals to positions of power in the city.

Islamists of more radical leanings carried out targeted assassinations of prominent Alawites across the country, killing not only *mukhabarat* and military officers but also sheikhs, doctors, professors, and university administrators. The regime responded with mass arrests, torture, and killings, and also by purging hundreds of Sunnis from the army, from intelligence services, and from the Ba'ath Party. Increasingly, those carrying out the repression of mostly Sunnis were mostly Alawites, who in many cases were determined to crush and humiliate their Sunni opponents. Thus when protesters set fire to a local Ba'ath Party headquarters in Jisr al-Shughour, a small city in northwestern Syria, the government responded with helicopter-borne special forces, and within days several hundred locals had been killed. While the origins of the animus may not have been sectarianism, the conflict between the government and the most pronounced and violent opposition had sectarian overtones.

The escalation of violence and what it said about the regime still wasn't enough, though, to dissuade my father from sending us with my mother to Syria that summer, nor from *le retour*. He was so utterly caught up in his own life that he couldn't see how all of the turmoil could have anything to do with him; after all, he didn't care about politics.

Then, shortly after our arrival in Damascus, the violence became more audacious. On June 26, Islamists attempted to assassinate Hafez al-Assad. Attackers threw two grenades and fired machine-gun bursts at him as he waited at a diplomatic function in Damascus. The next day, June 27, his brother, the feared Rifaat al-Assad, who the previous year had called for opponents to be

placed in labor and reeducation camps in the desert, extracted swift and brutal revenge. He went to the Syrian Desert, to the infamous prison in Tadmour
(Palmyra), and massacred over 1,000 Islamist inmates. Ten days later, membership in the Muslim Brotherhood became punishable by death; members
had a one-month grace period to turn themselves in.

The killings, though nearby, also seemed remote. The violence appeared
to be contained, and the victims were still being targeted for specific political
involvement. Both my parents' families stayed out of politics, for the most
part. Like other Syrians, they didn't feel directly implicated; it was all happening to *other* people. In this way, I think many Syrians learned to tolerate
the regime's voracious greed for absolute power: they were too busy being
grateful it wasn't them.

Syria might be having a bad summer, which to a more astute reader might
have portended an even worse future. Yet it was normal enough, contained
enough, that it didn't seem like it should get in the way of our summer of
family events—our baptisms, Suha's wedding, and many fun activities in
between.

But then, the very next day, on June 28, that violence came to our family's
doorstep.

༺༻

THOUGH MY GREAT-GRANDFATHER Abdeljawwad had already been dead
for a decade, his shadow loomed over his children, including my grandmother Salma. She continued to act like the word of her brothers carried
greater weight than that of her own husband. When Kamal and his parents
came to ask for Suha's hand in marriage, in front of Ameen, she told them
they'd have to wait for her brother the doctor to return from a trip abroad.

After Abdeljawwad's death, it was his third son, Nazir, who took over
his affairs. Salma's eldest brother had long ago been disowned for marrying
the woman he loved and cut out of any inheritance. The second brother
had died in 1964. With Abdeljawwad gone, Salma idolized Nazir, who had
movie-star looks, with his blue eyes and dark, slicked-back hair.

From the day Abdeljawwad died, his children began fighting over his financial legacy, which consisted of lands, other property, and money. But how
they cannibalized each other as they battled it out was his greater bequest.

Abdeljawwad had maintained his power in a family of many sons, where several of his children had inherited his egoism, by manipulating them—emotionally, financially, and even legally. Abdeljawwad had been at times as vindictively punitive as he was generous. He instilled in them all a tribal chauvinism while playing them off each other and cultivating jealousies among them. (For example, each morning, he'd hold private audiences with the sons living in the family compound in Hama. One by one, they'd come down in the morning to sit with him, and he'd often make them conflicting promises.) After his death, the family was bound in a contradictory vortex—they were selfish, petty, and possessed of an unwavering belief that their shared blood was better than everyone else's. They would love each other, swear at each other, rob each other, and even sue each other.

Honestly, one needed a cheat sheet to know who spoke to whom and who didn't, and when it came to squabbles, who lined up with whom and against whom—absurd results that meant siblings allied on one conflict might not be speaking to each other over another. Their children—the first cousins—tried to stay out of it, as many of them had genuine friendships, though not all were able to stay above the fray. Today, some of the second cousins (my generation) have warm relations while others maintain the grievances of their grandparents.

In 1980, most of Abdeljawwad's children were in their fifties or early sixties. Death seemed far away, and grudges were perhaps easier to assume, even those sworn for eternity; I guess they believed they had that kind of time. Yet that year, time would very much come up for two of them, though in drastically different ways.

When Abdeljawwad died, his daughters did not inherit any of his wealth. Salma trusted that her brothers would rectify this injustice. But in a culture where a woman joins her husband's family, her brothers did not see it her way. In 1980, Salma was already several years into a court battle with some of her brothers. Her sister declined to join in the lawsuit, finding it easier to use the power of guilt to get handouts from her brothers.

By the time we arrived that summer, Salma was no longer on speaking terms with the brother she most adored, Nazir. And we were barely settled in when politics, which supposedly had nothing to do with us, suddenly did. Even though Nazir lived in Hama, he was often in Damascus, where his son, who worked abroad, kept a house.

The day after Hafez al-Assad's brother massacred the prisoners in Tad-mour, uniformed men from the *amn*, or internal security, knocked on Nazir's son's door. They very politely asked Nazir to come with them, as they needed his help. He willingly went and got into an official car. Everyone later would say he had no reason not to. His family expected he would return shortly. When, hours later, he was still out, his family began to alert his siblings and any relatives (including their cousin Madhat) who might have *wasta* (a con-nection) to someone of influence in the regime.

Sari, who as a prominent surgeon in the capital was perhaps the most well-connected, called everyone he knew in the military and the *mukhabarat*, but no one had any information as to where Nazir had been taken. They promised Sari they would look into it. At Salma's house, the adults began a vigil, waiting for news and starting to panic. Salma also smoked.

Nazir oversaw the family lands, and as such he had many dealings with farmers and government officials. He was also involved in other entrepre-neurial endeavors that were making him rich. Whether or not he was fair depended on your point of view. Some people hated him; others loved him.

Two agonizing days after Nazir was taken, the head of the general *mukhabarat* called Sari. They believed Nazir had been found, and he told Sari to "come see him." Sari took cousin Madhat and drove to a hospital in the Nabak, about fifty miles north of Damascus. Though Nazir's corpse was bloated and his body bore at least five gunshot wounds, Sari was able to iden-tify him. Nazir was already dead when he had been found, dumped by the side of a road outside of town.

When Salma was informed of Nazir's death, she was stunned and then inconsolable. She immediately donned the black clothes of mourning and spent days on the couch in a haze of Valium, speaking to no one. Her grief was compounded by how horribly her brother had died: he had been mur-dered and thrown into the street with no dignity. She was also overcome with guilt, knowing that now they would never have a chance to reconcile over their differences.

Salma refused to go to the funeral in Hama, though Ameen, Lamya, and Suha tried to convince her otherwise. She was afraid to anger his widow, and she was deeply ashamed that she had not been on speaking terms with her brother. She was alone with her anguish.

When the family returned from the funeral to Damascus, Sari continued to push for answers. He went to police headquarters to retrieve Nazir's items.

They gave Sari what Nazir had had on him—or what had remained on him—at the time of his death: his wallet, his handkerchief, and a pen. The police told Sari that they would look into his brother's death. If the crime was what they called "an ordinary killing," they promised they would find the perpetrators; but if it was "an irregular killing," they demurred, "you will have to forgive us."

What this meant was that if someone connected to the regime had committed or signed off on this murder, then it wasn't going to be pursued.

Sari remained haunted until his own passing nearly thirty years later by what happened to Nazir. He wrote this account in an unpublished memoir:

> In the eyes of the authorities the matter was resolved; there were neither questions asked nor answers given. Like nothing had ever happened. It was like this crime didn't mean anything to anybody within the government, and of course no official bothered to make any promises that they would continue investigating this matter. It seemed as if this was an everyday occurrence for them, and that a citizen doesn't have that much value as long as the overall level of security is high and the government, as well as the officials doing its bidding, are safe.

When Sari urged Nazir's widow to insist on an investigation, she declined, fearing what the consequences might be. Despite her reluctance, Sari continued to push for answers until a fellow doctor came to him saying he had a message: "Stop pursuing this issue or the same will happen to you."

The family understood then that there would be no answers. In his memoir, Sari wrote, "I'm sure of one thing: history will not spare anyone. It will be written, and the truth will come out sooner rather than later."

⬥

LAMYA WOULDN'T—COULDN'T—TELL SHARIF about Nazir's murder until she returned to the United States. There was no way to discuss it privately. Calls in Syria were monitored—especially those between Syria and a foreign country. Although Syrians had a circumspect way of speaking about things over the phone, what had happened to Lamya's uncle did not lend itself easily to that kind of coded language. Because letters were also often read, she would have to wait to tell him in person. For the family to have talked about it would make it seem like they wanted to make trouble about it, that they weren't accepting it. The regime bought submission from Syrians in many ways. Silence was perhaps the most common.

In Lamya's ledger of life in the United States versus in Syria, *le retour* sustained a real blow. If the stories about people being disappeared or kidnapped or found dead in a ditch had been, until then, somehow abstract, her uncle becoming a statistic—one that no one could acknowledge—made what was happening in Syria much more real.

Of course, that summer, the adults kept all sorts of truths from us children. To me, Damascus was as magical as always. In the morning, my grandfather Ameen would bring warm flat bread from the bakery down the street, which I found more exciting than taking presliced Wonder bread out of a plastic bag. A tree whose upper branches I could reach from my grandmother's balcony, unbeknownst to me, was actually a cherry tree, and when all of a sudden it yielded fruit that I could pick and eat right away—I was ecstatic. I was fascinated by the man who would appear on the street with a pushcart of boiled corn at the exact moment that I craved it. Suha and I would pore over my sketchbook together, and she could draw anything I requested. We were surrounded by people who loved us. In Baltimore, I was acutely aware that we were alone, and always aware of my parents' loneliness.

I was also enamored with Stella, a beautiful young hairdresser who had long hair; I was already self-conscious about the short hair my mother forced on me. I was often mistaken for a boy, even though, in retrospect, I can see that the style was quite chic. Stella worked in Salma's neighborhood, and because her parents' house was too far away for her to go home for lunch, Salma insisted she eat with us every day. After Nazir's murder, Stella would try, as we all did, to distract Salma. She would tell Salma the gossip from the salon. But Salma barely ate and only smoked.

I didn't understand or know this then, but plans for our baptism and Suha's wedding were being rapidly scaled back. When a family is in mourning, as ours was for Nazir, it is expected to put off any kind of joyous events or outward celebrations lest we appear not to be adequately bereft. Our small baptism was scheduled for July 29 at the Church of the Cross. Salma would be my godmother, and Suha would serve as my sister's. My paternal grandfather, now an elderly widower, would be my brother's godfather. That day, my aunt was dressed in a beautiful cerulean dress with short sleeves, and my mother was in a sleeveless red sundress. My grandfather was in a gray suit and tie. Salma wore all black—dress, stockings, shoes, and bag.

I remember the ceremony clearly, because it was somewhat mortifying. The forty-day-old infants are usually dunked into the baptismal font naked. I was too old for that, and really too conscious. In the middle of the church, I had to strip down to my blue bathing suit. I remember some even laughing when the cold water was poured over me, startling me. The same ritual was repeated for my sister and my brother. After we dried off, and were allowed to put our clothes back on, I was relieved.

Back at my grandparents' house we had a celebratory lunch, but for very few people. Stella was there, as was her sister Nanette, who had pierced my ears when I was a baby. But I was already excited for what was meant to be the main event of that summer, Suha's wedding. She was clearly in love—even at my age I could see that.

My sister and I wouldn't let Suha enter any room or descend any stairs anywhere without preceding her and singing that American song, "Here Comes the Bride." But our enthusiasm and merrymaking was not shared by everyone. Much to Suha's dismay, Salma wanted to cancel the wedding until an adequate period of mourning had passed.

Suha was, like my mother, loved by her friends, and she and Kamal were an adored couple. People wanted to celebrate this union and have a chance to send them off to Paris properly. All that was meaningless to Salma; her brother was dead. Luckily, though, their trip to France had been booked long before, and it was socially inconceivable that a woman would travel and live with a man without being married. Salma had to relent.

Still, a compromise was reached. A church wedding was out of the question, and there was (and still is) no civil marriage option—unions in Syria must be religiously performed and sanctioned. So Salma made her terms clear: the marriage ceremony would be in Salma's house, but no one could come—none of their friends could be there, just the families. There would be no dancing and revelry at Salma's house. Any celebration to follow the ceremony also could not be in public; it had to be at Kamal's parents' house. And Salma would not attend.

Salma was sinking into a deep period of mourning that only got worse the more time passed. Suha was hurt by her mother's inability to partake in the joy of her wedding. They had grown close in the years of Lamya's absence.

Salma loved that Suha studied art. She had converted the small side terrace in their house into a room, and had given it to Suha to be her atelier. When, during university, Suha became distraught because she couldn't find anyone to volunteer to pose nude, so that she could study the human body as she drew it, Salma shed her clothes for her, sitting silently on a stool, smoking her cigarette naked.

The night before the wedding, we all stayed up late at Salma's house. Suha was taking dictation as Salma shared her recipes. After she had written the last of them, she laid her head in her mother's lap, and Salma stroked her hair.

The next day, August 2, several priests, including a bishop, came to Salma's house. Kamal came from a Catholic family, and Suha an Orthodox one. Suha had already met with the Catholic priest, who had tried to cajole her to convert, asking her if she didn't want to be Catholic like her future husband. Suha had answered that Jesus is one and that Allah was for everybody, an answer that did not impress the priest. Kamal, for his part, would have wanted a civil marriage were it possible.

Lamya witnessed for her sister, and my sister and I wore matching American dresses. Like Suha, we had jasmine in our hair. Salma again wore black. Even though it was evening, she wore her oversized tinted glasses to hide her eyes. The house was not decorated, and only candy-coated almonds were offered to those of us in the house in celebration.

Below my grandparents' house, the happy couple's friends waited for them, one playing a festive beat on a *derbekeh*, an Arabic drum. They would all go together to Kamal's parents' house, honking their horns as they drove in decorated cars toward Ain al-Kirish, where Suha had grown up, and where Kamal's parents still lived. Outside their door, Suha was given the sticky traditional dough to smack above her future in-laws' door. If it stuck, it would augur well for the marriage. It did.

At the party, I never left Suha's side, and insisted on posing between bride and groom for as many pictures as possible. I also stayed in between them for much of the night. There was food, dancing, and the notable absence of Suha's mother, who could not live in joy even for just that night. Salma had not allowed Ameen, either, to join in the celebration of their daughter's wedding.

As the party wound down, I watched my aunt leave for Hotel Vendôme, where she and Kamal would spend a few days before flying to Paris. However, they weren't allowed to check in, because they had forgotten to bring their marriage certificate—they had no proof they were married, and unmarried couples cannot share a hotel room in Syria. Seated in the lobby, Suha in her wedding dress and Kamal in his black suit and crimson bowtie, they waited until someone fetched it for them.

※

IMMEDIATELY AFTER THE wedding, Lamya's father and father-in-law came to speak with her. They both told her: "Pack your bags and go." They were afraid of the political situation in the country and how close violence had touched the family. They pleaded with Lamya to move up our departure date to the United States.

While, on her own accord, Lamya had already decided she preferred to raise her children in America, she wasn't ready to leave Syria sooner than expected. Finally, under pressure from both of them, she relented. But Lamya hesitated at the thought of leaving her mother in her current state. Salma seemed incapable of emerging from her mourning. Lamya proposed that Salma come that fall to Baltimore for the birth of her fourth grandchild. To her surprise, Salma agreed.

With Salma's promise to come soon, our departure was easier to bear. We left in early August, comforted that Teta would be joining us in October, just two months away.

5

LOCKED IN

Baltimore, Autumn 1980

S ALMA HAD NEVER BEEN IN BALTIMORE FOR THE BIRTHS OF HER grandchildren, and Lamya wanted her mother's presence, support, and help when the next baby came into the world. To her credit, Lamya had managed our chaotic household on her own until then. Our home was impeccably clean, the laundry never lingered, and our meals were always homemade. (I would not know what Chef Boyardee was until I was well into elementary school—and then, I envied the kids who got to eat it for their Americanness.)

Lamya also thought it would be good for Salma to get out of Syria for a while. The only times she had been able to overcome her grief, albeit fleetingly, was in the moments she spent with me and my siblings. Being away from Damascus and the constant reminders of what had happened to her brother—and what was happening in the country—might do her good. When Lamya delivered my sister Farah almost two weeks ahead of schedule, she didn't tell Salma, afraid she might use missing the birth as an excuse not to come at all. Lamya had already decided she would convince her mother to stay past her booked November 8 departure.

The abrupt arrival of the baby threw Lamya's plans off as well. My parents had bought a modest split-level house in a cul-de-sac in Baltimore County. It was important for Lamya that Salma be impressed by the home she had established, and Salma expected perfection in these matters. Lamya had planned a thorough cleaning before her mother arrived, but the baby's unexpected birth meant that she had to do it all when she returned from the hospital. After a day of recovery, she came home, scrubbed the house spotless, washed all the linens, and put out a freshly washed and pressed *aghabani* on the dining-room table. Embroidered in silver or gold thread in whirling patterns, these typical Syrian tablecloths had been part of her trousseau.

By the time Salma arrived, the house was flawless. Even though she was coming to a house celebrating the joy of a new birth, she still wore the black clothes of mourning. Salma was surprised to find the baby already there, but was delighted by Farah, cherubic as she was. Salma declared that she would be the most beautiful of Lamya and Sharif's daughters. That, however, was of little comfort to my father, who had been receiving condolences from the other Arab men in the community—three daughters! At least, they said, there was a boy in the mix. In my father's disappointment, a lot of cigarettes were smoked. Many of them, of course, were shared with Salma, who never stopped smoking, even though she was on blood pressure medication by then.

To entertain his mother-in-law while Lamya tended to a colicky baby, Sharif would take her out for little drives in the family Volvo. Dangling their arms out the windows with cigarettes between their fingers, they drove through old-moneyed neighborhoods, looking at real estate. They'd point out which houses they thought were smartly designed, which ones showed real craft in how their stone or brick had been laid, and, of course, what their likely cost might be. Though ranch-style homes were the fashion in newer communities, my father loved the classic American colonial. The style had imprinted on him ever since he had arrived in the United States; he found them functional yet stately. Along those established streets also stood deep-rooted oak and maple trees whose leaves had begun to change to saturated red and yellows, which delighted Salma. Fall in Damascus doesn't really take on the same brilliant hues of the American East Coast.

As I got older and began to ask those who knew Salma about her, I learned that Sharif was much more like her than Lamya ever was. Internally tormented, their moods dictated the humor of everyone around them. They both blindly idealized their own parents and siblings as being superior to those of their spouses (despite the fact that their siblings had caused each of them a lot of unhappiness). Both were irresistibly charismatic and often withdrawn—at times social, and at other times unexpectedly quite antisocial. They could both be extremely generous, and neither would ever turn away from someone needing help. My father often accepted home-baked cakes instead of payment from patients in Baltimore who were less financially fortunate.

I think they each also recognized *shakhsiyeh*—charisma—in the other. Sharif, who could quickly become dismissive of just about anyone, has never said anything dismissive about her. There are some photos where I believe she even looks like him.

On these little shared escapes they often ended up driving around the blue waters of the Loch Raven Reservoir, nestled among woods unadulterated. Surrounded by the quiet anonymity of trees, Salma often wept about her brother. According to superstition, displays of grief in a house with a newborn could jinx the baby, so she didn't let herself cry in front of Lamya.

In these moments, Sharif thought he saw more than sorrow for the loss of Nazir in her tears; he believed that Salma was ridden with guilt. She had been at odds with her brother when he was murdered. She also appeared tormented by the refusal of the regime to even acknowledge the crime. Like her son-in-law, Salma wasn't capable of expressing exactly what was eating at her. And, like her, Sharif didn't know quite how to comfort the emotional pain of someone close to him.

⪻⪼

ON SATURDAY, NOVEMBER 8, the day my grandmother was originally scheduled to leave, my parents planned to host a Lebanese couple for dinner. Lamya wanted to entertain and distract Salma. Even with a new baby, Lamya found herself splitting her attentions between her mother and her children.

Together that afternoon, Lamya and Salma prepared *tabouleh*, a salad whose main ingredient is finely chopped parsley. It involved gathering the parsley into small bouquets, splitting the sprigs, and lining up the leaves on one linear plane so that when chopped, no stems would make it in. It was labor intensive, a task my sister Manal and I would be conscripted to perform as we got older. Our job was to gather perfectly aligned bunches of parsley and hand them to my mother, who would quickly reduce them to flecks of green. Manal would later claim that parsley and *tabouleh* made her a feminist; she had resented how my brother was never called in from playing to help in the kitchen. He was often outside having fun as we pruned parsley inside.

For Lamya, it was usually a lonely task, as I imagine everything was in those early years in America. Now, with Salma there, they did it together, gossiping all the while (I would learn to appreciate that part of the ritual—gender politics aside—as I got older). But most of the time, Salma just spoke about the past, about the beautiful days back in Hama before she was married, and of a Syria before Hafez al-Assad. Of all the coups d'état Syria had lived through that century, the one that had made Assad ruler was so far the one that had stuck the hardest. He had already been in power a decade.

Once the parsley was gathered and chopped, Salma went upstairs to shower. As Lamya stood by the kitchen sink repeatedly rinsing the herb, I came running down to her. Teta had fallen in the bathroom, I laughed, thinking that my elegant grandmother was trying to be silly.

Lamya was much more alarmed. She ran up to find her mother just righting herself. Salma told Lamya that she was dizzy and that her head hurt. Lamya called Sharif, who was on shift at the emergency room, where he was the physician in charge. Given Salma's high blood pressure and history of painful migraines, he told Lamya to bring Salma in to see him. Once she was able to find a sitter to stay with us, she rushed her mother to the hospital. Salma, however, had quickly begun to feel better. Whatever had happened, it had passed. She lit up and puffed away at her cigarette during the drive to the city.

At the ER, Sharif ran the regular tests. Everything came back normal, and Salma wanted to go back home. With no reason to keep her, Sharif discharged her.

But when the next afternoon Salma stumbled again and lost consciousness for a few minutes, Lamya took her right back to the ER. This time the symptoms persisted. She was dizzy, her head ached, and she had fast, uncontrollable movements in her eyes.

My father decided to admit her to the hospital, and she was taken to the eleventh floor, where patients were suffering from everything from pneumonia to dehydration. Sharif alerted the neurologist.

Lamya had to return home to be with us. She figured that Salma's high blood pressure was simply wreaking havoc on her already bad migraines. With my father in the ER, my mother knew that Salma would be cared for and that he would let her know right away if anything happened.

Around 10:30 p.m., shortly before Sharif's shift finished at 11, the eleventh-floor nurses alerted him that Salma was suffering from a crippling headache.

My father rushed to her room. When Salma saw him, she cried repeatedly that she wanted to be able to see her son, Sa'ad, again. Sharif had often felt the loneliness of being a foreigner in this same hospital. He could not imagine being a foreigner and a patient as well. When he was alone here, he, too, used to yearn for family in Syria. He promised her that she would see Sa'ad again.

After administering a shot for the pain, he returned to attend to other patients in the ER. Then, as he prepared to leave for the night, around midnight, the eleventh-floor staff again paged him. Salma's breathing had become labored; she was losing vision, movement, and speech. He quickly had her taken to the intensive care unit, and the neurologist came in to see her. Sharif stayed until she stabilized. When she came to, Salma insisted that he go home to Lamya and get some sleep.

The next morning, well before his 3 p.m. shift started, both he and Lamya went back to the hospital. Salma told Lamya that what had happened had terrified her. She had been aware the entire time, even as she had lost speech, vision, and movement. She was so relieved to have come out of it. She quickly changed the subject. How were her grandchildren? she smiled meekly.

Their small talk was interrupted when a priest came by offering patients Communion. Salma—neither religious nor Catholic—asked for the rite. Sharif then performed a lumbar puncture to rule out meningitis. Salma told Lamya to go home and be with her children while more tests were run. She was okay, she reassured Lamya—Sharif was nearby. My mother was reluctant, but Salma insisted. Lamya walked out relieved that whatever had happened had passed.

In retrospect, it's clear my grandmother had suffered several transient ischemic attacks—or TIAs, as they are now called. In a TIA, a clot temporarily causes the flow of blood to the brain to be blocked or reduced. Today, these incidents are seen as possible warnings of something potentially much worse to come, and the standard of care is for a patient to be put on blood thinners right away to avoid the worst. But that wasn't the protocol in 1980, and later that night, the worst did happen.

Several hours after my mother left the hospital, Salma had a stroke. A clot completely blocked her basilar artery, cutting off the blood supply to her brain. Had this happened today, there would have been time (up to four hours) to administer a treatment developed in the mid-1990s that would have opened the blockage, preventing any further brain cell damage. Instead, the obstruction to Salma's brain was there to stay. It paralyzed her completely from the neck down.

The neurologist's diagnosis was as bad as it could be: Salma was "locked in." She could no longer move or speak, because all voluntary muscles were paralyzed except for her eyes. At first blush, patients can appear to be in a coma, until, with the eyes, they make it clear they are still there. Unlike in a coma, those stricken are completely conscious and aware.

My father called my mother. She understood her mother was dying, and Lamya thought she might lose her mind. Again she looked for someone to come stay with her children and raced back, weeping, to the city. She prayed fervently: Had she said or done something to precipitate this? It was supposed to be a trip to relieve and revive Salma. How had she let this happen on her watch?

When Lamya saw her mother, she knelt to kiss her and hold her hand. She begged her to recover and told her that the children missed her. In that moment, Lamya remembered her grandfather Abdeljawwad after he fell ill, and how Salma had tended to him. As what it meant to be "locked in" was explained to Lamya, all she could think of was how terrified Salma had been the day before, when she had been only temporarily rendered blind, mute, and paralyzed. That she was now in a similar state permanently was more than my mother could contemplate. Anything after that moment, she has blocked out.

To ease Salma's breathing and prevent her from choking on her saliva, Sharif performed a tracheostomy. When the neurologist saw what my father had done, he chastised him with words my father remembers, "What are you doing? She's trapped in a glass room. Let her go." The neurologist said that patients like Salma don't usually survive more than a few weeks. My father asked, was Salma still in there? The neurologist said that she was, that she could understand everything and see.

Sharif had a promise to keep.

⌘

IN DAMASCUS, TWO days before Sa'ad knew what had happened to his mother and on the day she had her stroke, he dreamed that he had gone to the airport with his father, Ameen, to greet Salma as she returned from her trip abroad. Without explanation, she had been carried out of the plane on a stretcher. The dream scared him, as dreams are seen as omens in Syria, but he figured it was just because he missed her.

Two days later, Sa'ad was coming home for lunch from university. He opened the door to their home, and as he walked in, felt a breeze across his face and saw what he was sure was his mother's shadow.

He walked into the kitchen laughing.

Ameen, solemn faced, asked him why.

"I was missing Mama," he said. "And I opened the door and felt her presence."

Ameen put his glass down and got up from the table.

"What's wrong?" Sa'ad asked, thinking his father might be jealous, interpreting his comment to mean that Sa'ad wasn't enjoying their time alone as father and son.

Ameen sat back down. "Let's eat," he said.

Sa'ad took a seat and then excitedly started to tell his father about the dream with the stretcher, asking him what he thought it meant. Ameen interrupted him by sternly putting his cutlery down and again getting up, this time leaving the kitchen.

Sa'ad saw he was actually shaken, and followed him out into the hallway. "What is wrong with you?" he asked.

"Let's finish lunch," Ameen said, turning back toward the kitchen. "We can talk after."

Sa'ad wouldn't relent.

Finally, Ameen told him that he had gotten a telephone call from Baltimore. Then he repeated what Sharif had explained to him. Salma had had a stroke.

Sa'ad was distraught. In those days, "stroke" was a word as bad as "cancer."

Ameen continued, explaining that Salma's case was very different from most. He told Sa'ad that Salma was paralyzed and unable to speak.

Hearing this about his mother, Sa'ad began to cry.

When Sharif delivered the news, he also told Ameen of his promise to Salma that she would see Sa'ad again. But Sa'ad had to come right away, he insisted. They immediately made preparations for Sa'ad to leave.

In France, Suha had been eagerly expecting a call from the United States with the date of her mother's arrival in Paris. She was excited to share the city with her and to have her there to help her set up her newlywed home. Instead, when Lamya called her, it was to tell her what had happened. "You should try to come here as quickly possible," she said. "To have a chance to say goodbye."

Suha had her first asthma attack in that moment. She continues to have them to this day.

The US embassies in Damascus and Paris (which seems hard to believe in today's world) expedited both their visas. Suha arrived first. When she walked into the hospital and saw her mother, she could not believe it was her. Salma was blue and swollen as if she had been blown up like a balloon. Suha fainted. When Sa'ad arrived, it was late at night, and Suha and Sharif met him at the airport. Because it was well after visiting hours, they drove to our house. That night the downpour was so forceful that the Volvo's windshield wipers couldn't keep up, and my father rolled his window down to see the road home.

With Sa'ad's arrival, I was ecstatic; I had never had my aunt and uncle with us in Baltimore before. Sa'ad was also thrilled to meet the new baby and to see us again. I understood that Salma was sick, but my parents had not let me see her. In fact, I never saw her again. We had been close—I was her first grandchild—and the adults chose to preserve my memory of her. Now that my mother is a grandmother, though, I think they may have chosen wrongly. If I put myself in Salma's place, I imagine she would have found comfort and joy in seeing and hearing all of us, and feeling our kisses on her face and hands. She must have been terrified, locked in both her body and in that hospital room, in a place where she barely knew the language, looking at faces that looked like no one she knew.

At the house, my father poured Sa'ad some cognac. Only twenty-one, Sa'ad had never drunk anything alcoholic other than beer and *arak*. Sharif would take him to see his mother in the morning.

When they all awoke the next day it was sunny and clear, the kind of sky only possible after the rain has purged it. Sa'ad wore short sleeves, thinking the blue skies meant it would be warm, and we laughed at him when we saw him.

After breakfast, my father drove Sa'ad to the hospital to see his mother. Rather than take him directly to the intensive care unit, Sharif gave Sa'ad a tour of the hospital first, the place where he had spent so many years of his American life. He also handed Sa'ad a sedative, which he took without knowing what it was. Sharif let it take effect before escorting him to his mother's room.

Before entering the ICU, Sharif told Sa'ad, "You will find her changed."

Inside, Sa'ad saw a stretcher attached to several monitors flashing and beeping, and someone sleeping underneath tubes and wires. The first thing Sa'ad noticed was Salma's head. It was at least two or three times its normal size.

He began to sob and kissed her.

It wasn't how Sharif had imagined fulfilling his promise to Salma.

Hours later, Sharif took Sa'ad to the nearby Inner Harbor to calm him down and distract him. They walked along the water, and he showed Sa'ad the old USS *Constellation*. Before taking him back to our house, Sharif took him to the reservoir he had shared with Salma. He told him how he and Salma had driven these same roads, smoking and talking. He also told Sa'ad how she would cry with him so as not to bother Lamya with her sorrow.

Every day they took the same trip to the hospital until all the arrangements could be made. Shortly after Thanksgiving, Suha flew back to Paris. Sa'ad would fly home via Jordan with Salma. Rami, Lamya's cousin and neighbor from the Tahaan, and who had been there the night I was born, would accompany them on the flight. My parents had decided it would be better to have Rami there should anything require a doctor's attention.

Because ambulances couldn't travel between states, one would have to take Salma from Maryland to Delaware, another from Delaware to New Jersey, and yet another from New Jersey to New York, where she would fly from John F. Kennedy International Airport straight to Amman, and then go by ambulance to Damascus.

The day Salma left the hospital in Baltimore, Lamya went to say goodbye to her mother, though she doesn't remember it. But my father has a clear memory of Lamya at the hospital's main entrance on a bright and crisp day. She was numb. She thought she would never see her mother again.

Salma was loaded into the first ambulance, and they set out, Sharif and Sa'ad following behind in our boxy beige Volvo. There were 180 miles to New York.

At each state crossing, the ambulances stopped on the side of the highway to transfer Salma to the next one. At each handover, Sharif and Sa'ad would get out to make sure she was okay and to thank the departing crew. The cold air that would blow on my father's face at these stops would knock him momentarily out of his stupor.

Rami met them at JFK, and Sharif stayed with them until they boarded. When the pilot saw Salma, he refused to take her unless he had a doctor's letter absolving him of any responsibility should anything happen. The airline had been alerted of Salma's condition but apparently did not understand how bad it really was. My father wrote the note by hand, and the pilot agreed to take her.

Rami had spoken to Salma a few times by phone since she had arrived in Baltimore and before the stroke. At JFK, he was stunned by her appearance, and worried that he would not be able to do anything if she stopped breathing on the flight.

But she survived it, and when Sa'ad, Rami, and Salma arrived in Jordan, another ambulance was waiting to deliver them to the Jordanian/Syrian border, which they reached with little difficulty. It was then that their luck ran out.

Sa'ad had expected to find Sari waiting with another ambulance to transport Salma back to Damascus. Instead, they had not been allowed in and were still stuck on the Syrian side of the border.

Sa'ad, Rami, and Salma had wandered into a (long-forgotten) crisis between Jordan and Syria. Hafez al-Assad had amassed hundreds of tanks and 30,000 troops along the frontier. He had accused Jordan's King Hussein of allowing the Syrian Muslim Brotherhood—which had carried out the attacks in Syria that summer—to operate from his country. Jordan denied the charge and had responded by moving 24,000 troops to the border.

Sa'ad decided to cross from Jordan to the Syrian border-control area alone. He explained to the Syrian soldier in charge the situation they were in, that his mother would soon run out of oxygen. At this thought, Sa'ad broke down.

After offering him a tissue, the Syrian soldier told Sa'ad to get in his truck. He promised to get Salma home, and he didn't ask for anything in exchange; not all who worked for the government were corrupt. In his vehicle they drove to the Syrian side and found Sari with the ambulance; they had been waiting for hours.

Despite the standoff, the soldier managed to escort the ambulance back into Jordan and then back to Syria again. It was the kind of intervention that Salma would solicit on behalf of the people who used to come to her in need—without it now, she would have died.

The ambulance delivered all of them to the hospital in Damascus, the same one where Abdeljawwad had died ten years before. Salma would stay there while they adjusted her house to her new needs.

In the United States, Sa'ad had clung to any hope he could find in what the neurologist had explained to him about his mother's condition. The doctor had said that sometimes, the body could invent a way to circumvent the blockage. But that would depend, in the first instance, on her body surviving.

⊗

SALMA DID SURVIVE, physically. Her body, however, found no such new pathway. Four months after the not-fatal-enough stroke, the Syrian neurologists told Sa'ad that there was no longer any hope Salma would ever regain anything.

But Sa'ad never lost faith. He put his life on hold to care for his mother. He skipped lectures at university, delaying his graduation by three years.

Sari's wife, Clara, a nurse, instructed Sa'ad daily for the first few months about how to care for Salma. Every hour or so he changed her position. He massaged her body. He bathed her daily, smoothed lotion onto her skin, and combed her hair. She never smelled of anything but her beloved Avon perfumes.

In fact, Sa'ad's care for his mother was so exhaustive that she did not die for seven more years. Though, maybe living that long was a much worse fate. To be locked in is to be completely alive—to be there fully—inside a body that is wholly paralyzed. It wasn't just her limbs that she couldn't control, it was everything from her eyes down. She couldn't sit up—she was like jelly. She required a catheter. She had no control over her lips or her tongue. She—of the acerbic wit and hoarse voice—was now mute. She could hear and smell everything, and the only things she could move were her eyes.

She was able to open and close them. Blinking was how she told the world she was still in there. Her eyes were also still able to cry, and tears often fell from them, staying on her cheeks until someone dried them for her.

Her eyes remained their mesmerizing green. When Sa'ad would check in on her during the day, finding her eyes closed though she was awake, he would urge her to open them, telling her to "raise those curtains to paradise."

He learned to ask all yes-or-no questions to try to figure out what she wanted or needed. They devised a system: for yes, she would blink, and for no, she would widen her eyes and slightly raise her eyebrows. Years later, Jean-Dominique Bauby would dictate an entire book—*The Diving Bell and the Butterfly*—with a more complicated blink system. In it he described being locked in as being "imprisoned inside his own body," "a prolonged and refined agony."

When nothing yielded a yes, Sa'ad would ask if what Salma wanted was a cigarette, and she would hold her eyes shut in a long, long yes. She had gone through withdrawal frozen.

He often read to Salma. She still loved poetry, and he read her lines from an Elia Abu Madi poem she had long recited to her children, in which the poet says:

> I came, I know not from whence, but I arrived,
> And before my feet a path lay under my stride,
> And I continue to walk be it my will or not.
> Whence did I come? And how will I find my way?
> I do not know!
> Am I new or old in this existence?
> Am I free or am I a captive in confinement?
> Do I lead myself or am I being led?

The bishop had given Sa'ad the Bible on cassette tapes to play for Salma. She never cared much for church, but with so many hours in the day, sometimes Sa'ad would play them for her. And although a night nurse was always there, Sa'ad would check in on her even when he should have been sleeping. He often found Salma awake, suffering from what I imagine was an excruciating insomnia, full of boredom, anger, regret, despair. She often tried to refuse food, answering "no" when asked if she was hungry. She clearly wanted to die, but no one would let her.

From Paris, Suha would make Salma mix tapes. Some featured new French songs, others were Suha reading her *1001 Arabian Nights*, and others yet were simply Suha making conversation with her mother. There was enough traffic between Paris and Damascus that the tapes were always hand delivered. Suha used her summer break from graduate school to come home. She, too, read to Salma, played music for her, and massaged her limbs. She used to caress

Salma's hair and hands. Sometimes she'd open Salma's closet and model for her that beautiful and abandoned wardrobe. Suha noted with remorse how much of it was black because of so many deaths—Abdeljawwad, Sara, and two of their sons.

Friends and family would visit, including Sabah, the beautiful former young maid who had married the neighbor at Salma's behest. Sabah wept each time she came, until the end calling her "my teacher" as she sat with her. Marianne, her friend, would stand in front of her bed and just repeat her name, "Salma," while my grandmother cried. Karawan, the singer, would serenade her.

Many visitors kept away from her room, preferring to stay in the living room. This greatly disappointed Sa'ad, who wanted people not to be afraid to see her. He believed Salma craved company, anything to break through the isolation. He didn't want his mother to feel forgotten. But guests would look away and say they preferred to remember her the way she was or that they simply didn't have the heart to see her like that.

Her daughter, my mother, was one of them. She only went back once in those seven years. Lamya had made a decision; she could either be in the United States while her heart and mind were always in Syria, or she could be fully with her family in the United States. She chose us. It had never been easy for my father to see her go back to Damascus while he couldn't. He still hoped to return to Syria, despite all indications that such a move would have been a bad idea. He felt that somehow it was my mother's fault that they hadn't gone back, but now they were even. She too had to share his exile.

Lamya sheltered us from her torment over having such a terrible thing happen to her mother while she was at our house—on her watch.

Our lives went on, Sa'ad's only slowly. He finally graduated in 1986; he had happily gotten engaged in 1985 and was able to introduce Salma to the woman he would marry. Suha went back to Syria permanently in July 1986, moving to the Tahaan. She lived in the apartment across the hall from Salma's, the one that had belonged to Ameen's sister Adèle and her blind husband Nikola. Every day, Suha had to see Hassan; he never apologized for taking her mother's house, but she'd greet him nonetheless. His wife, Hilal, had welcomed Suha, telling her how much Salma's kindness had meant to her.

By then, Salma's body was so small and her skin so thin. Suha's only daughter, just a baby, would crawl into her grandmother's room and caress her hand as she lay motionless.

A year later, in August 1987, on a rare day when Suha did not come over to visit, because Ameen was having lunch with her at her house in the Tahaan, and while Sa'ad was at his apprenticeship, Salma died.

They had gotten so used to her surviving that they had been lulled into forgetting that she was slowly dying. Looking back, though, both Sa'ad and Suha recognized signs from the previous few nights and days that her soul had been quietly leaving her body.

Lamya had stopped expecting the call. She now took it for granted that she would see Salma again. When she heard the news, my mother, who never rested, took to her bed, and in one of the few times I can remember, I saw her crying.

❦

A LITTLE OVER a year and a half after Salma's stroke shattered her, Hafez al-Assad broke her native Hama. In February 1982, he launched an assault on the city, which was still the center of an array of interests that had coalesced around the Muslim Brotherhood. Assad's forces commandeered Abdeljawwad's building in Hama, as it was one of the taller buildings, and from its roof set up surveillance of the city below.

The regime murdered, in a conservative estimate, 10,000 people.

I wonder how much Salma understood of what happened to her hometown. She'd listen to the radio, but the radio was silent on Hama, as silence was the official position of the state. Neither Sa'ad nor Ameen made a point of telling her the details.

Although Hama was the city in the crosshairs, the attack was a message to all Syrians: stay out of the regime's way. The news also succeeded in killing off much of the will of any Syrian to participate politically—making it clear that the punishment would be borne not just by individuals, but by families, neighborhoods, and cities. It was a price higher than most people could commit others to pay.

No doubt Nazir's death—and the impotence to object to it and to seek justice—had thrown Salma's soul into inconsolable despair. It's unscientific, I suppose, but I can't help but wonder what the regime's cost has been to the very bodies of Syrian people.

Not only did the Hama assault solidify Assad's power, it also brought Syria itself to a screeching halt. Governments had come and gone in Syria. But

Assad, especially after 1982, was going nowhere. The country entered a period of utter stagnation.

To my evolving consciousness, still that of a child, Syria was like my grandmother Salma—suspended between life and death. There and not there.

When Sharif's father visited us in Baltimore in 1984, he told Sharif, "Son, you stay here. People who live there are waiting to die." Only then did my father finally relent about moving back to Syria. (The three tins of delicacies sent in 1973 by his mother, however, still unopened, remained in the back of the extra freezer in our basement well into the 1990s.)

In Syria, the official position on Hama was to forget. Syrians never knew exactly how many were killed: family members still don't know who is dead, when they died, and who is in prison. This amnesia precluded any kind of national mourning, and the country remained suspended in the lack of truth, accountability, and reconciliation.

Although both had once been very real to me, all I had of Salma and Syria were memories, and both topics in our house were tinged in sadness. I remembered my grandmother, who was just taken away one day. There was no closure.

In choosing what to keep of her after she died, we, too, chose our official memory: even though it had been years since she could sit or stand, let alone walk, my mother, my aunt, and I kept Salma's shoes.

PART 2
Locked Out

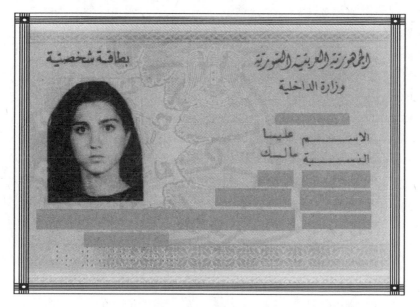

Author's first Syrian ID card.

Author's parents' wedding; the last time they would be in
Syria together, until their thirtieth anniversary, which they
celebrated in Damascus with all their children.

6

ANYWHERE BUT HERE

Syria, Summer 1992

I LANDED IN DAMASCUS ON JUNE 21, 1992, CURIOUS, EXCITED, AND tense—the advance instructions had been manifold: do not say anything remotely political; do not appear too American; submit to whatever anyone appearing official demands of you. Everyone is watching, my family warned me. Best not to draw any unwanted attention to yourself.

I was seventeen and traveling alone. On my shoulder, I carried a heavy camcorder; my father wanted me to be his eyes and film as much as I could. He hadn't been home since his one visit in 1986 when his father died. Around my waist, I was wearing a black fanny pack with "New Orleans" scrawled across it in neon pink. Through its band I had threaded a camera in its belt case, which declared "PENTAX" in red letters. I also wore a ridiculous straw hat.

I was arriving on a flight from Cairo that was packed with people from the region. Genetics aside, the way we dressed and carried ourselves was inescapably different.

I had left the United States four days after graduating from public high school in Baltimore, where the postgraduation ritual was to go to Ocean City, Maryland, drink, and celebrate this milestone of the American teenage experience. My strict Syrian parents didn't really care about the American teenage experience; nor were they particularly sympathetic to the milestones as they'd come up. I had only gone to a few dances and parties, and only after arduous battles to convince them I would not end up an alcoholic or a drug addict.

I knew a trip to the beach with my friends was never going to happen, so I didn't even bother to ask them if I could go. Yet they had no problem sending me by myself to the Middle East and Europe—first to Egypt, then to Syria, and lastly to Germany. Lebanon, still not two years out of its civil war, was not on the agenda. I would spend the entire summer abroad with relatives. To my parents, these places were much less frightening than a teenage nirvana two hours away from Baltimore.

It was with a heavy heart that I had left Egypt, where I had stayed with Ramez, one of my mother's favorite cousins, who was one of Nazir's sons. Ramez had grown up in Hama, but he was the same age as my mother, and when they were babies, Salma had nursed him when she had visited her parents in Hama. (My grandmother's milk was strong, and Ramez's mother had not been able.) He was now married to an Egyptian woman and had opted to live there after his father's murder.

I had been charmed by Ramez's children, my second cousins, who spoke fluent, if not Anglo, English, as well as Arabic with the endearing singsong Egyptian accent. Ramez's eldest, Kinan, was nearly my age and already terribly erudite and curious about the world (he went on to become a university professor of history). Kinan, along with his younger brother, the athletic and fun Jad, and their six-year-old sister, the rambunctious Dima, whose room I shared during my visit, were my guides, and a great part of my affection for Cairo was due to them.

It seemed to me they lived a magical life—as cosmopolitan as my life in suburban America felt provincial. Their maternal grandmother lived nearby, and both her house and theirs were full of art and antiques. We visited the pyramids and the Sphinx, sailed on the Nile, and spent hours in different museums. At the same time, Cairo was unexpectedly modern in some places. We shopped at malls, ate dinner at Chili's, and visited the opera. And we did much of this unaccompanied by the adults. With us were their first cousins, who were my second cousins as well: Ziad and Lina, who were visiting from Aleppo. We were all Abdeljawwad's great-grandchildren.

It hadn't taken much convincing to get me to extend my stay in Egypt, and my cousins assured me Syria had much less to offer. After all, they told me almost with a shudder, Syria only had three TV channels, unlike Egypt's five. (These were the days long before rooftops were congested with satellite dishes that received beamed programming faster than the censors could forbid it.) I would have stayed on even longer, and thought about changing my ticket again, but I had apparently already irritated relatives in Syria who had been expecting me days before. So I bid them a tearful farewell, and we promised to write.

Just a two-hour flight later, I landed in Syria. I could immediately tell from the looks of the airport in Damascus that maybe what my Egyptian cousins had said was true—Syria was years behind. At passport control, the uniformed man seemed initially amused by me as he took my American passport. When he saw my name, he asked me if I spoke Arabic. While my comprehension was fluent even then, I had yet to feel confident about speaking it. Also, as of 1992, my vocabulary was limited: I knew the words for ingredients and spices relevant to the Syrian kitchen, household chores, anything related to school, college, or grades, plus the Lord's Prayer and a bevy of cuss words. But with the edict to blend in ringing in my ears, I answered I did.

He asked me if I was Syrian. I reflexively answered, with barely suppressed indignation, that no, I was an American.

"Where are you parents from?" he asked.

"Syria," I answered, but couldn't help adding that they were Americans, too.

"Then you are Syrian," he chided me. "And if you are Syrian," he said, "you should have a Syrian passport. Don't you want a Syrian passport?"

I felt it was a trick question. I tried smiling and shrugged, "*Insh'allah.*" (While this literally means "God willing," in a pinch it is a polite way to demur, to avoid giving a straight answer, and to shirk accountability or responsibility.)

Was I married, he then wanted to know?

I bristled at the idea that he thought I might already be married. Couldn't he tell I was going to college at the end of the summer? It had always annoyed me as I was growing up that visiting Arabs would refer to me as an *'arous* (bride), and inquire as to whether I wanted an *'arees* (groom). Of course, no one had really been trying to broker a child marriage; still, it was an indication of what was generally expected to be the most important thing in a woman's life.

"Backwards Syria," I kept thinking, but then, in an effort not to seem too American, I simply answered the question—"No," I said, I wasn't married—and tried to look as dejected about it as possible.

Finally, he waved me through.

I could see the exit—it wasn't far—and readjusting my straw hat and the camcorder on my shoulder, began to make my way there to greet my family. Suddenly, a man leaning against a wall pointed at me and summoned me to follow him into the unmarked room behind him.

Apparently, a whole world existed in the short distance between where I stood and where I wanted to go, a world in which there were several different functionaries whose whims I could be subject to. I looked for some signage for an explanation, but there was none. (I realized later that I wasn't meant to understand what was going on or to ever feel like I was sure of anything. This would be the case with most of the interactions I had with the Syrian state. The arbitrariness was one of the myriad ways of controlling the society and extracting its submission.) I had no choice but to follow.

Once we were inside the small cramped room, he closed the door behind us.

We stood in silence for what seemed like an eternity as he stared at me. Who was I, he wanted to know? What was I doing in Syria? Where was I going to stay? Who was I staying with?

I answered to the best of my abilities: I was on vacation, I was visiting Damascus, I was staying with my grandfather.

He, too, asked me why I didn't have a Syrian passport—if I was Syrian, as I clearly was. I shrugged and explained: I was born in America.

Then he pointed to the camcorder still slung over my shoulder. Where was it from? He wanted to know.

"America."

What was I going to do with it?

"Film stuff?" I answered, hesitantly, afraid this was so obvious perhaps I hadn't understood the question.

Was it staying in the country?

"No," I answered, relieved to finally be catching his drift.

"Good. Make sure you take it with you," he told me. "Don't sell it to anyone."

He then said that I needed to register the camcorder, in a tone that suggested there was a regularity to this procedure, not that it was being made up as we went along. (In retrospect, I realized that "register" was a euphemism, and that what he really wanted was a bribe to let me through.)

"Of course," I said. "How do I register it?"

He held out his hand and beckoned for my passport and scribbled on the last page "RCA" (the make) and one of the numbers he found on the camcorder. There was nothing to suggest that the next official would even know to look there. All of it struck me as completely random. (I had that passport for another five years, and whenever I would see his illegible scrawl again, I couldn't help but grimace.)

Smiling at me, he asked me my age, which was simple math, considering that he had my passport in his hands, and before I could even answer, he asked if I was betrothed.

I was getting increasingly irritated. I had always been on the defensive in the United States about being Arab, as Arabs were endlessly maligned in the American imagination, often portrayed as hopelessly backward. I had tried, with the skill of a preteen and then a teenager, to explain geopolitics to my classmates and teachers while also trying to represent, in who I was, an alternative image of Arabs. The previous year's war with Iraq and my father's mistimed decision to grow a moustache that made him look like Saddam Hussein had made it all the more fraught. Now, in my first five minutes in Syria, I was frustrated by these Syrian officials proving some of the stereotypes correct.

"No, I'm not engaged," I told the guard. Hearing the annoyance in my own voice, I added, "*Insh'allah*, soon," and tried to smile.

The man then handed me back my passport, and as I took it, he held onto it a bit longer, so that we were both holding it at the same time. Was he going to change his mind? I started to wonder.

"Welcome in Syria," he said in poor English, finally letting it go.

I resisted the urge to correct him and backed out into the main hall. I quickly looked to see how many doors there were, wondering if I'd have to go behind any more. Then, a jittery man in an orange jumpsuit approached me; he was looking for an Alia Malek.

"Yes, that's me," I said, surprising him as I went to shake his hand, which he took hesitantly. He had been hunting everywhere for me, he said. While never looking me in the eye, he ushered me toward the exit.

When he saw Sari, who was waiting outside, he hurried me along and delivered me to my great-uncle. Then he began obsequiously asking forgiveness for the delay, addressing Sari repeatedly as "*Ya istaz, ya doctour*" (Oh professor, oh doctor).

Of Salma's siblings, I knew Sari the best, as well as his beautiful American wife Clara and their six kids. We'd visit them in Cape Cod where they would summer.

I was so relieved to see a familiar face, but he was cross with me for having taken so long. In English, he snapped at me: Why had I not met with the man in the orange jumpsuit? (I didn't know I was supposed to meet him.) Turning to the man, my great-uncle thanked him and dismissed him, and as he did, I saw Sari slip money into his hand. "God keep you, *ya istaz, ya doctour*," the man bobbed his head, bowing. Suddenly embarrassed about my handshake, I hid my hand behind my back.

છ૭રૄ

WHEN I WALKED into my grandparents' house for the first time in twelve years, it felt more familiar to me than I had expected. Hardly anything had changed, even with my grandmother Salma already five years gone.

The *salon* looked as I always remembered it. The heavy green velvet curtains with white chiffon trim were drawn, but even in the dark I could see the matching green velvet of the nineteenth-century walnut wood furniture she had reupholstered in her favorite color, after inheriting it from Ameen's parents.

My grandfather looked much older now. The way my siblings and I had experienced the entire notion of grandparents had been just another thing that had set us apart from what looked like the idyllic American family experience. From our bay window in Baltimore, which looked out on a cul-de-sac, we had watched our neighbors receive visits from their grandparents frequently. Ours were more like imaginary friends; we could only talk to them on the telephone, and even then, only if it would connect, and only on holidays. Once we connected, it seemed like we had to yell to be heard across the world. Of course, once Salma was locked in, there was nothing to hear, except maybe the sound of her breathing. With my grandfathers, who both outlived their wives, we would exchange pleasantries and not much more. There was just too much they didn't know about us; it seemed pointless to share the minutiae of our days.

Now Ameen, my last remaining grandparent, stood before me, more than just a disembodied voice. He was eighty years old, and the skin on his face was thin and almost translucent. What remained of his hair was white. He wore an ivory-colored short-sleeved shirt (much like an unadorned *guayabera*) that looked like it kept him cool in the un-air-conditioned house.

"*Ahlan*," he welcomed me, as we maneuvered an awkward embrace. The last time he had seen me was the summer of my baptism, when Nazir had been murdered and he had told my mother to take us and leave the country. Just how much of my life he had missed was readily visible now, as I stood taller than him.

My uncle Sa'ad—nine years younger than my mother—was newly married, and he and his wife, Nuha, now lived here, too. She was a wonderfully gregarious woman, only ten years older than me. I caught a hint of green in her beautiful hazel eyes.

Nuha had spent a few months, years before, studying English in Britain, and she was eager to speak it again with me. She already had two children under the age of two. A pharmacist and a talented seamstress, Nuha had mended the green curtains, which had become worn with age and had been neglected in my grandmother's illness, and to spruce up the kitchen she had sewn little red-and-white-checkered curtains for the windows and a matching tablecloth. But the heart of it remained the same 1950s Frigidaire that my grandmother had moved from her apartment in the Tahaan back in 1970, after having used it for twenty years there. (It still works to this day.)

Nuha's mother was Syrian, but her father was a Palestinian, forced out from Jaffa in 1948. As such, Nuha had only become a Syrian citizen once she married my uncle Sa'ad, as neither wives nor mothers can pass on their citizenship to their spouses or children in Syria. She spoke Syrian Arabic, not the Palestinian dialect that I associated with the Palestinians I had known in the Arab American community in Baltimore.

My uncle had refused to join the Ba'ath Party, and to his credit (or naïveté, depending on whom you ask), he was an honest lawyer. He was therefore not a particularly wealthy lawyer. Nuha was much more enterprising, working as a pharmacist and sewing much of her own clothing. Together, they seemed quite happy.

It felt good to see Sa'ad in this new life. Caring so lovingly and diligently for Salma in those terrible years of her locked-in life had left him little time for much else after work. Both Nuha and Sa'ad were clearly excited to have me; they had been putting aside money so we could travel together in Syria. I hadn't realized how disappointed they would be when I had delayed my arrival from Cairo.

But we didn't have much time right then and there to catch up: a big dinner was being hosted to welcome me back after twelve years away. I had to quickly freshen up and change.

On my grandmother's dining-room table, Nuha had laid out an enormous spread of food and delicacies. People I was told were my relatives poured in. I really only knew the names of my aunts and uncles and immediate cousins. I barely understood who the vast majority of these people were or how they were related to me. But after all those years in the United States with just my nuclear family, I was excited to suddenly have a houseful of relatives. Right away, I could see the resemblance on several faces to my mother and father. I had never experienced this before.

People wanted to know how my parents were. Would they come back? Why hadn't we come more often? They also told me I was too thin or too freckled and that there were places where I could have had my hair done. Several took me aside to ask when I would be coming to their house for lunch—after all, they really made the best *kibbeh*, or stuffed grape leaves, or *fatteh* in the family.

෩

UNFORTUNATELY, THE OLD hot water heater at my grandparents' house broke, consuming the money Sa'ad and Nuha had set aside for our travels. Instead, Nuha's younger brother was dispatched to accompany me on little day trips to some of the nearby archaeological and cultural wonders.

In his parents' old white Volkswagen bug, we visited the well-preserved crusader castle Krac de Chevaliers, 120 miles northwest of Damascus, in the rolling green hills above Syria's Mediterranean coast. We also went to Ma'loula, some forty miles northeast of the capital, a scenic village built into barren rock hills where people still spoke Aramaic. I visited the mountain monastery and convent at Saidnaya; the Damascus church where St. Paul fled the city, lowered from the city walls in a bucket; and the Old City's brilliant Umayyad Mosque—built on the site of a Christian basilica dedicated to John the Baptist, who is honored by Christians and Muslims alike. Before becoming a church, the site had served as a Greco-Roman temple to Jupiter, and before that, it had been a temple to an Aramaean god.

My guides always encouraged me to film and photograph what I was seeing. "A Muslim miracle happened here!" "A Christian miracle happened where you are standing!" "Look at this vista! You are seeing what they saw thousands of years ago!" "This is sacred!" "This is historical!" "This is important!" I'd then switch between the video recorder on my shoulder and the regular camera attached to my waist. (Either way, my relatives would stand rigidly, occasionally waving once they remembered one of the devices could capture motion. "Hi Lamya and Sharif!" they'd say.)

They even made me pose for pictures with the kitschy mannequins dressed up in clothes from different eras, meant to show us how people inhabited the palaces or *hammams* (communal baths) once upon a time. In all these pictures I'm sporting the tourist-tool-belt look—the fanny pack and the camera.

The pictures I like best from that trip, however, remain the ones of old Damascus streets, with their quiet testimony to all the centuries they have endured. I took those on my favorite excursions—the ones with my aunt Suha. As an artist, her sensibilities were always focused on the aesthetic, the refined, and the pleasurable. She always seemed interested in getting to know me, too, without ever being disappointed by what she learned. She never dropped the casual admonishments I was growing used to as the price to pay for having relatives.

Suha and her husband had now been in Adèle and Nikola's old apartment in the Tahaan for nearly six years. Suha was thus living across the hall from the very house in which she had grown up, and across the hall from the very man who had taken it from her family. But with Hassan having long refused to leave, with the law on his side, and with my parents resolutely in the United States, she decided to just be a friendly neighbor, knowing her daily life would otherwise be miserable. To smile in the face of those who stole from you to make life easier was, after all, a decision many in Syria made.

Art also helped to bring them together. In addition to writing poetry and dialogue for Arabic television, Hassan had begun to buy and sell paintings from Syrian artists. Hassan had not studied art himself, though he dabbled in painting. Several of the artists were Suha's friends, or had been her classmates at the Faculty of Fine Arts in Damascus. Sometimes Hassan would therefore solicit her opinion, which she would give—because she did love art. She even admitted that Hassan had a way with words. His writing could be entertaining and even beautiful, as Salma had found all those years ago. And while other artists had submitted themselves to the regime, Hassan had at least always refused all requests that he pen any kind of poetic ode to Hafez al-Assad.

But like everyone else, Suha was much more fond of Hassan's wife, Hilal, than she was of Hassan. Hilal always reminded Suha about how much she had learned from Salma, especially about how to run a house and prepare certain dishes, what with Hilal's own mother far away in Dara'a. Hilal's eagerness made Suha think she was lonely, and she knew Hilal had suffered in her marriage to Hassan. He slept during the day, waking up only to go out in the evening. He came home intoxicated every night, and was known to the police as a drunkard. They would drop him off in Ain al-Kirish without ever having to ask where he lived. He'd often return well after midnight with friends, including women, and rouse Hilal from her sleep so she could prepare something for them to eat and drink—but he refused to let her join them, or even be seen. When she would knock on the door to the salon, where he entertained his friends, with a tray of food and beverages, he'd snatch it from her hands and rudely dismiss her.

Hassan forbade Hilal from going out on the street except in the company of her upstairs neighbor, Fatima, the woman whom Salma had looked after when she moved in as a new bride in 1965. As much as Hassan fashioned himself a bohemian, some of the women in the building saw him as "typically shar'ee," meaning Eastern, as a husband. Others saw no contradiction at all in the double standard he applied in his marriage—after all, how could he trust anyone when he himself was not trustworthy?

Hilal and Suha had now been friends for a long time. Not a morning passed that one of them didn't go over to the other's home for coffee, or they joined Fatima upstairs, while Hassan slept late into the day. Over that morning break, Hassan's wife would often weep about his latest insults. Sometimes he only hurled words; other times he overturned his lunch plate when he didn't like the food that she had served him. Yet Hilal would still rhetorically ask her friends why he couldn't, just once, go out with *her* on the street, so the world would know that *she* was his wife, that the great poet belonged to *her*.

Hilal's son, now twenty-five, had gone to Ukraine to study dentistry. She had a nine-year-old daughter at home, only a year younger than Suha's daughter, and they had become friends as well. The girls crossed the same hallway to ask the other to play that Suha had as a child to draft her cousins, though mostly the girls came to Suha's. The building's children had always avoided Hassan. Even his son Shadi spent most of his childhood at Fatima's house upstairs, with her son Amjad. The boys were the same age and had been best friends growing up, even though Shadi attended a public school and Amjad attended the Laïque.

Suha sometimes entered her old home as a guest. Hassan had kept a few pieces of her mother's furniture, but it no longer felt like Salma's domain. When Salma had lived there, the door between the dining room and the salon was never closed, and the light from the front windows and balcony spilled in. The house was usually full of guests and commotion, with a woman, Salma, at its center. Now the woman of the house cowered in the kitchen and in the bedroom. The only time Suha could feel her mother's spirit was when she stood on the front balcony and looked down on the bitter orange tree Salma had planted when she had been born, the one Salma had told Hassan to take care of.

Hassan hadn't forgotten his promise. Every now and then he would recite from the poem he had written about it that began: "This tree, its name is Suha." It went on, perhaps in Salma's voice: "I watered it and raised it tall and then I used to call to it, where are you oh Suha?"

The apartment had become a painful reminder to Suha that nothing had gone as it was meant to in their lives—for the house, for Salma, for the country. So many of the residents had changed that the building—and for that matter, the country—no longer felt the same.

The children of the top-floor neighbors, Abu and Um Ali—everyone agreed—had indeed grown to be *z'araan* (hooligans). No one had any doubts that they were involved in criminal activity. They even siphoned off electricity from other apartments.

Above Suha, the apartment where the improbable couple Baheej and Lili had lived was now owned by Abu and Um Mustafa. He sold birds in a small pet shop near the citadel—from a shop no larger than a bathroom. The gossip was that they had been able to buy the house only because their son was a smuggler—perhaps of birdcages, or perhaps of drugs. Things between Um Mustafa and Suha were tense, as Um Mustafa insisted on beating her dusty carpets over Suha's balcony. This not only dirtied all the freshly wrung laundry Suha had put out to dry in the sun but also exacerbated the asthma that had plagued her ever since she had seen Salma in the hospital in Baltimore. The stairs were no longer as clean as they used to be, despite Suha, Fatima, and Hilal's best efforts.

Until that summer in 1992, I didn't have any memories of the Tahaan. My memories of Salma had been at the house she had moved into after she had left Ain al-Kirish. If I had ever been in the Tahaan before, I couldn't recall it. To me, it was simply where Suha's house was and where we'd meet before our outings. Together we strolled through the Hamidiyeh Souk, a bustling marketplace covered by a vaulted iron roof where the sun poked through in beams—thanks to a constellation of bullet holes perforated by the machine-gun fire of French planes in 1925. We visited the neglected yet rich National Museum. And we dropped in on the ateliers of her friends.

I began to see that Syria was a place of great beauty and civilization, but comparing my recent experience in Cairo, I was frustrated, because Egypt exploited its tourist attractions so much more effectively. In Syria, museum placards were handwritten, some in French, others in English, and not enough in Arabic. I told my family how Egypt had made a fortune off of me, charging me, my camera, and my camcorder separate entrance fees at their sites, while in Syria I could have likely walked off with some priceless antiquity and no one would have noticed. I was immediately shushed for even implying that the government was not doing a good job at something.

But it was impossible not to notice how rundown everything was. American cars from the 1950s and 1960s still crowded the streets, as well as old Citroëns and Mercedes. The other cars were Eastern European models I didn't recognize. Electricity came and went. But my family assured me it had been worse. In the late 1980s, there had been extreme shortages. Specifically, people had hoarded the tissue paper used as both napkins and in the toilet. Bananas were such rarities that neighbors would invite each other over to share them when someone brought back a few kilos from a trip to Lebanon—a country in the middle of a civil war that still had better commercial goods than Syria.

An essential legacy of the ostensibly socialist 1963 Ba'athist coup was a bloated and politicized public sector. In Syria, it was rife with cronyism—staffed largely by utterly unqualified and corrupt regime loyalists—and burdened with political goals such as near-full employment of college graduates. It was bound to fail as the population expanded. By 1986, the government had run out of money. To restart the economy, the regime decided to abandon its socialist model and began to reach out to the previously sidelined and skilled business community, as well as making businessmen out of regime loyalists to create its own private-sector network.

At the same time, the regime turned its back on labor and the peasantry, which had been integral parts of the original Ba'ath coalition. Gradually it dismantled the state economic sector and began to shrink state payouts (such as food subsidies) to the population in the hopes that private business would compensate for the smaller public sector.

Thus began the unofficial and strategic networks between the regime, the traditional business community, and their regime-created counterparts. These new private endeavors used the savvy of the old commercial class, the acumen of the new entrepreneurs, and the power of regime bureaucrats who were eager to take part in high-earning economic partnerships previously unavailable to them. The wealthiest of the business elites and the regime were now partners. However, because the regime did not want to see its power diffused, these relationships were never symmetrical or transparent, which meant the private sector was never able to flourish naturally. In sum, Syria economically went from an authoritarianism of the Left to one of the Right, as the political ecomomy scholar Bassam Haddad succinctly puts it.

But by 1992, not only could people in Syria find toilet paper, they also had easier access to the kind of foreign goods that were usually only available on the black market, smuggled in from Lebanon or Turkey. This was such a marked improvement that many at first didn't resent that in certain quarters in Damascus there were signs of new and much greater opulence and prosperity. Over time, as opportunities were largely confined to certain groups, this disparity created fissures in Syrian society; before, the crisis of toilet paper and bananas was felt by Syrian society in its entirety, fostering a sense they had all been in it together.

Even so, if you had asked me about the Syrian economy in 1992, I would have likely told you it was awesome. I bought several bootleg cassette tapes— the Police, Madonna, and C+C Music Factory—all for less than a dollar.

No matter how much people might be struggling economically, they were never anything short of generous. Hospitality that would have been extended to my parents, if they had come, was passed on to me instead, sometimes in such amounts that I thought people were making up for years of lost time.

⛥

ALTHOUGH THE PLANS Sa'ad and Nuha had made for a more elaborate trip were dashed, we did still travel together to Hama for a big family wedding. We went by bus for the three-hour drive north of Damascus.

For the first time I would visit the house and garden of my mother's childhood lore and even stay there. I would be sleeping in the flat that had belonged to one of Salma's brothers and in which now his widow, and their son the groom, lived. I knew one of her daughters, Rania, well, as she lived in New Jersey and had married Rami, Adèle's son. Although Rania and Rami were both my mother's cousins, they were not related at all to each other. However, Rania, who had grown up in Hama, had come to Damascus for university and had coincidentally rented Rami's parents' old apartment in the Tahaan.

My mother, who hadn't been to Hama since before she had married and left Syria, had asked me to see the *noria* in her place. When I did, I understood why. Standing since Byzantine times and still used to irrigate the surrounding fields, the waterwheels were, in Syria, unique to Hama; once you saw them, you knew exactly where you were. And as she had told me, there was indeed a soothing rhythm to the sound of the water as it was lifted from the Orontes River and poured onto the ancient aqueducts.

A decade had passed since Hafez al-Assad had crushed the Muslim Brotherhood (and other opposition) by killing tens of thousands of people in Hama and destroying large parts of the city. I had only a vague understanding of the specifics, but a clear sense of the takeaway: Assad was to be feared; his wrath could be terrible, and we were supposed to act as if we never knew it had ever happened.

We arrived at my great-grandfather's house a few hours before the wedding, and I looked up at it in the sun. At five stories, it stood higher than most buildings in Hama. I wasn't surprised then when someone whispered in my ear that in 1982, Assad's snipers had commandeered its roof as they decimated the city. The house was right behind the church where the wedding was to take place. The church had been destroyed in 1982, but the Christian community in Hama had quickly repaired it. I understood later that swift restoration was essential to the collective public amnesia everyone was supposed to have about what had taken place.

We changed into our church attire. I put on the white suit I had worn to my high school graduation a month before and a world away. My uncle's wife, Nuha, wore her new dress—one she had made herself, a perfect replica of a dress I had brought with me from Macy's in the United States, and which she had seen when I had unpacked my suitcase.

As we walked in heels on the uneven streets of Hama, the people on balconies above us watched the procession. Nuha stumbled but quickly regained her balance, grabbing my arm. She whispered to me that it was the fault of the lady on the balcony to our right, who had given her a look that Nuha was sure was the evil eye, as her dress was so different and so pretty. I turned my head to see, but couldn't be sure, as the woman was now smiling. Nuha said that *that* was the proof. I was charmed; it all reminded me of southern Italy, where I had never been, but which was the backdrop of some of my favorite films.

As for the wedding itself, I barely could focus on it, as I was much too hot during the entire ceremony. But to have taken off my suit jacket and exposed my arms and shoulders would have been inappropriate. When we were finally allowed to file back out of the church, those of us staying at the family house walked home to rest and change before the soirée.

Back at the house, I was chatting with second cousins whom I had just met, more of Abdeljawwad and Sara's great-grandchildren, when I heard a commotion. Rushing to a window, we saw a procession of men in village dress preceding the bride and groom. They were approaching the door. Some beat drums, others a kind of animal-skin tambourine, while singing about the new marriage. Women in the street ululated.

Once inside the building, the bride climbed the stairs to her mother-in-law's house and was handed a piece of kneaded dough the size of a flattened soccer ball. As the percussion got louder, she slammed it above the door and the audience that had gathered took a breath to see if it would stick. It did. *Alhumdullah!* (Praise be to God!). The marriage would last.

That night, we went to the party on the terrace of a beautiful hotel, where the tables were set up around a lit swimming pool. We were served more food than anyone could possibly eat, which, as I had seen all summer, was always the case.

I met even more relatives, all of whom I organized in my head according to which floor of Sheikh Abdeljawwad's house they belonged to. I danced with them all night as if I had known them all my life, and when a small drunken scuffle broke out between the groom's and bride's families, I was sure to stand on "our" side.

At some point, the hotel staff rolled out the wedding cake. It was several tiers high, and one of them appeared to be a layer of columns. When I looked closer, I saw it was actually a cage, and inside there were doves. With a sword—cakes at Arab weddings are often cut with swords—the bars made of sugar were slashed, and the hesitant birds, with some coaxing, flew out and away.

I was impressed; I had never seen anything like that in Baltimore. The Damascenes who had come for the wedding applauded, but they were much less awestruck than I was.

"What they think is a big deal here in Hama," they explained, "has already been done many times in Damascus."

⚕

THE NEXT DAY, Sa'ad and Nuha went back to Damascus. I stayed on an extra day in Hama, where I had become fast friends with one of the groom's nieces, my second cousin Laura, who was close in age to me and spoke fluent English. She had come to the wedding from Lebanon. Like me, she was the eldest of four—three girls and one boy—whose order mirrored my siblings and me. We had all been staying with their grandmother—the mother of the groom—at our great-grandfather's house.

Laura invited me to go shopping in the souk with her mother and sisters. As we got ready to leave, she wrapped her long blonde hair into a bun and put a baseball cap on. She suggested I hide my hair as well. Like their mother, the girls were all naturally blonde. As we walked through the market, we kept hearing as we passed, "*Ajaanib, ajaanib*" (Foreigners, foreigners). Hama was clearly more conservative than Damascus, but also, as a group we were more noticeable. We just kept walking along, pretending, as we were told, that we weren't aware of all the attention.

It was slightly jarring then to pass by the lingerie shops, which carried items that were much more racy than anything I had seen before. Years later, the lingerie stores in Syrian souks would become a recurring story for Western journalists, but back then, I hadn't known to expect it.

At the different stores we went to, Laura's mother expertly bargained the prices down. She often caught the merchants off-guard; they were surprised to hear her speak not only Arabic, but Arabic with a Hama accent, as she had grown up there. Soon we had acquired towels, bracelets, and spices.

When we were walking back, a donkey suddenly bumped us from behind at a tight junction, and we had to stop and untangle while giving way to shoppers coming the other way. The chorus of "Foreigners, foreigners" intensified, and Laura's mother told us to huddle in and not talk to anyone. Unwelcome hands rubbed up against us, and she yelled at everyone around us to show some manners and be ashamed, again startling those who didn't expect the slight blue-eyed blonde to be one of them.

⚜

FROM HAMA, I went on to Aleppo to visit Salma's only sister. I had met her before in the United States, because her two sons had emigrated there. Tante Hind never failed to remind me that because she was a fair-skinned blonde with blue eyes, she was considered to be prettier than my darker grandmother. And in fact she told me that again in Aleppo. Like my grandmother, Hind, too, always seemed to be irritated with her husband. And like my grandfather, Hind's husband was sweet, erudite, and soft-spoken. Of Greek extraction, he spoke the language and had served as the Greek consul in Syria's second city. His family's centuries-old traditional-style house would go on to become a popular restaurant and boutique hotel, though eventually it would be destroyed with much of Aleppo after 2011.

In Aleppo, I was also reunited with Ziad and Lina, whom I'd come to adore in Egypt, and met Hind's daughter and grandchildren. I visited Aleppo's famous citadel and its stunning Umayyad Mosque, and I ate in its wonderful restaurants. Aleppo, with its proximity to Turkey and its huge influx of Armenians fleeing the Ottoman genocide decades before, boasted a cuisine that, I had to admit, was perhaps even better than the Damascene kitchen.

The pomegranate molasses used in many Syrian dishes, but even more in Aleppan ones, was unlike what made it over to the United States. Before I returned to Damascus, Tante Hind packed an unmarked glass bottle filled to the brim with the thick ambrosia to take with me. Her supplier was a farmer from the countryside, and I understood that what I was being entrusted with was sacred.

When I arrived back in Damascus, there was one bureaucratic matter to take care of before I moved on to Germany. In fact, I couldn't leave Syria without doing it.

When I was born, before my parents had given up the idea of raising their children in Damascus, they had registered my birth abroad with the Syrian state. At age fourteen, I was supposed to have presented myself to the Syrian government so that I could receive my national identity card. Now that I was seventeen, I was already three years late.

Sa'ad filed the necessary paperwork. But I still had to be interviewed by the government, essentially to explain why there had been no trace of me in Syria since I had been born. I had to go to a building quite close to my grandfather's house. It was an office of the *mukhabarat*.

Once I arrived, I was ushered from room to room. Every single one of them had a picture of Hafez al-Assad leering at me from the wall. I had seen versions of these portraits throughout my trip. They had been in every store, every restaurant. Wallet-sized varieties had been affixed to every dashboard of every taxi I had ridden in—these were often pasted onto hearts cut out from red construction paper, which in turn were pasted on to other hearts cut from lacy doilies. (Taxi drivers were notorious informants, so we never spoke as we rode.) Some portraits were stories-tall and draped down the sides of buildings. I found all of them, even the delicate arts-and-crafts ones of the cabbies, menacing. To me, Assad looked like Mr. Burns from *The Simpsons*, though in the offices of the *mukhabarat*, I quickly stifled the snicker that thought started within me.

Finally, I was escorted into a dark room and seated at one side of a table. There was a light bulb suspended from a wire in the ceiling, and I couldn't help but think of a movie set's interpretation of an interrogation room. Inside, there were two men waiting for me.

The *mukhabarat* wanted to know why I was so late in filing for my ID card.

"Because I wasn't here."

"Where were you?" they asked.

I didn't know why this was all so hard to understand. I had clearly been in America, as I was born in America. Who were my people in Damascus? they wanted to know.

They already knew who my relatives were in the country—probably even better than I did. But I answered with as much deference as I could muster. I began to rattle off, "my grandfather, my uncle, my aunt, my cousin, my other cousin—" and mercifully for all of us, they stopped me.

Then came the only question I stumbled on. They asked if I had any friends in Syrian *sijun*? "What's a *sijun*?" I said. That word had yet to make it into my Arabic vocabulary.

They look at each other and repeated, "*Sijun, sijun*," in an ineffective effort to explain to me what a *sijun* was. Finally someone translated it: "Brison," he said, making the common substitution of a "B" for a "P," a phoneme that doesn't exist in Arabic.

I think I produced a sound that sounded like a laugh, though I was too nervous to think anything was funny. Suddenly the anti-Soviet literature that had been part of my Cold War–era social studies curriculum in Baltimore seemed not so remote and irrelevant.

"Prison?" I repeated in disbelief. I was a seventeen-year-old student from Baltimore.

As sure as I knew the sky was blue, I knew this was all absurd. As they already knew, the last time I had been in Syria, I had been five and a half years old. Now, twelve years later, I had only been there for six weeks. Were they really asking me if I had contacts in their prisons?

And yet I also understood that if I wanted to get on with my day and be able to leave the country, I had to play along and not let on that I thought this was ridiculous. I had to become an active participant in all of this.

"No," I said. "I don't know anyone in prison."

I was then fingerprinted, and my picture was taken. Shortly thereafter, I had in hand my Syrian national ID card. I was officially Syrian.

⸙

DURING MY TRIP to Syria, I rediscovered many of the people from my memories, matching real flesh to the shadows that had followed me around for twelve years. But there were several women whom I had not yet seen again. I looked everywhere for Nanette, who had pierced my ears as a toddler—setting me apart from most American girls my age until high school. I also wanted to see her sister, Stella, who used to lunch with us at Salma's house before returning to the salon where she worked. I had expected them to reappear at a lunch or dinner, or to receive an invitation to go see them. I had been quite passive on the trip—going where I was told to go, eating what I was told to eat. But now I was about to leave, and I had yet to see the sisters. I asked where they were.

Only then did I learn that these women were Jewish. A few months before my return, Hafez al-Assad had lifted a long-existing discriminatory ban that prevented Syrian Jewish families from traveling together. Ever since the onset of the conflict between the Arab countries and the Jewish state of Israel, being both Arab and Jewish had become an identity no-man's-land, as Arab Jews' very existence complicated both Israeli and Arab narratives of the conflict. For Syrian Jews, the decades since Israel's 1948 founding had been, at best, complex, and in Syria they were often regarded as a potential fifth column. In 1992, changes in long-standing geopolitics allowed any inconvenience that Syrian Jews posed to both Israel and Syria to be resolved: Syria lifted the ban, and American Jewish groups sought (arguably cynically) to encourage the community to leave and go populate Israel (passing through the United States first, as direct travel between Syria and Israel remained prohibited). The resulting mass exodus meant that the Jewish Quarter in the Old City, thousands of years old, was suddenly without its people. I had just missed them. But that summer, I was unaware of the entire context. All I knew was that women whom I'd always thought of as Syrian and nothing else, and whom I eagerly wanted to see, were now gone.

While I had loved my trip to Syria, I was also relieved to have grown up in the United States. So what if Hassan was still in the house intended for my mother to raise me in? Despite the complexity of being an Arab in America, we had electricity, water, and cars. We had bananas and toilet paper. Best of all, there were no *mukhabarat* or pictures of the leader or corrupt government officials looking for a bribe.

I saw it more of a blessing than a tragedy that my grandmother's old friends Stella and Nanette might now be in a place far less chaotic and "backward" than Syria. In my teenage confidence, I shrugged, thinking I'd rather live anywhere but here.

I, for one, was not in a particular rush to get back to Syria.

7

NO-MAN'S-LAND

Palestine/Israel, Summer 1998

S IX YEARS LATER, I WAS WORKING JUST ACROSS THE BORDER FROM Syria, wanting—almost desperately—to go back. But my relatives in Damascus would not hear of it.

I was twenty-three years old and had just finished my first year of law school. My plan was to become a human rights and civil rights attorney. For the first time as an adult, I was living in the Middle East: I was spending the summer in the West Bank, working in the Occupied Palestinian Territories. I had come here because I had needed to see the place for myself. Here lay not only the root cause of the animus directed toward Arabs in the United States, but also the source of much upheaval, instability, oppression, and radicalization across the Middle East.

Syria was never far from my mind, especially given how close it was geographically. My mother would be visiting Damascus for the first time in eight years with my brother and my youngest sister. I wanted to join them there. Naïvely, I thought traveling to Damascus from the West Bank would be an easy excursion, as long as I made sure to travel via Jordan. But communications from my Syrian relatives via my family in the United States urged me to reconsider—they were afraid that no matter how cautious I was about what stamps were on my passport, Syrian officials would know I had been in Israel.

Anyone who has been in Israel is supposedly not allowed in Syria. "Israel" was such an unlikely place where a Syrian might go that Syrians would refer to it as "Disneyland." They were not only afraid for me, but for themselves; after all, they could be forced to bear the repercussions of my recklessness.

Israel, too, hadn't been particularly welcoming. From the minute I boarded my flight for Tel Aviv, the tension had been palpable, mainly because of a hierarchy that put anything or anyone Arab at the bottom. As was par for the course, I was interrogated upon my arrival, while other Americans—non-Arab ones—were let through. I could see them stealing glances at those of us who were pulled aside and was reflexively embarrassed. After two rounds of interrogation, which focused on my ethnic heritage, I was finally let through.

But what made my first day in Israel/Palestine memorable was the *sherut* (Hebrew for a group taxi) ride from Tel Aviv to Jerusalem. When I had first approached the driver who had been next up in the queue, he had greeted me pleasantly enough. However, upon hearing my destination was Sheikh Jarrah, a Palestinian neighborhood in East Jerusalem, he looked me over with a raised eyebrow and interrogated me as to where exactly I was going. Then he gruffly reached for my average-sized suitcase and complained about how hard it was to make it fit in his white minivan.

His humor deteriorated further before we even left the airport. Two hefty ultra-Orthodox men in their black Borsalino hats squeezed into the back seat, and from what I could tell, they objected to being put in the back. The driver, who appeared disdainful of them and their request for preferential treatment, ignored them and pointed to all the women he still had to fit in, whom, per their religious beliefs, they couldn't sit next to anyway. (We women were put in the first two rows.)

After taking my seat, I noticed who the universe had cruelly wedged between the Borsalino men: a professor from my first year of college that I hadn't been particularly fond of. His foundational class had been one that international studies majors like myself couldn't opt out of. He was a noticeably small man who loved to tell us he was from the Bronx, where folks were tough, and he often argued that violence was a justifiable means to resolve conflict. (He didn't appear to be the kind of man who had ever been in a physical fight.) His examples of justifiable victims were mostly in what he called "the Third World." Much of his scholarship was on Israel and its conflicts with Arabs. I got an A in his class but frequently felt the sting of his offhand remarks (made to the laughter of the students who adored him), which relied on caricatures of the developing world's peoples, from Colombians to Vietnamese to Arabs.

After begrudgingly saying hello on that *sherut* ride, I answered his question as to why I was there. When I told him that I would be doing human rights work in the West Bank, he snorted, and I saw the young American woman next to me straighten up and glance over. For the rest of the hour-long ride from Tel Aviv to Jerusalem, he played guide to his companion, who did not seem very familiar with the Middle East (yes, I was eavesdropping), recounting a history of the place that did not include the Palestinians. It was a narrative I was familiar with—a land without a people for a people without a land—that erased the *other* people, the ones critical to any truth of the place.

I hadn't known then what to say, or if it was even my place to say anything. I was the only non-Jew in the van, and worse, I was an Arab. Minutes after landing in Tel Aviv, I had been made aware of the power of the Israeli state, and whom it viewed as unwelcome.

The driver delivered everyone else to their coordinates in West Jerusalem, before finally taking me to the East, where I was the last one to be dropped off. We reached a neighborhood of old stone houses seemingly built around the olive and birch trees, the former with silvery leaves, the latter of white bark. The driver pointed at the address that was my destination, where I'd be getting a lift to Ramallah in the West Bank, and dumped my bag on the sidewalk before speeding away.

Though I had remained intimidated and silent in the minivan, this time—unlike the last time I had been to Syria—I had a much better grasp of the regional geopolitics and history, with its nuances and discontents, and I was eager to connect that knowledge with the very people whose lives were being lived against this backdrop. Both of my mother's siblings were married to Palestinians who had been born in Syria. Now they were more than just aunts and uncles; suddenly, they were unlocked stores of experiences, and I wanted to know so much more: Where in Palestine were they from? How had their families left? When? What had remained behind? Did they feel Syrian or Palestinian? Would they go back if they could?

When I had made the decision in my first year of law school to spend that summer clerking in the West Bank (as opposed to at a law firm in the United States), my parents weren't thrilled. They worried that I would forever be stigmatized by potential employers. Like many Arabs of their generation, they were also jaded by geopolitics and ashamed of the collective Arab inability to do anything for the Palestinians despite years of alternating wars, peace summits, and rounds of diplomacy. And, of course, they were sure the Syrian government would find out I had been to Israel and never allow me to enter Syria again.

The opportunity for me to go to Palestine came with an American non-profit organization (started by an Arab American) that placed first-year law students in Palestinian institutions for the summer. We were a group of eighteen, representing twelve different law schools. The group included three Jewish Americans and one Israeli American, and nine of us were Arab American. Only one of the students was Palestinian—including me, there were two Syrians, five Egyptians, and one Lebanese (Americans and Canadians). But even if we weren't Palestinians, we felt implicated by the country's fate. The creation of Israel had set off huge influxes of refugees into neighboring Arab countries, where our parents came from. It also meant sustained military conflict, the loss of territory (Israel has illegally occupied the Syrian Golan Heights since 1967), and a constant state of emergency for most of the Arab world. With such a convergence of interests, many people both in the Arab world and in the Arab diaspora had subscribed to Arab nationalism and pan-Arabist sentiments.

And with an external existentialist threat in Israel, Arab regimes, including the one in Syria, had long been able to justify stifling internal dissent and opposition, consequently racking up thousands of human rights violations across decades. Meanwhile, the failure of these regimes, which exacted a heavy toll from their populations in terms of civil rights and liberties, to either defeat Israel (militarily or politically) or improve the lives of their own people helped delegitimize the very idea of secular governments, which the authoritarian regimes claimed to be. People were turning to religion for comfort, and then to the Islamists for alternative ideas of government (as if there were only these two extremes). This gave those who claimed to represent religious authority—such as wealthy and hypocritical Saudi Arabia—worrisome influence in other countries' societies. It felt like the entire region's development would be stunted as long as the Israeli-Palestinian conflict festered. For the Arab Americans there that summer, we had a sense that the fates of many countries and peoples relevant to our own lives rested on some sort of resolution to this central conflict.

Though I was so close and yet so far from Syria that summer, there were reminders of Syria everywhere, whether I was noting how different or how similar Palestine was. After all, Syria was my benchmark, and comparisons between the two were a running conversation in my head.

※

THAT SUMMER, I clerked at the fledgling Palestinian Authority's Ministry of Agriculture, tracking the cruel attacks that Israeli settlers and the Israeli state carried out on Palestinian farms, farmers, and the environment. I sat silently with octogenarian farmers as they wept in the middle of their groves of olive trees as old as they were, after Israeli settlers had hacked and sawed them down. I visited families driven to ruin by the acid that settlers sprayed on their almond trees and grapevines, or by the army's confiscation of their herds that had wandered into Israeli-controlled zones (the boundaries between these areas weren't always readily clear to humans, let alone sheep or goats). I also surveyed hilltops cleared of all their trees and vegetation to make way for more illegal Israeli settlements, whose toxic wastewater runoff turned downstream Palestinian plants bright fluorescent green.

As an Arabic speaker—albeit with a Syrian accent—I felt welcomed by Palestinians. I was also a curiosity. With no formal relations between the Syrian and Israeli states, there weren't many Syrians one could meet in person in the West Bank. (While in the Golan Heights, people did speak with Syrian accents, permits to leave the West Bank were only sparingly issued.) Even though a lot felt familiar to me—some overlap in cuisine, and of course language—there was much here that was different from Syria.

Damascus and Aleppo were large, bustling cities. Ramallah and Bir Zeit, where I worked and lived respectively, were much smaller and much less urban. In the West Bank, it was easy to get away from buildings and lights. At night from our rooftop, the stars seemed to be right above our heads. I provided farmers with endless entertainment on my visits when they'd quiz me as to what plant I was seeing. Usually it was already plucked, and I was being asked to identify it essentially by its leaves. For every plant I answered sincerely, "*Ban-a-dora?*" pronouncing the word for "tomato" in the very different Syrian way (Palestinians say *bin-doura*). They'd erupt in laughter at both my city slicker ways and funny way of speaking.

Despite the fact that the Israeli Occupation had robbed Palestinians of many freedoms, I found Palestinians freer than Syrians ever were in their conversation. People freely cursed everyone from the Israelis to Palestine

Liberation Organization (PLO) chairman Yasser Arafat to even Hafez al-Assad (Saddam Hussein was the most popular Arab leader, as far as I could tell). They also had a much more sophisticated understanding of other people's struggles across Europe, South America, Africa, and Asia than what I had ever discussed with Syrians, whose small-talk skills were honed to excruciating perfection. They possessed solidarity as a people, fortified by the external and existentialist threat that Israel posed to them. In Syria, I had been instructed to never speak of anything, because "even the walls had ears," meaning that you never knew who might sell you out to the *mukhabarat* and the regime. That had always felt like an internal rot.

But these were all observations based on old impressions made of Syria—I wanted to get back to Syria now as an adult.

⊛

BY MIDSUMMER, MY mother and siblings had arrived in Damascus. I, however, had finally acquiesced to family there and renounced any intention to go; they had remained adamant that there would be no way around the questions I would be asked at Syrian border control. And then they would all be suspected and guilty of my guilt. (It was my last chance to see Ameen, who would die the next year.)

I decided instead to visit Egypt (which had relations with Israel, albeit strained), thrilled to see family and to return to the country that had charmed me in 1992. From the West Bank, I traveled to Cairo with my friend Daalia, an Arab American from California whose parents were Egyptian. Not only were we classmates at Georgetown Law, we were also roommates that summer. Back in DC, Daalia had entertained me with stories of how theatrically Egyptian her parents had remained in Los Angeles, eating lupini beans at the mall and belly dancing around the house. But what fascinated me most was their love story: her father was Muslim, her mother Jewish. Neighbors back in Cairo, they had fallen in love growing up. They were both practicing their respective faiths, and their marriage worked.

In Palestine, people often used the word "Jews" to refer to Israelis (the Jewish ones; Christian or Muslim Israeli citizens were considered Palestinians). Israel, of course, called itself a Jewish state and used a Jewish symbol on its flag; what made Palestinians outcasts in their own land was that they weren't Jewish. It was not an arbitrary shorthand, but it nonetheless obscured many complexities, including the diversity of both Arabs and Jews. Daalia was proof that once it *hadn't* been impossible to be both Arab and Jewish, that there was a time when it wasn't an identity no-man's-land. Yet it was something she didn't disclose to either side. As I became more familiar with Palestine and Israel, it wasn't hard to see why there wasn't room to be both.

When we returned from Egypt, we again had to line up at Ben Gurion Airport for a *sherut* at the same stand I had been at almost two months before. Again, I told the driver where we were headed, "Sheikh Jarrah," and braced myself for the quick change in demeanor.

There was none. He didn't react; instead, he said something to me in Arabic, and I exhaled, assuming he was a Palestinian with Israeli citizenship or with a Jerusalem ID—the only way for a Palestinian to work here in Tel Aviv. I got the last seat, which was next to him. Not wanting to draw attention to the fact that he was an Arab with the other passengers, I didn't utter any more Arabic, and rode in silence.

Again, all the passengers with West Jerusalem coordinates were dropped off first. When it was just Daalia and me in the *sherut*, the driver asked me courteously where exactly we wanted to go.

Then we began polite conversation. Quickly I noticed that, unlike when I spoke to Palestinians, I was not converting his words from Palestinian Arabic to Syrian Arabic, as I had been doing daily, and by then, reflexively. He, too, dropped his Ks and Qs and negated his verbs by preceding them with *ma* instead of with the suffix *–ish*.

I realized I was speaking to a Syrian. I was stunned; after all, Syrians are prohibited from traveling to Israel. After a moment of mutual recognition, we began excitedly exchanging the relevant details, the hows and whys of who we were that allowed us—two Syrians—to be in Israel/Palestine. He was Jewish, and I was an American.

I had to catch my breath. I had been so utterly immersed in the Palestinian-Israeli conflict that it hadn't even occurred to me to wonder, let alone look, for any pockets of Syrian life here.

"Arab" was such a derogatory word in Israel, despite the fact that Jews across the Arab world had immigrated to the country. If there was any celebration of Arab culture, I hadn't seen it (appropriation, however, was another matter). Left-wing Israelis whom we met that summer had told us that Arab Jews didn't want to be seen as Arab, or as anything that suggested they were like the Palestinians. That, these good liberals explained, was why, they hated to admit, Arab Jews often supported right-wing parties. (In retrospect, there was clearly some internal Israeli racism at play in this kind of analysis.) But had I thought about it more thoroughly, I would have realized that it made sense for there to be fragments of Syria here, as Jews had lived in what would become Syria since before the common era. Syrian Jewish communities had flourished in the cities of Damascus, Aleppo, and Qamishli, enlarged by influxes of Jews fleeing the Crusades and those expelled from Spain in 1492.

Yet as we neared the end of the twentieth century, Jews were virtually gone from Syria. Considerable numbers had left for the United States at the end of the nineteenth century, when many other Syrians, predominantly Christian ones, also began immigrating to the Americas. They had left primarily for economic reasons, but also to avoid conscription in the Ottoman Army, from which minorities were no longer exempt as of 1909. Under Ottoman rule, Christians and Jews were also often vying for a better position in the empire. Scholars have noted that in some instances, Jews were the preferred minority, since they did not have any perceived natural allegiances to the Christian states of Europe. Ottoman Syrian Jews had enjoyed a considerable degree of prosperity and communal autonomy in matters of religious worship, education, welfare, and family status. Rabbis had exercised authority in administering their communities and enjoyed official status in the Ottoman state.

But what had set off the greater emigration in the first half of the twentieth century was Zionism and its call for—and eventual success in—creating a Jewish homeland in Palestine. European-grown, Zionism called on the world's Jews to eschew any other national identity and embrace Jewish nationalism, putting it on a collision course with the era's burgeoning Arab nationalism. This left little room for people to be both Jewish and Arab. The conflict between Arab nationalism and Zionism had culminated for the Syrian Jews in the Aleppo Riots in 1947 on the eve of the founding of the state of Israel. While between 1942 and 1961 about 9,000 Jews from Syria and Lebanon would arrive in Israel, the majority went on to the United States.

With the onset of the Arab-Israeli conflict, Jews who remained in Syria were unfairly made scapegoats for Israel. Things for the community were arguably at their worst in 1965 when Syrian authorities publicly executed Elihu Ben Saul Cohen, an Israeli spy who had infiltrated Syrian political and social circles. Although he was Egyptian born, his parents were Syrian Jews who left Egypt for Israel. There he had been recruited to serve as a spy in Damascus. For six hours after he was hung, his body was left on display in Damascus, swinging from a noose.

The Syrian state had then imposed severe restrictions on Syrian Jews' property ownership and on their ability to travel both internationally and domestically. But with the rise of Hafez al-Assad, himself from a minority sect, Syrian Jews had seen their situation improve somewhat. Restrictions were gradually lifted until the only remaining travel restriction had been the prohibition against emigration of full Jewish families. That finally changed when the Syrian state-controlled radio announced on April 23, 1992—not two months before I arrived in Damascus with my straw hat and camcorder— that the restriction had been lifted. It was the seventh day of Passover, when Jews celebrate the biblical exodus from Egypt.

This development grew out of the ill-fated Madrid Peace Process, which had begun in 1991. Syria, after its participation in the First Gulf War, had earned an invite. Assad, whose cunning was widely recognized, knew he had in the Syrian Jews a card he could play in his negotiations with Israel. It's not clear what he got in exchange for lifting the restrictions, as supposedly the most contentious issue between Syria and Israel—the latter's occupation of the Syrian territory in the Golan Heights—remained in firm Israeli control.

At the same time, American Jewish organizations had seized on the thaw in relations to facilitate the emigration of the 4,000-strong Syrian Jewish community to Israel. So it was that this community that had been part of Syria for thousands of years quickly began disappearing; by December 1993, most of them were gone, and of Damascus's twenty-two synagogues, only four remained. The Syrian state said it would safeguard the property they left behind, and in fact it did. But most Syrian Jews were leaving, not knowing if they'd ever return.

In 1992, for a Syrian Jew, leaving Syria was a reasoned gamble. Back then, it looked as if peace between Israel and the Arab world might become a reality, and with it the problem of being Arab and Jewish might disappear; perhaps leaving Syria wouldn't have to be permanent. (Of course, that peace had yet to happen, and I had a front-row seat to that failure on the West Bank.) There were also no guarantees that things would not change in the future, especially one without the aging Assad. Who knew what the whims of Syria's next ruler might be—even if Syrians were frequently promised that Assad would rule forever.

Never mind that the whole calculus only made sense because citizenship as a concept had long been gutted in Syria. No people should have to depend on a specific leader for their rights to be recognized in their own country. But then, who did Syria belong to really?

Because we had long understood that Syria didn't belong to its people, we believed ourselves absolved when it came to what was happening in the country. At the time, if Syrians thought about it, they likely were resolved that the case of Arab Jews was a particular one, without implications for the rest of us.

But after all these months in Palestine, with its injustices in the forefront of my mind, in that *sherut* from Tel Aviv I was thinking much less about the ills of the Syrian regime or the fickle and precarious nature of Syrian citizenship. I thought I was savvier in 1998 than I had been in 1992, but I still had much to learn. So instead of asking the kind man next to me how he was navigating this divide between the parts of himself that were congenitally linked yet dissonant in both Syria and Israel, I quite bluntly inquired, "How can you live in a state that does what it does to the Palestinians?"

He was quiet as we drove around the wall that held old Jerusalem, the golden Dome of the Rock rising in front of us.

"It's not easy for me here," he simply said.

I thought, at the time, that his answer was merely nonresponsive. I only realized later that that's the way the balance sheet works in Israel and Palestine, and even the region. As long as you are unhappy, or have been wronged, you cannot be complicit in someone else's tragedy.

As he dropped us off, he helped me with my luggage and wished me well.

I watched him drive away in his white minivan. Living on the West Bank, the Israelis I had encountered were mostly soldiers and settlers, the primary agents of the Occupation. In the Occupied Territories, these Israelis, with their guns slung over their shoulders, were easily distinguishable from Palestinians, in whom I had found something familiar. Yet in this young Syrian Jewish Israeli, I recognized the warm mannerisms of the people I knew in Damascus, and he spoke to me in my parents' tongue. He was the most familiar of them all.

Only then did I think to ask him, did he know Stella—she had long hair? Or Nanette who had pierced my ears?

But he was already making his way back up the hill to the main road, and I watched his white minivan quickly disappear. Surely easier fares awaited back at the airport.

8

THEY DID IT TO THEMSELVES

Lebanon and Syria, 2000–2004

ONE MONTH BEFORE I FINALLY MADE IT BACK TO SYRIA, THE IM-possible happened: Syria's longtime ruler, Hafez al-Assad, died. Posters and banners in Syria had regularly promised that he would rule forever. Instead, "forever" came to an end on June 10, 2000. A sudden heart attack took him at the age of sixty-nine.

Even though public gatherings were not permitted in Syria, thousands of weeping Syrians took to the streets of Damascus under the watchful eyes of uniformed security officers and plainclothes *mukhabarat*. The United States even sent an official delegation to Hafez's funeral in Damascus. Madeleine Albright was the highest-ranking American on the delegation, and selected Syrian Americans accompanied her. The doctor who had informed my father of his mother's death back in 1973 was among them.

Mourners grieved not only for Hafez but also chanted their devotion to his son Bashar al-Assad, saying "God, Syria, and Bashar only." Hafez was dead, but in the preceding years he had laid the groundwork for a way to rule beyond the grave, by grooming his son Bashar as his heir apparent.

Becoming president of Syria had not always been Bashar's destiny. The intended heir had been Bashar's elder brother Bassel, who had been in his father's inner circle, had pursued a military career, and had been leader of the Presidential Guards. But in 1994, on a foggy morning, Bassel had crashed one of his many sports cars while madly speeding to the airport to catch a flight. His unexpected death demanded the immediate shuffle that would forever change Bashar's life. My mother's beloved Laïque high school, which had been renamed the Freedom Academy once the Ba'athists came to power in the 1960s, was again renamed—this time as the "Martyr Bassel al-Assad School." (Undeterred, people continued to refer to it as the Laïque.)

Unlike his brother, Bashar was known for being mild-mannered. He was a doctor and had specialized in ophthalmology—supposedly because it was a bloodless medical specialty—when he was recalled from the United Kingdom, where he had been furthering his medical training. (Salma's brother was an esteemed professor at the University of Damascus Medical School. When Bashar sat before him and other professors for his final exams—which were oral—my great uncle was politely dismissed and told to leave the room. Bashar inevitably passed.)

In the years since the death of his brother, Bashar had been quietly groomed for succession, with his military credentials and rank steadily advanced and a public image carefully cultivated. He was said to be an advocate of the Internet and modernization, becoming president of the Syrian Computer Society. He was also put in charge of an anticorruption campaign and in charge of Syrian affairs in Lebanon, which effectively put him in control of Lebanon, as Damascus exerted much more than just influence on its small neighbor's affairs. Both of these duties allowed Bashar to clear the military, the security services, and the government of any opponents to his automatic ascension. After all, their loyalty to his father did not mean they would automatically embrace him. Indeed, some fled the country while others went into retirement or committed suicide.

After Hafez's death, technical obstacles to Bashar's assumption of the presidency were quickly dispatched. The Syrian Constitution was immediately amended to reduce the minimum age for the presidency from forty to thirty-four—conveniently, Bashar's age. He was also promoted to lieutenant general and named commander of the armed forces and head of the Ba'ath Party Regional Command. Parliamentarians then endorsed him by acclaim in a session that ran an extra day because so many wanted their support duly recorded.

In July, right before my arrival, his presidency was put to national referendum, in which voters were given a ballot with a green circle signifying "yes" for Bashar or a gray circle for "no." There were no other candidates, as had been the case in the referendums on his father's presidency. Voters could opt to mark the circles with their blood instead of ink, and several polling places offered safety pins or sewing needles perfect for pricking a thumb. Ninety-seven percent of voting Syrians supposedly said "yes" to Bashar.

I arrived later that month, after graduating law school and sitting for the bar. I was taking advantage of the three months before starting work to come back to the Middle East. I would again volunteer in the West Bank, this time with the British organization that advised the Palestinian peace process negotiators. Learning from past mistakes, though, I would visit Syria before making my way to Disneyland. So it was that eight years after that Syrian summer as a teenager, I finally returned.

The ubiquitous photographic reminders of authoritarianism had changed. Whereas before it had been creepy pictures of Hafez al-Assad everywhere, now it was a photo trinity: recently crowned Bashar flanked by his long dead brother and newly dead father. Or, as Syrians wryly referred to them, the Father, the Son, and the Holy Ghost.

That summer, I found people in Damascus as tightlipped as ever, especially as there was a fear of potential instability. Regardless of his new rank and powers, Bashar was essentially untested. And his assumption of power was not uncontested—there were older Ba'ath Party loyalists and regime seniors who felt passed over. This included his uncle, Hafez's notorious brother Rifaat al-Assad, who was making noise from his exile in Paris, claiming that he was the rightful heir to power. (Syria is not a monarchy, but in the past two years power had passed to the sons of long-ruling monarchs in Jordan, Morocco, and Qatar—rule by bequest was thus in the air.)

Some people did express optimism for the future—Bashar was young and hopefully had a fresh and modern vision for the country. State-controlled media had credited him with choosing younger and more forward-looking ministers. "Maybe this new generation will be different," they told me. Since Hafez's death, a new openness had in fact begun to flourish, known as the Damascus Spring. It saw the establishment of *muntadayat*, salons, which became informal forums where participants discussed political, judicial, economic, and social reforms. (Bashar would crack down on them within a year.)

Like me, some in my family, and some of their friends, were troubled by how power had been passed on like an inheritance, but they only responded to my prodding with raised eyebrows, a roll of their eyes, or a sheepish smile. The walls still had ears, after all.

The state of the economy was also alarming. After abandoning the fully socialist model in 1986 (when the government essentially ran out of money), the regime had cautiously allowed a private sector to begin to flourish. But it was so plagued by cronyism and corruption that the economic boom that followed was illusory and short-lived. The business ventures that appeared in the wake of that shift (such as commercial services) provided little or no added value to the economy; they neither used labor nor created exports. They did, however, greatly enrich a small group of regime insiders, bureaucrats, and their business partners.

Unemployment had gone through the roof, and at the same time, the contraction of the public sector had deprived people of the state largesse—in the form of subsidies, salaries, and pensions—that they had come to rely on. Salary increases were evaporated by inflation. Although the calculated embrace of a private sector was supposed to stimulate trickle-down benefits, it was so handicapped that it was bound to only make the gap between the few rich and everyone else much starker. People whose parents had been comfortably middle class were increasingly just getting by.

If Syria was on the precipice of great change with Bashar, it wasn't yet perceivable at the level of my family. Everyone still lived in the same houses they had before, and none of them had been updated: they still had old plumbing, old appliances, and erratic electricity. Sa'ad still drove his old Romanian Dacia car, which to me embodied the bleakness of the Eastern Bloc in the 1980s. Suha was still in the Tahaan—as was Hassan, firmly ensconced in Salma's house thirty years after she had first rented it to him for a term of one year. Noticeably, many of the women in the building now wore hijabs.

In conversation, people avoided like the plague any talk of my legal studies or experiences, lest anyone overhear us say "civil rights" or "human rights," or really, "rights." Instead, as always, people preferred to chat (often passive aggressively) about when I would get married, as I was older, after all (twenty-five). Everyone seemed to know a dentist to introduce me to, reassuring me my American passport could make up for my age.

This time, I was much less put off by these remarks and just much more curious about who my relatives were. Whereas back in 1992 I had been overwhelmed by how big and old our family tree was—in Baltimore, we were just a sprig—now I wanted to make sense of it. I asked endless questions of my uncle's and aunt's spouses, both Palestinians, matching up their personal histories with what I knew of the situation in Palestine, which was becoming substantial. When they asked me, in return, what their parents' cities were like today, I told them about what still stood and what was long gone.

After several weeks, I left Syria—eager to go back; unlike when I had left in 1992, I no longer felt I had to outrun Syria. I wondered if my skepticism would be proven wrong, and if Bashar al-Assad's rule might turn out to be a transition to a better future. However, in 2000, of all the former Greater Syria lands I'd visit, it was Lebanon that beckoned to me as a possible home.

༺༻

EVEN THOUGH MY father's family's origins—over a century ago—are in its Beqa'a Valley, I had never visited Lebanon as an adult, mostly because of its civil war. That finally changed when I arrived in Beirut later that summer.

The Lebanese and Syrian capitals couldn't have been more different. Beirut sits on the sea, a ready outlet to the world. Landlocked Damascus could feel cut-off and suffocating, heavily controlled by the state and full of hovering relatives. (I had yet to master the art of managing them, of keeping them at a healthy arm's length.)

My Lebanese relatives were mostly new to me. (I had family members from both my parents in Lebanon, including Ameen's sisters and their families, and more fellow Abdeljawwad great-grandchildren.) They were much less sheltered than their Syrian counterparts—for better and for worse. While the Syrian state had oppressed its people, and the threat of violence was ever present, there was a logic to it: stay out of politics, stay out of the way of the regime, and you will be safe from physical injury. But in Lebanon, war had indiscriminately disrupted and mutilated lives irrespective of class, religion, age, and gender.

Like the Palestinians, the Lebanese couldn't afford not to have opinions about their country. Of course, the conclusions some came to were fascist, sectarian, or otherwise problematic. Others were chillingly fatalistic, while some were remarkably Zen. In Syria my questions about Syrian society, politics, history, and prospects for the future were met with silence; in Lebanon the cacophony was what was deafening.

Part of that was because the Lebanese had much more freedom to say what they thought. The country already had a long tradition of such freedoms that had survived the war, if not fully intact. True, Syria essentially occupied Lebanon (to the cheers of some Lebanese and the ire of many others), running it like some satellite state, with 30,000 Syrian soldiers and unknown numbers of *mukhabarat* based there. Yet in Beirut, I personally felt free of the watchful eye of the state, whereas in Syria it was bored into my skull, a sort of third eye (though not in any kind of enlightened yogic sense) that followed me everywhere, even as I slept.

Unlike in Syria, in Lebanon, the public sector had not been the main engine of the economy, which had always had a relatively free market and private banking. (For example, it was possible to get home mortgages. The inability to do so in Syria partly accounted for people opting to stay on in houses where the landlords wanted them out.) Despite the existence of community-specific fiefdoms, there was much more room for private initiatives and development, whether in business, commerce, medicine, education, culture, entertainment, or civil society. While many of these endeavors went ahead with no licensing or oversight, it still allowed for a lot of Lebanese to use their talents, to embrace some agency. In Syria, the regime's stranglehold on both the public and ostensible private sectors meant that ideas and potential were often held back or impossible to actualize—in turn depriving the entire country of the talents of its people.

I found Lebanon more open to the world than Syria—with a multiplicity of foreign educational institutions at all levels, foreign investment, and an internationally recognized banking system—and many of its people had been driven into exile abroad by the war. Lebanese from varying backgrounds therefore had been exposed to and part of different societies and were hybrids of more than one place, more like me. Though this camouflaged increasing inequalities and deep corruption, Beirut could feel more cosmopolitan than Damascus.

Also, Lebanon's topography is intoxicating. Syria has some of the same dramatic dips and climbs, but Lebanon is small and its beauty more tightly concentrated. A sensual coastline curves its way to what seems like infinity while the mountains reach past the clouds. As that annoying but true slogan goes: In Lebanon, you can ski in the morning and go for a swim that very afternoon. It has the ethos of other Mediterranean countries (and much of what I had loved about Italy), but with the added layers of Asian and African influences and a heritage I could claim as my own.

But there was already sobering evidence of the kinds of shortsighted alliances both within Lebanon and with foreign powers that would fester in the entire region well beyond the exigencies that had brought them about (the region's fate). On that first trip to Lebanon in 2000, I visited many of the must-see sites, from Roman ruins to ancient port cities, religious shrines, and cedar forests. But as of that very summer, one could now also travel to southern Lebanon: it had been under Israeli control since 1982, but Israel had just withdrawn from the south in May.

For Hezbollah, the Iranian-backed Lebanese Shiite militia that had resisted Israel's eighteen-year occupation, it was a victory further solidifying its position as a powerbroker in the country and of Iran in the region. Saudi Arabia and the political class it favored in Lebanon—which were often in competition with Iran and Hezbollah—watched those developments warily.

Signs of Hezbollah's sense of triumph were ubiquitous in the south, from the group's yellow flag to banners exalting its soldiers and especially its leader, Hassan Nasrallah. By the side of the road, people posed with a life-size cutout of Nasrallah atop a captured Israeli tank. Symbols of Israel's former dominance had been turned into rudimentary museums. I visited what had been a prison set up by Israel and its Lebanese collaborators. Our guide was a former prisoner. The cells were so recently vacated that he told us to cover our noses and mouths, so as not to inhale the germs of diseases that he was convinced still lingered. Hastily painted Arabic and English signs explained what we were looking at. A small courtyard between the buildings was labeled "suffering yard." What could have been a rudimentary prison yard chin-up bar was instead identified as the "suffering column," a pair of handcuffs still dangling from it. One set of arrows pointed to the "Women Prison," and another to the "Detectiveness [sic] room & suffering by electricity." (Suffering was their translation of "torture," and "detectiveness" was for "interrogation.")

There were plenty of Lebanese (and other Arabs) who were willing to overlook that Hezbollah (or its patron, Iran) pinned its legitimacy to religion simply because other parts of their political agendas—namely, being pro-Palestinian and anti-Israeli—lined up. Similarly, those political classes in Lebanon who accepted Saudi patronage in their quest for dominance in Lebanese politics forgave the Gulf country's same exploitation of religion.

But drawn to their natural conclusion, both Hezbollah and their Sunni Isla-mist counterparts were inevitably exclusionary and divisive; the region, after all, was made up of nearly twenty different sects, religions, and ethnicities.

Peace talks between Lebanon's neighbors, Syria and Israel, had broken down in mid-January 2000. The withdrawal of Israeli troops, Hafez al-Assad's death, and the ascension of Bashar al-Assad in Damascus, all within weeks of each other, made for great unease in Lebanon as well that summer. What would the balance of power within the country and among the competing regional players look like in the new millennium?

I wasn't ready to leave when the time came; I wanted to stay in Lebanon and learn more. The possibility of understanding what the future might hold for the region seemed to be partly in this small country. Living in Syria, given my line of work, seemed impossible, but Lebanon appeared to be much more feasible.

As I left Lebanon, I promised myself to come back, and if possible, not just as a tourist. Everything that would come after, from that fall through the next three years, I'd see as a reason (or pretext) for making the move.

※

AFTER LEAVING BEIRUT, I made my way circuitously back to Palestine via Jordan, arriving in the West Bank two years after having left it, with two more years of hope forestalled. The whole West Bank felt on edge, as if all it would take would be a spark to set the place aflame. Within weeks, former prime minister Ariel Sharon seemed to happily light the match, taking a po-litically calculated stroll around the Al-Aqsa Mosque accompanied by 1,000 armed Israeli police. What followed that meant-to-provoke provocation was completely predictable, and thus, the Second Intifada began.

The peace process had long become more about process than peace, but even those frenzied periods of meetings and negotiations were coming to a grinding halt. The work in the negotiations legal unit didn't stop, however, and I worked until I had to head back to Washington, DC, at the end of October—a job I had accepted nearly a year before was waiting for me.

I returned to the United States thinking there was something to capi-talize on. The violence I had just witnessed was so wanton and one-sided that I thought perhaps American and global leaders might finally take real action to resolve the Palestinian-Israeli conflict. If it could be put to rest, then perhaps the entire region, Syria included, could begin to move forward. There would be less need for strongmen and emergency rule. With peace could come stability, economic prosperity, and a new future.

But drastic changes were coming to the United States—though no one fully foresaw them. I had competed for a position in the Honors Program in the Civil Rights Division of the US Department of Justice in my last year of law school in the fall of 1999. At my interview, when I asked if the division would change a lot should a Republican win the upcoming presidential election, a remote possibility then, I was told not to worry. When I was hired—under a Bill Clinton presidency and a Janet Reno DOJ—I accepted without fear of the election's outcome. But within weeks after I reported for work, George W. Bush became president. Promising to be a "uniter not a divider," he went on to appoint as attorney general John Ashcroft, the conservative senator and Pentecostal Christian from Missouri who had just lost his own attempted reelection to the US Senate to a dead man.

Shortly after he settled in, our new boss sent out a memo on his stylistic preferences for our official correspondence. We were to refer to married women as Mrs. "Husband's First and Last Name"; we were never to use the word "pride," as pride was sinful. Then, we received invitations to attend his prayer group—held at the department—where I imagine we could have learned more about his views on sin. He also sent us the lyrics to the patriotic paean he had penned, "Let the Eagle Soar." (You can find him singing it on YouTube.)

Not a year after I had started at the Civil Rights Division, 9/11 happened. Like other Arab Americans, I found myself simultaneously grieving for the innocent, wondering what backlash might befall Arab and Muslim Americans, and processing that the kind of violence I usually associated with the Middle East had just happened right here on US soil.

It was a painful time to be an Arab or Muslim American in the United States, or to be anyone generally invested in civil rights and liberties in the United States. The 9/11 attacks ushered in an era of nativism, racism, and Islamophobia as well as a pursuit of domestic and foreign policies of questionable legality, constitutionality, and morality.

Ironically, following the United States' lead on terrorism discourse (i.e., you're either with us or against us), rulers in the Middle East used terrorism as a pretext to go after their enemies, from Islamists to secular civil society opponents. And as the Bush administration talked about protecting

American values from the evils of the Middle East, it sent prisoners to be tortured by governments there—including to Syria. While Syria hadn't made Bush's "Axis of Evil" list—which included only Iran, Iraq, and North Korea—it had been named, along with Cuba and Libya, to the "Beyond the Axis of Evil" list enumerated by Bush State Department official John Bolton.

During those years as an unhappy DC bureaucrat, I traveled to both Syria and Lebanon in the summers. In Damascus I heard an earful of conspiracy theories, mostly about the impossibility of Arabs being able to pull off 9/11, and about how Israel or the CIA must have done it, especially given alleged CIA support of Osama Bin Laden. There was always an overreliance on French sources for these ideas.

At the end of one of those summers, I tacked to the wall above my desk in DC a postcard of where I dreamed of being: Beirut at sunset.

With each day, my job at the Civil Rights Division became more and more meaningless. Other parts of my very same department carried out policies that I believed would ultimately harm the United States as a country and as a society. If I had felt that in entering the new millennium, maybe we would also be in a new era—one that accepted Arabs as Americans, one with a more robust defense of civil rights, one that might mean progress for the Middle East by resolving the festering Palestinian and Iraqi wounds—those hopes had been resolutely dashed by the Bush presidency and its reaction to the 9/11 attacks.

The last straw came in my third year at the Civil Rights Division. The Bush administration began its path to war with Iraq, fabricating a pretext out of the 9/11 attacks, abetted by the hyperbole and hysteria prevailing in the country that made a traitor out of anyone who questioned hastily passed policies and actions. As the administration—aided by a lapsed media—beat its war drum, I was reminded of the 1991 Gulf War, of how my father had once looked like Saddam Hussein, and of how people who could have been me or my family had once had their lives overturned and now would again.

I resigned my post and decided to move to Lebanon. I had agreed to work with a local NGO that helped the large population of refugees who made it to Lebanon from other parts of the Middle East and Africa prepare their asylum cases with the United Nations. With war and its paybacks imminent in Iraq, a flood of fleeing Iraqis was expected to make its way to Beirut.

LATE ON THE evening of March 16, 2003, I arrived in Beirut straight from the airport. I was on my way to see an apartment for rent when, across the street, I stumbled upon a noisy and agitated crowd. A white minivan had just spectacularly crashed into the side of a building, and its tail end was now emerging from a concrete wall. Miraculously, no one was seriously hurt by the impact.

The now crumpled vehicle had collided with an all-hours bakery, and the smell of fresh-baked dough mingled with that of spilled diesel and cigarette smoke. My second cousin and good friend Pamela, who had picked me up from the airport and lined up apartments for me to check out, gave me a look as if to ask, "Are you sure?"

But all I could think was, "Good riddance, Washington, DC." I felt relief, even if the move to Beirut hadn't happened in an ideal fashion. Instead of through careful planning, it was sudden, and almost seemed like an admission of defeat. In retrospect, I think I was looking for a place to hide from what was happening in the United States, admittedly able to do so in Lebanon because I had the privilege of an American passport. (I'm sure plenty of those on the street with me that night would have happily traded places, First World woes and all, for that luxury.) I shrugged my shoulders and signaled to Pamela to keep walking. The apartment was just the first I would be visiting that night, and I saw no reason to delay. (Sometimes there are benefits to being in a region full of nocturnal people.)

The flat was perched on the eighth floor of a seven-story building. The last floor had been added on after the building had been completed, perhaps as an afterthought, and the elevator didn't reach it. We had to climb the last flight of stairs to the top. But it was nevertheless a profound postscript, a room with a wall of windows and a balcony with distant views of the snow-capped tips of Lebanon's mountains and the breaking waves of the Mediterranean Sea. All around me was evidence of how humanity had saddled the country with an erratic pattern of buildings—urban planning a casualty of war—that echoed in the flickering lights of the surrounding hills. I silently decided to take it, but went through the motions of seeing a few more places just to be sure.

Several days later, I returned for the keys. By then, the American invasion of Iraq had begun. The bakery's wall, where the white minivan had pummeled it, had incredibly already been patched up, secured, and repainted. There was no sign of the accident. The Lebanese, I would learn, had a knack for quickly moving on, or at least appearing as if they had.

When I had seen the apartment that first night after the crash, I had failed to see in the dark both the minaret directly across the street, with its speakers pointed precisely in the direction of my windows, and the mosque's adjoining school, silent and barren of children at that hour. I learned of both on the first morning I was there—the former at 4 a.m., when an off-tune imam called the faithful to prayer, and the latter when, shortly after sunrise, a school bell summoned its squawking flock.

But soon I was heading off to work every morning. I stayed with the refugee NGO—where I was volunteering—until I was fired for suggesting that the head of the organization could not sleep with refugees, or take advantage of their desperation to have them do tasks that she wouldn't be fairly compensating them for. Luckily, I found paid work shortly thereafter teaching human rights at the Lebanese American University (though I had to engage in an epic administrative battle to get paid as someone who had a juris doctorate and not a bachelor's degree, simply because the person in charge of the department had personally never heard of JDs—only MDs and PhDs).

Despite all these inane realities of life in Beirut, I was happy. Something that had been missing, a longing that had shadowed me throughout my life (likely inherited from my parents), was finally being soothed.

෪

WHILE LIVING IN Lebanon, I frequently visited Damascus, going every month to see family. Syria was also much cheaper than Lebanon, and I bought many of my household needs—like custom-made curtains—in Damascus.

Upon hearing I was living in Lebanon, I'd often be asked, "Why?" by everyone from distant family to friends of relatives to overly inquisitive shopkeepers searching for some morsel of information about a Syrian American that might ingratiate them to the *mukhabarat*.

Did I prefer it to Syria? they wanted to know, quickly reminding me that I was from Syria.

Any answer I gave—such as that I could work there in my field or that it felt freer or more anonymous or more cosmopolitan or more welcoming—

often triggered strangely smug conversations and caricatures. Syrians snickered that Lebanon was nothing but a fiction that the French had created out of Syria; implied that the Lebanese thought themselves better than the rest of the Arabs, because they could speak French fluently; criticized the Lebanese for being frivolous, spending money—that was borrowed—conspicuously; denounced them for shamefully abandoning that most revered of pan-Arab causes, the Palestinian struggle; and blamed them for the vicious civil war that had destroyed Beirut several times over.

"They did it to themselves," I would hear.

When I felt safe enough—never in public spaces, where who knew who would be reporting what to the *mukhabarat*—I would push back. Yes, both Syria and Lebanon had absorbed huge influxes of Palestinian refugees after the creation of the state of Israel and again in 1967, I'd start. But the PLO only set up in Lebanon, and only used Lebanese territory to stage attacks on Israel. (In both countries, Palestinians remained stateless—they had been denied citizenship even after several generations in Syria, the spouses of my aunt and uncle being examples of this.) Some Palestinian fighters even targeted Lebanese in their own country. Then when Israel invaded Lebanon in 1982, ostensibly just to root out the PLO, an estimated 17,000 Lebanese (many of them civilians) lost their lives in the process, in addition to Palestinian refugees who died in the slaughter of Sabra and Shatila. Of course, Israel did this with the acquiescence and cooperation of certain right-wing Maronite militias and their backers, but that hardly incriminated all Lebanese. Similarly, Lebanese resistance to Israeli occupation over the past twenty years meant they knew firsthand Israel's military wrath; meanwhile, the Syrian government had essentially abandoned the Golan Heights.

I'd also ask what role other countries had played in the Lebanese war, and whether that might not be a reason to resent foreign interventions, whether from Iran or Saudi Arabia. I'd often then ask cautiously but provocatively, "What role had the Syrian regime played? After all, Syria occupied Lebanon—then and today, even though the war is over."

To that last point, the responses were often a variation on the following: Syria had to be there to stabilize the situation, to stop it from spreading. The Lebanese were devouring themselves and would devour the region. And if the Syrians left now, the Lebanese would do it all over again to themselves.

I would point out how I had been stopped at Syrian checkpoints inside Lebanon, and that it felt as unjust as Israeli checkpoints in Palestine had. That Syrian soldiers were easily as disrespectful as the Israeli soldiers—and unlike them, were often open to, if not actively soliciting, bribes.

"Those are soldiers. What do you expect?" they would respond defensively. "The government and the people aren't the same."

Besides, I would also be told, if people close to the regime had benefited financially or in other ways by occupying Lebanon, the Syrian people—like them—hadn't. Look at how the government treats us. And as they got more defensive, they'd ask, "What could we have done? We don't have control of our own lives here." (There it was, that balance sheet that had helped me understand my conversation with the Syrian Jewish driver of that *sherut* back in Jerusalem years before.) The debate never went much further in Syria, but everyone always seemed to agree that the Lebanese civil war was tragic, and we were relieved that it could never happen to us in Syria.

As for Syria itself in those years, Bashar al-Assad, with his new charming and photogenic wife, Anglo-Syrian Asma, projected youth and modernity (if not democracy). The fact that she was from a prominent Sunni family helped to blunt the Assads' "Alawite-ness," which to many quarters had remained objectionable. In addition to using his marriage to bolster his Muslim and sectarian credentials, Bashar al-Assad was consolidating his rule in Syria. Although he had in 2001 symbolically closed the infamous prison in Tadmour, located in the same desert as the glorious ruins of Palmyra, he had actually rearrested several activists and shut down the political salons and initiatives that had begun in the Damascus Spring. His consolidation of power had significant consequences for the economy. With many of the Old Guard of his father's regime further embedded in the economy, thanks to the symbiotic (if not asymmetrical) relationship between the business community and the state, power had been to some extent diffused. To reconcentrate power in a much smaller circle, the new leadership diverted the most lucrative opportunities to a tight number of individuals who were loyal to the president's family, most prominently his cousin Rami Makhlouf, while making most other economic opportunities more open to a larger segment of the business community. Still, most of Syrian society was not feeling, or benefiting from, these developments.

In those monthly trips I had finally decreed that I would only stay with Suha in her house in the Tahaan, to avoid the same tug-of-war each time over which relatives would host me. (Syrians are good at finding slights in seemingly banal actions.) By then, I knew fully the story of Salma's apartment, where she had once made herself into a *sheikha* and which was now in my mother's name. I also knew the consternation it had caused my grandmother and that my family's fate—and decision to remain in the United States—was linked to its being taken from us. I had inherited Salma's frustration and impotence.

I would often try to furtively peek in at the apartment across the way, when a door was opening and before it shut. Only once was I invited in—for a cup of coffee. Finally, I was inside Salma's house. It was horribly rundown, so much so that I found it hard to even imagine what it once had been.

As I sipped my demitasse, Hassan and Hilal asked me how my parents were and said to please say hello to them on their behalf. I was struck by how we could all be so polite to each other even though we were bound to each other by the great injustice that had passed between us. But if there was courtesy, there was also shame. We were all part of a society that had compromised our dignity. My family had been robbed of a house; theirs had been made thieves—an outcome sanctioned and desired by the state. After all, Hassan had only chosen to exercise the rights the state had given him. Of course, he could have picked what I would have considered a more honorable path, but his choice wasn't incomprehensible to me, especially given how hard it was to make it in Syria, owing largely to how the regime had run the country. I know I felt ashamed as a Syrian that these kinds of morally ambiguous choices were a daily part of life there—we were complicit, even if not completely at fault.

Hassan seemed unapologetic about what he had done, but I saw evidence of his wife's shame in her obsequious manner. While I was in the apartment, she avoided full eye contact with me, excessively complimented my parents, and insisted on serving me more and more coffee. In my discomfort and embarrassment, I stole glances instead at the house. I looked for Salma, for traces of her, but the house had become someone else's, with the shadows of other lives upon it.

※

I TOOK ADVANTAGE of being in Lebanon to visit the regions to which my father's parents traced their roots. I got to know my Lebanese family, filling in the family tree and soliciting their stories. I was particularly drawn to those who had known Salma and looked for ways to know her through their memories. The more I heard, the more I wished she could have had more time.

I also stood for long periods on my balcony, gazing on the waters and mountains that had drawn me here, sometimes entreating them for a modicum of clarity. I imagined they were often laughing at me: As privileged as I was, was I still not satisfied?

My neighbor Wissam, who lived in the other apartment on the eighth floor, had a much larger balcony, with different and more expansive views. Although you could glimpse the mountains from his balcony, it faced away from them and toward the sea. He could see the mosque that shouted into my window and the bakery below us, the site of that first night's crash. His terrace also overlooked the Tareeq al-Sham, Damascus Road, which led to my parents' native city and was, in fact, the road I took every month to leave Beirut. But it was also the Green Line that had separated West from East Beirut during the civil war. Our building was just over the boundary on the east side.

Wissam, only two years older than me, was a somewhat enigmatic director of music videos and major ad campaigns. He had a closetful of nearly identical loose white collared shirts that he wore everyday untucked over his jeans to complement his carefully cultivated tousle of hair. He operated in flawless French, as many Lebanese can, and for whatever reason, it earns them the disdain of other Arabs. But his mother tongue was actually Arabic, and he had an excellent grasp of the written language (which is different from the spoken) as well. He consumed Arabic literature, media, and pop culture. He could just as easily do the same in French. He had a profound knowledge of history, and I used to probe his memories of the war, as I did with others. But what always set Wissam's responses apart was that he was utterly nonpartisan; as far as I could tell, he was disgusted with everyone and hated all the politicians and leaders equally.

We were on his balcony one night looking down on that demarcation between the West—which, speaking in broad strokes, had been anti-American, pro-Palestinian, pro-Russian, and leftist—and the East, which was its opposite. The PLO had operated in the West, and that part of the city had been essentially under the PLO's control, and then jointly with the Syrians, and then it was just the Syrians. East Beirut was considered free, in that only indigenous Lebanese madmen controlled it. Or, as Wissam put it, reverting to the boy he had been for the entire duration of the war, East Beirut was M-16s and the West, Kalashnikovs.

He explained that night on his balcony that growing up, on some level, he had liked the war. When it started in 1975, he was only three years old. Yet even though war had become his generation's normalcy, he knew that it was not an ordinary life. It was better! One morning he might have school, and then the next day school would be closed. He felt free and played endlessly, even when in the dark in the underground bunkers where he had spent days and nights as the war raged on—a constant—above them.

It was what he saw in American movies come to life. He knew that without conflict, there would be none of the stories of heroism and drama that entertained him endlessly. And like in the movies, he didn't see anyone directly get hurt. Death was meaningless, just like it was on the big and small screens. Like many Beirutis, his family would migrate to relatively safer regions each time things heated up where they were. Intense clashes in Beirut? They would head to the mountains to wait it out.

If the war tormented his parents, they kept it from their children. But when Wissam was around other adults, he found the anxiety palpable. By a very young age, he already knew the names of several different brands of sleeping pills just from eavesdropping on the conversations of grownups.

Then one day in March 1990, during the intra-Christian war between the Lebanese Army, led by General Michel Aoun, and the Lebanese Forces, led by Samir Geagea, his parents' house suddenly came under intense shelling before they could reach the relative safety of the ground floor. Apparently the Lebanese Army was trying to target a building next door that was supposedly used by the Lebanese Forces. The five of them huddled in the bathroom together until a break in the shelling, and then they ran to the stairwell to make their way down to the bunker. But the shelling quickly resumed, and they were trapped on the first floor.

Within minutes, he heard his brother cry out and saw him fall. Shrapnel had struck him in his back and lodged itself in his intestines, centimeters from his spine. His blood was everywhere. Wissam gathered him in his arms and moved him to the ground floor, and then, in a fit of heroism or insanity, he ran into the street to find help. He ran into an ambulance that had come too late to save another man, and so they diverted to Wissam's building as the shelling continued. They loaded his brother in and disappeared with him and his father.

After a childhood in war—in a war that he loved—Wissam suddenly decided he wanted it to stop. Three weeks later, he turned eighteen. Six months from his birthday, the war was over.

His brother lived. Aoun went into exile in France, Geagea to prison. Many of the other faction leaders, warlords, militia commanders, and weapons and goods traffickers quickly transitioned into lives as politicians, developers, and businessmen. Everyone else was expected to move on, too.

I remember thinking then that this was a uniquely Lebanese condition, and that nothing similar could ever happen in Syria.

※

A YEAR INTO my life in Beirut, my parents decided they wanted to celebrate their thirtieth wedding anniversary in Syria with their children. They wanted to throw a party in Damascus, where they hadn't been together since their wedding day. We had also never all been in Syria at the same time.

My mother, Zayn, and Farah had been to Damascus six years earlier, when I hadn't been able to meet them, but my father had not visited for eighteen years—ever since his father, the carpenter widower, had died. My sister Manal—who had not been since 1990—flew in from the US city where she was a medical resident. My brother, Zayn, an economist, came in separately, and my other sister, Farah, who was about to start a new job as an engineer, flew in with my parents. As it happened, of all my immediate family, I was the one who had returned most frequently by then to Syria.

Instead of staying with relatives, we stayed in the Cham Palace Hotel at the center of the city. This was uncharacteristic of my father, who, despite being successful in the United States, was disdainful of certain kinds of expenditures, fancy hotels and vacations—basically fun—among them.

My siblings and I were introduced to an even wider circle of family and friends, who had never seen all of us together. We were sized up, of course. As far as anyone knew, we were all—in order of importance—single, had American passports, and were fairly attractive and well-educated. My sisters, a doctor and an engineer, were considered smarter than my brother and I, who had studied law and economics (Zayn at an Ivy League university, for what it's worth).

After all, in Syria, how a student performs at the age of eighteen on standardized nationwide exams determines what (not where) he or she will study.

The university system is public, and as such—because the state is providing the education—the student studies what it tells him or her to study. (Private universities had only just begun and were untested.) The smartest were herded toward medicine, pharmacy, and engineering. Lower scores got a person into the faculties of law and business (which is how my brother's degree was understood by many). I always figured the reason was that such professions, what with their notions of justice and market economics, were more threatening to the power structure than the legions of really good Syrian doctors out there, many of whom went on to serve populations abroad, as my own father did.

I was happy to have my entire family there. I had always visited Syria on my own as an adult, and I was regarded by many of my distant relatives as much too unconventional. People had been suspicious of my having lived in so many places, all of which were not my parents' house. Unmarried women living on their own were suspected of sexual promiscuity. For the smaller minded (and there were many of them, I'm embarrassed to say), the fact that I lived in Beirut only confirmed the suspicions. According to their mentality, people went to Beirut to drink and have sex. (That all seemed much more plausible to them than my working with refugees or teaching at the university.) But with my parents there, who were successful in the more conventional way, I was hoping their legitimacy might rub off on me.

The night of their fete, my parents were more than just legitimate. Sharif wore a tux and Lamya a lovely black lace dress; they both looked beautiful. There were copious amounts of food (as there always is in Syria), toasts, and dancing. Nearly a hundred family members and friends, many of whom they hadn't seen in years, came to the party.

My parents noted the differences that time had wrought. Everyone was older, some were richer, and many were fatter. Friends who had worn miniskirts at university were now veiled. Others with whom they had often shared a beer or whiskey no longer consumed alcohol. In the years since my parents had married, many of their friends had worked for some time in the Gulf countries and embraced their ways; similarly, the rulers of certain Gulf countries had worked hard to change the more secular and tolerant culture of places like Syria.

We accompanied our parents to all the places they wanted to show us, often having fun at their expense. We laughed at their own discomfort in their native country, which my father had always idealized in diaspora. They seemed to bristle at the lack of personal space on the street, the ease with which merchants and taxi drivers tried to blatantly rip us off, or the expectations of government officials to be paid bribes to make things happen. My brother, who had lived in Egypt and Morocco, and I were on some level more accustomed to it. Manal and Farah, who had never been as enamored as Zayn and I with the Arab world, didn't seem bothered, because they expected Syria to be less than perfect.

We went to the Midan, the neighborhood my father had grown up in, and which, all our lives, he had described in mythical terms. There the men were real men—tough and street-smart, and no one was tougher or ruled the streets more than my dad and his brothers (according to him). He showed us the house where he had lived, an old enclosed traditional-style house with a fountain in the center. His parents—to his shame—had never owned the house. When they were finally able to buy one, it was only with the help of their grown children.

We walked through the souks together, and my father was surprised to find the same shoemaker that his mother used to buy her children's shoes from in the 1950s—and they were still sold by the centimeter. Many things in Damascus were indeed impervious to time.

With Manal, the doctor, my father went to the hospital where he had done his training. She was a resident at a tough inner-city hospital in the United States, and in comparison to what she saw in Damascus, her hospital seemed like the Ritz-Carlton. She was aghast at patients lying on the floor, and at family members holding their bags of IV fluids because there was no IV pole. She told us later that our father had gone silent, shocked that the hospital was so much worse than when he had been there in the 1960s. He wondered to her how the military could have equipment and weaponry but the public hospital was woefully underresourced.

Both my parents were further disillusioned when we all went to Jordan for a brief side trip. My father had always dreamed of seeing Aqaba, and I had raved about Petra for years. We went via white minibus with a Syrian driver. As we crossed into Jordan, my parents again went silent. They were in shock at the modern infrastructure—paved highways and stoplights (that people actually stopped at). And they were annoyed that the Assads, who had acted like a hereditary monarchy, hadn't delivered even a fraction of the kind of development the Jordanian kings had. They started to complain to us before stifling it, lest the Syrian driver note their criticism and duly inform on us.

With each day on that trip, my father seemed to seek to distance himself further from Syria. In the United States, he had always used Syria and being Syrian to separate himself from the country where he had made his life. Now it was the other way around. At social visits, he was nearly bragging about the success he had found in America, attributing it to how individual merit was valued there. All of a sudden he was firmly in camp USA. Naturally, that was annoying to people. They couldn't deny that perhaps there was more personal opportunity in the United States for Syrians than in Syria itself, but they challenged my father to justify America's foreign policies. Of course, my father agreed with them that the United States had betrayed its own values in its actions in Palestine and Iraq. But where the Syrians saw sanctimony and hypocrisy, my father, particularly after that trip, saw that for all the supposed honor there had been in the Syrian regime's position on Palestine and Iraq, it had failed to improve the lives of Syrians.

Staying at the hotel had been somewhat extravagant, and it wasn't private. Hotels, being places where foreigners frequented, were often under the watchful eye of the *mukhabarat*. We knew our belongings had probably been rifled through. The management had also swindled us, adding on costs that had not been disclosed (and that likely went to them personally). But what bothered my parents the most about the experience was that a home in my mother's name was just a walk away, and we should have been able to stay there. Despite their frustrations during the trip, my parents knew that when they returned to Baltimore they would again miss Syria. And there was no reason they couldn't visit more frequently, if only they had access to Salma's house.

Later that year, Sa'ad told my parents that perhaps they should take advantage of the newly passed property law. It allowed landlords to pay unwanted tenants—like Hassan—to leave their property, to the tune of 40 percent of the property's value.

It would still require a court battle, as it was to the tenant's benefit to assert a higher value. Nonetheless, my parents asked Sa'ad to file the papers that year. They wanted to take back Salma's apartment in the Tahaan.

PART 3

In the Eye of the Belly

View of the front balcony from author's grandmother's house after the renovation was completed;
visible is the bitter orange tree planted in 1953.

Author's mother and aunt as little girls
on the same balcony, c. 1955.

9

RETURN

Damascus, April 2011

I MOVED TO SYRIA ON MONDAY, APRIL 25, 2011. IN FEBRUARY OF
that year, schoolchildren in the southern city of Dara'a, near the Jordanian
border, had scrawled graffiti mimicking the slogans that had been chanted in
the Arab countries that had risen up against authoritarian rulers. Though
it was just a prank, the regime responded by arresting the boys, aged ten to
fifteen, and torturing them. Grown men beat them, burned their bodies, and
pulled out their fingernails.

In what became a widespread telling of what happened next, the devastated parents went to the authorities asking for their children. They were
told, "Forget your children. If you want children, make more children. If you
don't know how, bring us your women and we will make them for you."

The arrest of the boys (not to mention the threatening response of the
government) sparked protests in the center of the city, with people demanding the resignation of the mayor and of the local *mukhabarat* head. People
called for an end to corruption—but not the fall of the regime. Regardless,
security forces opened fired on them.

A high-ranking delegation of government officials to Dara'a assured elders
there that Bashar al-Assad was committed to bringing to justice those who
had opened fire. In a gesture of goodwill, the children were released. But

within forty-eight hours, Syrian forces raided a mosque in the city. Since then, the protests had spread across Syria, and by the time I moved there, already more than four hundred Syrians were dead. The same day I set out for Damascus from Beirut, the regime carried out a new predawn assault and siege of Dara'a.

I was only minutes across the Syrian border when I saw a fresh colorful billboard on the side of the road. A non-Arabic reader could easily be forgiven for thinking it was geared toward children. It was instead a brazen and implicit threat by the regime intended for Syrian adults. In bright colors and with a glossy finish, it declared, as if in the voice of an enthusiastic child, "I am with the law!" The word for "I"—in Arabic, *ana*—begins with the letter *alif* (ا), and on the poster it was drawn as an arm topped with a raised, volunteering hand. It had the feel of a youth-targeted civic education campaign, but in the coded language between dictator and dictated, I understood "I am with the law"—seemingly innocent—to really mean something entirely different and menacing: "Submit."

"Welcome back 'in' Syria," I thought. I had not been back in nearly seven years but had made this border crossing—from Lebanon to Syria—more times than I could count. All of its motions were familiar, as was that boot-on-my-neck feeling—recognizable, loathed—that immediately returned once I was across the border.

The government had created and posted these billboards (I would see various iterations all over Damascus) soon after the peaceful civil demonstrations had begun. It felt like a collective scolding, as if we were all wayward children. The slogan, "I am with the law," begged the question, "Which law?" Syria, after all, had been, for decades, under "Emergency Law"—because of myriad existentialist threats to national security. It was a country where laws had been routinely amended to accommodate a dynastic presidency, where an extended family was above the law, and where government officials down to the most minor of functionaries would flout it for a measly crumpled note of 50 Syrian lira (1 USD) pressed into a sweaty palm. Yet here was this same government invoking *the law* in admonishment of any Syrian who might be thinking about exercising their basic rights of citizenship. Every time I saw that poster, with that raised five-fingered hand around Damascus, I wondered how long until someone took the risk of severe punishment and defaced it, transforming it into what it really was: a middle-finger salute by the regime and aimed at its people.

The shabby booths and buildings at the border crossing, where bribes were as necessary as travel documents, were covered with pictures of the Syrian trinity: Hafez al-Assad, Bashar al-Assad, and his dead brother Bassel al-Assad. Lebanon and the week I had just spent there were quickly receding.

Much had changed there since I had left in 2004—the explosive (literally and figuratively) murder of Rafiq al-Hariri had upended Lebanese politics and forced Syria out of Lebanon after fifteen years of military occupation. And then, in the summer of 2006, Israel had decimated Lebanon in its war against Hezbollah. For a country that had been brutalized and traumatized almost continually since 1975—my entire lifetime—Lebanon seemed to have reached a tipping point. Meanwhile, Syria continued to use Lebanon for its own proxy aggressions against Israel, the United States, and Saudi Arabia, while allowing Lebanon to bear the consequences of its actions.

When I had called from Beirut to announce my arrival the following day, my Damascus relatives asked me warmly, "When will you be leaving?"

Their anxiety was audible in the practiced banality of our conversation despite there being plenty of newsworthy happenings to discuss, digest, and process. Everyone else in the world was talking about Syria. Yet no one would dare acknowledge as much on the phone, other than in the most oblique remarks about weather: forecasts were cloudy; it was unseasonably warm; hopefully, it would cool down soon. Just as audible were the clicks on the line and that large emptiness of space that suggested someone else was listening, one of the ever-present and intimidating reminders that we were never alone. These relatives trying to shoo me away were of course afraid for me: Why opt in to the risk and uncertainty facing Syria when, as an American, I didn't have to? No one wanted the responsibility should something happen to me. But they also didn't want anything—like my suspicious presence—to cast a prying eye on them.

After the border checkpoint, the road was nearly empty, and from a cloudless sky, only the late afternoon sun followed us, appearing and disappearing behind hills and bends in our road. There were new housing developments well outside the city limits of Damascus, and banners announcing others in the works. But for a long stretch, the land was relatively empty—a blank canvas here, at that moment, much like the country, for which there were about to be many competing visions.

I was eager to be moving to Syria in this new era. I couldn't help but think of when my grandmother had moved to Damascus from Hama, a new bride coming to the capital when Syria itself was a newly minted independent republic. It was Salma's house that I hoped would give me cover now, an easy answer to every would-be informant or curious relative who might demand to know why I was in Syria *now*.

My parents' bid to get her house back had been successful, but Hassan had fought them, exhausting the appeals process. Though he had paid very low rent for forty years, he haggled in court over the value of the house, so that he could extract the maximum amount of money from my parents—who by law had to pay him 40 percent of its worth to get him to leave.

He still had some of Salma's furniture, but rather than give it back to her family, he again sold it off. When Suha found out, she finally lost it. She screamed at him, "Why didn't you give me a chance to at least buy my mother's things?"—as absurd as it was that she should have to pay to have something of Salma's. (Or that Syrians should have to beg and then bleed for simple reforms.) He merely turned away.

Hassan had saved so much money from selling paintings and not paying market rent that together with the ransom from my parents, he was able to buy a large house in central Damascus. We had at last gotten our house back from the man who had refused to leave, and he had extracted a heavy price from us in the process. I wondered now if Syrians could get their country back and what it might cost the people.

As we approached Damascus on the Mezzeh highway, excitement made me giddy. I would soon see family whom I hadn't seen in years. Little cousins would now be young women and men. I would be able to sit with the older generation and ask them what they remembered of Salma. I could again wander the streets of Old Damascus. This time, there was no rush. The city was mine to know, I hoped, without the filters and buffers of a passing visitor.

The fact that I had—like most Americans—moved out of my parents' house at eighteen had for ages cast my honor in questionable light for the more conservative elements in my family. If their criticisms were silenced by my professional accomplishments, they were vindicated—in their minds—by the very unconventional way I had married and then divorced, the most egregious part being that I hadn't invited them all to a grand wedding. Worse, having done this terrible thing, I then did what one rarely does, no matter how unhappy one is, or how betrayed many are in their marriages in Syria: I left. For people who could spend their whole lives gearing up for marriage, it was just too much of an affront. Luckily, my closest family, like our matriarch Salma, was not so small-minded.

By the time I reached Damascus, the sun was lower in the sky and gave Mt. Qasiyoun, which cradles Damascus to the north, a rosy gold color. Even though it had been seven years, very little had changed with the roads and avenues, and I easily directed the taxi driver to the Qasour house. My uncle Sa'ad now lived there alone.

Nuha, his enterprising wife, had applied for a visa to immigrate to Canada, not because she wanted to permanently leave Syria but to give her sons—who would have to serve in the Syrian Army—opportunities beyond Damascus. She had moved to Ottawa with them in 2006—they were sixteen and fourteen years old at the time—and Sa'ad stayed in Damascus to continue working.

When I got out of the car, the jasmine lining the trellises and iron gates was already fragrant with the scent that perfumes the entire city. Clusters of loquats (one of my favorite fruits) hung from the trees. I looked to see if any were in reach before ringing the doorbell.

When he opened the door, I hugged my uncle—who was much thicker in the middle than before. My mother had come to Damascus to meet with the contractor who would restore Salma's house. Both of us would stay with Sa'ad while she was there. She was already out and about with her sister in the neighborhood, so I quickly dropped my bags and went to join them.

Within a block of Sa'ad's house, I saw armed men guarding a branch of the Interior Ministry's *mukhabarat* that stood on the other side of the street. I had only been in that building once, when I was seventeen, when I had to explain why I was several years late in applying for my national ID card. Now, a large empty bus—having discharged its unfortunate riders—acted like a barricade at the entrance. I wondered when, if ever, and in what state, those who had been rounded up and bused in would emerge again into the light of day.

Rather than occupy buildings in remote and abandoned parts of town, the different *mukhabarat* branches had long ago deviously inserted themselves within residential neighborhoods. Their presence, and our imaginings of what unspeakable things were being committed inside, kept us actively threatened, and in line. But most insidiously, no matter how much we averted our gaze, the fact that we knew what was happening inside and yet went about our lives made us complicit. Later, as the situation in Syria grew more violent,

I wondered how much of the obsequious pro-regime support wasn't really a way to deflect a sense of guilt. We had started to hate ourselves for that complicity.

As I walked past the guards, I tried to see as much as possible without turning my head, just from periphery vision. I wondered how I looked to them. Did I seem suspicious? Did my gait or my clothes betray that I was American? Could they tell what I thought of the regime? Did they already know that I had just crossed into Syria on an American passport and Syrian ID card, that I was a journalist, and were they watching me? When I finally passed them and turned off that street onto another, I let myself exhale.

I arrived on the main drag of the Qassa'a quarter and made my way down to the gates of the French Hospital where my mother and aunt awaited me. The street was packed with evening strollers, shoppers, and hordes of young people checking each other out. They spilled off the sidewalks and into the paths of cars that nonetheless tried to wade their way along, often with windows open and riders peering out to people watch. It was a Syrian passeggiata. There were smokers and partisans of heavy cologne and perfume. Girls in tight jeans and hijabs, widows in black with varicosed calves. Boys with gelled hair and others with beards. Plopped down along the shop-lined sidewalks were also *fellaheen* (rural peasants) selling *jaanerik* (small sour plums) and *'aoujeh* (green almonds in their fuzzy husks) out of woven baskets. I looked for signs of optimism or fear on people's faces. What were they thinking or feeling about what was coming?

As I walked with this human current, I spotted my mother and aunt across the street—I waved large and ran to them. My mother shook her head with a smile and a look of resignation when I joined them.

When we were still in the United States, she had asked me, "How are you going to justify your presence in Syria *now?*"

"I'll tell them I'm there for the house," I had said, and it wasn't untrue.

Now, in Damascus, as I leaned down to kiss her, she held onto me as she whispered in English in my ear, "Be careful what you say and keep your thoughts to yourself."

ℰ◊ℨ

IN THE MORNINGS, while my uncle prepared his coffee in the kitchen, my mother and I would quickly change the TV channel in the family room to

BBC or Al Jazeera English. My uncle—at least in front of us—would only watch news on the state channel, Syrian TV or Addounia. In Syria, we had begun to divide ourselves according to TV station. For those who supported the regime, or feared the alternative, or feared any appearance of not supporting the regime, the previously derided government-controlled networks suddenly became the only channels they would watch. Previously venerated, the Arabic satellite channels Al Jazeera and Al Arabiya, based in Qatar and Saudi Arabia, respectively, became alleged tools of Gulf interference and propaganda. For those who supported the uprising, those networks or foreign-language services were their sources for news. There were also many who watched a sampling of all the channels as a way to piece together something approximating truth.

By April 2011, as far as I could tell, state TV had become an unwatchable mouthpiece that required Syrians to suspend logic, believe blatant lies, and deny what they knew or at least suspected to be truth. There were days when Syrian state TV showed a "live-cam" shot of city centers that were empty, while on the other channels, we saw live shots of the same areas filled with peaceful demonstrators. At one point, the Syrian government claimed that Al Jazeera had built a set to look like certain Syrian cities.

For his entire life, Sa'ad had refused to join the Ba'ath Party. Now he began exhibiting signs of the sort of Stockholm Syndrome that had gripped many people in Damascus, who all of a sudden were afraid of any change in the status quo, no matter how much they had formerly despised the regime. They would ask, "*Shoo al-badeel?*" (What's the alternative?)

When a telephone call came to Sa'ad's house from "the West"—a stressful event nowadays, as we imagined it flagged us to the *other* listeners—he made a point of reassuring concerned callers, not just with, "Everything is fine," but also, for good measure, "All those Gulf channels are lying. Only Addounia and Syria TV can be believed."

At first I bristled at the underlying idea behind "*Shoo al-badeel?*"—that chaos, violence, sectarianism, or fundamentalism were inevitable—because I thought it undersold the Syrian people. But I came to understand later how deep the intimidation of the population ran. In its quest to hold onto power, many already understood—consciously or subconsciously—that the regime would work to unleash all those forces without a second thought. Before that winter's "Arab Spring," no one disputed that the state of democracy and freedom were bleak, and had been for generations. At some point, something had to give—in the entire region—but how and when had become an over-whelming and depressing mystery. Everyone had just gotten used to it.

Then, that January, Tunisia had erupted in revolution. Many Syrians shrugged—Tunisia was, after all, like a distant cousin in the Arab family, and it could have been a one-off. But then Egypt—the family's elder statesman—began to teeter. People in the Middle East and the diaspora were at the edge of their seats as something finally did—miraculously, joyously—*give* in the Arab world. The night that Egyptian dictator Hosni Mubarak stepped down, my cousin from Egypt, Kinan, posted on Facebook: *R.I.P Despair: June 1967–February 2011*, citing as birthdate the disastrous defeat of Arab nationalism during the Six-Day War with Israel. Watching from the United States at the time, I had felt like a moment I had been waiting for since 1967—even though I wasn't born until 1974—had finally come. Many of us, even in the diaspora, had been nursed on our parents' disillusionment with the catastrophic failure of the greater Arab nation, and it felt as if it was our own.

But the euphoria at watching Mubarak forced to step down under popu-lar, revolutionary, non-Islamist, and nonviolent pressure had already given way to caution for many Syrians. Simple candlelight vigils in front of the Egyptian and Libyan embassies in Damascus—which did not address the Syrian government—had been broken up by the regime, and people were arrested. February 5, 2011, called for mostly by Syrians abroad as a day of protests in the style of Egypt and Tahrir—came and went in Syria with nary a whimper.

Whether the regime felt specifically threatened by the vigils is debatable. For years, it had worked hard to abort any efforts that fostered solidarity among Syria's people, prohibiting any civil society initiatives that weren't under the regime's direct control or patronage, and construing any agency exercised by Syrians (even on environmental issues, for example) a slippery slope that might lead to people wanting to vote in free elections one day. In the wake of the first salvos of the Arab Spring, Assad had declared that he didn't think he would share Mubarak's fate. Meanwhile, his wife, Asma, posed in American *Vogue*.

Many things did, in fact, separate Assad from Mubarak. He was relatively popular. He had supported Palestinian and Lebanese resistance to Israel. (Syrian resistance to Israel, however, did not involve anything more than rhetorical and logistical support; during Assad family rule, no shots were fired from Syria's shared border with the Zionist enemy after the 1973 Arab-Israeli

War.) He wasn't taking millions of dollars in aid from the United States every year, as far as anyone knew. He wasn't a real military man; he was ostensibly an eye doctor. He wasn't old. He didn't look menacing, but rather goofy, long necked and chinless. His wife was fresh-faced and natural, unlike Susie Mubarak, and heavily involved, not just ceremoniously, in social and charitable initiatives. They cultivated their image, even hiring a pricey PR firm well before the uprising to mount a charm offensive on their behalf. The airport in Damascus featured a large version of the oft-disseminated photo of Assad in jeans, planting trees with peasants.

Plenty of Syrians thought Assad had a chance of winning an election if he would call for one—definitely not with 99.5 percent of the vote as in years past, but potentially by over 50 percent. If nothing else, caution and a fear of instability might very well have tempered a rush to change things. And although political restrictions remained *a la père*, economic restrictions appeared to be loosening. Western brands and goods were increasingly available. You could finally get a Coca-Cola and a lot more in Syria. However, political tyranny extended to economic tyranny: the best financial benefits of any privatization were reaped mostly by the Assad family, their inner circle, and the businessmen they had long co-opted.

When larger peaceful and civil protests had begun in earnest in March, they had not even called for the fall of Assad or even the regime, asking, rather, mostly for reforms and *huriya*, freedom. But if there were Syrians who hoped for a nonviolent and speedy end to their own dynastic dictatorship and the beginning of a new opportunity to participate in their own political future, the regime soon disavowed them of any such notion. The demonstrations were not tolerated; people were arrested and tortured—including children—and the regime did not hesitate to open fire on peaceful demonstrators. It was determined not to make the same mistakes Mubarak had made in Egypt: the foreign press was not allowed in; the Internet was strategically blocked and monitored; on Fridays, access to any public space that aspired to be a Tahrir Square was heavily guarded. Friday is the Muslim day of prayer, and mosques were one of the few places where a critical mass of people (including non-Muslims) could form.

Even after the police and then the army opened fire on peaceful protesters, many Syrians retained a stubborn belief that Bashar al-Assad himself was a good-hearted modernizer who was powerless against an old guard that was calling the shots. By April 2011, it was still easy for most Syrians, particularly in the major cities, to feel removed from what was coming. Central Damascus itself had yet to witness any significant unrest—we saw more on Al Jazeera than we did with our own eyes—but we swapped accounts about the things we had heard were brewing in hushed tones.

Syria TV and other pro-regime outlets, such as Hezbollah's Manar network and its followers, worked hard to counter any reports hinting of a popular movement to assert more political participation, or of a regime crackdown in violation of civil and human rights. They presented a version that explained what was happening as essentially a Western plot to destabilize Syria because it had steadfastly resisted Israeli and US hegemony, and/or as Gulf-funded Islamist terrorism that sought to destroy Syria's supposed secularism. History and geopolitics—from European colonialism to unwavering American support of Israel to Gulf campaigns to spread Wahhabism and political Islam—made that version of what was happening in Syria plausible, especially for anyone who was trying to justify looking the other way while the government shot at and rounded up its own people.

In my first few days in Syria, I did not heed my mother's advice, and let my own thoughts seep into conversation, especially when I was confronted with people who engaged in logical gymnastics to deny that the demonstrations might have been peaceful and civil and native to Syria.

"So what are they?" I would ask.

"The US, orchestrating everything happening here and in the region."

Any retort I gave was inevitably answered with, "Didn't the US lie about weapons of mass destruction so it could invade Iraq, which allowed violent chaos to explode there?"

That's where the conversation usually ended, because I could not deny that that was true. There seemed to be little room for parallel truths: that the United States had lied to invade Iraq *and* that Assad did not legitimately hold power; that the United States had supported Israel's brutalization of Arabs *and* that Syria needed reform; that Islamophobia informed to some degree US foreign policy *and* that the Assad regime had tortured children from Dara'a who had scribbled political graffiti.

Explaining the United States to people in the Arab world had never been easy. I had often been asked versions of the question, "How can the US have such great ideals but have such terrible foreign policy?" The years after 9/11 and George W. Bush's tenure had made it that much more difficult for me to answer.

My first few days in Damascus had flown by. I'd had meetings with the contractor for Salma's apartment and lunches and dinners with relatives, where my politics and likelihood of being a CIA agent were often probed. Then, on my first Friday—the day of rest in Damascus—I braced myself. Since late Thursday night, the Internet had become almost impossible to access, as it would be every Thursday night thereafter. The streets were deserted, much more so than they should have been on a beautiful spring weekend, one of the first of the season. I joked to my mother that everyone must be staying in to watch Prince William and Kate's wedding.

The morning had been like the others—we snuck in some non-Syrian-government broadcasts, looking for news from across the region. Fridays were particularly explosive everywhere: Libya had stalemated; Egypt had come under contested military rule; tensions in Tunis between secularists and Islamists were mounting. My mother and I also took the time to draft a marathon to-do list for the house to be accomplished before her departure the following week. That afternoon we had been invited to lunch at the home of my mother's cousin Renée, the daughter of the son that Abdeljawwad disowned, who lived within walking distance in a building across the street from a mosque. No one was booking social obligations on Fridays that required traveling anywhere by car.

"We should get there before prayers let out," my uncle told us. The *mukhabarat* would be on high alert as large groups of people began pouring out across the city from the mosques.

We walked in the opposite direction of the security branch down the street where I had been "interrogated" as a teenager and toward the mosque. The streets were empty and quiet. Traffic police on their motorcycles watched us as we passed, and I stared at them through my sunglasses. I vaguely remembered how I had felt when I was a teenager in high school, resentful that my parents—who were more strict than other parents—had so much authority over me, and that I had to just accept it. It was jarring to know that someone might be watching us wherever we went.

At Renée's house, the smells of lunch promised a feast. But first, we were ushered to the sofas near the TV, which was already on, and offered drinks and nuts.

"What channel are you watching?" asked my uncle as he reached for the remote, preparing to deliver his news network manifesto.

Recognizing the provocation, Renée intervened and said, "Let's watch the royal wedding," diffusing any tension that might raise voices that could then be heard outside the apartment and reported.

I thought about mentioning how the Syrian ambassador to the United Kingdom had been disinvited from the wedding, but thought better of it.

"Isn't her dress pretty?" Renée asked, pointing at Kate in white lace, slipping into polite and meaningless conversation, a skill many Syrians had perfected in all those years.

※

WHILE MY MOTHER looked at tiles in a ceramics store for the renovation, I pretended to take a photo of a bathtub displayed in the window. What I was really taking a picture of was the man on the street on the other side of the glass.

When she saw what I was doing, my mother glared at me, and in a moment when we were alone, she said, in English, "You took a picture of the guy with the gun, didn't you?"

"Yes, but don't worry, he didn't see me," I said.

"Why did you do that?" she asked, tense.

"Because somebody should," I said, with misplaced bravado. I didn't like how we were all acting as if this were normal, that armed men not in uniform but with the look of the regime were implanting themselves onto more and more of the streets. This man was young, gun slung across his chest, and unapologetic for the intrusion.

"Don't do it again," my mother said.

When we left the store, we passed right in front of him, and I could feel him assessing us as we walked.

"This is not normal," I said again as we got back into the car and headed to Ain al-Kirish. Since arriving, I'd yet to see the now vacant apartment in the Tahaan.

We sped down Aleppo Street, happy to leave the armed man behind. Our road to the house was easy and short. Unlike Beirut—where the chaos of war and corruption meant buildings sprouted in cacophony—Damascus at least had had decent urban planning that made it easy to navigate. Veering onto Revolution Street, we came upon the four small streets that make up Ain al-Kirish. Once we parked, I practically sprinted to the Tahaan and up the stairs to Salma's apartment.

It still had the three traditional entrances, a vestige of another time: two side-by-side doors, one for the men and one for the women, and another leading directly to the kitchen, originally for the servants. I entered through the door for women into the large room that had been for formal dining. A ladder stood in its middle, a door removed from its hinges leaning against it. Empty and open, the house seemed so much brighter than when I had last seen it, when Hassan still lived there.

The floors, now covered in pulverized plaster and dust, were still the original ones from the 1940s. It was hard to believe this gem had been hidden beneath the dark rooms I had seen years ago. Finally the elegance I associated with Salma—from what I remembered and from all that I had heard over the years—was in view.

My mother was talking to the engineer, who was delivering a litany of excuses as to why things were so behind schedule. When she pushed him, he just named the towns the workers had to come from—all implicated in the *mishaakel* (troubles)—as if to say things really were beyond his control. I left them, because I had quickly come to dislike him and his condescending way of speaking to us. When my mother's or father's brothers were with us, he directed his answers to them even when we were the ones who asked the questions.

I walked into the front salon. The men's door from the hallway opened into it. It had two internal doors that led to the front balcony, and I stepped out into the warm sunshine. Beneath me were the higher branches of the fifty-eight-year-old bitter orange tree my grandmother had planted in 1953. This was the first time I had ever been able to touch it. I tore off a leaf and scratched it, releasing its citrus scent.

I looked out across the street at the neatly spaced buildings. Many had the old green wooden shutters that were swung open every morning and hooked in place. Others had more practical rolling shutters, which were honey colored. My mother had decided to keep the original shutters, several of which had already been removed to be sanded and eventually repainted.

I looked up and down the block full of loquat and citrus trees. I noticed the women on the balcony across the street looking at me. I looked back at them and smiled. They knew Lamya, and I hoped they could see, even at that distance, that I must be her daughter.

Behind me another door took me back inside the house, into the room adjacent to the front salon. There were bags of plaster, cement to be prepared, a stool, and someone's baseball cap. The wall had been painted with three different color swatches for us to consider. My mother had shared this room with her sister when they were children. It was this room they were constantly ousted from when relatives visited from Hama.

Hearing the engineer approaching as he talked to his crew, I used yet another door to exit onto another balcony. This one was narrow and ran about two-thirds the length of the entire flat, along the side of the building. I walked the tighter passage, used mostly to dry laundry, peering back into the house through the windows. I spotted my mother and her sister on another little slender balcony, which jutted out from the same side of the building I was on. That balcony was only accessible from the master bedroom. They were chatting and leaning over slightly to pluck leaves from a prolific grapevine with roots in the ground below that was now old and strong enough to be reached from our floor. Suha had prepared *tabouleh* for lunch, which we would scoop with these fresh leaves. I paused to look at my mom and aunt, adult women in the house in which they had grown up, doing a chore together the way they had as little girls.

I stepped back inside and found myself in what had been the family room in Salma's day. In addition to the door to the balcony, this room had two internal doors. One led right back into the big dining room, and the other into the more private parts of the house. There were the master bedroom, the bathrooms, and the kitchen. Looking around at this room, I claimed it in my head: "This will be my office," I thought.

I followed the voices of my mother and aunt—they were still on the balcony attached to the big bedroom that had once belonged to Salma and Ameen and that, as little girls, they had often shared with their parents. It was sunny, with windows facing south and east. Before joining them outside, I paused and looked around the room. I wondered—at the beginning, when Salma and Ameen had been newly married, what had they imagined their lives and country would be? And when did they understand that much of what they had dreamed would never come true?

When my grandparents and my mother and her siblings all slept in this room, had Salma imagined that Lamya would leave, make America home, and not return to Syria for so many years? Did she sense her own life would be cut short, even before she died? Would she have been happy that we had now won the house back, and that we were restoring it to look almost exactly as it did in her day? If she could stand here now, what would she say about what had become of her life and Syria? Of where Syria was headed today?

"Don't be late," my aunt said as she stepped back into the room, my mother behind her. Suha took both their stacks of selected grape leaves; she'd wash them back at her house before lunch.

I went to see the kitchen with my mother; it was a disaster—the entire back wall of the kitchen was nonexistent. My parents had decided to enclose what had been a balcony to extend the kitchen. This was out of code, but everyone did it, we were assured. The workers would leave the kitchen open and exposed to the elements until the city signed off on the renovation and certified it was habitable; luckily, by late April, there would be no more rain for months.

After the engineer left, my mother and I walked through the house again, making sure to lock all the doors.

"Are you really going to live here?" she asked, moving away from me. What she was actually telling me was, "Don't live here. Don't stay in Syria."

She was leaving to go back to America the following week, and urged me to quickly follow.

10

TAHRIR SQUARES

Damascus, Cairo, Homs, May–July 2011

As I settled into Damascus, nearly every day I passed through the city's Tahrir Square. *Tahrir* means liberation, and Arab countries are full of Liberation plazas, boulevards, and buildings—though freedom has been in short supply in all of them. Earlier in the year, Egyptians had electrified the world with *their* Tahrir Square, filling all 70,000 square feet of it with thousands of people seeming to speak with one voice.

In Damascus, Sahet al-Tahrir is also, like in Egypt, a traffic roundabout, though four and a half times smaller than Cairo's. At its center stands an abstract sculpture of three pillars in different sizes that resemble totem poles. There is some suggestion they were meant to represent the short-lived federation of Syria, Egypt, and Libya. My aunt Suha and her friends from art school, who hated them, used to call them the three *khowazee'*—for the notorious impaling sticks that the Ottomans used as a dreadful punishment, driven up the rectum and through the torso in a way that left the victim to die over a few days. (In common Syrian Arabic speak, it's a way to say you got screwed in a really bad way.)

I'd pass through the roundabout whenever I'd return from the Tahaan to Salma's last house in the Qasour, where I was staying during the renovations. I'd take Baghdad Avenue, the crosstown thoroughfare that started on the west side of town at Seven Fountains Square (where Ameen used to work), and that dead-ended on the east at Tahrir Square. Along the way, I'd see dilapidated traffic signs to the square in English and Arabic. I began to feel as if both the signs and the roundabout itself were taunting me.

It was already clear, after three months of only escalating developments, that there would be no quick and cathartic revolution for Syria like what appeared to have happened in Egypt. Syria wasn't going to remake itself in a similar neat eighteen-day arc—apparently the perfect amount of time to hold the world rapt without overly taxing short attention spans. Egypt's story had been inspiring, and it was impossible not to cheer on the young, social-media-using "regular Egyptians" who brought down the dictator straight out of central casting. It also had been—for the most part—bloodless.

Instead, in Syria, in the first three months of the demonstrations—not even for regime change, but just for reforms—1,000 Syrians were already dead and reportedly 10,000 in prison. Whereas in Egypt the military had stepped in to stabilize the situation (arguably to protect its own vast economic interests), in Syria the military was killing (or being ordered to kill) Syria's own people.

As if that wasn't bad enough, the state media (TV and newspapers) continued to batter Syrians with an almost ludicrous version of what was happening in the country. Every day, we heard justifications for the brutal military crackdown. There was the proffer of evidence that the ongoing protests against the government were being orchestrated—or infiltrated—by foreign-armed terrorists. We were treated daily to alleged confessions by Syrians who supposedly had been paid to be terrorists; to bedside interviews with allegedly wounded Syrian soldiers, with zoomed-in shots of bloodstained sheets; to videos of alleged arms caches; and to footage of alleged protesters, their weapons circled in red.

Whether people actually believed these reports or not, the regime was cuing Syrians as to what the accepted narrative would be. This was made easier because, unlike in Egypt, in Syria the regime was not allowing in foreign journalists who might have been able to pursue the story without the consequences that could be unleashed on Syrian citizen journalists. (Never mind that there was no free press in Syria.) Because the regime seemed to be fighting for domestic rather than international legitimacy, it didn't care if it looked like it had something to hide to the outside world.

There was much that was infuriating about all this—but when it came to the propagandizing, I resented being treated as if we were children, and I looked at Egypt with envy and wonder. When early in the summer I got the chance to go to this promised land where Arabs no longer feared their rulers, I went to see it for myself. There, much more than just the difference in the sizes of the Tahrirs was quickly obvious.

The opportunity came with an invitation to a family wedding. Dima, the second cousin who had captured my heart in Egypt in 1992 and 1998, was getting married. Because of the distance between us—caused by our parents seeking better lives outside of Syria—we had missed out on the mundane in each other's lives. Before social media and cheap modes of communication, I heard about many of my relatives only at the landmark moments: graduations, weddings, births, and funerals. Dima was to me always a wild little girl; I wasn't going to be able to imagine her as anything else until I saw her again. And I was very keen to go to Egypt and learn more about how people had broken through the fear that was still so prevalent in Syria. I wanted to know what might be gleaned about Syria's own future from what Egypt was living now.

The last time I had been in Egypt, Syria's once overbearing partner in the United Arab Republic (UAR), was in 1998, when I had visited from Palestine. Thirteen years later, the Egyptian airport had been expanded and updated, and I was once again annoyed by how much nicer it was than the Syrian one. I was starting to suspect that the Syrian dictatorship kept things rundown on purpose. Maybe it was to keep people occupied with the need for material improvements (as opposed to political ones), or to maintain the ruse that Syria was always under siege and that everyone was in it together, or to convince Syrians we didn't deserve any better.

I might have been imagining it, but it did seem like everyone was smiling in Egypt, as if they knew they had done something big.

At customs, I handed my American passport to a clean-shaven and handsome Egyptian policeman in an all-white uniform. In a charming Egyptian accent he asked me the perfunctory questions, welcomed me as a "sister from Syria," and then let me in. Simply, without creeping me out the way Syrian border control did every single time.

The Egyptian Revolution still had its newlywed glow, and it was such a universal high that even corporations were cashing in on it. As I made my way down to baggage claim and the exit, I saw a billboard-sized advertisement for Mobinil, an Egyptian telecom provider. It featured a man waving an Egyptian flag in the sunlight with a quotation: "There is nothing new in Egypt, Egyptians are making history as usual . . . "

The words were attributed to Silvio Berlusconi, perennial Italian prime minister. Of all the praise to be proud of, Berlusconi's was an odd choice. After nearly twenty years of Berlusconi rule, many in Italy were hoping to dump him just as unceremoniously as Egyptians had Mubarak.

※

IN CAIRO, I stayed in Zamalek, long home to Cairo's old money families and ever popular with foreigners living in the city. It was less conservative than other parts of Cairo: one could easily find a drink or be foreign without attracting too much attention. On Gezira Island in the middle of the Nile, with bridges connecting it on both the east and the west to the rest of Cairo, it felt like a bit of an oasis in the crowded city.

The wedding was to be held in a church in Heliopolis, a large sprawling area where many of the city's wealthy had built stately villas. On the afternoon of the wedding, I left Zamalek and crossed back to the east side of the Nile, where I almost immediately found myself on a ramp that passed over Tahrir Square. There it was—symbol of change and hope—right beneath my taxi. It was a Friday, the day of rest. The square was almost empty and its size made it much grander than Damascus's; I tried not to take it as a sign of Syria's chances for change. When I caught sight of the burnt-out headquarters of Mubarak's National Democratic Party (NDP), I gasped so loudly that the taxi driver looked back at me in his rearview mirror.

He asked me if I knew what the building was. We had exchanged very few words so far, but when hearing my accent as I responded, "Yes, it's NDP headquarters," in Arabic, he said, "Oh! You are Syrian," while shaking his head in what I understood to be sympathy.

Gesturing back to the building as it faded from our sight, he said, "Like the Ba'ath Party."

"*Ya rayt*," I answered, now shaking my head. I wish.

On a weekday, the city's horrific traffic would have easily kept me sweating in the back seat of a taxi for an hour. Instead, on a Friday, when the streets are generally deserted, I arrived in fifteen minutes to Heliopolis.

Not all the guests could fit in the church, so many watched from the door. I had found a spot in the pews toward the front by the aisle. Dima, a grown woman in a luxurious gown, entered on the arm of her father. She beamed, and in that giddiness, I still saw the little girl who had delighted me in that first summer in 1992.

No less than five priests officiated her marriage—one to represent all the different Christian denominations of the bride's and groom's families.

The church was full of Cairo's wealthy. Between the ceremony and the reception, several women changed into even more formal attire. The celebration was held at a posh hotel, and many more guests came for the party. When the newlyweds made their grand entrance, it was by driving a convertible into the ballroom. How that was possible still remains a mystery to me.

The guests at the reception included Egyptians from Egypt's long-established Greek and Syrian communities, a remnant of more cosmopolitan times. Once large and vibrant, and dating back to the nineteenth century (Egypt, too, was Ottoman), their numbers (along with other communities like Jews and Egyptian-ized Italians) had dwindled in the 1950s when Nasser's nationalist reforms saw their fortunes diminished and their presence much less welcome. The guests generally represented Cairo's business elite, and included both Christians and Muslims. Many had been educated at the American University of Cairo or abroad. Dima and her siblings had all studied in Canada. Everyone spoke at least Arabic and English.

Conversations were superficial and shouted over Arabic and American pop music, but I met many young Egyptians eager to play a bigger role in their country's future—something they hadn't imagined possible before. Even though many of them came from families that had found a way to do business and get rich under Mubarak, they had always understood that real political and even economic participation weren't welcome.

One of the more painful realities of the modern Middle East is that so much native talent has gone unharnessed by the countries that would rather cast out anyone who might challenge their power. And so, many Arabs have chosen to pursue their ambitions in other countries, enriching those other societies. That appeared to have changed in new Egypt. People—even these children of the wealthy who had found a way to thrive financially in dictatorship—believed their country was destined for better days. I didn't hear the suspicions of their fellow countrywomen and men that riddled Syrian society. It felt more cohesive.

Many had tales to share of the days when everything had changed—January 28 in Tahrir Square, the first Friday of the revolution, and February 11, when Mubarak had been forced to step down. It wasn't all rosy; there was concern about the antidemocratic measures of the current rulers—the military—and almost universal disdain (at this wedding) for the Muslim Brotherhood. But that feeling that nothing was in their hands when it came to their country was, at least at that moment, banished.

Members of my extended family had also come from Syria. Dima's grandfather was Salma's brother Nazir, who had been murdered in the months before Salma suffered her terrible stroke. All of Nazir's grandchildren were at the wedding. In addition to Dima and her siblings, my other second cousins (all Abdeljawwad great-grandchildren) had come from Aleppo and Damascus as well as Saudi Arabia.

The latter were superlative examples of the Syrian social circles they moved in—beautiful, married, rich, and procreating. Although these circles had the trappings of cosmopolitanism—they were multilingual, had perfunctory university degrees, and traveled the globe frequently—they were also rigid in what they valued and somewhat insular. Despite the fact that we were all Abdeljawwad's great-grandchildren, we were so different, and I wondered at which generation the die had been cast. I speculated about the reasons for that—the differences between our parents, differences in how sons and daughters are raised and treated in matters like marriage and inheritance, differences in the countries where we had all grown up.

But I was really much less interested in those questions than I was curious about getting to that other Tahrir Square.

᳓

IN MY BRIEF trip to Cairo (the first of several over the next year), protesters returned to Tahrir more than once. Sometimes the gatherings were small; other times, such as on Friday, May 27, they were quite large. On that day, tens of thousands of mostly liberal protesters filled the square for a demonstration billed as "The Revolution Part II."

Cairo's Tahrir Square—as has been written over and over—was now much more than just a traffic roundabout. It had transcended its intended purpose, becoming a vehicle of change itself, and Egyptians would keep returning to it. The space clearly belonged to them, and they could exercise some control over their lives and future from within its concrete embrace.

When I entered the square at that large Friday protest, Egyptians had set up lines and security checks to ensure order. In the women's line, I opened my bag and let them peer in. When asked to show ID, I handed over my Syrian card. With excitement, a group of them began to cheer and said a word that means, essentially, "We hope it will be your turn next!" (They used the plural second person, meaning "you Syrians!")

I answered "*Insh'allah*." But what I was seeing in Cairo was currently unimaginable in Syria. If a place to gather and make reasonable demands was impossible back in Damascus, everything else that was happening in Egypt seemed like science fiction.

During that trip, I attended political salons, went to meetings of nascent political parties, and overheard many conversations in public places about what should happen next in Egypt. I even went to the "Liberal Corner," a sort of adult literacy program in civics for Egyptians who were teaching themselves about alternatives to dictatorship, theocratic states, or military rule. The Liberal Corner was being held at the Egyptian Democratic Academy (EDA), which was founded in 2009 by liberal activists to raise political awareness among Egyptians.

Those in attendance were educated, but for most of them, not in foreign-language schools. They were not the wealthy elite of the wedding; they were mostly students and salaried employees who made their way to the EDA after a long day of university or work, eager to do something good for Egypt. The classes were taught in Arabic, and the teacher on the nights I attended was a twenty-five-year-old medical doctor still in training who believed strongly in Egypt's future, liberalism, and John Stuart Mill. Her father was a not-so-junior member of the Muslim Brotherhood who spent many years and three sentences in Mubarak's prisons. She wore a hijab and black Converse hi-tops and was rather fluent in political science thought, having herself come up through the classes of the Liberal Corner. It was all so earnest: Egyptians from different walks of life seemingly intent on doing good for the country.

Of course, post-revolution Egypt was messy and imperfect. Days after the wedding, new sectarian tensions between Christians and Muslims erupted and protests at the Israeli embassy turned violent. The military council ruling Egypt in the interim between Mubarak and elections enacted several antidemocratic measures, such as arresting activists and discouraging demonstrations. The Muslim Brotherhood, which had skipped the large protest in Tahrir, was quickly proving itself to be power hungry and unwilling to really change Egypt as much as put itself in power. But despite all those realities, Egyptians were politicized and seemingly headed into the future. They had also (for most part) been untouched by the kind of violence already claiming lives in Syria, violence that would consume it whole and eventually damage the collective mental health of its people.

Even when I wasn't looking, I was reminded how different things were for the previously united countries. On one of my last nights before heading back to Damascus, I had dinner with a few Egyptians who were much more like me than my second cousins from the wedding. Some of them had graduate degrees from top American universities, and they were all members of the country's intellectual class. Over dinner in Zamalek, we had spoken generally about everything that was happening in the region, and specifically in Egypt. When the conversation turned to Syria in detail, I dropped my voice lest anyone hear what I had to say about the regime. I did it without thinking.

Suddenly one of them, a member of Egypt's foreign service, started to laugh. "Why are you whispering? You're not in Syria, you can speak!"

He was correct. But Syrians had long ago internalized the *mukhabarat*, even in diaspora. It was a fear rooted in the belief that they had unlimited reach. If I had thought I was free of that kind of fear, it was clear I wasn't. What I used to regularly call "not normal" had become secondhand to me. In Egypt, I was reminded that there was nothing normal about the situation in Syria. I was also inspired that the people could triumph.

I would try to hold onto Egypt as I returned to Syria. As usual, I flew via Beirut. It seemed easier for the government to disappear people from the airport in Damascus than from the land border crossing between Lebanon and Syria. Whether in actuality that was true, I don't know. We would learn that the regime was willing to act with a stunning level of impunity—a level, in fact, that I would not have imagined possible in a hyper-connected era when the rest of the world couldn't claim it didn't know what was happening.

When I landed in Lebanon, it was to news of the death of Hamza al-Khatib, a Syrian thirteen-year-old. I thought this would either quickly force a Syrian Tahrir Square or see to it that there wouldn't be one anytime soon.

HAMZA'S SCHOOL PORTRAIT became ubiquitous. It showed a chubby boy wearing a polo shirt under a baby-blue sweater. The background looked like a blue sky swirled with the yellow of the sun, rays of light radiating from the center that almost cast a halo around Hamza's head. Where other boys might start to look like young men at thirteen, Hamza was still on the childish side of the age. Everyone in Syria became familiar with this portrait of him and one other, a still taken from a video of him after death: a naked and bloated corpse, no longer the color of flesh but nearly purple from all the bruising.

Security forces had arrested Hamza on April 29 in Dara'a four days after I had arrived in Damascus, for attending a rally with his family. But no one would hear of it until nearly a month later when Hamza's body was returned. According to activists at the time, it was released to the family on the condition they say nothing. A video, however, was made and circulated, soon reaching global networks like Al Jazeera.

The body showed many signs of torture. There were bullet wounds on his arms. He had black eyes, cuts, injuries consistent with electric shock devices, bruises, and whip marks. His neck had been broken, and he had been castrated. While American media often sanitize what viewers can see of what can be done to a human body, the same cannot be said for Arab audiences. Images from Iraq and Palestine had not been sanitized for years. And yet what we saw of Hamza—which clearly showed violence done to a Syrian boy by the Syrian regime—shocked those who were willing to look. Hamza's father was briefly detained when the video came out.

Syrians were put on notice: an exposé to be shown on state TV would give us the truth. When it aired, doctors on camera made the case that these injuries were acquired after Hamza's death, and certainly not while the regime had him in its custody. The doctors who testified on TV said the marks on his body were not signs of torture but had been faked by conspirators who wanted to agitate the Syrian people. To allay any doubts, Hamza's father and uncle appeared on state TV in a pre-recorded conversation and said that they trusted Assad, who, they added, had pledged to look into the circumstances of Hamza's death.

At first I wondered why the regime had bothered with the charade—no one around me seemed to believe that anyone else but the regime had done this to the child (even though some insinuated that he or his parents were at fault for ignoring what they should have known were possible consequences for participating in the rally). But I began to understand that we weren't meant to be convinced. This was how the regime could hide a threat in plain sight. As state TV lingered on the bodily mutilations, speaking calmly about how the wounds were inflicted postmortem, we were meant to actually look at and commit to memory the damage that can be done to a body, even to a boy. The message: be grateful this is not your child.

It was a master class in how to hear, read, and speak this coded language, the one that exists between dictator and dictated.

What happened to Hamza taught me that what many Syrians who were hesitant to confront the regime feared most was not instability or the *badeel*—the alternative—to the regime. They had (whether consciously or subconsciously) understood that the regime would, like an abusive parent, punish them severely for their misbehavior—as if Syrians demanding reforms were just children.

Really, the regime had survived for years on an intricate architecture that made children out of adults. To remind anyone getting any ideas to the contrary, the regime began to make corpses out of children—as they did with Hamza.

৪৩

ANGUISH AND OUTRAGE over the violent deaths of young people had sparked revolution in both Tunisia, where a twenty-six-year-old fruit vendor had set himself on fire after police officers humiliated him, and Egypt, where plainclothes police had dragged a twenty-eight-year-old man out of an Internet café and killed him a block from his home.

I was again in Cairo in July, this time for work, and Egyptians had retaken their Tahrir Square, occupying it fully with an encampment. They were protesting the slow rate of change since the fall of Mubarak, and they accused the military council of protecting him. Activists had hung a giant canopy overhead to shield people from the unrelenting daytime sun, and tents sheltered them as they slept or discussed Egypt's past, present, and future late into the night and into the next morning. The canvas surfaces also provided space to display slogans, party and coalition names, and political demands.

Again a tent-city, the square soon acquired the necessary trappings: vendors sold both goods and sustenance, barbers provided a good shave, electricity was being siphoned from street lights, entertainment was available on stages and screens, and a cup of mint tea was never far away. There was also the trace of carnival, perhaps inspired by revolutionary euphoria, or just by the sense of community that came about by spending summer nights together in the open air. Its cause made little difference to the entrepreneurs who had the right trinket, balloon, or souvenir to sell. If in Cairo they were staying up all night claiming a say in their futures, in Syria it felt that some people were voluntarily going into slumber.

As triumphant as things felt in Tahrir, the reality was that elections were coming. The Muslim Brotherhood had fully mobilized and was organizing new and old supporters far beyond the square. But Ramadan—the month that would soon bring the country to a halt—was approaching. As a reminder, the festive lamps of the holiday already hung from cables that crisscrossed above the camp. Liberal activists feared that Egyptians would go the polls after Ramadan without really understanding what they were being asked to vote on, making it easier for the Brotherhood to get want it wanted. At the end of July, the Muslim Brotherhood—which had stayed out of Tahrir until that point—took to the square with other Islamists, vastly outnumbering the liberals in a show of organizational force that would portend their fortunes in the coming elections.

The following Monday, the military forcibly dispersed the protesters who had remained in the square, to the cheers of many of the merchants and residents of the area, who were fed up with the camp. There were Egyptians who felt that Tahrir belonged to the days of revolution. Now they were in the age of elections. The interim military rulers clearly wanted the people to understand that transition, and the Muslim Brotherhood was eager to see it complete, because its members knew they would benefit greatly.

Whether that shift was premature or sincere, it had happened, while Syria was still casting about for its Tahrir—both the figurative one where Syrians were united, optimistic, and no longer afraid, and the literal one, where they would take a stand against the regime. Wherever Syria's Tahrir might be, it was clearly not going to be the sleepy roundabout in Damascus that I daily passed through. That summer, it looked as if it could be Hama, Salma's hometown, which had a long history of standing up to the regime (and to power). The American and French ambassadors had made surprise visits to Hama in July, angering the regime, which then deployed tanks to the outskirts of the city.

I wanted to be closer to Salma, and to return to Hama with all the knowledge I had gained about the region, the country, and my grandmother. But so many in my family objected. They were sure that if I went to Hama, they would pay the price. I deferred to them—I wasn't comfortable gambling with their safety.

But when after the start of Ramadan my mother's university friend Athena invited me to Homs, which had also begun heavily protesting the regime—and which would become the "capital of the revolution"—I readily went, but I told no one until I got back.

✪

WHILE ALEPPO AND Damascus have competed through the centuries for mantle of Syria's greatest city, Hama and Homs have been locked in their own rivalry. Some say it dates back to when two tribes from Yemen—who didn't like each other there—settled in Syria. One made its home in Hama and the other in Homs, and the enmity continued. There was also the matter of the Orontes River (Asi in Arabic), which flows from Lebanon to Turkey; like the Nile, it flows northward, which has always given the advantage to Homs.

A veritable comedic canon has been born out of this Hama/Homs beef, always at Homs's expense. (The proverbial Homsi, or person from Homs, has long been the butt of Syrian jokes, independent of Hama.) For example: The people of Hama tried to imitate the idiocy of the Homsis, so they built a dam in the middle of the desert. The day after it was completed, they found Homsis fishing in it. (However, given what Homs has withstood since Syria's war began, these laughs may make no sense for future generations.)

There are explanations for why an industrious city full of many clever Syrians (Steve Jobs's father was Homsi) has a reputation for being daft. Folklore says it goes back to when Timur, seeking to restore Genghis Khan's Mongol Empire, invaded Syria, eventually sacking Damascus and Aleppo. Having conquered Aleppo, he had begun his march toward Homs, whose people knew they were no match for the fierce armies. Homs's citizens decided that instead of facing Timur on the battlefields, they would just bluff. With red dye, they painted their faces with dots, giving the appearance—from a distance—of leprosy. They also shredded their clothes and roamed the streets of Homs as if they were all crazy. At the sight of such a spectacle, the historically inaccurate story says the Mongolians decided to skip Homs as they tore their way through Syria. With time, what was remembered was not Homsis' cunning, but rather that they were dimwitted. Before Homs became the capital of the revolution, Homsis prided themselves for being the capital of laughter and comedy.

According to my mom, at university, their friends would often tease Athena for being from Homs. (Her grandfather had been a Greek laborer on the railroad in Greater Syria who married local and stayed—hence her name.) Athena, who during university had boarded in Damascus and was far from her own mother, also became a frequent visitor to Salma's house in Ain al-Kirish, as Salma made a point of looking after her. Athena had married another classmate of my mother's, Faris, who was from Hama. For all the talk of rivalry, there were a lot of Hama/Homs marriages in Syria. If Athena had Homs's light heart and gullibility, Faris had Hama's generosity and stubbornness.

Athena came to Damascus several times a month for work, so we met at the bus station to travel together to Homs. Buses, not trains, connected different parts of the country. (Sometimes I wondered if this was to keep Syrians less easily connected.) While we waited for the bus to arrive, fanning ourselves in the heat, we overheard a man say that the Ba'ath Party newspaper was reporting that in Hama and Homs "ID-card killings" had started to occur. That was something that had happened during Lebanon's civil war, when people were executed for being the "wrong" religion after they presented their ID card at checkpoints. Athena couldn't help herself and told him that could not be true, before catching herself. While the Syrian national ID card does not mention religion, there had been in previous weeks sectarian killings between Sunnis and Alawites.

Before we boarded the bus, she told me to pretend I was sleeping for the two-hour trip, so no one would hear my accent, which eventually always came out. She would handle giving my ticket to the bus driver when he came back to collect them. She would also show him my Syrian ID if he asked for it, or in case there were any checkpoints along the way.

I slouched a bit in my seat and dropped my head to the side. From behind my large dark sunglasses I looked out the window. If I expected to get on a highway, the kind that would facilitate travel between major Syrian cities, I was about to be reminded how little had changed in Syria. After forty years in power, the regime had failed to make important infrastructure improvements—which I was beginning to suspect was by design.

Soon we were passing through Harasta, where car dealerships and flush showrooms had opened, taking advantage of the town's location just outside the capital, its cheaper real estate, and its location on the main artery north. I had already looked there for appliances and furnishings for the ongoing renovation. While Syrian consumers had welcomed relaxed access to foreign goods, the private Syrian investors who owned the dealerships or franchises, of course, still had to share their profits with the Assad family or others close to the regime. Consumerism seemed to be the regime's preferred opiate, a substitution for real reform or change. From Harasta we made our way north, passing through Adra (home to the prison of the same name, where political prisoners are forgotten), and several other towns before arriving on the periphery of Homs.

Since mid-March, regime security forces and troops had surrounded Homs, and several residents had been killed, many shot at Saturday funerals for protesters who had been killed during Friday demonstrations—the week now had a certain routine. In recent weeks, the regime had been tightening its grip, arresting scores of people in house-to-house raids. The sound of gunfire was now frequent enough that Athena said she and Faris could tell what sort of weapon had been fired and how far away it was. They had learned when to stay inside, and when the risk outside was manageable.

Bashar al-Assad's wife—Asma—originally hailed from Homs. His marriage to a woman from a prominent Sunni family was meant to help assuage the tensions that kept arising over an Alawite family ruling over a Sunni-majority country.

We arrived in the city by 3 p.m. and went straight to Athena's house. If Hama's defining feature was its beautiful waterwheels, then Homs was known for its characteristic black stone. Quarried from volcanic rock in the Basalt Desert, it has been used as building material for centuries. Old traditional-style houses, churches, and mosques in Homs have been built with it. I caught glimpses of it as we passed through town.

Athena and Faris lived in a mixed neighborhood—Sunni and Christian. Their apartment was large, and their only son had moved out after getting married. We ate a modest lunch together and took siesta. I had reluctantly finally given in to this. Siesta in Syria is not a mere short nap. It's a two-hour pause in the day. There are many reasons to do it, particularly in the summer. It can be too hot to make being outside pleasant. And before air conditioning, it wasn't really pleasant to be moving. More convincingly, everything is closed and everyone else is sleeping. Syria and Syrians are very nocturnal, and since one will be staying up late anyway, a long siesta helps keep a body rested. I came to appreciate how it also reset the day and how in Syria, the days thus happen twice.

But with the risk of violence increasing, the central part of the city already, for the most part, no longer reopened for the evening. Athena, however, determined that I would still get a glimpse of what normal life in Homs was like, took me to the nearby Hotel Safir following our nap. Hotels in the Middle East are spaces for the locals as much as for out-of-towners. Syrians like to go to hotels. They have coffee, order food, or sit on the verandas or poolside and smoke a cigarette or *argheeleh*, the waterpipe.

The sun had yet to set, and those fasting would have not eaten or drunk anything since it had risen. We took a table on the deck of the pool, in which no one was swimming. It was already dusk, and other patrons who had ordered juice (or beer) were counting down the moments until the mosques would let us all know the sun had set.

We didn't linger much longer. The rules of engagement then were still relatively clear. Weapons would only come out after the fast had broken and night had taken over. It was a short visit to the hotel, but I imagined it was something Athena would treat visitors to back when people still visited Homs from outside. It felt like a performance of normality, even as it was slipping away, and giving way to a new one. In those early days, visible evidence of the growing conflict in these central parts of town was still hard to see, but it was there in the altered rhythms of the city.

Athena was apologetic that we wouldn't be able to stay out during the night, which was when Syria used to come alive, especially during the summer and during Ramadan. She outlined for me all that we would see the next day—she'd show me Homs as she knew it and loved it, all her favorite things. She promised to show me the souk, which was miniature compared to Damascus's but special nonetheless; the old Christian neighborhood, the Hamidiyeh, where my grandfather Ameen was from; the church of *Um al-Zanaar* (Mother of the Belt), which housed a relic believed to be the Virgin Mary's belt; and the Agha restaurant, located in a refurbished 150-year-old house. It would be a beautiful guided tour, ominously prescient that many of these places would only be preserved in memory.

But for the evening we'd stay in. We quickly made it back to Athena's house. The prayers would be ending soon, as well as the breaking of the fast, and the men would spill out of the mosque or their homes into the street. To socialize, to protest, or just to get from point A to B.

At home, Athena and Faris changed into their house clothes and slippers and we all met back in the living room. Usually they'd sit on the balcony and enjoy the breeze. But now they stuck to the relative safety of their living room.

"The symphony will start soon," Faris deadpanned, gesturing with his head to the balcony and the street behind him. We had left the sliding doors open to let the fresh air in.

Almost on cue a few gunshots sounded. Then a barrage of automatic gunfire. I was slightly startled, but Athena and Faris didn't flinch. He looked up at me from his newspaper and said, "Even if there are things that are wrong in this country—and there are—this is not the way to approach the regime."

I asked him what other recourse the people had. But then the house phone rang. "*Ahlayn, ahlayn*," Athena said, answering the phone—Welcome, welcome. "How are you? When did you get back?"

The gunfire got louder, and she raised her voice to be heard and to hear. "Hello?"

As her ears readjusted to the competing sounds, those from outside and the one inside her receiver, she said, "You were saying? Yes, go on."

11

PSYCHODRAME

Damascus, August 2011

O NE SUNDAY DURING RAMADAN, MY YOUNGEST COUSIN, TALA, suggested I accompany her to see the Jesuits. She was sure I'd be interested in their *psychodrame*.

"What's that?" I asked, unfamiliar with the French term and generally uninterested in anything church-related.

"A place to talk about fear," she said.

I did a quick search online and found out that psychodrama (as it's called in English) is a method of psychotherapy, often done in a group, that uses role-play and spontaneous dramatization to probe participants' lives—their worries, anxieties, and any other issues.

Tala was right; I was super-intrigued. In Syria, very few people readily admit to needing mental health care, let alone seeking it, largely because, as in other societies, it carries a stigma. In the context of what was happening in Syria, where the collective anxiety, anger, and sadness was inextricably related to what was happening in the country, a public discussion seemed pretty bold, even subversive. Of course, the *mukhabarat* would know this was happening.

Tala was currently enrolled in three universities. She was studying economics at the public University of Damascus; marketing at a newly opened private institute; and music at the conservatory. A pianist, she was going to the small Jesuit church to accompany the chorus on organ.

We had long finished lunch at her house, where she lived with her parents and two elder sisters—one a doctor and the other a pharmacist. They lived in the house that my paternal grandparents had moved to in the 1960s. Their middle-class neighborhood, the Tijara, was just north of the Qasour, where Sa'ad lived. At the foot of their building was the *mu'assissah*, where people came to buy subsidized fruits and vegetables. Not far was a public garden where my uncle took his daily walks, and there was a bakery near the neighborhood mosque known for its delectable *ka'ak* (sesame-covered breadsticks).

My uncle Majed had earned a doctorate in engineering in Germany—like my fathers' two eldest brothers. His wife, Randa, had also finished her medical training in Germany. But unlike my other uncles, who had chosen to live their lives in Germany, Majed and Randa had returned to the country they loved and wanted to raise their children in it. Now in their sixties, they had been looking forward to their golden years, to their daughters' marriages, and to grandchildren. They both still worked—he at the university as a professor and also in his own engineering firm, and she as a pathologist at a nearby hospital.

Majed waved me off each time I suggested he needed a plan B, given current events in Syria. He believed everything was about to be resolved—at the next UN meeting, after the next US election, at the next Arab summit. He thought nothing was in Syrian hands, not even the regime. His daughters were a bit less sure. They had reason to doubt the state's version of events. A common refrain was that the protesters were violent jihadists. But a good friend of theirs had just been taken days earlier by the regime. She was caught handing out pamphlets. She was also Christian. No one knew yet where she was and what might happen to her.

Just as the city was starting to wake again, Tala and I made our way to the Jesuit offices and small chapel. The sun had still not set, and during the month of Ramadan, when many people kept the fast or kept the illusion of keeping the fast, the streets were generally empty.

The chapel was sparse and modern, unlike most other Syrian churches. Tala played the organ beautifully, but I was eager for the Mass to end; when it did, we all headed downstairs to the meeting space. There were refreshments and conversation. Eventually, we were invited to take our seats; by then, others had joined us, people of different faiths. I found out later that the group was 60 percent Muslim and 40 percent Christian. There were in fact Sunnis, Druze, and Alawites there. Most people appeared to be in their thirties.

The same priest who had officiated Mass, Father Mazen, stood before us—without his vestments, only his collar identified him as clergy. In addition to being a priest, he was a psychotherapist and had studied in France. With Hala, another psychotherapist, they had started the psychodrama the month before to give people an opportunity to talk about their fears in the face of an impending unknown, where violence was already promising to play a big part.

I looked around almost in disbelief at how many people were there—they easily numbered fifty.

Father Mazen began with some introductory remarks—reminding those gathered that we weren't there to discuss politics, but rather people's fears and feelings. That seemed impossible, but perhaps the disclaimer was an effort to persuade the informants present (surely they were there) of the innocence of the project. If the informants and *mukhabarat* were, as was said, not particularly sophisticated, I figured there was a chance the simple ruse might work.

Father Mazen then called for volunteers to start off the role-play, the main therapeutic vehicle of psychodrama. It was up to the participants to decide what form it should all take. Three men and three women volunteered, and they each took a chair in the circle at the front of the room. Anyone else who wanted to could join the circle at any point in time. They would have thirty minutes, at which point Father Mazen would tell them the time was up.

A man (Man 1) carrying worry beads in one hand began. He had a suggestion: "We've been going around and around about who has been shot, who's armed. Let's instead talk about the opposite of fear—dreams. Let's talk about our dreams for the future. What are our dreams?"

"How would we do that?" asked another man (Man 2). "What's the scenario? The context for this conversation?"

"We could pretend we are being interviewed about our dreams," Man 1 responded.

A woman (Woman 1) spoke up: "It's hard for us to dream given what we are seeing. My biggest dream is for the killing to stop; I can't dream past this."

"Actually, before this [the conflict], I couldn't talk about my dreams," said Man 2.

Another woman (Woman 2) joined in: "Even if we are afraid to dream, we can close our eyes and imagine. It can help us escape."

The last woman (Woman 3) added: "It's relevant—we can talk about how we dream change to happen. Because change is frightening."

But then Man 2 objected to the idea of an interview. It wouldn't be a real conversation, he said. He looked to Father Mazen for guidance, but the priest did not interfere.

After some back and forth, they decided to pretend they were attendees of a conference for Syrians to discuss their dreams for the future.

Conferences in the Middle East—photographs of which are oddly in society and airline magazines—are often more about prepared presentations than free-flowing discussions. In Syria, they are also frequently held under the auspices of a ministry or the First Lady. It seemed the most stilted way to imagine how such a conversation could happen. I felt sad that they couldn't come up with another, less official scenario where ordinary Syrians would be speaking openly about their dreams and hopes for the future.

"Then we need to represent different groups—the youth, the government, the revolution, civil society," said Woman 1.

Man 1, not to be dissuaded by the rejection of his interview idea, made himself a sort of moderator. "Welcome to the conference," he announced. "We're going to talk about Syria's future and what we most want to see in our country."

"Can I begin?" asked Woman 3.

The moderator man nodded in encouragement.

"I'm keen to see how we teach change; that's what's killing us. There's a military structure to our education—from how books are written to how questions are asked," she said. "I want to destroy and rip apart the current books."

"But there are some positive results in our education," the conference moderator said. "Engineering, for example."

"I think it starts from the mother-child relationship," said Woman 2. "That's the basis of society. I dream of paying more attention to our girls from the start. After all, they will become mothers and raise our children."

"What you are talking about is making a cultured, enlightened society—that's not just education," said Man 2. "It's in the upbringing."

Then the woman who said she couldn't dream past wanting the violence to end, Woman 1, decided to represent civil society. "Civil society needs to be stronger," she said. "People start out wanting to do something for their country. But when we realize it's for nothing, we stop thinking to try, to do. It does start from how we educate. You're forbidden to exercise your mind, to think. If a child asks the teacher questions, he yells at you, shuts you up, and tells you just to memorize. Something starts from there, from when we are being told not to think, not to express what's inside of us."

The third man, Man 3, who had yet to speak, said, "I want to be like Europe in some way—advanced, with liberties and freedoms. But I also fear its bad sides, like their societal ills."

Man 2 then announced he'd represent the regime, and I caught my breath.

He spoke at length. "Look at this society, the people. The taxi driver is a thief. The bureaucrat, the cop—they take bribes. We have an elite. These people can think and organize our lives, tell us what our dreams are. You, don't bother yourselves with your dreams, we will organize your dreams for you. Otherwise, with this guy and his dream from here, this other guy from there, there will be chaos. The people [Syrians] are incapable; their thoughts and feelings are not good—"

Woman 3 interrupted him: "How can we know who these elite are?"

He ignored her: "—with the international conspiracy against Syria and the armed groups—they will get the advantage."

I had heard this before, of course. The insinuation from members of the regime that they were the best Syria could do—because otherwise the masses, unsophisticated as they were, would ruin the country—was an integral basis of its power and Syrians' acquiescence to them. It was built on an idea that Syrians needed to fear other Syrians. Because points of national dialogue were heavily monitored, and because geography and class kept Syrians from each other, no one would ever really know where reality stood exactly. And in that vacuum, the regime continued to play on such fears.

"Why are there weapons if all they want is reform?" the role-playing government man asked, echoing the constant rhetoric of state channels. Then, tongue-in-cheek, he said, "You want reforms? We've been talking about reforms for thirty years, so obviously we have no problem with reforms."

Everyone began to laugh, and someone shouted that it had been forty years.

"We're ready for more reforms," he continued. "We'll give you more banks and Internet, but not too much, because then the bad ideas will get in and there will be chaos, people will attack each other. Western ideas will get in, and then, there is the CIA, the Mossad. The Saudis hate us, the Turks hate us, half of Lebanon hates us, three-quarters of Iraq does, and all the rest. It's a really big conspiracy."

There was more laughter at the easily recognizable and almost spot-on mimicking of the regime.

He continued, "If you want to dream . . . I want to dream with you. But without you dreaming. That's the way. Do you know another way? If there's something wrong we can change it—education system, politics, economy."

Even though it was an absurd statement, Woman 2 engaged him: "Yes, but who gets to decide what's wrong?"

He waved her off easily—his script was ready made, so loud and unchallenged was the regime's messaging in Syria.

At this point the mood changed from laughter—there was something cathartic in being able to mock the regime—to anxiety and frustration.

Woman 3 beseeched him, "*Ya istaz,*" she said, calling him "professor," as Syrians do as a sign of respect. "I don't want to change the wrong; I want to change, I want to change!" Raising her voice slightly, she said, "I want to try, I want to do, move—try another way."

The man trying to moderate the conference asked her for patience (as many Syrians were asking of those more willing to confront the regime), but she interrupted him: "People can't learn if they don't try!"

To me, she sounded like a teenager nearing adulthood and asserting herself to her parents. I had been that teenager in my day, though the regime didn't appear to be acting out of an instinct to protect Syrians as much as maintain their power. I could see her asking to be seen as more than just a child, but then she turned to the moderator and said, "I want to ask him—does he allow us to dream? Can we dream or not?"

I winced; there it was, that infantilizing of adults. The pretend government man ignored her.

"I don't see how the two roads can converge," Woman 2 addressed the moderator. "He's telling us not to dream."

The government man answered. "All of us want what is best for our country, isn't that correct? We don't need foreign ideas as to how to do it."

This set off Woman 3 again. "I'm against the fact that each time we open a bit we say that 'it's from Europe.' A human on his own can't see and think thoughts? Why can't our ideas be ours? Why do we instead dismiss such thoughts with 'Oh, you like foreigners?' We're not foreigners, but what if we are? Why this fear of the foreigner, of the other? Why not open toward people? They're people like us—they're not beasts; all people have good ideas."

Woman 1 challenged her: "We fear anyone who is different from us. We can't accept our own differences: How can we accept others?"

Woman 3 continued, "As if there's only one way. There's no brain in that."

While she became increasingly agitated, the government man kept his cool. "Can this *sha'ab* [people, masses] dream? Do they deserve democracy? Freedom?"

"That's the question," said the pretend moderator.

Imitating a common refrain, the government man added, "When the demonstrators are asked, 'Why are you demonstrating?' they say they're out there because they're being paid—Is that democracy? Those people don't deserve democracy. Syrians can't even stand in line; our nature is *fawda* [chaos]."

Woman 3 continued to engage him: "I want to reach a point of understanding, commonality—you don't want us to dream? Or we can dream, but only after you give us permission if it's a correct dream—right?"

"Right."

"You have to approve?" she asked again.

"Yes, yes, correct."

Man 3, who had been long silent, finally blurted out, "Who are you to make these decisions?"

"Are you the father?" asked Woman 2.

Reformulating something he had said earlier, the pretend government man said coolly, assertively, and with finality, "Don't dream. We will dream for you."

Father Mazen raised his hand—thirty minutes had passed. The participants moved their chairs back into the bigger group and the feedback portion began. First the participants would give their reactions, and then everyone else would be invited to join in.

The pretend government man wanted to speak. "That was not my real opinion, but I wanted to represent that point of view. Right now, I can't think of bringing a child into this situation. Once I felt I could dream, I could think of children. I don't fear dreaming. I fear the end of dreaming completely. I want to hope for a day where we can say, 'Come, let's do something, let's build.' Where we can have results here. Why is it that only when a Syrian leaves Syria, he can have results?"

Woman 1 reiterated what she had said at the start. "The very idea of dreaming is distant. I can't live in a dream; a dream is beautiful, I can't associate it with this period. I feel responsible for my family. I didn't feel like I could enter role-play."

Woman 3, the one who had argued the most with the government representative, then spoke. "What bothered me wasn't what he was saying. I'm used to these opinions. What bothered me was how important he made himself. The rest of us couldn't talk to each other anymore. I thought about how we have someone in our house like this. It angered me that we allowed him to take over, that we couldn't put him to the side and talk to each other. He had taken the whole space; he was central."

"So why didn't you tell him?" asked Father Mazen. "Why did you wait for someone else to?"

She paused and thought. "I don't know. I didn't want to get into it because it's never a real conversation; it's not give and take. It's just rhetoric. I don't want to talk to him," she said. Pausing again, she added, "I wanted someone to talk to me. But no one is talking to me."

Woman 2 also answered Father Mazen. "I did in the role-play what I am trying to do in my life. I want to like the other so I can reach a recognition, a point to agree on." Turning to the man who role-played the regime, she pleaded, "You wouldn't even let us dream."

The man who barely participated, Man 3, said, "I didn't like him. I felt he blocked the conversation. I didn't like his role-play. I was eager to talk about how we can change things; instead we couldn't. But maybe we will have to work on ourselves, by ourselves, and that would be beneficial."

"Correct," agreed the man who played the moderator. "If the government falls and creates a vacuum, we will need to fill it with conversations of our dreams. We need to be ready, to imagine what to do if the time comes."

"We don't want to eliminate him," said Woman 3. "He, too, is a part of our society."

A man from outside the circle then spoke. Gesturing to Woman 3, he said, "She called him *istaz*. Why do we respect the person with authority? It really bothers me that no one can stop him," he said, using the present tense, as if he knew such a person in real life. "I was shaking. It was the first time I thought of getting up and confronting him, the first time I thought of getting up and telling him he's not someone to dictate."

More voices began to chime in, some with observations, others with reactions, still others with their current fears. Many voices quivered as they spoke. Some with what seemed to be anger, others anxiety.

"I don't know if I can't dream or can't feel."

"We're on a path, but to where? I fear this path, and where it will lead, and will it lead all people? There's too much chaos. Too many unknowns."

"The focus on the government man, that's something in our nature. We laughed at the caricature, but his words should be red lines."

"I wanted to hear, was waiting to hear, the dreams. He canceled even uttering a dream. He killed the dream of all who want to help in new Syria."

"Let's stop looking for where we differ; let's look for where we agree. The role-play started so nice, discussing education. The big wound for me is that we are seeing how much we differ. The picture we had of Syria is upside-down; now we see blood. Is this our culture?"

"Only he who tries can dream. Those who dream went to the streets— they'll die, but at least they're not just going along."

"We've minimized the role of the father in the family; the revolution eliminates the role of law. Where are we going? Let's be patient. When I think of doing something I think of doing something with little blood."

The man who represented the regime, after listening closely, then spoke: "I only wanted to show reality. I wasn't trying to stop the conversation. I was strong because you were weak, not because I am strong. I wanted to show what we have to go through."

At that point, the other psychotherapist shared her observations: "Even in a country where mental health care is stigmatic, we still are more willing to participate in group therapy than open political conversation. Why? We fear differing too much; you didn't want to fight even though there was difference and disagreement, and in the process your dreams weren't really spoken of."

"The man who role-played the regime had no weapon to silence you here, he didn't threaten you," added Father Mazen. "You silenced yourselves."

೮૪૭

"So much for not talking politics," I said to my cousin once we were alone in her car.

"I knew you'd like it," she smiled at me.

"Yes, that was the most compelling time I've ever had in church," I said. "Finally, a priest living his faith rather than just performing its rituals."

She laughed and then fiddled with the old car until it started.

The psychodrama hadn't been fun; in fact, it had been deeply disturbing. But there was something refreshing in how truthful it felt. Unlike many of my interactions and observed interactions with strangers in Damascus so far, this hadn't felt like a performance—even as it was role-playing. I was also saddened by the fact that that the situation was such that Syrians had no forum in which they could talk directly to each other about what was happening in their country. At the psychodrama, they were only able to begin to talk to each other by pretending to be just pretending.

The session had effectively captured so many of the dynamics of Ba'athist society in Syria for these past decades. It was stunning to see adults infantilized in a moment, at the mere suggestion of the regime—and this wasn't even a real interaction with it.

I hoped for Father Mazen's sake that the disclaimer of psychodrama not being political and only a place to talk about fear would work. Because what I saw felt very subversive, especially as it was happening right under the regime's nose.

෧෬

LATER THAT FALL, Hala, one of the psychodrama founders, had my aunt and uncle over for lunch in Damascus. They were friends, as Suha's husband, Kamal, was also a psychiatrist. Hala, a woman in her sixties, was leaving later that day for Europe to visit her daughter, who was about to give birth. Lunch, Suha later told me, was delightful, and she was happy Hala would soon meet her grandchild.

But Hala never made her flight. At the airport, before she could board, she was taken.

The place to speak about fear immediately disbanded, because people were too afraid to come, even though Father Mazen would have gone on. He did continue to see patients for individual therapy.

Hala's disappearance tortured Suha and Kamal, and my aunt often invoked Hala's sixty-eight-day detention as she warned me over and over not to do anything to catch the regime's eye, and better yet, to just leave. Suha would grab a fistful of her hair at the top of her head and tug it, telling me, "I can't be dragged by my hair across the floor. I just can't," referring to what we had heard about the treatment of women in detention by the *mukhabarat*.

"That's what they will do," she warned me. "They will take all of us if you do something."

12

FATHERLAND

Damascus, November 2011

M Y FATHER ARRIVED IN DAMASCUS THE FIRST WEEK OF NOVEM-
ber 2011 to oversee the final payments for the renovation of Salma's house.

It was his longing for Syria, fueled by fantasies of long stays in Damascus,
that had been the driving force for getting Hassan out. He wanted to work as
a doctor with patients in the country that had educated him for free. After
our family trip in 2004, my father had returned again in 2008, and it looked
to him then that Syria was improving. Private universities were opening up,
people seemed to have more wealth, and the country appeared to be stable.
By the time he arrived in 2011, eight months after the first protests, 3,000
Syrians were dead.

The government had continued to use lethal force to stamp out protests
and to lay siege to restive cities. Formal agents of the regime—the police, the
army, and the *mukhabarat*—were aided by pro-regime militias. (In Arabic,
they were called *shabiha*, meaning "ghosts.") But some anti-regime Syrians
had taken up arms as well—by October, 10,000 Syrian officers and soldiers
had allegedly defected from the armed forces and coalesced around the new
Free Syrian Army (FSA). Based in Turkey, the FSA had called on officers

and men of the Syrian Army to join in its cause: to overthrow the regime and protect the protesters.

As counterintuitive as it may be, this seemed to suit the regime. Its primary strategy thus far appeared to be to make it too perilous for Syrians to object to its rule or to get Syrians to resort to weapons. If enough did, their actions would simply validate the regime's narrative that it was not opposing nonviolent Syrian protesters but defending the country from an armed, foreign-funded, terrorist insurgency. It was maddening. Those who took up weapons walked right into the trap—even if their intentions were honorable. Others opposed engaging the regime militarily precisely because they understood that was what the regime most wanted. This group included activists and other early protesters, dissidents, and opposition members within the country. They knew the regime was much more terrified of a peaceful uprising, but that in the murkiness of moral ambiguity, it could thrive.

In the month before my father arrived, the UN Security Council had tried to pass a resolution condemning the violence, but both Russia and China had vetoed it (just as the United States often did for Israel). Toward the end of the month, the United States had recalled its ambassador because of threats to his safety. Then Syria agreed to a plan by the Arab League to halt the violence and to dialogue with the opposition within two weeks, though many doubted (myself included) that the government would change its tactics so abruptly. Indeed, in the few days between the plan's announcement and my father's arrival, 240 more Syrians were killed, mostly in Homs, which by then had emerged as the focal point of the uprising, becoming an urban battlefield.

My father's trip had gotten off to a bumpy start. He had flown in via Istanbul, landing in Damascus well after midnight. I had returned to the region from a trip to the United States a few days before my father, but to Beirut. I was still convinced that flying directly to Damascus on an international flight would draw too much attention. I'd be arriving via land a few hours after him. My father had told both of his brothers, as well as my mother's brother, what time he was arriving. He exited customs expecting to find them waiting for him. Instead, no one was there.

My father didn't have a cell phone that worked in Syria and didn't have anyone's number readily accessible. He prided himself on being a Luddite and never expected that no one would show up. He tried to keep his cool, even as men he called "Syrian secret agents" kept approaching him and asking, "Are you okay, 'Amo?" (calling him "Uncle," as is the Syrian way).

Every few minutes, a different one would walk up to him.

"Are you sure someone is coming for you, '*Amo?*"

"Do you want us to call someone, '*Amo?* Just tell us their names and numbers." (No one ever said they were subtle.)

My father wasn't afraid—"as a son of the Midan," as he liked to say, he feared nothing. He also thought they were being sincere in wanting to help him—after all, what could they possibly want from him? Having left Syria when he did, he didn't fully understand that these interactions were never innocent.

As it turned out, Sa'ad was late because his car, the old 1993 Dacia, had broken down along the dark road to the airport. He had called a friend to come, and together they fixed the car, finally arriving hours later. My father, meanwhile, calmly waited outside the entire time, his trench coat draped over his arm, his suitcase by his side.

By the time I arrived from Beirut later that morning, he was still in bed, exhausted from his trip. But he was already fixated on sleeping in the Tahaan as soon as possible. My father saw that house as *his* house—it was his money alone that had gotten Hassan out and renovated it—and he wanted to stay there and not anywhere else. He was never comfortable being a guest in someone else's home. I think it required too much intimacy and the sort of niceties he wasn't particularly good at performing. Which is why, despite his long-held belief that he could have been successful in Syria, I was less sure. Performances—like joining the Ba'ath Party even if you didn't believe in it—struck me as necessary.

Indeed, when he had visited Syria in 2008 for Christmas—his first since 1969, when he had left Damascus for America—he had refused to stay with any relatives, instead opting to rent a room in the old folks home run by the Orthodox Church. It wasn't any cheaper than the nice hotels, but he figured he'd rather his money go to the church. He had been supporting two orphanages run by the archdiocese for years.

When I had seen my father in the United States earlier that month, I had overheard him on the phone with the contractor discussing final details and payments. He had always ended these calls with, "But it will be ready when I come, right?"

"Don't count on it," I would tell him when he put the receiver down, much to his ire.

In my absence, the renovation had slowed down, though the contractor would tell my parents otherwise. When I had returned from Damascus to

Baltimore that fall, I warned my parents repeatedly that the engineer was, best-case scenario, being overly optimistic about what he would accomplish in time for my father's upcoming trip. But having a home in Damascus was an obsession for my father, so much so that he couldn't conceive of it not happening. He didn't want to even consider that the growing violence in Syria might prevent him from returning again, either to the house or to the country.

On the morning of his arrival, as we had our first coffee together in Damascus, he declared that his first priority was to get the apartment—still an uncompleted renovation site—cleaned. He was unconcerned that it would be dirtied again.

So we went to the Midan and bought mops, brooms, buckets, and detergents for the cleaners he'd hire. He also bought a folding laundry drying rack.

"Do we need this now?" I challenged him.

"Yes, of course. We are going to have to wash the sheets and towels," he said. (We didn't have any sheets or towels, let alone beds or mattresses.)

The cleaning squad that showed up consisted of two men in their twenties who lived in Harasta, a suburb where residents had protested the regime. Both of them were as lean as boys; one had a deformity of his hand but wielded the mop like a virtuoso. They rolled up their pants and worked barefoot; cleaning the apartment took them seven hours. My father stayed with them as they worked. Despite being an expat, a professional, and comparatively wealthy, he had never stopped seeing himself as the son of a poor carpenter.

If my father had been ashamed of it growing up, coming from poverty had long become a badge of honor for him—so much so that he didn't ever want his children to learn how to play tennis or golf, because those were the sports of the rich. How poor my father had been as a child was a constant part of the narrative we heard growing up—for a long time, we didn't know anyone who had known him as a child, so all we knew was what he told us.

And he told us how, on the rare occasions when his mother cooked meat, neither of his parents had eaten any—it was just for the six children. He remembered with bitterness how in school, when it was cold, a better-off boy had gloves to warm his hands, but he did not. In my father's telling, that particular boy was also terrible at school, while my father was always at the top of his class—for him, these two facts were intimately related. When as a little boy he'd harangue his parents as to why their family was poor, his father would tell him how, when they had come from (modern-day) Lebanon, their vast lands had been stolen. His mother, Alia before me, on her more generous days, attributed it to luck and Allah. But often enough she'd also imply that it was her husband's fault: although he was a talented artisan (the pieces I'd seen were clearly the work of a master), he didn't have a real mind for business.

My father's affinity with the poor had followed him into his medical practice in the United States, where he often didn't charge those who couldn't pay. He was like Salma in this way. His generosity, like hers, was rooted in solidarity, and, like her, he didn't feel sized up by those who were less well off the way he did by the wealthy.

For lunch, my father went to fetch *shawarma* sandwiches for the Harasta men, bringing two for each man.

When they finally took a break, they each ate only one. They wrapped what was left carefully and asked if they could take the rest home.

༄

A WEEK INTO my father's visit to Damascus, the Arab League moved to suspend Syria's membership from the organization. Assad had refused to stop using violence against civilians who were merely demonstrating, despite agreeing just ten days before to do so. (The Arab League itself is by no means a bastion of moral authority.) It gave him four more days to comply with the plan's original requirements—to halt the violence directed toward civilians, withdraw all security forces from civilian areas, and release the tens of thousands of political prisoners. Government newspapers in Syria criticized the Arab League's decision and suggested that the organization be renamed the "American League." Several thousand Syrians attacked the embassies and consulates of Turkey, Qatar, Saudi Arabia, and France, countries that for months had already been among the principal villains in the regime's narrative of a foreign-funded insurgency.

In Damascus, pro-regime supporters threw stones and bottles at the Turkish embassy, burning Turkish flags and pictures of Mustafa Kemal Atatürk, before the Syrian police intervened. At the Turkish consulate in Aleppo, crowds tried to enter the grounds and lower the Turkish flag, but failed. Another group attacked the honorary Turkish consulate in the coastal city of Latakia, breaking windows and burning flags. Mobs armed with sticks and knives also attacked the Saudi and Qatari embassies in Damascus, as well as the French consulate in Latakia. At the Saudi embassy, which was near

Assad's office in the Abu Rumanneh neighborhood, hundreds shouting slogans in support of Assad beat a guard and broke into the building, shattering windows and causing other damage inside the compound. Another crowd forced its way into the Qatari embassy, where some protesters made it to the top of the building and replaced the Qatari flag with the Syrian one. And the next day, tens of thousands of government supporters poured into the main squares of several cities, expressing their anger at Arab officials and shouting their support of Assad.

The Arab League called for an immediate meeting of Syrian opposition leaders in Cairo, but the opposition was bitterly divided and had little on-the-ground legitimacy. The opposition and the international community (which desperately dressed the opposition up like a shadow state) had gotten ahead of themselves.

So had we. During all of this, my father and I were on a frantic shopping spree—even if the restoration of the house wasn't finished, we wanted to make it look like home. We went about acquiring all sorts of appliances and waited for them to be delivered at the Tahaan. Only after everything had been purchased did we panic—delivery trucks were never going to make it down the narrow street, let alone quickly unload all the large appliances before traffic was backed up to the top of the block, garnering unwanted attention.

In the end, our worries were quickly allayed: no delivery truck ever came. The first new purchase to arrive, the furnace, came strapped to a wooden board attached to a bicycle. "Syrian technology," my father laughed. The refrigerator, the dishwasher, and the washing machine (the item my father cared the most about) showed up in a miniature three-wheeled pick-up truck, all stacked on top of each other. The vehicle was small enough that—like a regular car—it could park half up on the sidewalk, pedestrians be damned. Then, one by one, while the driver remained behind with the goods, the deliveryman strapped each appliance to his back and walked them up to our floor.

While I was on the street watching this scene, bemused, a man casually came up to me.

"Who's moving in?" he wanted to know.

I had been caught off-guard, but before I could answer, he told me, "That's Lamya al-Hakim's house."

"Yes, I know," I said, wondering how *he* knew that. Maybe he was from the neighborhood?

"Are you renting from her?" he said.

"Excuse me?" I said. "What business of yours is that?"

"Well, she's not here. I don't see her," he said. Was he a neighbor? I wondered again, not sure whether to be rude or pleasant.

"I'm her daughter," I said, though I'm not sure why. Maybe I was asserting that I belonged, and I thought it would make him back off or at least tell me who he was. Or had I just given him more information than he already had?

He offered nothing about himself, and then my father summoned me from the balcony to come up and help with the placement of some of the appliances.

I walked back into the building, chastising myself almost immediately for not being particularly savvy. I told my aunt what had happened when I saw her on the landing, and she demanded an immediate description of the man, but couldn't be sure who he was.

Once the appliances were in place, we set out to get lighting. From the Tahaan, we walked down one evening to the Souk al-Kahraba, literally, the Electricity Market, a few alleyways where an assortment of chandeliers, lamps, sconces, lanterns, wiring, bulbs, and switches for every taste were sold. We'd do the same for doorknobs, bathroom hardware (towel racks, medicine closets, toilet paper holders), and kitchen accessories (cutlery, flatware, salt and pepper shakers), which each had their own souk.

Thematic shopping had its conveniences. It allowed us to see a wide variety of stores and their selections side by side and made it easier for us to negotiate prices (though it also made it easier for merchants to collude). Many of the merchants were from the Midan, and my father would excitedly seize on that fact to get a better price. But it also felt like he sometimes prolonged these interactions just to hear about the old neighborhood and reassert his sense of belonging to it.

Nostalgic conversations about the old neighborhood aside, we raced to complete the house so my father could stay there, at least for some days before his trip was over. And crucially, there could be no sleeping at the Tahaan without beds. My father's brother joined us for the mission of acquiring them: the sons of a carpenter, both of them loved furniture.

Majed was eager to take us to a Turkish store out in Harasta. As soon as we arrived there, I saw the army everywhere outside my car window. In America, a military uniform makes its wearer look neat and spiffy; these guys looked dirty and underfed instead. I couldn't help but think, as I looked at them, "What an army."

While I was curious to see this Turkish furniture showroom that Majed kept raving about, I also wondered if it was prudent to go there, given the anger of the regime and its supporters against Turkey. The country had quickly become one of the principal villains in the regime's narrative, which still contended that it was not pursuing and killing unarmed civilian protesters but vicious terrorists who were being given safe harbor in Turkey.

What a difference the past eight months had made. Before the first demonstrations had started, relations between Assad and Turkish prime minister Recep Tayyip Erdogan were so warm that the two heads of state had even vacationed together. But for most of their history as modern nation-states, Turkey and Syria had had a strained relationship. After the fall of the Ottoman Empire, Syria's time as part of it had come to be retold as one of Arab subjugation at the hands of Turkish rulers. There was also that matter of the Antakya region—which Syrian maps still showed to be a part of Syria. There were disputes over water as well, as upstream Turkey had constructed dams on both the Tigris and the Euphrates rivers. Hafez al-Assad had also sheltered Abdullah Öcalan, the leader of the Kurdistan Workers' Party, or PKK, for years. Relations had only begun to slowly improve in 1998 with his expulsion from Syria.

The real rapprochement between Turkey and Syria, however, had been recent, with a free trade agreement signed in 2004. To a person on the street, the thaw was evident: Turkish soap operas became a Syrian national pastime, and Turkish goods—like the furniture store in which we were now shopping—became available. My father had instantly dubbed it "Turkish IKEA."

We decided on a bedroom set, paid, and made arrangements for immediate delivery after siesta. As we left Harasta, I learned that my father's father had once had a workshop there. He had invented a machine that improved upon wheat cultivation, and was even awarded a limited patent. It had been his chance at redemption in his wife's eyes and a more lucrative career. But his attempts at mass production had failed.

Now his son—my father—could easily afford whatever he wanted from this Turkish IKEA of sorts, though none of it could ever rival his own father's craftsmanship. Yet with my father unwilling to squabble with his siblings over what remained after the death of their parents, he could also never possess any surviving work crafted by his own father's hand.

IN BETWEEN OUR manic shopping runs, my father constantly asked me, "What do you think will happen in Syria?" We had these conversations under our breath and often in English. Both in Syria and the United States, my father had always stayed away from politics. My mother, on the other hand, had joined my siblings and me several times at protests in the United States against Iraqi sanctions and the invasion of Iraq, for Palestinian rights, and so on. She had written letters to Congress and signed many petitions.

When I asked my father what he thought, he shared a memory from his high school days with me. One morning in 1960, the children were lined up single file in the schoolyard, being called by age group to their classrooms to start the day, beginning with the oldest. As a tenth grader, my father was still in the schoolyard when he heard a commotion from inside, and a twelfth grader came running back out, blood all over his face. The kids whose fathers were communists had beaten him up because his father was in a rival political party. For my father, that sealed the deal. He would not join any political party in Syria. Indeed, he had many such stories at the ready, specializing really in these sorts of single moments in which his views on vast subjects in life were neatly crystallized.

He even had one for Hafez al-Assad. Back in 1968, a year before my father left Damascus for America and two years before Hafez seized power, my father was something like the chief resident in the pediatric division at the university hospital. Around 4 p.m., two men all in black arrived via motorcycle. They wanted to know who was in charge of pediatrics, and my father presented himself. The men had a message from the minister of defense— Hafez al-Assad. They told my father they had been sent to inform him that Assad was gifting the hospital with two oxygen incubators for children. They had them with them, ready to deliver. It turned out that a few months before, a relative of Assad, a baby, had had a lung infection and had required such an incubator for treatment. To my father's knowledge, no hospital in Syria had one until Assad made the gift. So when my father heard a few years later, thousands of miles away in Baltimore, that the same minister had taken power in Syria, his first reaction had been "Hallelujah." Not that he was or ever became a fervent believer in Assad, but back then he figured if the guy cared enough to donate needed equipment for the benefit of everyone's children, then maybe there was something redeeming in him.

But my father's expectations weren't particularly high for Syrian leaders. He had been raised on a national narrative of persecution, the widely accepted idea that no leader could succeed as long as so many threatening powers had Syria and its people always in their crosshairs. As he once described it, the news in Syria was, "They want to eat us, they want to take our land, they want to shoot us"—with "they" being a combination of Israel, the United States, the Soviet Union, Turkey, and other Arab nations. He believed this, too, to some extent, but he also saw a lot of rot from inside Syria. As he told it, "Syria never had a break, and the people who never gave it a break were the insiders—coup after coup or the Ba'ath Party. Syria never had a government that could claim they were better than another."

He also asked me rhetorically once, "Do you really think the Alawites are alone in controlling Syria?" Of course I didn't. But I was still optimistic—then—that the status quo was untenable, that something would have to give. Was the regime really going to double down and just kill many of its own citizens? Displace them? Bring to fruition the nihilistic jihadist alternative (*badeel*) they had been threatening/promising? Would the world really let that happen? (Clearly, I was naïve. This was before I fully understood the lengths to which the regime and its primary backers, Iran and Russia, would go to maintain power. Or how unconstructive the international community would be.) I told my father I thought that eventually the regime would go—at least its symbolic head—but that the state apparatuses would remain, and that Syrians would take the reins, and it would all be okay.

Many of my father's relatives spent their time contradicting me when they had his ear at family gatherings—they were highly proficient in the regime's narrative and in geopolitical conspiracy theories. I don't fault them for their "analysis" now—I have come to believe that many of them already understood the regime and what it was capable of much better than I did. I also believe that a portion of them were suffering from the same kind of Stockholm Syndrome with which I had diagnosed others. Some actually fully believed the regime and its narratives; others knew it was prudent to just act like they believed it. Thus we had inane conversations over pistachios and beers in their living rooms. I was told more than once by some Christian relatives that they didn't need democracy if democracy meant gay marriage, which, thank god, Islamic law would never allow.

But it was through these relatives that we connected with Gabriel, the son-in-law of my father's cousin and an engineer who also did renovations. Both of us took a liking to him, and my father asked him (at my urging) to audit the restoration's expenditures and to arbitrate between us and the contractor (who I suspected was trying to rip us off). He agreed. When we met with him a few days later, he had run the numbers and receipts. He showed us what looked suspect to him. There were items we had been charged for that wouldn't have been needed in the quantities listed. While the overage was immediately clear to someone in the business, it wasn't to us.

I felt vindicated and relished how the crooked contractor was about to be finally held accountable. I didn't really care if he had been an acquaintance of my uncles or from the same church. But it rubbed my father's brothers the wrong way. They believed that we had to show *thiqa*, trust, in our contractor. After all, we had shaken hands with him. While Majed was fond of me, even when he disagreed with me, my other uncle was not. He had been the reason, all those decades ago, that my mother had broken off her engagement to my father.

One day, he joined us at Salma's house, walking around with his arms behind his back like an inspector. I was the only woman there, and he contradicted me at every turn, especially in front of the project manager. I could see my father was torn. As a father to three daughters, he had learned never to underestimate a woman's potential, and he had turned over what he had inherited from his parents to his only sister. But in that moment, in front of his brothers, my father took my uncle's view and rudely dismissed my counsel.

I was incensed. We were in Salma's house, and I was the only one there who was her blood relative. I walked away in a huff and left for Suha's apartment across the way. Happily, I found her there. She and Kamal had been joined by their good friend Amer. A transplant to Damascus from Qamishli, he was Kurdish, an ethnic minority that had been discriminated against by the modern Syrian state. As such, he was long politicized and able to have critical conversations about what was happening in the country.

I breathed a sigh of relief. Suha's house, like Salma's before it, was a place of ideas and openness. It was an oasis.

૭૪૪

THREE DAYS AFTER my father and I had gone to Harasta to shop at the Turkish IKEA, the Free Syrian Army struck the notorious Air Force Intelligence building there, its boldest attack yet, coming on the heels of an FSA ambush in Dara'a that reportedly left thirty-four government soldiers dead. The same day as the Harasta attack, several thousand people attended rallies in Damascus and Latakia in support of Bashar al-Assad, marking the anniversary of Hafez's seizure of power back in 1970. On the same day as the attacks and the rallies, France also recalled its ambassador, closed its consular offices in Aleppo and Latakia, and shut down its cultural institutes.

While that was a further sign of Syria's increasing political isolation, for people like Suha and Kamal, it felt like the walls had closed in around them just a little tighter. They loved to attend events at the cultural institutes. French friends and friends of friends traveling to Syria had often visited Suha and Kamal in Damascus. Kamal also went almost yearly to France for psychiatric conferences, and Suha eagerly awaited his return, when he would bring her souvenirs. Now these small outlets to the rest of the world—to moments of respite—were disappearing and being cut off to them.

Not by coincidence, the attacks and rallies came ahead of an Arab League emergency meeting in Morocco, where the League was scheduled to ratify the previous week's vote to suspend Syria. It would also discuss the possibility of taking further steps. Turkey, which was not a member, was also attending the meeting. There, the foreign ministers of Turkey and Qatar had harsh words for Syria; Syria, which did not attend the meeting, condemned the suspension as "shameful and malicious," accusing Arab countries of being conspirators with the West.

Between shopping, grimly following the news in the country, and fretting with Suha as to what would happen to Syrians as the world abandoned them, I received an email from a Turkish journalist and novelist urging me to come to Istanbul for an important trial.

᭢

BEFORE MY FATHER returned to the United States and before I went to Turkey, Suha's daughter, her only child, became engaged. Her fiancé was a charismatic, handsome, and quite successful diamond jeweler, who had spent many years growing up in California.

Suha and Kamal avoided a lot of the bourgeois circles in Damascus that many of Abdeljawwad's grandchildren belonged to. They weren't interested in their gossip or their incessant focus on appearances, wealth, and the orchestration of socially beneficial marriages. They had raised their daughter to value education and culture and to have a more cosmopolitan outlook. Suha had put off her own artistic ambitions and diverted almost all of her energies to raising her daughter, and I think she had hoped her daughter would become the working artist Suha had not. But her daughter gravitated toward those same circles Suha and Kamal had shunned. That may have been partly because of her impressive physical beauty. Slender, fair skinned, and blue eyed, their daughter had long, thick, straight black hair and a perfect nose, one that other girls referenced with their plastic surgeons.

On my last night in Damascus with my father, we went out to dinner with the daughters of Abdeljawwad's disowned son and bumped into Suha's daughter and fiancé. When I went over to their table to say hello and chat, I sat next to the fiancé's childhood friend, who mentioned he was ethnically Armenian. At some point, he said that he traveled frequently to Turkey. I found that curious—I asked him if his family came from Turkey originally, and then mentioned casually that I was going to go in the coming days. I left out the reasons why.

In the bathroom, my cousin reprimanded me, saying that no one needed to know anything about me or the fact that I was going to Turkey.

Wasn't that extra paranoid? I asked. The guy himself had just said he went there frequently.

She grabbed my wrist. "Yes, and he informs on people," she said. She was always prone to the dramatic, in grand diva style. (She demanded perfection in her appearance—a small tear in her nylons or a chip in her manicure was enough to send her household into crisis mode.) I dismissed her concerns and went back to my table.

The next day, at my father's final lunch and family visit in Syria, he announced that he would sleep at Salma's house and depart for the airport from *his* home. He had washed the new bed linens and towels and spread them on the newly arrived beds. His flight was in the dark hours before dawn the next morning. I left him to spend the night there alone. He slept a few hours, woke up, showered, and indeed left the country from the Tahaan.

Later that morning, I left for Beirut, and from there I went to Turkey to report a story about imprisoned journalists. I was very curious about this place that was being touted as a model for a post–Arab Spring future. For admirers in the Arab world, it was a path to emulate: economically successful, modern, powerful, and Muslim. And for those concerned by the success of Islamist parties at the ballot box, Turkey's ruling party appeared to offer a comforting model of what Islamist political parties and leaders could look like. But for many who would hear I had gone to Istanbul, it was more confirmation that I was likely a spy.

The same day I left for Turkey, Syrian soldiers attacked a convoy carrying Turkish pilgrims returning from Mecca. (Turkey had already long been warning its citizens not to visit Syria.) They had been stopped at a checkpoint near Homs, and once they were known to be Turks, Syrian soldiers had emerged from behind the sandbags, cursed the Turkish prime minister, and opened fire. Amazingly, no one was killed.

But other things happened that day that in retrospect portended what was to come. The severely mutilated body of a Syrian journalist who had been filming antigovernment protests in the Homs governorate was found in town on the side of a road. His eyes had reportedly been gouged out (Syrian *mukhabarat* are not subtle in their symbolism). And the offices of the ruling Ba'ath Party in Damascus had come under rocket-propelled grenade attack, hinting at a shift toward a protracted armed struggle. November was by then the bloodiest month yet, with 3,500 dead.

When I returned to Beirut from Istanbul, Suha's daughter asked me to cool my heels there. Her fiancé's friend had asked her too many questions about why I had gone to Turkey.

13

IN THE CARDS

Damascus, December 2011

I RETURNED TO DAMASCUS IN EARLY DECEMBER, AND WHEN I crossed the border from Lebanon, it felt as if the world outside disappeared behind me more quickly than usual. In Beirut, the morning had been sunny, but as we climbed toward the Syrian border, we drove straight into gray clouds. On the Syrian side, rain was coming down in fits and starts.

My trip to Turkey had started off with Erdogan issuing his harshest words yet for Bashar al-Assad. He compared him to Hitler, Mussolini, and Romania's Nicolae Ceausescu. He also warned Assad that he should learn from what had just happened to former Libyan leader Moammar Gadhafi, who had been ousted from power and unceremoniously killed. "For the welfare of your own people and the region," Erdogan had advised, "just leave that seat."

Yet in Turkey, I had interviewed lawyers, human rights activists, Kurdish activists, journalists, and the family members of imprisoned journalists who felt Erdogan's words were rife with hypocrisy. He might not have been mowing down his citizens by the thousands, but he was consolidating his power in an arguably antidemocratic manner. Those worries were finding little room in the global narrative about Turkey, which was being exalted as a model for how Islam-based politics could be compatible with democracy. More realistically, NATO member Turkey was also being eyed as a Muslim alternative to Iran and its influence in the region, specifically in Syria. When I asked the wife of one the most prominent jailed journalists if she thought Turkey was a model for the post–Arab Spring Arab world, she told me, "I hope the Arab Spring is the model for us."

When we reached Damascus, the rain was a reminder that it was now winter. My father had left with the last few days of fall, and gone with him were the manic but easily filled hours. The days were short and all too quickly turned into night. People still didn't know why I remained in Damascus in times like these, and my trip to Turkey confirmed for many the likelihood that I was up to no good. If these rumormongers had backed off while my father was there, providing a clear reason for my presence, now they would quickly resume their efforts to get me to leave. I thought about this with a mix of annoyance and apprehension as my taxi crawled through traffic. In the city center, I saw long queues for cooking gas and heating fuel—shortages had led to hoarding, price gauging, and theft. Pedestrians, caught under alternating drizzle and downpour, looked up at the sky, seemingly to plead for some consistency. A donkey-drawn cart cut off a Range Rover.

I would be staying with Sa'ad for what remained of the year; my father might have been able to pretend Salma's house was ready for his one-night stay, but there were still tasks to finish to be able to more than just sleep, wake, shower, and leave. When I arrived, Sa'ad made it clear he wanted to talk. So I put my suitcase down, and we sat to discuss what essentially would be the rules of my engagement in Damascus.

The government's propaganda campaign had been unrelenting. He reminded me of the key points: Turkey was clearly considered to be Syria's enemy. As was the United States. And journalists, of course, were not welcome. So I was "welcome," he said, if I wanted to just live in Syria—it was my right as a Syrian. But I had to know that many in my family were nervous about the fact that I'd gone to Turkey, nervous that I was an American, and nervous about all the journalism.

I knew his fears were legitimate. Nonetheless, I tried to explain that my past work had been critical of the US government, and that the story I had just reported was also critical of the Turkish government. He listened to me closely, but his response was quiet and frustrated: "These people don't read, Alia."

It was the first acknowledgment since the crisis had started that he *did* know that there was something wrong about it all. But we were not going to talk about it again.

೫◊ಕಿ

I RESUMED THE routine I had established before. In the morning, I had tea with my uncle while he watched the news reports from state TV. I ignored both the news and his tut-tutting of the captured *z'aran* (troublemakers)— who always confessed they had only protested against the government and/or taken up arms because they were being paid to do so by some foreign country. Only when he was showering would I flip to BBC or Al Jazeera International. I'd then head to the gym, walking past the same *mukhabarat* building of my teenage interrogation, wondering what horrors were happening inside and how we could all live with it.

At the gym, I tried not to notice the stares. Even after months of going there, I had remained an oddity—as far as I could tell, I was the only woman not wearing makeup and perfume to work out (hijab or no hijab) and who actually was sweating. The gym was small and spare, and conversations were easily overheard (they were often meant to be overheard). One of the trainers there—who the guys called "Coach" and who clearly used steroids—had taken an intense disliking to me, especially as I had not shown any interest in him, was American, and had once reflexively rolled my eyes as he delivered an ode to Bashar al-Assad while doing an impressive number of pull-ups.

The other trainer was naturally fit, seemingly happily married to an athlete, and didn't react with condescending amusement each time I went to the weight rack. He and I had never joined in when others denigrated the demonstrators and had quietly understood that our opinions potentially aligned. After my workout, I'd get on with my day: reading, interviewing people about Salma, and finishing her house.

To get it done, I met several times with Gabriel, who had audited the renovation expenses. His office was well appointed, even lavish. He clearly was successful, though always honest and never pushy with me. He also was curious as to why I would be in Damascus, and based on instinct (which could have been reckless), I let on a little more than usual. I told him I wanted to write a book about my grandmother and that I wanted a chance to live in Syria, to not just be a visitor.

Slowly, we did that waltz to feel out what the other might really think about what was happening—irrelevant non sequiturs became indirect observations and then subtle questions. Out of the blue, for example, Gabriel told me that his mother-in-law (who was never fond of me) didn't like his politics. This only recommended him to me even more. One day, leaning forward from behind his grand desk and whispering, he eventually came out to me: he was secretly going to protests. He would meet at mosques outside of central Damascus with other like-minded friends—both Christian and Muslim—before they took to the streets. He beamed with joy and told me that he finally felt alive.

I was happy Gabriel had come onto the project for so many reasons. Not only did the end of the renovation finally feel attainable, but he also renewed my hope that even the comfortable and the co-opted in Damascene society weren't fully surrendering. He was in his forties, not ideological, had never been in the party, and skilled. He had much to lose and still thought it was worth the risk to come out onto the streets. Such people would be needed in the new Syria. (In 2013 though, he'd be arrested and detained for two months. After his release, he quickly moved to the Emirates.) With his help and the help of his team, I was rapidly able to cross off remaining tasks from my to-do lists. It would soon be possible to move into Salma's house.

But for these surreptitious conversations and exchanged glances, there was little indication in the capital of the upheaval occurring across Syria. In Damascus, things seemed relatively calm and orderly—offices, schools, shops, and restaurants were all still open and bustling. The regime appeared invested in maintaining an impression of a serene Damascus unaffected by events in the country, as a way to both deny that a popular movement threatened its control and cut off any uprising's momentum. By going about our lives, we had become bit players in the regime's efforts to maintain the fiction that everything was normal. No doubt many residents voluntarily participated, hoping that by performing normality, they could will away whatever was coming to Syria.

Of course there were signs that things weren't normal. There were daily electricity cuts, with different neighborhoods losing power on a rotating basis for several hours a day, and these hours changed without much rhyme or reason. Some of the wealthy had generators, but not among my family and friends. It required a leap of faith to start drying your hair or washing your clothes, because the electricity could disappear before you were finished. People already had little control over their lives; the inability to exercise authority over the most banal tasks was a constant reminder of that.

The prices of basic food items were rising. (Sa'ad came home one day saying he had not been able to afford beans.) The Syrian lira had already lost a quarter of its value since March, and it was still falling. The Four Seasons Hotel had few tourists or visitors. Though Christmas was soon approaching, Christians did not publicly put up lights or decorations: so many Syrians had died that any sign of outward celebration would have been in poor taste.

The regime kept tight control of all the potential Tahrir Squares in the capital. Internet access disappeared late every Thursday night to keep people from organizing Friday events. I inquired at the telecom office about why my wireless USB wasn't working one Thursday evening (I was being cautiously provocative), and the representative told me with a straight face that the "Internet was broken." Every Friday started off tranquilly enough, with silent streets, but I always remembered soon after waking up what Fridays had become in the Arab Spring, wondering how many Syrians would be dead by evening.

One afternoon, I found myself unable to nap during siesta—even the sound of the rain was distracting. I flipped on the TV while Sa'ad slept, stumbling on an extremely bad direct-to-video American movie. A female FBI agent was working to bring a notorious drug lord to justice. After he had several key witnesses brutally murdered, she was put in a safe house until his trial; the drug lord nevertheless found her, and she barely escaped an attempt on her life. Someone in the government had betrayed the citizen he was sworn to protect and was colluding with the criminals.

I found myself utterly immobilized, even as I was aware of how bad the film was. I felt genuine anger that at each turn, the villain was evading justice. His impunity made me furious, and I could feel my anxiety rising—even though I knew this kind of formulaic film would have a happy ending. Only when the credits started to roll did I realize that I had lost hours there, never having settled back into the sofa's cushions, the remote control still in my hand. I had waited just to see this bad man get what was coming to him, and I couldn't move until he had.

As Syria geared up for the local December 12 elections, promoted as part of a reform process announced in response to the months of antigovernment protests, the regime continued its violent crackdown on the demonstrators and the armed opposition. While some of my relatives refused to vote, others reluctantly did: the regime was keeping track of who participated and who didn't, and those who didn't could be suspected of a lack of enthusiasm for their government.

In the capital, there were increasing public shows of support for Assad. When I watched these demonstrations on TV, I was convinced they were mostly staged. I winced when people—aware the cameras were upon them—made sure to kiss glossy portraits of Assad. Caravans of pro-regime cars regularly drove through the city, the drivers honking their horns with pro-Assad music blasting from their vehicles. Huge pictures of Assad were plastered to their hoods, and Syrian flags flew from their car windows. It was as if he had just won the World Cup, all by himself.

Sometimes I was on the street when they passed; other times, I watched from Sa'ad's balcony. These spectacles repulsed me. I was angry at those who supported Assad out of conviction—those who actually believed in him. But I felt a kind of skin-crawling embarrassment at the nonbelievers who nonetheless *chose* to be obsequious, and even theatrical, in supporting him. Many Syrians—including those who hated or faulted the regime—chose survival over solidarity with those who were suffering in Syria, and with those who were putting their lives on the line to fight back.

Mercifully, no one I knew was a sycophant, and only occasionally on the street did anyone pump a fist in support of the passing convoys. Yet there was still a sort of delirium to it all. Those who weren't prone to being undignified were nonetheless long accustomed to these displays, having been initiated in the practiced cult of the Assads since the days of Hafez al-Assad. It had become normal, and for more than one generation, it was the only normal they had ever known.

But whether intoxicated or numb, many seemed to snap out of their trance or stupor—even if just briefly—when, thousands of miles away, the North Korean dictator Kim Jong-il suddenly died on December 17. For days, our TV screens were cluttered with images of maudlin displays of North Koreans in deep mourning at the funeral of their leader (with retrospective footage of them worshiping him during his life). It was as if Syrians—especially those who knew it was all a farce—were only self-conscious of the depths of their own submission, long ago extracted, in those brief moments when they were outdone.

§⊗§

DESPITE THE ABSENCE of Christmas and New Year's decorations, the devaluation of the Syrian lira, the increase in prices, and the general mood of the country—much of it already suffering and mourning the loss of loved ones—families still made modest plans to celebrate the holidays. I had long lost a taste for Christmas after spending it in Bethlehem in 2002, when Israeli tanks pulled back just for the day (and for the international press) after having pummeled the city for months. But Christmas is a national holiday in Syria, so businesses would be closed. I decided to split my time between relatives on both my parents' sides.

But just before the holiday, on December 23, the first big explosion rocked Damascus. Two suicide car bombs exploded outside of Syrian military intelligence agency buildings, killing 44 people and injuring 166. The regime quickly blamed Al Qaeda and took Arab League observers, already in Syria, to the site.

I felt certain the government itself was responsible for the strike, that it wanted to rattle Damascenes, and perhaps specifically Christians. Dutifully, priests were paraded on TV to state their support for calm and the regime. A group of Christian women I had gotten to know had met with the clergy and tried to convince them at least to stay silent if they couldn't speak out on behalf of the protesters. The women believed that failing to speak out was immoral and callous to the suffering of other Syrians. In the long run, they argued, the regime would someday fall, and those Syrians who would come to power in that day might very well hold the actions of the priests against all Christians. The priests asked the women, "Do you think we have much choice?"—implying that to protect Christian communities, they had to play along with the regime.

Whoever carried out the bombing, it was a frightening development. Either agents of chaos were now in Syria and would operate by their own opaque rules of engagement, or the government had cynically targeted itself to give credence to its narrative and to dissuade Damascenes from rising up. Both of these explanations meant we were on a slippery slope: a Pandora's box was opening that couldn't be emptied.

Sa'ad had a different reaction: he was almost euphoric at the first word of the explosion. "See, I told you so! *Irhabiyeen!* Terrorists!" he said, using the English word in case somehow I didn't know it in Arabic. He was in no way celebrating the violence itself; rather, I understood that he was relieved because it validated the regime's narrative. If the regime wasn't lying to us, then we couldn't be blamed for our submission. Even if Sa'ad and I no longer discussed anything political, my silences, deep sighs, and sarcastic snorts made it impossible—even in the supposed privacy of his own home—to forget that we were complicit. Understandably, he had chafed under my barely disguised hints, I think in part because he agreed with me, and we both hated ourselves for it. Now, with a terrorist attack in Damascus (whether real or manufactured), we had momentarily been absolved—or at least had plausible deniability.

Sa'ad wasn't alone; many others seemed to need relief from the simultaneous shame of living under such a regime and of looking away—of being both a victim and a bystander. In some ways, the interaction between the regime and its citizens seemed similar to the dynamics of domestic violence. Except that instead of giving us flowers or a box of chocolates after blackening our eyes, the regime had given us the twisted absolution of chaos. That winter I gave myself a course, of sorts, in comparative dictatorship. I read books about East Germany and the Stasi, about South Africa and apartheid, and I recognized this strain of shame there as well. The South African poet Breyten Breytenbach had written something that resonated with me: "The two of you, violator and victim (collaborator! violin!) are linked, forever perhaps, by the obscenity of what has been revealed to you, by the sad knowledge of what people are capable of. We are all guilty."

৪৩

ON CHRISTMAS EVE, the day after the explosion, Majed and his family picked me up for a quiet evening together to celebrate with his in-laws. They lived near the *mukhabarat* branch of the Syrian Air Force, but we decided to take a route that kept us well away from it and parked some distance from their house. We walked in the drizzle to get there.

Randa's brother hosted the gathering, and their other brother had flown in from Dubai, where he was a diamond dealer. Their sister lived in America. They were each married and had adult children or teenagers. We were all smartly dressed, but lounged casually in the family room, not the formal receiving room. Gifts were exchanged, with the wealthy uncle from Dubai handing out to each of his nephews and nieces an iPad, like they were candy. The conversation at one point turned to what was happening in Egypt, though what we were actually talking about, I'm fairly sure, was Syria. Discussing another country in the midst of large changes was a safer way to vent anxieties, thoughts, and hopes.

The Dubai brother had a lot of opinions, and everyone seemed to defer to him (after all, he had just won that last round of gift giving). He hadn't been to Egypt recently but nonetheless explained to us with great authority how the Salafists were coming to power there, and how the days of Christians in the Middle East were over. When I pointed out that the military was actually in charge there, and had deep economic interests and privileges to protect, he waved me off, and he was similarly dismissive of any other observations I shared, many derived from my trips to Egypt earlier in the year and conversations with actual Egyptians.

I had already heard the main points of this logic before: Christians were here centuries before Islam; the continued presence in their homeland had to be protected; only this regime could protect minorities from a majority that didn't really want them. I looked around the room: it was Christmas Eve and no one had gone to Mass or had any plans to go to Mass the next day. But because identity, rights, and fate in Syria and the region are wedded to religion, what we were talking about was personal and existentialist: whether they could belong in their own country if they weren't Sunni Muslims. This sad state of affairs, linking so much to religion, was thanks first to the regime, which gave power a sectarian face (even if plenty of non-Alawite Syrians were part of it and beneficiaries of it), and second to the exclusionary discourses of political Islam—Shiite and Sunni—and the problematic nature of the Islam promulgated by Gulf countries, which had outsized influence because of their satellite TV channels and mosque building projects abroad.

"Shouldn't everyone just be equally protected?" I asked. The answer was the same that I had frequently heard: the Muslim Brotherhood wouldn't protect everyone. When I asked if the Brotherhood was the only alternative, the *badeel*, I was told to look to Egypt and Tunisia, where democracy had ushered them in via the ballot box.

Given that it was a major Christian holiday, I took a different tack: "If Jesus were alive today, what would he do?" I asked, noting that essentially,

Jesus had led an uprising against corruption and the status quo. "After all, what is being Christian about?"

I glanced at the wife of our host, who was related to a longtime opponent of the regime, who was now a high-profile opposition figure. They shared the same not particularly common last name, and at times it was a burden to her. I could see I was making her uneasy. In fact, looking around the room, it was clear that everyone else seemed to want the conversation to end, too. As they had kindly invited me to join them that evening, I backed off. Talking about Christ and revolutions was ruining Christmas.

꧁꧂

A FEW DAYS later, on my birthday, at the top of my to-do list was buying the still missing lights for the kitchen and what would be my office. I headed to the Electricity Souk only to find that the electricity had been cut, which made it difficult to evaluate lighting fixtures. The salesman assured me that the power would be back soon, as it had already been a few hours.

In the meantime, I negotiated the discounts I would want. After the electricity came back on, and I made my final decisions, he gave me his card, which had his name written in English. "Showpan" was supposedly his last name. I commented that it was an odd name, especially considering there was no "P" in Arabic. "Where are you from?" I asked. It turned out that he was from my father's neighborhood, the Midan.

He explained that he had chosen his last name himself, for the music that he liked. I stared at him, not sure what kind of music Showpan was. Then, finally getting it, I exclaimed, "Chopin!"

"Yes," he smiled, "He was from the Midan too," he winked at me.

I laughed as I left the store and put in a call to Gabriel, who promised to send me an electrician that day to install the lights. As it was, Suha was making me a birthday lunch back in the Tahaan, so I made my way there.

Remarkably, the electrician—a skinny youth no more than twenty years old—was there almost as soon as I was. With the electricity working, he quickly and efficiently installed everything I had bought. When it was all done, I wondered if Salma would have liked them.

Across the hall at Suha's, Sa'ad arrived for lunch, which, as always, was a culinary treat. After the meal, over cake, Sa'ad gifted me cologne, made in Lebanon and crafted in the image of foreign perfumes. I could see that it must have cost him a lot. He had adopted Salma's love of perfume after all those years of taking care of her in her locked-in life, when he had daily applied to her unfeeling skin the Avon scents she so loved.

While we cleared the table, Suha's daughter made sure I still wanted to celebrate New Year's Eve with her, her new fiancé, and their friends. Then she gave me some rules: his informant (or informant-friendly) best friend would be there, and he was already asking a lot of questions about me.

"So?" I asked.

"So don't open your big mouth," she answered sternly.

⚳

IF PEOPLE WERE dying in Syria, you wouldn't have known by seeing how these Damascenes—from all sects—celebrated New Year's Eve. My cousin's fiancé had taken us to an impeccably renovated house in the Old City in Damascus with its traditional courtyard open to the winter sky. It was meant to be a boutique hotel—before the Arab Spring, tourism to beautiful Syria had been on the rise.

For hours that night, the glamorous adult children of the rich and elite danced, drank, and snorted cocaine with incredible hedonistic abandon. At midnight they blew noisemakers, tossed confetti into the air, and paraded around in glittery hats and gag glasses. They wore European designer clothes, and when my cousin saw me wearing sleek black pants, high heels, and a blouse from New York City, she balked in distress. My top, in her opinion, was "too afternoon." I wasn't worried: her critique was more an indication of how Syrian women of a certain class dressed for lunch than of my being inappropriately dressed for the occasion.

The informant friend had begun asking me questions as soon as I arrived. As he had gotten more and more drunk, his body language had become more menacing and invasive of my personal space. What did I think of Syria? What was I doing here? Did I have a boyfriend? Did I like Bashar al-Assad? Did I like Syrian boys?

I blew my noisemaker and cupped my ear to pretend I couldn't hear him, mimicking those around me the way heroes do in zombie movies, when they don't want to have their brains eaten, and he finally stumbled off.

The revelry lasted into the early hours of morning. As drunk as everyone was, they insisted on driving and walked to where their luxury cars were parked, outside the city walls. The other ruins of Syria's other civilizations were still lit up in the receding darkness. With dawn already breaking across the sky, there would barely be enough hours to sleep before everyone would head to their next New Year's Day social engagements.

⁂

I SPENT THE first day of 2012 visiting family members to wish them the best for the coming year. That included Odette, the widow of the only adult child Abdeljawwad lived to bury (his son's death was one of the few times people could ever remember seeing him broken). Odette had been married off at nineteen, and the pictures of that day capture a flurry of lace and ribbons and fear. In one photo, the bride is clutched by her sister, and they are leading a procession in Hama down a stone street. Everyone is looking at the photographer, who must have been to their right, ahead of them, walking backward to keep pace. Salma is perfectly composed, in a tailored suit and heels, a brooch on her lapel. She is holding my mother's hand, who is only two years old and dressed in white, her hair gathered in a white ribbon. She is in the full chubby glory of a toddler.

Despite the look of absolute terror on her face in the photograph, Salma's sister-in-law had a happy marriage, though it was cut short by my great-uncle's sudden death. She was a favorite in the family, considered a great cook and a keeper of the many recipes passed down from my great-grandmother Sara. I liked her for her stories and ability to read coffee grounds and tarot cards.

On New Year's Day 2012, we sat together on a little settee in the corner of her living room. I asked her about Salma. What was her voice like? Her accent? How did she walk? What did she smell like? What did she talk about? What was the Tahaan apartment like when she lived there? The neighborhood? Who were her friends? Why did she help people? What made her happy? Was she happy? Why wasn't she? Did you visit her after she was locked in?

Before I got up to leave, I asked her if she'd read my fortune. It was, after all, the start of a new year. I'd leave it to her which method to use. From the drawer of a side table she pulled out a clear plastic bag containing a notebook and some other items, and she withdrew from it her worn tarot cards. She spread them in front of me, face down, and we began the ritual. I kept my pen and notebook ready.

In the cards that were drawn, she saw travel, a bad man, and sickness. She told me that what I wanted to happen would happen, but not now, and only much later. There would be harmful gossip about me, and a bad friend would betray me, revealing publicly hidden information about me. My luck and my health would prove to be good, however. And something that I didn't know would happen would in 2012.

14

ROUTINE

Damascus, January-March 2012

O N THE DAY I FINALLY MOVED INTO SALMA'S APARTMENT IN THE
Tahaan, my cousin who would help me was running late. In Ain al-
Kirish, the electricity had consistently been disappearing for several hours
starting at 6 p.m. When she made it with twelve minutes until darkness in
the building, I was waiting on the curb with my suitcase.

Thankfully, we were able to park near the Tahaan, and the power was
still on when we arrived. We were on edge and rushing, aware that the lights
could go out at any moment. But that night, they stayed on until 8 p.m. I felt
blessed by the small miracle, happy things had turned out slightly better than
expected. Anxiety, fear, and guilt were always weighing on us, even if in central Damascus we were still mostly sheltered from the violence. I even caught
myself being *grateful* for the mercy of the regime for deciding we could have
power that night, momentarily forgetting the same incompetent, corrupt,
and now murderous government deserved my ire. "Bananas and Kleenex," I
thought to myself.

The first order of business was making sure I knew how to work the furnace. It ran on diesel, and I had enough to last the winter. I also had an
electric heater that was easier to use—when electricity was available. It was
best to keep both options ready, with all the cuts and shortages. Everyone was

adapting, including businessmen. As each scarcity created a new need, the market would be flooded with Chinese goods perfect for our ever-changing situation. Chinese-made rechargeable lights became ubiquitous; I had already bought a few for Salma's house and kept them fully charged.

A series of firsts soon gave way to a daily rhythm in the house. Each morning I'd let in the light by opening up the wooden shutters from my grandmother's day—no longer emerald green but an ugly honey brown that my mother had inexplicably chosen. They were over sixty years old now, and no longer completely kept out the draft or the light, but there was comfort in using them just as Salma had so many times.

I had set up my office in the room that Salma had used as a casual family room. My aunt had an old foldable plastic table that I used as a desk, and the room was now completely ringed by Suha's previously stored artwork: canvases, sketches, and prints. It was the same room where the furnace was, and I kept a pot of water atop its metal plate for when I wanted tea. A red sofa from the Turkish IKEA could be converted into a bed for visitors.

When I was in the kitchen, I could sometimes see my neighbor across the way in what was the building that Salma's housemaid's suitor had lived in all those decades ago. Thanks to the renovation, there was now a big window along the back wall that looked out onto the same expanse of space across which Sabah and the young army recruit had fallen in love. Suha didn't know the woman who now lived there; she had only recently arrived. All I knew about her was what I couldn't help but see and hear daily: her young son drove her mad, and she often yelled at him loudly, sometimes hitting him. I'd hear the ruckus even when my shutters were shut.

We'd smile or wave at each other every day, usually in the morning when we were both making coffee. She seemed to be looking at me with curiosity, as if she couldn't help wondering why a woman was living by herself, with no family. Sometimes I'd be caught at the window while she screamed at her son, who ran from her crying—I could trace his movements as he appeared in and out of different windows. Even when she knew I'd seen one of her fits (or his—I don't know who triggered whom), she would assume the same friendly posture as when we waved over morning coffee.

I visited Suha daily, often for coffee, sometimes right after my first cup, other times midmorning, after lunch, or after siesta. When we were alone, we'd have a chance to talk about Salma and the other people who had passed through the building. It was on one of these occasions that Suha first told me about Um Ragheed, Salma's neighbor and friend so many years ago from the apartment downstairs. I had never before heard about her and her husband, the pro-Nasser colonel, and their family's exile in Cairo.

"Why didn't you tell me before?" I exclaimed to Suha, before chastising my mother for the same over email. After all, I had been to Egypt and would soon be returning; maybe I could find them. If she was still alive, Um Ragheed could tell me so much about Salma. I decided to try tracking them down in Cairo and prayed for luck.

By the time I moved in, many of the tenants of the building had changed. The ground floor was in fact empty. In the basement apartments were a doctor's office and a lawyer's office. Above me lived Fatima, and above Suha, Um Mustafa. Above Fatima was the family with the troublemaking children. (Indeed, one of them was briefly imprisoned in 2003, suspected of helping a relative, who wanted to wage jihad against the Americans, get to Iraq.)

Salma's home was enormous for one person. I lived in the back, where the kitchen, bathrooms, master bedroom, and my office were located. I'd taken to using the servant's door to go in and out of the apartment, and keeping the others locked. I also kept the doors to the unused rooms—the dining room, the formal salon, and what had once been my mother and aunt's bedroom—closed, lest any heat slip way. All those rooms remained empty, though sometimes I paced through them, imagining Salma when she lived there as her heels clicked against the marble, a trail of cigarette smoke in her wake, reciting lines of poems from centuries before. Although I was living there alone, it felt like I was sharing the house with her, and that I could almost hear the echoes of another time and other lives.

I found myself laughing out loud sometimes, like when I'd have the bucket and mop out, my hair up in a scarf like a caricature of a gypsy, as I cleaned the parts of the apartment I lived in. While Salma wouldn't have done that sort of housework, she also hadn't had the opportunities I had had for an advanced education. What had she wanted for her daughters and granddaughters? Would she have believed that it would take forty-two years for any of them to ever live in this house again? (Or that the Assads would still be ruling forty-two years later?) At the end of the day, I'd close the shutters, locking them into place, like a ritual. Alone in the large bedroom, I marveled how Salma, Ameen, Lamya, and Suha had all slept in there together when visiting family members had taken over the girls' room.

Though it happened in the years after she had left this house, sometimes I'd lie there still, as if I were locked in the way Salma had been after that stroke. At first I'd try a minute of motionlessness; since Salma couldn't turn her head to see a clock or a watch, I'd count in my head from 1 to 60, pausing between each number, to get to one minute. In that time, I'd feel keenly aware of my face and how it bothered me—I'd want to scratch my ear, lick my lips, rub my nose. But I wouldn't let myself. I'd keep counting to 120, and then I'd want to crack my knuckles, wiggle my toes, or move my arm, bothered by how it pressed into my armpit. I made it to 180, 240, and finally 300—just 5 minutes—before desperately contracting my muscles and leaping out of bed, needing to feel the cold reassurance of the ground beneath my feet.

I added it all up one day, how many seconds were in those seven years of imprisoned paralysis. With 60 seconds in a minute, 60 minutes in an hour, 24 hours in a day, 7 days in a week, 4 weeks in a month, and 12 months in a year, over nearly 7 years, it was 203,212,800 seconds of being alive in a dead body, waiting, waiting, waiting for something to happen.

༄༅

SINCE I HAD visited Athena in Homs in August, the city had become the epicenter of armed confrontation between the regime and its opponents.

Already in the fall, Homs had seen sectarian bloodshed to a much greater extent than the rest of the country. People without clear ties to any side in the conflict were nevertheless being murdered, and by late October there were fierce clashes between the Free Syrian Army (many of them defectors from the Syrian Army) and the government's security forces as well as paramilitary groups affiliated with the regime. Casualties now came from both rebel and government ranks, although unarmed civilians still bore the brunt of the death being meted out.

In the new year, fighting had at points tapered off in the midst of a flurry of potential diplomatic efforts. But if we thought that might augur a coming to the senses on all sides, we were about to be brutally proven naïve. Instead, on the first Friday of February, the government launched an all-out attack on parts of Homs in an attempt to rout out FSA members and other armed rebels. On that first day of the offensive, at least two hundred Syrians reportedly died under mortar and heavy machine-gun fire. It was the bloodiest episode yet since peaceful protesters had first taken to the streets demanding reforms.

It would be a month-long assault, and though February, with its condensed, dark days, was also the shortest month of the year, it seemed endless. It was also the thirtieth anniversary of the Hama Massacre, when Hafez al-Assad had definitively quashed the uprising against him by leveling Salma's native city. Was the timing coincidental, or intentional? I leaned toward the latter, and I often felt (and still feel) that the regime took some glee in taunting the people and gloating in its victories.

After all, in 1982, in Hama, the regime had gotten away with killing its opponents as well as innocent civilians. Crushing Homs on the anniversary seemed to be a clear threat that they could and would massacre the people without consequence again. But back then, the regime had gotten away with it because almost no one inside or outside of Syria knew for sure what had happened. For thirty years, people in the country had been left to wonder— what would have happened if the world could have seen? Unlike in 1982, in 2012 we now had social media, and photographic and video evidence could be readily disseminated and accessed.

To adjust to this new reality, the regime stuck to what had become its playbook: Syrian state television denied that a massacre was taking place in Homs and blamed purported violence on "armed gangs." To preempt any easy contradiction of its narrative, it continued to ban foreign journalists from the city. This is not to say there is anything inherently better about foreign journalists—but local journalists faced the risk that the regime could retaliate against their families. The regime also cut the power and Internet and cell-phone service to the city. Landlines were erratic, at best, and they were also traceable.

Over the next month in Homs, government forces would use tanks, helicopters, artillery, rockets, and mortars essentially against civilians—it became its standard modus operandi. In Homs—and elsewhere—the regime would bombard a territory into submission no matter the expense to civilian life, or infrastructure, rather than engage the public or address grievances.

But thanks to the efforts of a local media center and the foreign journalists who did sneak into Homs, news, photos, and footage of what was happening were making it out of the besieged city. What we learned—if we wanted to learn—was that people were dying daily. Entire families died together. Civilians were living in multiple layers of clothing to keep warm, rationing their use of diesel for heat and hot water. They were hoarding foodstuffs, like bags of rice and sugar. On the few days the bombardment would let up, they'd rush out to buy formula for babies, food for their children, water, batteries, and flashlights, if they could find them. Stinking piles of garbage rotting on corners, and oftentimes set aflame inside the city to create cover against government snipers, filled the air with rancid smoke. There was no safety even in the public hospitals: injury had become an admission of guilt that you were a fighter or from one of the neighborhoods identified by the government as sheltering fighters. Why else would the regime be shelling it?

Condemnations of the regime by other countries reached a fevered pitch. Then the "international community" mobilized to issue more formal condemnations. Action at the United Nations Security Council was promised. But Assad's foreign allies seemed more committed than the critics. Days after the assault on Homs began, the Russian foreign minister arrived in Damascus to a rapturous welcome from the regime's supporters. It was a potent visual affirmation that Russia had Assad's back. Russia also vetoed—along with China—any Security Council resolution demanding Assad share power with the opposition.

In addition to propping up the regime both militarily and economically, both Russia and Iran had English-language news channels that worked hard to challenge activists' or journalists' reports coming from Homs while validating the regime's version of events. (A young British journalist appeared on both channels to refute any reports that contradicted the official narrative.) Legitimate news reports or reporters were dismissed as tools of Western imperialism, a Zionist plot, or a Gulf agenda for regional hegemony. In the meantime, the regime said it was cooperating with the international community.

Those dark days in February became darker. Parts of Homs were incessantly shelled, and two powerful car bombs exploded outside of two security headquarters in Aleppo one Friday, killing twenty-eight people, including military and police personnel as well as civilians—both adults and children. People outside of Syria (and outside of the regime) believed it might be Al Qaeda. Not surprisingly, the chaos and deterioration of the security situation in Syria had provided an opening for opportunistic foreign actors. Meanwhile, the government assault wasn't limited to Homs. Many towns and large areas of the countryside in Idlib Province had declared themselves government-free zones, and defecting soldiers were basing there as well. Dara'a, where the uprising had first started in March 2011, was also in the regime's sights, and there were reports of massacres in Hama.

In Damascus, we worried for friends and family in all these places. I personally was able to breathe more easily once I heard that Athena and her family had managed to leave the city and had made their way safely to the capital.

&0&

WE LIVED THROUGH the first part of February in a haze, the days bookended by the darkness of the morning and the night. I dreaded getting out from under the covers in the morning, as any heat that had survived the night once the electricity had been cut or the furnace turned off had long dissipated. When I did get up, I immediately put warm layers over my flannel pajamas: a thick robe, a big alpaca wrap, a wool hat, and bootie slippers over my wool socks. One of those days, midway through the month, I walked across the hall to Suha's flat for coffee. While she made it in the kitchen, I sat in her family room. My phone automatically connected to her Wi-Fi, and my emails started downloading. I was glancing at the subject lines when I saw one that said, "Mourning the death of Arab American journalist."

I wondered which old-timer had passed. Then I saw an email from my brother; its subject was a name—that of a good friend, a mentor, and a great Arab American journalist.

My heart started to race, resisting the obvious summation of those two email subject lines. I opened my brother's email to me, my mom, and my sisters. He had written, "Wow, can't believe he is gone. Sad." I knew that my friend had snuck into Syria and was reporting from Homs. Had the regime just murdered him?

I started to hyperventilate. I leapt out of my chair, ran over to Suha, and said something incomprehensible to her. I ran back to the TV and flipped to find English-language news. There was nothing about him. Had I misread my brother's email? I looked back at my phone. There was email after email, each one a devastating blow to my denial.

When Suha's daughter saw me shaken, she coldly faulted my friend; he shouldn't have come to Syria, she said. He had in fact died trying to leave Syria—not by the regime's hand—at least not directly. He had been traveling by horse when his allergy to the animal triggered a respiratory attack. Without any medicine, he had suffocated to death.

I wasn't able to mourn his loss publicly in Damascus. I felt bitterness, shame, and guilt that the country had become a graveyard—for so many

Syrians, and now non-Syrians, who had chosen not to abandon the nation in the darkness.

My friend wouldn't be the last foreign journalist to fall. Not a week later, the regime attacked one of its fiercest opponents, one that could threaten it more than any gun or armed group—the local media center in Homs. The activists, the civilian journalists, and the foreign correspondents who had snuck into Syria had long infuriated the authorities. In that late February attack, more foreign journalists died, while others were seriously injured. Their Syrian hosts unselfishly risked their lives to successfully smuggle the foreign survivors to freedom, and several Syrians died in the process. The government denied targeting journalists and rejected any responsibility for the deaths of those who "infiltrated Syria at their own risk without the Syrian authorities' knowledge of their entry and whereabouts." (A 2016 civil lawsuit in the United States would proffer evidence to the contrary.)

By the time February came to an end, hundreds had died in Homs. The rebels withdrew from the city, but it was devastated. All the previous warnings from the international community about serious consequences appeared to have been empty threats. However, even Russia and China—which had repeatedly blocked international action—joined in calls demanding immediate humanitarian access to the city.

The regime had lacked the manpower to subdue all the rebellious cities at once; with Homs defeated, it could now move on. But first it made sure to block any access to those who would deliver humanitarian relief.

⚬

WE WERE ABLE to see Athena again a few weeks after the rebels had withdrawn. She was now in Damascus, where much of her pharmaceutical business operated. She rang Suha one night to tell us she was nearby and would walk over to visit us in the Tahaan.

The power had already been cut in our area, but it was due to come back on soon. Sometimes in a city we can forget how dark the night can be, but with the electricity shortages in Damascus, we were often reminded. In some windows, I could see the glow of the Chinese-made rechargeable lanterns, but plenty of folks had taken to simply going to bed earlier, especially as it was warmer in bed and under the covers. I stood on Suha's front balcony with a bright flashlight to guide Athena when she got closer. As I waited for her to arrive, two boys rode past silently on one bike. I only saw them because the passenger's cell phone lit up his face as he scrolled through it. I watched them until the glimmer I knew was them disappeared.

Athena then shouted up to me, and I waved my beacon at her. Me, the balcony, and my flashlight—we had become a lighthouse. She used her own cell phone to navigate the Tahaan's entrance and stairs. When she arrived at our landing, she was a bit out of breath.

Suha and I happily embraced her. "*Hamdallah al-salameh,*" we both said. Thank God for your safety.

We moved into the family room and closed the balcony door for privacy. We put out a brown paper bag full of sunflower and pumpkin seeds and plates for the shells as we discarded them. Huddled close together, we smiled in relief.

We had many questions. What had happened? Did they witness it from where they were? How did she get here?

She told us that many of those who made up the FSA were indeed people from Homs who had taken up arms to defend themselves, not only army defectors. Anyone who wanted to declare themselves FSA could do so. By the third day of the assault, she and Faris had decided to try to get to Damascus, having heard that others had made it there from Homs. Baba Amr, the part of Homs under regime attack, was about 1.5 miles away from their neighborhood. The city had been completely closed down, and they were afraid that the battle might expand to other areas. Residents were shut inside their houses, terrified to go outside. All around had been the sounds of gunfire and explosions. Athena and Faris left in one car and their son and his wife in another. The cell-phone network was down, and there was no way to communicate with each other once they left their respective homes, where they had been stranded. They had agreed on a meeting point outside of Homs, but it would take a long time to make the spot because of all the checkpoints. They made it through, though, and finally reunited. Once on the highway, they were able to make Damascus in regular time.

But Athena—like many Syrians—hoped that now that the assault on Homs seemed to be over, things would get better, and they could go home. The regime was clearly the stronger military player and would not be dislodged by ragtag militias. Otherwise, what might ensue? A civil war? That seemed unfathomable.

We were staring down the one-year anniversary of the first demonstrations in Syria. Surely, with everyone taking stock—the kind of reckonings that anniversaries force upon us—people might come back to their senses.

But we had blown through all the meetings, elections, holidays, and other dates that Syrians kept assuring themselves would be the event that would bring these "troubles" to a definitive end. Now, 8,000 were dead and 230,000 displaced. The regime was stronger militarily than the rebels, and the fractured opposition was clearly ineffectual.

෨෯෮

THE DAY BEFORE the anniversary of the first protests in Dara'a, March 11, 2012, I returned to the 'Asrouniyeh souk with Tala. There were a few more things I needed for Salma's kitchen. The souk was full of people, and I found myself again looking at people's faces and trying to read their minds. After all, we weren't really able to talk to each other—directly or indirectly. In freer societies, indirect exchanges can take place in spaces of national conversation, such as the political, media, and pop-culture arenas. Of course, those other societies are never as inclusive as they could be, but it was nothing like the invisible yet almost tangible barriers between people in Syria.

As we made our way through the different khans and alleyways, Tala spotted a friend, Akram, who lived in Homs. He had a bohemian spirit with long hair, an earring, and a wooden cross around his neck. She told me he was always singing and dancing and laughing.

"You two must meet," she said. She flagged him down and introduced us. He had an errand to run but would meet us in thirty minutes for tea.

Tala knew Akram because she had visited the initiative he worked for in Homs, called Al Ard, The Land. A Dutch Jesuit priest had started it—Father Frans, who had been in Homs for nearly fifty years and spoke Arabic almost like a native. He had started the organization with a donation of twenty-three hectares full of olive, almond, and cypress trees and vineyards, and it had grown to include a guesthouse, where the poor who couldn't afford a vacation could come to a beautiful place, eat, and sleep for very little money. It also had a free school for the disabled (with free transportation) and a guesthouse for tourists, and it employed locals in farming activities as well as in business initiatives that made ceramics and wine. There was a simple café on the premises.

Before 2011, Syrians of all walks of life could come to Al Ard and get to know one another in a natural setting. Father Frans wanted to foster these exchanges, and he wanted urban Syrians to appreciate the problems caused by rural depopulation. He wanted them to feel involved in the social development of the country. Father Frans also organized annual multiday hikes open to Syrians of all ages, religions, and classes, which my cousins had attended. They'd start walking in the morning, and no matter how many hours it took, they wouldn't stop until they reached their campsite for the night. They met many of the Syrians who lived in the towns, villages, and remote areas along the route. The purpose of these hikes, and of Al Ard generally, was to give participants a chance to meet different people from all over the country and to discuss things not normally talked about in Syrian society. I was surprised the government allowed it.

We met Akram again as planned at the Nawfara Café, steps from the Umayyad Mosque, where some believe the head of John the Baptist remains. The old coffee shop's wood paneled walls were covered with all kinds of framed pictures, maps, and portraits, though, to my eye, it seemed the enormous framed photo of Bashar al-Assad was the largest. At the center of the back wall was an elevated chair for the *hakawaati*, the storyteller who would entertain those gathered with wonderful tales in the Syrian oral tradition.

Akram, who was twenty-six years old and originally from Homs, confirmed a lot of what Tala told me, but explained how the focus of Al Ard's activities had shifted. Now the organization was distributing food and other forms of relief to families and giving shelter to many of the displaced from the besieged parts of Homs. When I asked how he had gotten involved, he told me he had run away from home at the age of thirteen. Akram came from a middle-class family that was respected in its circles, but he hated his father, who was abusive toward his mother. So one morning, Akram took a bus to Damascus. By day he had slept in the Umayyad Mosque, just a few steps away from where we were sitting. An old imam there kept an eye on him but couldn't let him stay past 10 p.m., when he had to lock the mosque's doors for the night. After adult men tried to prey on him, Akram went back to Homs, where he said Father Frans took him in at the monastery, saving him from the street. Akram then worked side by side with Father Frans and the other Jesuits, but without the expectation that he would join the order. He grew up under their care.

Akram explained how, before the revolution had started, he had hated the rigid society his parents belonged to. When he pierced his ear, he said, no one who knew his parents would even say hello to him. He also hated certain agents of the regime—especially the officer who insisted on bribes from him when he did his compulsory military service. When the officer had demanded a TV from him, the Jesuits had helped him secure one. But Akram said his eyes weren't fully opened to the regime until he saw the police open fire on protesters.

"It was then I understood that the regime was like my father. I hate my father, and I hate the regime," he said.

I looked at everyone around us to see if anyone was listening, and I tried to smile and not look like we were in a dissenting conversation. We had both noticed a man who had taken a seat above us on a mezzanine. He had been staring at us as we talked.

That same officer in the army who had demanded bribes had also threatened Akram after the demonstrations started. He came to Akram and told him he had been seen at demonstrations and that he better show up at the pro-regime manifestation coming up. "You have a lot of girls among your relatives," the officer had said, and Akram understood the threat.

Akram felt he had no choice but to go, but this got him in trouble with an anti-regime fighter who was new to Homs. In the summer of 2011, Assad had released the man from prison, along with many radicalized prisoners who the regime knew were likely to take up arms against the government. This fighter had put the word out that he wanted Akram's head because Akram had been spotted at the pro-regime manifestation, sending Akram into hiding in the small villages outside of Homs. What saved him was that both the regime officer and the ex-prisoner died within a month of each other in 2011. When Akram came out of hiding, the FSA told him he was safe. They all knew about his work at Al Ard.

His friend Bassem soon joined us; we barely had enough space for another chair around our table, but Tala had to leave, so he took her seat. Like Akram, Bassem was Christian and also against the regime. He was flustered about something that had happened recently to two of his friends, both young women—one Christian, the other Muslim. They had been active in distributing medicines to both Hama and Homs, something I'd soon learn was a transgression in the regime's eyes. For their "crimes," and in the light of day, they were taken from a Damascus café. Someone they thought was a friend had informed on them.

I was silent. Criminals or radicalized prisoners being released by the regime, young women being arrested for providing medicines to civilians—it
was all so cynical, calculated, and dirty.

"*Shoo?*" What? they asked me, detecting my distress.

Of the many things bothering me, I told them how what worried me
was that communities were being seen monolithically—people were being
judged not as individuals but collectively. I told them how even people I
was sure were fundamentally good had made some problematic statements,
such as, "All Alawites would have to pay for what the regime had done,"
or that "all Sunnis wanted a religious state." I told them how a Kurdish
friend had criticized Christians for not being vocal, once asking me, "Why
haven't they come out in Bab Touma?" referring to the Christian quarter of
Old Damascus.

Akram scoffed right away, saying, "Why haven't they come out in Mezzeh?" referring to a well-to-do neighborhood where many of the rich Sunni
families lived. With a smile and conviction, he added, "It will all be over
soon. The regime can't survive this." But he did fear that the regime would
do as much as possible in the short term to weaken its opponents' position.

I looked up at the man who was watching us. He slowly looked away as he
took a drag of his cigarette. Akram was watching him, too. It was now well
after 10 p.m. Even if the Middle East is more nocturnal than other places, in
light of events, people were getting home earlier these days.

Akram turned out to be staying with the Jesuits, very close to Ain al-
Kirish, and we set out together. As we walked, we talked about the man who
had been watching us. Akram didn't think he could hear us, but that he was
likely trying to read our demeanor.

From the café, we soon passed in front of the arch and columns that remained from when the Umayyad Mosque had been the site of the Roman
temple to Jupiter. They towered above our heads. The arch stood at one end
of the Hamidiyeh. On the other side was the long vaulted bazaar. I had never
been there so late; every last shop was closed. As far as I could see, besides us,
there wasn't another single soul around. To get to the other side, to Revolution Street, we'd have to traverse the entire length—a quarter mile—of the
bazaar in pitch blackness.

"Should we go around?" I asked—there were still lights on behind us and
around us.

"But this way is so much shorter," Akram said.

So we took one step into the darkness. The more steps we took, the darker it became. As my eyes adjusted, the outlines of the Hamidiyeh became more visible and familiar, like the ink drawings I had bought years ago of this same spot, the entire souk suggested by just a few scratches of black.

We also lowered our voices, lest their echo escape us and alert anyone we were there, but also because the bouncing of any sound waves testified to the vastness of the space and how imposing it was. Our low tones kept it human scale. I couldn't help thinking that it was impossible that no one else was there. Was the man from the café following us?

I quickened our pace to make it out to the other side, where the light and noise of the street awaited us, outside the walls of Old Damascus.

⚜

ON THE MORNING of March 17, I was dreaming that I was renting an apartment where water was flowing on top of me. Even in my REM state, I realized I might be hearing actual running water, and I opened an eye in panic, staring at the ceiling. No water.

As I became more fully awake, I guessed the sound was coming from a neighbor washing her balcony. I looked at the time; it was close to 7:25.

I began to drift off again when a massive "boom" ripped through my sleep. It was quickly followed by another explosion. The windows, the shutters, and the doors shook, and I felt the reverberations throughout my body.

I jumped out of bed and ran to Suha's. She had her cell phone already in hand and was in a panic about Kamal. He had left home for work but had yet to arrive there. She ran out onto the balcony to see if anything would reveal what direction the sound had come from. I followed her and saw many of our neighbors in their pajamas and robes on their balconies. They looked as startled as we did. Kamal answered his phone; he was safe. But no one knew anything else yet, so we retreated to our televisions.

We'd learn where the blast had happened when my cousin's fiancé called, as he lived in the building exactly facing the target: the same security building we had avoided going near on Christmas Eve. All the doors and windows, as well as the external walls on that side of his building, had been shattered and blown out. I'd see the site the next day—it looked like a doll's house, opened to reveal its inner workings. Each floor belonged to a different owner, with a different aesthetic, now exposed for everyone to see.

I spent the morning of the blasts at Suha's: although we weren't far from the explosion, we had family and friends who lived much closer, and we spent hours trading calls and texts with everyone to make sure no one was hurt. I braced myself for when my family would wake up in the United States and begin the barrage of emails pleading with me to come home.

If Suha's daughter had been hiding from or escaping the country's problems, thinking about her impending wedding and marriage, the morning had been a rude awakening. The government was already saying it would compensate those affected for their damaged property, but no one believed much money would be forthcoming.

I had my suspicions as to who was behind the attack. State TV immediately began blaming the protesters, and a lot of other people did the same. In this region of seemingly long memories (the telling of a story about yesterday often begins a century before), memories of the past year had been remarkably short. Scrubbed from any remembrance was the reality that the demonstrations started peacefully and that the government used violence first.

There were voices in the opposition calling for arms to fight the regime. If it was forces opposed to the regime who had just caused the explosion, I wasn't reassured. Instead, I was convinced that the government could win, or at the very least survive, in the moral ambiguity of an armed uprising.

I went back to Salma's apartment to make myself a small lunch. I hadn't raised the shade that morning in the kitchen as I usually did, having rushed over to Suha's. My neighbor across the way did not know I was there. Through her sobs, I heard her beat and yell at her child with more vigor than usual. Though he bore the blows, I suspected they were not meant for him this time, but for some invisible threat that she'd never be able to confront.

෴

A FEW DAYS later, spring arrived—the skies were a clear blue and the temperature was in the high sixties.

Suha and I were going to spend the morning together in the parts of Old Damascus that we both loved. She had errands to run, and I needed a wedding gift for my friends who would soon be getting married in Cairo. We had also tracked down a few phone numbers to help me find Um Ragheed. On our way out of the Tahaan, we bumped into the neighbors from the small flat Salma had built all those years ago. They were surprised I spoke Arabic; the news that had gotten to them was only that I was a foreigner. Long gone were the days when the building was a well-integrated hive.

Suha and I savored our time in the historic Old City, a major stop on the Silk Road and the pilgrimage to Mecca. In no rush to complete our to-do list, we paused to admire superlative examples of different eras' architecture. We walked through the Bzhouryieh, the spice market, buying dried figs stacked on a wooden skewer and olive-green laurel soaps. We passed by the boutique hotel where Brad Pitt and Angelina Jolie had stayed when they visited. That Damascus was now a world away—no tourists were coming back anytime soon.

As we walked, Suha told me she could never imagine leaving Damascus. How could she be away from here? she asked. I, too, loved Damascus, and it had fascinated many others for centuries. We then strolled into the old Jewish Quarter. Many artists had set up their workspaces and studios there. We ran into several old friends of hers and had a look at what they were working on. There were painters and sculptors. Suha was easily as talented as many of them, but she had put it all on hold for her husband and daughter. I saw her genuinely excited to be among her friends and peers. For a minute, everything felt normal.

The city had quickly resumed its daily rhythm after the explosion. Even near the blast, the very next day, the restaurants and streets were packed with people enjoying the sunshine. Because the regime had placed its *mukhabarat* branches so deeply within residential neighborhoods, many Syrians had no choice but to walk past the site as part of their daily routine. Others made a slight detour out of morbid curiosity.

Either way, it was a visual reminder that the regime would tie the fate of all Syrians to its own.

15

SUSPICION

Damascus, Spring 2012

Several months after Salma's widowed sister-in-law Odette read my fortune in her cards, she invited me to her house for her birthday lunch. En route, I picked up a large bouquet of Gerbera daisies—in Syria, florists are true artisans of ribbon, gauze, cellophane, flowers, and foliage. After I selected an assortment of colors, they were wrapped in a kind of burlap and held together by a blade of hay that the flower designer assured me said "spring." By American standards, the flowers cost practically nothing. I met Sa'ad, who was also invited, on a nearby corner, and we strolled over together.

When we arrived, we found the whole clan already there. Besides Odette, there were her two daughters—Mimi, who was unmarried, and Mona, who was there with her husband, a jeweler, their two adult children and their spouses, and a toddler grandchild. To our surprise, they were already seated and eating. "You're so late we forgot you were coming," said Mimi, who often ignored pleasantries.

We were in fact not at all late, but arguing with Mimi was generally pointless. Her sister Mona waved her off and invited us to sit and join them.

I found myself across from my newly married second cousin, Lahab, Mona's son. He, too, was a great-grandchild of Abdeljawwad. Short and balding, he was a decade younger than me and worked with his father. He had stubble on his cheeks and beads of sweat on his forehead. His new wife, now sitting next to him, had been his high school sweetheart. In an effort to make conversation with them, I asked how their honeymoon had gone. She started to answer when he cut her off, correcting the itinerary.

For what was not the first time, this family asked me why I was in Syria. I repeated that I had come to finish the restoration of Salma's house and to work on a book about her. There was a chorus of snorts in response. Trying to change the subject, Lahab's sister, who had been interested in journalism before she was married and had her first child, asked me about my first book. It was a kind gesture, and I thought maybe if I were more transparent about my work, whatever anxiety I caused them might dissipate.

I began to answer her question just as Sa'ad reached for a second helping. At the same time, Mimi abruptly got up from her seat to take plates into the kitchen. When everyone protested on cue that she take a break (throughout lunch she had complained about how tired she was from all the preparations), she snapped, "You don't care, you are here for my mother."

Rising to help with the dishes, I was motioned to sit back down and ignore Mimi. Lahab pushed back from the table and reached for his wife's hand. "It's Friday, no one's in a rush," he said. "Let's chat." He began to interrogate me about America, Barack Obama, and Zionist conspiracies against Syria; his questions were nearly verbatim regurgitations of the regime's narrative.

I stared at him, at his gold chain around his neck, and at his sweaty forehead, and was somewhat insulted that he thought I would take such obvious bait. I instead asked him what *he* thought, and he proceeded to go on a diatribe against the United States and Americans.

I listened politely then excused myself to wash my hands, and when I returned, the guests had dispersed. The women were in the kitchen helping to put away the excess food, and I decided to join them. As soon as Mimi noticed me there, she responded to whatever had just been said with mock shock, exclaiming, "Oh no, not the Virgin [meaning saintly] America!"

"Thanks for a great lunch, Tante," I said to Odette as I did my best to disregard the passive-aggressive remarks and walked toward the kitchen's enclosed balcony. My second cousins and their spouses were there smoking, with the little girl twirling around in front of them as they cheered. Lahab sat on a stool with his slender wife on his knee, his arm firmly around her. Out of the blue he asked me where I had spent New Year's Eve—even though we were already several months into 2012.

I told him it was a new place—but an old house—in the Bab Touma neighborhood. "Strange you don't know its name," he said.

I explained that I had been with my cousin and her fiancé, and that they had bought the tickets. I had just tagged along.

"Oh you mean it was in Mezzeh?" he asked, naming an area quite far away from Bab Touma.

"No, I mean in Bab Touma."

"That place in Abu Rumanneh?" he said.

"No, it's still in Bab Touma," I said, feeling that he wanted to catch me in a lie.

We had this same exchange, going through several more neighborhoods, until I finally asked him, "What are you getting at?"

He flicked his cigarette over the windowsill.

Mona then summoned us for coffee, and he didn't have to answer.

When we returned to the living room, I sat near her, avoiding her son, while he told his wife to sit next to him. They were on the same settee where I had sat to talk with Odette on New Year's Day, the table with her cards and little notebook right next to him. She sat under her own oil portrait, unquestionably the family's matriarch.

In Syria, the groom's family puts on the wedding (because a bride-to-be and her future mother-in-law really need one more battleground), which gave me plenty of fodder for conversation with Mona—because what else could we possibly have to talk about in Syria in the spring of 2012?

Sipping at my coffee, I asked, so what did she wear? How was the party? Had she recovered from all that planning? Before she could answer, her son turned toward us and began listening keenly.

She then began to explain to me that there was much more than she had imagined needed doing. After all, they had to buy her future daughter-in-law a lot of new clothes, which had been more difficult now that Turkish fashion was no longer in Syrian stores. She said that tradition required the bride to enter her new marital house with a whole new wardrobe. (This was not part of any tradition I had ever heard of.)

I couldn't help but laugh and said smugly, "It's the year two thousand and twelve."

"Meaning what?" she asked me, not sure why I was laughing.

"Meaning, aren't there more important things for a woman to bring to her new marriage than her wardrobe?"

Her son interjected, "Well, we do things differently in Syria."

Finally unable to hold back, I responded, "On that we do agree," forcing myself to wink at him in an attempt to keep things light.

As for the newlyweds, they'd be in the United States within eight months; they were expecting a child, and his wife had American relatives. My charmless second cousin who hated America and hated me for being American wanted his baby to be born an American and then become one himself. How they got a visa while thousands of deserving Syrians were rejected, I'll never know.

🕉

A WEEK LATER, while I was at the gym, the trainer who I liked mentioned to me that the other trainer, Coach, had told him not to speak to me, that I was a spy.

I laughed, "A spy for whom?" wondering what had suddenly brought that on. I knew Coach was good friends with Lahab. Could that be the reason? I tried not to make too much of it.

A few days after that encounter, Suha asked me to come over for late afternoon coffee. Kamal was there as well, which wasn't too out of the ordinary, but they appeared quite serious. They were sitting on the edges of their seats.

Odette had telephoned Suha that morning and summoned her, saying there was an urgent matter to discuss. Suha recounted what came next.

Odette told Suha that she must make me leave Syria immediately. The *mukhabarat* had come to Odette's house asking about me, wanting to know about the girl who had visited her a few weeks ago with a "fat man," carrying a big flower bouquet. She told Suha that the *mukhabarat* were reading my Facebook page and monitoring my phone, and that they knew I was coming and going each time on a different passport. They had someone specifically watching me in the gym. Odette had told her no one believed I was writing a book on Salma, because, after all, who was Salma? "She was no one."

I sat there listening in silence, slightly stunned. Suha and Kamal told me I should probably leave Damascus as soon as possible.

I could feel my heart beating in my throat; admittedly, I was terrified. But then I started thinking it through. I had said nothing of consequence on

Facebook, or on the phone. I didn't speak publicly, and in fact I didn't use a different passport each time I entered Syria. Why would the *mukhabarat*—who were hardly subtle or interested in investigating before arresting someone—go to her house and not come straight to me? And the way they gratuitously referred to Sa'ad as "fat" smacked of a certain kind of passive aggressiveness that was a bit too personal for the *mukhabarat* but typical of Mimi. Also, the gym was awfully specific.

I started to sense that Lahab had a part in all of this. I explained my thinking to Suha and Kamal. Also, Mimi was known to make things up, and she could involve her mother. This was a big thing to make up—but could it be possible this was simply all untrue?

After thinking it over, Suha looked to Kamal for his take. He agreed that the source was highly questionable and certain things did not add up.

Did he think any of this was true? I asked.

Taking a drag from his cigarette, Kamal said, "You will only know when there's the knock on the door."

"I can't see anything happening to you," said Suha. She urged me to consider leaving.

That night, I met up as planned with the two grandsons of the son whom Abdeljawwad had disowned for marrying the woman he loved. They were both in their twenties and generally sober about what was happening in the country. They never uttered pro-regime sentiments or regurgitated its narrative. They also didn't think the uprising was a good idea, a position held by many of the pragmatic Syrians I had been meeting in Damascus.

I told them the whole story, starting with the tense lunch, the incident at the gym, and Odette's summit with Suha.

The younger brother, who worked out at the same gym I did, then told me that the friendly trainer had told him the same thing—that Coach had said I was a spy. He then asked me if I remembered that time our second cousin Lahab—who rarely made an appearance at the gym—happened by when both of us were there.

"Yes, of course," I answered. I had made a point of saying hello—despite how little I cared for him—and had asked if everything was okay at his parents' house. A recent explosion near their street had shattered all their windows. Politics aside, I did not wish them ill. Lahab had spoken to me at length and thanked me several times for my concern. "What of it?" I asked the brothers now.

"As soon as you turned your back, he started pointing and laughing and saying '*jassousseh, jassousseh*' [spy, spy]."

I was incensed; it was one thing to say stupid things privately—even though such recklessness could easily endanger my safety. It was another matter to say that out loud in public with the veneer of legitimacy he would have because we were related.

The brothers saw I was upset. Both reassured me there was no reason to leave, especially as I was headed to Egypt in a few weeks. Don't change your plans, they advised. Lahab and Coach, they said, were "idiots."

"There are a lot of idiots like them in the regime," I said.

I decided to seek advice from my mother's brother and my father's brother as well. When I asked Sa'ad, his first reaction was annoyance that Suha had been summoned and not him. But to him, the fact that Odette went to a woman and not a man meant it was likely all made up.

"Don't run. You've done nothing wrong," he said. "Leaving makes it look worse." He would soon be heading to Canada for a protracted stay—an opportunity at Canadian citizenship that many Syrians would have been ecstatic to have. But even under the current circumstances, he didn't want it; he loved Syria. He understood if I didn't want to leave Damascus.

After listening to the whole ordeal, Majed said, "Stay." And he also told me not to switch gyms.

Within days, Sa'ad left for Ottawa, joining his wife and two sons. I decided to remain in Syria, and ended up leaving for Egypt just as I had planned, and no earlier.

The same day I arrived in Cairo, I made my way in a taxi to an apartment, my heart once again beating fast. Suha had jotted down the address for me on a piece of paper torn from a notebook, wishing she could have come with me. I couldn't arrive soon enough and encouraged my driver's Formula 1 instincts. Waiting for me were Um Ragheed (now widowed) and her daughter, and her daughter's children. "Tell her," Suha had said, "that the bitter orange tree still stands."

❧

WHEN I RETURNED to Damascus, I found a chair stationed on the landing in the Tahaan between my floor and the one above it. Suha later explained that Um Mustafa, who lived upstairs, had placed it there because she was tiring easily when climbing the stairs. It would take her so long to recover that while sitting on that chair she had taken to shelling fava beans or preparing other spring vegetables for her winter's *mouneh*.

Um Ragheed and her family had given me a warm welcome, and we had talked for hours. Her memories were vivid, and I was eager to find a research assistant I could trust in Damascus to verify and fill in details that were missing. Shortly after I returned to Damascus, I met with a doctor of social science who I had been assured could help me.

Through him, in fact, I would meet many brave, ordinary Syrians, all very different individuals. Many of them didn't believe in taking up arms, were civically minded, and espoused secular politics. Outside Syria, they would come to be called activists, but at the time, they were simply moved to act because they were horrified by what was happening and couldn't ignore the suffering of their countrymen. Both the regime and the jihadists would want to eliminate them. In my cell phone and notes, I gave everyone aliases to avoid putting them in jeopardy, should my materials ever be seized by the *mukhabarat*—or if I was seized myself.

I nicknamed this social scientist "the Mustache" because, in a region of great mustaches, his was truly superlative. He was a longtime dissident who, both before and after 2011, organized many civil society initiatives. Even before 2011, he was always looking to the new day that would come in Syria—when the regime would fall or change. In his work, he sought to prepare people to assume the duties of citizenship in a new Syria. He came from near Latakia and was Alawite.

At our first meeting, we talked briefly about my research needs. But once he mentioned that he was involved in an underground aid network, our conversation quickly changed to more urgent matters. I sensed that he had a story to tell, and something about it reminded me of Salma.

As the violence across Syria had become more treacherous and the numbers of displaced and injured continued to swell, he explained, what had been individual and ad hoc efforts to provide relief had grown into an increasingly organized underground network of volunteers. Together they were trying to get food, clothing, medicine, shelter, services, and money to those who were trapped, wounded, or displaced by the fighting—whether they had fled to Damascus and its periphery or were still in their besieged cities and towns. The Mustache, like the others, had been moved to act by the realization that the government had no intention of responding to the humanitarian crisis caused by its own siege of Syrian cities, which had resulted in the internal displacement of hundreds of thousands of people. The Red Crescent had estimated that as many as 1.5 million people needed help getting food, water, or shelter.

The regime, as it had done in Hama in 1982, had already made it clear that it would hold entire neighborhoods responsible for any opposition that appeared to have come from its quarters. Now, it had also demonstrated that it considered any aid to such areas, even humanitarian, as a comfort to its enemies. So even though Syria has a strong cultural practice of giving, with several hundred charitable institutions in place, anyone who wanted to provide aid, the Mustache said, had no choice but to act in secrecy.

Not that people hadn't tried to work openly. In March, after the government's month-long bombardment of Homs, a few Damascenes had created a nonpartisan Facebook page called "Carrying Homs in Our Hearts," with a logo of a hand holding an olive branch. The page identified organizers' real names and phone numbers, offering to receive donations they would take to Homs. In three weeks, they had gathered forty tons of food and signed up two hundred people to deliver it to the stricken city. On March 19, they set out in a convoy of three buses and vans, wearing white hats emblazoned with their logo and large identification tags hanging from lanyards around their necks, just like organizers had done in the public service outings that were carried out before the conflict began. (Those, of course, had always been regime approved and regime controlled.) Minutes after their departure, they had been stopped by the traffic police in Damascus. It took a day of wrangling with security services and a call to the satellite television channel Al Arabiya to strike a deal in which the Red Crescent was allowed to deliver the goods to Homs. The volunteers, however, were prohibited from going. While the regime was caught off-guard that time, it had since ramped up its efforts to keep aid from those in need. The Mustache believed this was important to the regime for another reason as well: it was determined to keep civil society from gaining any foothold.

So it had begun to go after those working in secret. The regime had already detained people who had been caught distributing aid—especially medicine. Two women had been taken in broad daylight from a café last month, the Mustache told me. I realized he was refering to the same women Akram and his friend Bassem had told me about. This month, the son of a doctor was taken for helping stockpile and deliver medicine. Another man was arrested after collecting Easter chocolate to send to children (Christian and Muslim) in Homs. A psychiatrist who was training volunteers to help children who had been traumatized by events was also taken.

The reasons were particularly insidious, as the Mustache explained: "They want to get rid of the idea that the people can help each other. They don't want there to be solidarity among the Syrian people." I would hear the same sentiment echoed elsewhere—both from the people I interviewed and from my own family and friends. Some said the regime thought the aid network undermined its efforts to divide and conquer, whether on sectarian, ethnic, or class lines. Resentment was also growing based on geography—residents of the besieged towns and smaller cities felt abandoned by the major cities like Damascus and Aleppo, because residents there had not risen in significant numbers to protest. Aid from the cities, particularly from the relatively un-affected capital, however, subverted that narrative. By taking an active role in the conflict, these underground volunteers were pushing back against the capital's facade of relative normalcy and complicity.

At first, the government had tried to appear responsive to the crisis. In April, Bashar al-Assad and his wife, Asma, were shown on state television at a stadium full of euphoric volunteers filling bags with sugar and rice to be distributed to those in need throughout Syria. The undertaking was staged by Syria Trust, a nongovernmental organization, that Asma chaired. It was through Syria Trust that since before 2011 most civil society initiatives had to be run. "They want to make it look like only the government can provide," the Mustache explained, meaning that, by implication, the government can also just as easily take away.

So now every stop on that underground railway of aid was shrouded in secrecy, from requesting supplies to confirming the needs to delivering goods to fundraising to collecting donations. Separate cells carried them out. Par-ticipants only knew the identities of the people they dealt with directly. He estimated (and others agreed) that there were hundreds of people working in this network in Greater Damascus, and thousands more within Syria. Citi-zens of all genders, sects, classes, and geographies were contributing money and supplies and working to avert the further tearing of the social fabric. While the rest of the world became obsessed with the fall of Assad and when that would happen, these citizens were more concerned with the loss of Syria.

※

A FEW WEEKS later, I waited outside my mother's old school, the Laïque, for the Mustache; he was giving me a ride to a meeting being held at a small farmhouse outside central Damascus. It belonged to a Syrian who lived abroad. He had only described it to me as being "a meeting on citizenship."

In the car with him were two young women, college students, one in architecture and the other in economics. Both said that since what they excitedly called the revolution had started, it had consumed them much more than their studies. The architecture student was from Dara'a, where the uprising began, and I would later come to refer to her as Carnations.

When we arrived at the farmhouse, people were already gathering, preparing their mugs of instant coffee or tea. The house was full of windows, and it was a sunny spring day. People were good natured, kissing each other hello and asking after parents, children, siblings, and friends in common. The crowd was divided equally between women and men, of varying age. Of the women who appeared to be over forty, none were veiled. Other than Carnations, I only saw one other woman, also in her twenties, with the hijab.

We took our seats, with people balancing their mugs with their notebooks and pens. The Mustache got up to speak. He seemed slightly deflated. Word had come from a credible source: "Obnoxious guests will be joining us soon," he said. We all understood. The *mukhabarat* were on the way to the farmhouse at that very moment.

Someone asked for more details. One of the organizers explained that they were coming with a bus. They offered everyone who wanted to leave an opportunity to do so.

I began to wonder what I should do. My first thoughts were about my mom and aunt. I had already begun to feel that I was betraying them by going about and doing my work, or at least possibly putting them in danger. I also had my recorder on me, and I didn't want to lose the audio of my meeting in Cairo with Um Ragheed. People around me were discussing what to do. Some felt we shouldn't be intimidated, that we should stay and not give the regime what it wanted. Some of the women around me began packing up their things; they wanted to go. Others suggested we take a vote—twelve people decided to leave and fifteen wanted to stay. With nearly half of the attendees leaving, the organizers decided to adjourn until a later date. They'd have to try to set this up all over again.

Although they didn't seem discouraged, I found it all so depressing. It was also frightening. I had seen those buses parked in front of security buildings.

Some came and went; others were used as barricades or potential blast absorb-ers. (There was nothing special about these buses. Though they were not yel-low, they looked like the ones I had taken to school as a child in Baltimore.)

In the car, on our way back to central Damascus, I asked the Mustache what they would have talked about had the meeting taken place. He said he had wanted to guide a real discussion or dialogue on citizenship.

I asked the young women how and why they got involved. Carnations came from a conservative family. She was obsessed with Hamza al-Khatib, the boy from her town who had been castrated and killed, and whose father was forced on TV to deny it was the regime. In Dara'a, she had tried to visit his family, but there were always *mukhabarat* watching the house. Without her parents' knowledge, she had already participated in many demonstrations as well as in confrontations with regime supporters at the university.

"All our lives we were raised to be afraid," she said. "But you get to a point where you realize you are strong *because* you can speak and act."

Her companion had gone to her first protest in April 2011. It had made her feel alive, invigorated, and like she was part of a community. Once, after the government had started to regularly open fire on protesters, she saw a man die in front of her. Still, she wasn't dissuaded.

She had also snuck into Homs for four hours recently to deliver aid. She said the people there inspired her. "It was the greatest four hours in my life," she said.

If only Syria were to fall into these women's hands, I thought.

Of course, these activists and initiatives were not funded by the would-be saviors of Syria in the Gulf countries, Turkey, or the West; at the same time, they were aggressively hunted by the regime.

৩৩

TWO DAYS AFTER our stillborn meeting on citizenship, I met up again with Carnations on another beautiful spring day in a Damascene house in Sarouja, not far from Salma's. Like many other old houses with the classic courtyard, it had been converted into a coffeehouse. I was casually interviewing her for what would become a front-page article for a major newspaper.

She was stunningly beautiful and dressed like an average college student anywhere in the world—jeans, a sweater, sunglasses, and a book bag. She was hardly the terrorist villain of the regime narrative. When I asked her what she was planning for her next protest, she smiled and bent toward me. That day was the one-year anniversary of Hamza al-Khatib's death. She was going to campus, but class wasn't really her priority, she told me as she reached into her purse. She had made stickers with Hamza's picture, and below it she had written: "The Martyr Hamza al-Khatib," with the date of his death. She was going to spread the stickers across campus and around town. She had more than a hundred of them.

We weren't alone in the enclosed courtyard. There was a woman there in a long black veil and black *abaya*. She had a friend and a child with her, and Carnations kept looking at them even as she spoke to me. I had perfected a way to appear while having serious conversations in public. I smiled and nodded and hoped anyone watching figured we were only talking about shopping. But when the woman seemed to take a photo in our general direction with her flip phone, Carnations snapped at her. "Is there a reason you are taking our picture?" she said. The woman was taken aback—maybe we were being paranoid—and said she was just photographing the stunning architecture.

We had been at the café for nearly two hours, and both of us needed to leave. As we parted, we kissed and each said, "*Deeri balik 'ala halik*" (Look out for yourself).

The next evening I texted her: "How are you? everything good?" It went unanswered. After several hours, I called her phone. When the call connected, I said hello, but the person on the other line told me right away that she wasn't the young woman I was looking for. I had a bad feeling. "Who is this?" she asked. I mumbled my name quickly. She told me my new friend wasn't there. I heard concern in the other woman's voice.

I said something like, "Ah, okay, she's out, but she's okay?"

She paused. "I don't know," she answered.

Not thirty minutes later, I received an email from the Mustache, in French. In between banal sentences, meant to hide the nature of our conversation, he indicated that Carnations had just been arrested and that she was the fourth person he knew who had been taken since we had met to discuss citizenship at the farmhouse just two days earlier.

I responded right away, telling him I had just called her phone, that another woman had answered, and that she didn't know where Carnations was. I asked him if we were at risk. His response was short and swift: "Erase her number from your phone right away."

Then he emailed again to say, "Stay calm, and above all, don't speak about what happened to her to anyone. ANYONE."

I wrote back, "Calm, that's difficult. She's so sweet. I'm afraid it's because she sang with me yesterday." (Songs had become our word for "article.") He didn't know how or why she was taken, but he told me to try to get some sleep—we might know more tomorrow.

I wasn't going to be able to calm myself down easily. Why had she been taken? Was it because she had spoken to me the day before? I was specifically terrified of what might be happening to her as a woman in detention.

I had been transparent with her about the fact that I was working on an article for an important newspaper, one that was read by many people; even though my name wouldn't be attached to it, I told her, the article would make the regime very unhappy—especially as it would undermine the appearance of normalcy it was trying to project about Syria, and the idea that the troubles were confined to a few bad seeds. They might try to figure out who had written it, and when they did, they would want to find out who had spoken to me.

Like a child, I felt guilty. Had I transgressed the limits by which the regime tolerated my presence? Had I just endangered us all? It was too late to head to Beirut—almost 10 p.m. I decided to pack a bag just in case, so I would be ready to leave if necessary. I also took one of the chef's knives I had bought for Salma's kitchen and slid it under my pillow.

Suha knocked on my door. She was cheerful and wondering if I wanted to come over.

I told her I couldn't.

"What's wrong?" she asked, her smile disappearing.

I couldn't answer her: I had promised her I wouldn't do anything to jeopardize them, and the reality was, I just had.

"It's okay," I said. "But, please, can you check tomorrow morning and make sure that I'm still here?"

"What have you done?" she asked me fearfully. "I told you, I can't. I just can't be dragged by my hair."

❧❧❧

I DIDN'T SLEEP that night. I also didn't close the shutters before going to bed; if anything happened, I wanted witnesses to see and hear it. I was fully dressed under the covers, staring at the framed picture of Salma, my sister Manal, and me on the nightstand. In case she was listening, I asked Salma to watch over me. I asked her to watch over Carnations, too.

When the sun came up, I was still there. Not long after, I got word that Carnations had been taken for something she had done the evening before. With a few other friends—who were also young women—she had walked around downtown Damascus handing out carnations to pedestrians in the city's center. Each flower bore a tag that said simply, "Stop the killing."

That's all. The tags said nothing about who should stop killing, nothing about the regime, nothing about the opposition.

Six agonizing days later, Carnations was released. She had not been sexually assaulted. She was safe with her family. We agreed to meet at a café. Starbucks was operating in many Middle Eastern countries, and though the region had cafés that were centuries old, the Starbucks model (comfy chairs and couches, collective magazines, laptops) had its imitators everywhere.

When I saw Carnations, I hugged her tight, and then over frothy iced coffees we talked about her arrest, her cell, and her interrogation. As she told it, the flowers operation had been a few days in the making: four young women were to carry bunches of carnations and hand them out to passersby on the street. They wanted to counter the regime's image of the activists as terrorists or foreign-paid agents, and they wanted to register some resistance to the regime's demand that Damascenes act as if nothing were happening in the rest of the country.

On that afternoon, the young women had set out in pairs. Her partner had finished handing out the last of her flowers, and Carnations still had three left and was about to cross a street when an Opel station wagon (they didn't need to be marked, everyone knew these belonged to the *mukhabarat*) pulled up next to her. Two men with large guns across their bodies jumped in her way.

"We got her," yelled one of them. "Go find the other."

But the other woman, without flowers in her hand, wasn't so easy to spot. She had kept going even though she saw Carnations get stopped. They had agreed beforehand that if one got detained, the other should just walk away. The man sent to find her returned alone.

"What's in your hand?" asked the man blocking Carnation's way.

She nervously laughed and answered, "Flowers."

He snatched them from her and read the tag. "'Stop the killing'? Who are you saying that to?" Before she could answer, he told her to get in the car.

"You don't have a warrant," she objected. Telling me this, she giggled at her own courage. "I don't know where I thought I was! Europe? America?"

"Get in the car!" the *mukhabarat* man yelled again.

"On what grounds are you taking me?" she challenged him.

"Get in the car, or I will humiliate you on the street and drag you off in front of everyone."

"Fine, I will walk," she said, catching the two men so off-guard that they agreed. One man got back into the car, while the other walked alongside with her. They quickly reached the offices of the political affairs *mukhabarat*.

They took her bag and left her in a waiting room. Her mother and brother were coming to Damascus from Dara'a that evening for a dentist appointment the next day. She had told them to come a day early so they could go out that night, since in Dara'a, for safety, they spent a lot of time cooped up at home. Knowing they would soon panic, she was preoccupied with how to tell them she was okay.

After a long wait (though she had no way of telling time), she was led into a room with a man who was seated behind a desk, going through her bag.

"How much did Qatar pay you?" he asked with a heavy Deir al-Zour accent.

"Nothing," she answered.

"You must be crazy," he said as he rifled through her things. "Do you think you and your kind can do anything to the government? Think you can make revolution?"

As he flipped through her wallet, he saw she was from Dara'a. "So you are a terrorist," he said. And when he found simple blueprints (from a university assignment), he became agitated and suspicious. He asked her what the plans were for.

She was so afraid that she couldn't stifle her laugh, and told him she was an architecture undergraduate.

"Shut up," he told her. Then he turned to what he wanted to know. "Who was the girl who was with you?"

At first she denied there was anyone with her. And then she said it was a girl she had just met. He asked for a description, and Carnations said she was a very tall, fair-skinned girl, when in fact she was short and had olive skin. The other young woman had already been taken once, and Carnations didn't want to give her up. When he asked for a name, Carnations invented one, "Lina."

For the next several hours (how many she didn't know) she was taken in and out of different interrogation rooms. Similar questions were asked while she remained standing: Who paid her? Who was the other girl?

Finally she was placed before a man who seemed to be in charge. Referring to the tags attached to the carnations, he asked, "What do you mean, 'Stop the killing'? Who are you telling to stop?"

"All those killing people," she said carefully. This is why they had left the tags ambiguous.

"Do you mean the Syrian Army? Do you mean the president?" he urged her.

"Is the president killing Syrians? Is the Syrian Army killing people?" she asked, in a way that turned it back on him for suggesting it.

On hearing this, I was in awe of her composure.

He got angry, hurling insults at her.

She decided to play the part of a vulnerable girl. "I'm afraid," she said. "Afraid for the country and for the people."

Seeing she was from Dara'a, he criticized the town with disgust, calling it the place "where you have your revolution and demonstrations."

She asked for water and to sit down; both requests were denied.

He wanted her email and Facebook accounts and passwords. She kept two different ones, and one of them was clean in case she was taken.

After he could find nothing incriminating, he said to her, "Do you think you are smarter than me? I know you have another [account]."

"I am a student, in class from morning to night. I don't have time to be on Facebook all day," she said.

Then he found a Lina among her Facebook friends. "Is this the Lina that was with you?" he asked triumphantly.

Carnations suppressed laughter. That Lina, from the university, was notoriously pro-regime.

He then moved on to who her father was, and what he did for a living, and whether anyone from her family had ever been in political prison.

Her mother was from Aleppo, which had once stood up to the regime (in the years when I used to come to Syria as a small child). Her maternal uncle had in fact been taken in the 1980s, and they still didn't know where he was or if he was even alive. She also had a cousin from that side of the family who had been in political prison for ten years. But her interrogator didn't seem to know, and she didn't bother to tell him.

They took her back to the first interrogator from Deir al-Zour. She was finally allowed to sit and drink water. She thought maybe she was going to be released.

"You are so stupid," he said. "Your father is a respected merchant in Dara'a. Why are you doing this? Who used you, who got you to participate?" He was sure she hadn't been capable of deciding to get involved on her own.

Again, she insisted, truthfully, that no one had paid her.

"I want to talk to my parents," she ventured.

"Forget your parents," he said.

She was taken back to the room where she had been left waiting. Then at some point, maybe after midnight, two men escorted her to a car.

"Are you going to let me go?" she asked.

They started laughing and put her in the car. They then blindfolded and cuffed her and told her to keep her head down. As they drove away, she started to cry.

"Shut up. Don't lift your head," one of them yelled. "If you do, you'll see something you won't like."

When they arrived at their destination, her blindfold was removed, and they walked her down some stairs. She saw blood everywhere and then a sight that made her scream and cry. In the room before her, several naked men were hanging from the ceiling and were being flogged.

One of the men doing the whipping came over to her escorts and said, annoyed, "Don't tell me you're bringing in a girl now. Wait." Carnations assumed from his accent that he was Alawite.

The tortured men were roughly let down and led out of the room. A woman arrived to search her.

Throughout it all, Carnations wept. She was then taken to a cell and heard them bring the men back and refasten them to the ceiling. The beatings resumed.

The cell she estimated was no more than about three by six feet and smelled of rancid bodily fluids.

Another woman was in there as well; Carnations was aghast—she was eight months pregnant. She told Carnations they were in the Khatib.

When Carnations told me this, I had to gasp. That was the *mukhabarat* branch across the street from Salma's Qasour house, the one that I often walked past with a shudder. Like many branches, it had a prison in its basement.

It was only then, when she heard its name, that she fully understood she was in prison. "You start to remember everyone," she said. "I thought of my friends who were well. Do they know I'm here?" she said. "I even thought of you."

"I didn't stop thinking of you," I said, telling her that I had been distraught, thinking she had been taken for speaking to me.

She smiled. "I know." The Mustache had told her.

She continued. "I was afraid most for my parents. I knew I was still okay, but they didn't. I was afraid their fear and worry for me would physically hurt them."

She also thought a lot of the boy she liked. She used to make him promise that if something were to happen to her that he wouldn't do anything stupid. But he would never make her that promise.

"What's the good of that?" she'd chastise him in that recurring argument. "Because one day when I come out, no matter how long it is, I want to find you."

After her release, he told her that each time he thought about doing something while she was taken, he remembered that she wanted to find him. And so he had waited and tried to hope.

If initially the pregnant woman was distrustful of Carnations, her crying so uncontrollably convinced her cellmate that she couldn't possibly be an informant sent to extract a confession. She told Carnations that she was from the Zabadani and had been taken from a sewing workshop; the regime was trying to get her husband to come out of hiding. But even when they caught him, they still didn't let her go. She had been in for almost three weeks.

Before Carnations came, she said, she had had another cellmate, whose name was Mary.

Mary? Carnations believed she knew exactly who Mary was. She had even been to her house. Mary and her husband were a young Christian couple— both of them were doctors, or maybe one of them was a pharmacist. She knew they had been heavily involved in getting medicines and food to the displaced Syrians who had come to the periphery of Damascus. A few days after Carnations had been to their house, the *mukhabarat* had come and taken both husband and wife, in front of the children, reportedly threatening to kill the children if the couple didn't cooperate.

Carnations didn't know where Mary was now or if she was well, yet it made her feel momentarily better to know that someone she knew had been in that same space.

From the other side of the cell's wall, she listened to the beating of the men, who cried and begged for mercy even as they screamed and moaned under the blows.

"Say your God is Bashar," Carnations reported hearing the torturers command.

"The sound of grown men crying . . . " she told me now in the café, beginning to tear up.

That first night, she cried so much that she fell asleep. She dreamt of her mother. When she woke up, she saw a light above her cell and thought it might be morning. She was happy she had managed to pass a few hours unconscious. She smiled.

But the pregnant woman disavowed her of that comfort—she had been asleep maybe twenty minutes. The light was a lamp. Carnations often looked for any natural light to indicate what time it might be. But she was underground, and whenever she thought she saw the daylight, it always turned out to be a bulb.

The food they were given was inedible, but the stale bread could still be swallowed. The pregnant cellmate was hoarding the bread so she would have something in the moments when she felt faint. She would hide it in the itchy, fetid blanket they were given.

The next morning, guards led Carnations from her cell. She asked if she was being released. They laughed. Indeed, each time she was taken out, she asked the same thing, and they laughed every time.

At her first interrogation, there were two investigators. Again, they wanted to know who she intended the message "Stop the killing" for.

She again answered, "To whomever was killing anyone."

One listened to her politely, while the other yelled at her. "Who? Who? Stop who? Think we're blowing up our own guys?" He told her she was stupid and just wanted to be famous like Rima—a woman who gained some foreign media attention for standing alone in a busy intersection, wearing a red dress and holding a sign that also said "Stop the Killing" in silent protest.

"So you mean from all sides?" the quieter investigator said. Carnations thought she then saw him erase something from her file.

She asked when she would be released.

The rude one laughed, "We like having you here, so never." He added, "Depends on what you say and your luck."

The other one said, "*Insh'allah*, everything will work out."

Later that night, she was taken out of the cell for another interrogation. She walked into the room to find the three remaining carnations in a glass of water. "What are these?" this new man asked her, pointing at them, as if they were dangerous contraband.

After the same sorts of questions she had been asked already, he said, "I want to ask you something. Don't get upset," and his demeanor became more respectful. "You are from Dara'a, and people with your last name are both Sunni and Shiite. Are you Shiite or Sunni?"

It wasn't necessarily easy for her to know which way to play it. Initially, any demonstrators or activists from the minority sects—Christian, Druze, Alawite, or Shiite, for example—were treated much better in prison than Sunnis. But as the uprising had stretched over several months, the regime began to punish members of those groups sometimes quite harshly, as if they were traitors.

Carefully she answered, "Our roots are Shiite" (though her family had long ago become Sunni).

This interrogation was now over. Another man came back to escort her back to her cell.

On her second morning, she met with a man she thought was a lawyer. Apparently, the other woman who had been handing out flowers with her had that same evening informed Carnations' parents about what had happened. The family had immediately begun working to secure her release. She luckily had an important doctor among her relatives. But at the time, she didn't know they were working behind the scenes. Every time she asked to call her parents, the interrogators had laughed at her.

Over the rest of her time in custody, whenever she was in her cell, she heard the beating of the men. When she needed to use the bathroom, she would knock on the door to get her jailers' attention. They would then go to the torturer and she'd hear them ask, "You done?" to know if they could let her pass.

But, Carnations told me, the torturer was never done. He would only pause while the men were moved so she could pass. It was futile and absurd— she could hear the torture, so what difference did it make if she saw it?

Then, for whatever reason, the regime did decide to let her go. When she got out, Carnations promised her family she would stop being an activist.

"Is that true?" I asked her.

She smiled. "When I got out, I felt like I was stronger than before. I want to work more. You see the blood, the humiliation, the evil—you can't stay silent," she told me. "I'm so upset when I think of how many are inside. We couldn't protect them."

The day we met, the article for which I had interviewed her came out. I didn't dare bring it up online on a computer over public Wi-Fi, but I had a picture of it. I leaned over close to show her where her very own words were—on the front page. She giggled excitedly, and to anyone watching, we would have looked like any pair of young women, talking and laughing about the sorts of things young women everywhere are imagined to talk and laugh about.

胣

IN THAT SECOND spring of the so-called Arab Spring, I met many more activists. Several of them had been taken but had had the fortune (i.e., the ability to pay the right bribe, good enough *wasta* [connections], or the right sect membership) to be released. I heard about many more who never made it back out.

One man was key to introducing me to many activists, lawyers, advocates, and regular people just trying to stop their country from falling apart. I had nicknamed him Clark, for Clark Kent, because he was a journalist by day. Like my friend Amer, he was Kurdish and lived in the same quarter of Damascus as many other Kurds.

Like the Mustache, Clark had been part of the underground aid network. When doctors in Homs needed empty blood bags, so that they could collect blood for transfusions, Clark himself had set out to deliver what the network had collected. When he and his companion found the roads impassable by gunfire, they abandoned their vehicle. Instead, they carried five hundred empty bags each on their backs and found a shepherd to lead them through back roads and dirt paths, hiking sixty-five miles to the city.

It was Clark who gave me my own fake name one day as we walked to an interview at a safe house in Jaramana (a Damascus suburb) with a recently released prisoner. As we approached the door, he turned to me and said, "By the way, your name is Rita."

"Why?" I asked. "I can't trust this guy?"

"Rita," he said, "You can't trust anyone under torture. Anyone would give up a name. Better they give up the wrong name."

He was right; I admonished myself for being so stupid.

Inside I met someone I called Mate (for the Argentinian tea yerba mate, because he was Druze—many Druze who had emigrated to South America had returned, bringing the tea back with them). He had just been released after forty days inside. The *mukhabarat* had spotted him at a peaceful demonstration in the city center, chased him down, and dragged him away. It was his second time in, and he had only gotten out both times because different *mukhabarat* branches had taken him, and clearly they weren't coordinating.

What emerged from my conversation with him and many others was that there was an unrelenting campaign of arrests snaring tens of thousands of people. The arrests seemed to focus on two groups: first, secular activists, including those who were organizing humanitarian aid, and second, men and boys from the towns that the Syrian Army had besieged or had retaken from the armed opposition. Noticeably absent were actual fighters. Those who were arrested were being dumped into a system devoid of meaningful judicial process or oversight and subject to torture.

Lawyers and activists said that pacifist Syrians had redoubled their efforts to make sure that the fighters' voices were not the only ones being heard—both inside Syria and abroad. The government had responded by arresting them in greater numbers. These nonviolent people were trying to build up civil society and the country's institutions. Removing them from the streets not only deprived the opposition of its more sophisticated members but also allowed the regime to say its opponents were only militants and religious extremists.

A lawyer involved in monitoring and defending these cases explained that "in the beginning, they were taking everyone and putting them behind bars. Little by little, they figured out who is important and who isn't important."

According to Mate, "with more information gained over these months, they have been able to go after and find the key activists. We are talking about pacifist activists, who know exactly what they are doing. By putting them in prison or finding a way to get them to leave the country, they have emptied the street of that strategic voice." But just because he was against using weapons didn't mean he necessarily faulted those who did.

Simultaneously, men and boys were being scooped up from the regions where the government crackdown had been the harshest. They were being taken from their hometowns while attending funerals, participating in protests, or walking down the street. They were also being arrested at checkpoints if their IDs showed they were from a town under government siege or under opposition control.

Detainees from this group were being forced to confess to possessing weapons. Mate told me it was because the regime needed to "prove" both to domestic and international audiences that there were armed fighters in the areas the regime was bombarding, to back up its version of events. Mate had met, in prison, an elderly man named Abu Riad, who had apparently been arrested after asking the authorities where his sons were. His three sons, construction workers, had been arrested at a checkpoint as they returned from a job. The men were all from Dara'a. When Mate met Abu Riad, he was thin and his body was covered in cigarette burns. By then, Mate said, Abu Riad and his sons had all confessed to having carried weapons against the state.

These generally less-connected men and boys from the besieged regions rarely saw release. Mate said that the Sunni prisoners were often forced to kiss photographs of Assad, or to say, "There is no God but Bashar," a riff on the Muslim declaration of belief: "There is no god but God." He also said they were forbidden to pray and were subjected to taunts against God and the Prophet Muhammad.

But Mate wasn't spared the torture of the other prisoners just because he wasn't Sunni. He had been beaten and hung by his arms for hours, with a car tire placed around his neck. Once, the agents blindfolded him while they were hanging him. When it was removed, he saw a coffin in front of him full of what looked to be blood. They left him for hours to contemplate it.

With about two hundred other prisoners, he had been kept in a small cell about fifteen by eighty feet, where they tried to sleep standing up and to not piss or defecate until they were escorted elsewhere.

During his interrogations, the Alawite inquisitors had told him that Druze and Alawites were both minorities and had to stick together. "You know how these Muslims and Gulf Arabs are."

Mate ashamedly admitted to me that he had said, "Yes, that's right." And when his torturer had said, "You're either with us or against us," he had responded, "Of course I am with you."

To me he said, "I was someone else inside."

. In the easier moments of the interrogation, he had been asked, "What was missing in your life? Wasn't it better before?" This was a common refrain pro-regime commentators had been cued to say over and over on state TV.

So what was missing? I asked Mate.

"My voice, a feeling that I was a citizen, my rights in this country," he said. "The first thing you think of when you become an adult in Syria is to go outside of the country because there's no opportunity here. The opportunities here are for those who have *wasta*. But with technology and globalization, your friends are from everywhere and you get jealous that your country is not like another."

When I asked Mate what his plan was now that he was "free," he said he planned to lie low for a few weeks. "Just for my mom," he explained.

"But then, of course, I'm going to continue," he said. "I won't shut up."

16

UNRAVELING

Damascus, May 2012, and Yerevan, September 2012

O VER A CUP OF ARABIC COFFEE AT SUHA'S APARTMENT, SHE EX-
plained to me that her daughter's fiancé was going to Armenia later
that week to find out about becoming an Armenian citizen.

"How is he going to get Armenian citizenship?" I asked.

Unlike other Syrian Armenians—who were fluent in Armenian and
whose Armenian identities were strongly rooted in their everyday lives—he
hardly spoke a word of it, nor did his parents.

That's when I found out Armenia was offering any Syrian Armenian a
fast-tracked visa. Ethnic solidarity was no doubt at play, but surely luring
them and their wealth to the struggling country was also a consideration.

Moving abroad was increasingly looking like a smart choice for any Syrian
who had an opportunity to do so. My cousin's fiancé, a diamond designer with
considerable stock, could practice his trade anywhere. But there was a slight
hiccup slowing him down—my cousin had no passport, because she had no
citizenship.

Even though Kamal's mother was Syrian and Kamal himself had been born
in Syria, his father was a Palestinian who got stuck in Syria on the wrong side
of 1948. Since nationality in Syria is paternal only, and with Israel now where
Palestine had been, Kamal had no passport. So unfortunately for his daugh-

ter, despite having a Syrian mother and having lived only in Syria, she, too, was Syrian solely in feeling. Both she and her father had only *laissez-passer* papers. While once she married she would finally become Syrian, her fiancé still needed a place to move his business to and was considering all options, including moving to Armenia.

I looked over at the wall where a framed portrait hung. In charcoal strokes, Suha had rendered Marianne, the daughter of Teta Marie, whom my family had taken in after she had fled the Armenian genocide. With Marianne's marriage to the Laïque's principal's personal cook, she had been a frequent visitor to Salma's house in the Tahaan. Suha had drawn just her face, a few wisps of hair on her forehead, with her characteristic short scarf tied around her head.

I was curious and profoundly sad about the further disintegration of Syria into its parts. Something was familiar in this story.

"It's a bit like what happened with the Jews," I said to Suha. "To Stella and Nanette."

"You found them, right?" asked Suha. "But you never told me the details."

"Yes, it's true," I said. It was also true that I hadn't told her the full story.

I had found them—sort of—when I moved to New York City in 2005 to complete a master's degree in journalism. Shortly after I arrived, a Lebanese acquaintance told me how on a recent flight he had been seated next to an Orthodox Jewish man. After they exchanged a few pleasantries, he learned the man was in fact Syrian. They switched to Arabic, and the man told him of a large Syrian Jewish community in Ocean Parkway. That's when I remembered that many of the Syrian Jews who had left Syria had ultimately settled in Brooklyn. It no longer seemed impossible to find the sisters, especially as I too was living in New York City.

I had called Sa'ad in Damascus; he might know what had happened to Stella and Nanette, because after the stroke, even as many relatives couldn't bear to see Salma in that state, the sisters had come often to sit with her. When I asked Sa'ad if he had heard anything about where they might have gone, he said he thought Stella had wed in Argentina, and that Nanette had married a Lebanese doctor and moved to Brooklyn.

In 2005, I was so close, I set out to find them. When I arrived in Ocean Parkway, in the south of Brooklyn, I encountered a landscape that was 100 percent New York, but Syria was never far from the senses. I ducked in and out of grocery stores and bakeries. Syrian arts, like copper and mother-of-pearl mosaics, decorated the walls. Syrian-accented Arabic was the lingua franca. Its curved calligraphy advertised grocers' goods, and the smells reminded me of the spices souk in Damascus.

I saw the natural immigrant re-creation of home, yet poignantly different. In Ocean Parkway, no new clergymen were coming from the old country to tend the flock, and no relatives were visiting with up-to-date gossip and stories of the old neighborhoods. There would be no visits "back home" with suitcases laden with gifts, evidence of the prosperity that made the painful separation from family worth it—because most of the people living there had resigned themselves to exile. Later I'd hear that keeping the community relatively intact in Brooklyn nevertheless seemed to have mitigated the ache of losing what had been cut away over a decade before. For the time being, many Syrian Jews were marrying either other Syrian Jews or other Sephardic Jews, especially Arabic-speaking ones.

I told Suha how I had walked around Ocean Parkway, noting down all the hair salons, thinking that maybe Stella was working in one of them; after all, she had been a hairdresser in Syria. But it would be in a bakery with particularly appetizing *baklawa* in the window where I'd find a clue. Inside, the baker's wife, who was Moroccan Jewish, didn't really know the community, though that did not stop her from gossiping about them at length to me. I had been ready to leave when another woman entered. She was perfectly coiffed and unnaturally blond. I could smell her perfume and noticed her gold jewelry. She was overdressed for a Brooklyn weekday at 4 p.m. She must be Syrian, I thought, and when I heard her speak, I was sure.

I had yet to master the journalistic art of invading people's personal space, out of the blue. But I didn't want to lose the opportunity. I introduced myself and told her I was looking for friends of my grandmother. She was eager to help, speaking to me in that utterly feminine Syrian way that I have also never mastered. I asked her if she knew Stella and Nanette, who I thought might be living in Brooklyn. I knew it sounded crazy—it was like looking for a needle in a haystack.

"Of course I do!" she told me. Stella was in Mexico, she said, and she could get me Nanette's phone number.

At the same time, completely coincidentally, my mother had called me, and I told her what was happening. Excited, she asked me to ask the woman about several other names—friends she had lost track of ever since her own immigration to the United States. The woman was in a rush, but she gave me her cell phone number and told me to call. I called her several times, and each time, she had yet again forgotten to obtain the numbers for me.

Over the years, I had asked many Syrians, both in Syria and in the diaspora, what they thought of the exodus of Syrian Jews. Most expressed remorse. Some spoke from genuine feeling, invoking the memories of friends, neighbors, and classmates. Others regretted that the Jews' departure or forced expulsion from Arab lands had deprived the Arab world of full moral authority on the issue of Palestinian dispossession. Others shrugged it off; they were resigned to the changing reality that was transforming Syrian identity to an exclusively Muslim one. Many even preferred it, cheered or incited by sectarian preachers and Islamists supported by foreign money. Some Christians expected that with such a diminished sense of who Syrians were, their existence in the Middle East would eventually no longer be tenable.

A month had passed in New York after I had started my search, and I was beginning to doubt I'd hear from the Syrian woman. Maybe no one wanted to reopen old wounds, or maybe the sisters didn't want to see me. But then she had called me from a noisy party. Stella and Nanette's youngest sister was with her; the sister didn't understand exactly who I was. Would I mind explaining? she asked me, before handing the phone to the sister.

"I am Lamya's daughter, who is Salma's daughter," I shouted over the Arabic music, which I could hear through the receiver. In a culture where men and women take their father's name for their middle name and where many last names use the construction "son of," plus a name, it was gratifying to trade instead on my mother's and grandmother's names and their reputations.

The woman was much younger than her sisters, but she knew Salma. She gave me Nanette's number; Stella, it turned out, lived in Israel.

I had called Nanette the next day. We spoke for almost an hour—we had twenty-five years of life to catch up on, since we had last seen each other when I was just a child, the summer of my baptism. There were things she had waited for so many years to say. She wanted to thank my father for the medicines he had sent her in the 1980s. And she wanted to tell me that for Salma, there were two important things in life: Allah and Alia.

We made plans to see each other the next day for lunch.

When I arrived, she was waiting on the street. Unlike Stella, whose image was burned into my memory, I only recognized Nanette because I had been staring at pictures of her from my baptism for years. She took me in her arms and then looked at me again, trying to find the child she knew. Inside her apartment were the sister I had spoken to, the sister's daughter, and another friend. They were all Syrian women. The lunch spread was bountiful, with Syrian delicacies my mother no longer executed with the same disregard to fat. We swapped pictures and talked about the relocation to Brooklyn. We then called Stella in Israel, who was expecting us.

Stella had moved to Israel after her marriage failed. There, the state had provided heavily subsidized housing as well as health care for her aging mother. I felt a pang of regret; I had again been working there and had just moved to New York from Palestine/Israel that fall. We could have met there. Stella still spoke broken Hebrew, and she no longer worked. When I asked if she was happy, she answered that life had not turned out as she had planned, but she felt blessed to be living close to her family.

I answered all their questions, too: Did Suha have more children? Did Sa'ad find love? Was my grandfather still alive? Stella told me how it had broken her heart every day when she had visited my grandmother after her stroke. Before she was locked in and before her brother's murder, she said, Salma had been so full of life. She said that what had always cheered my ailing grandmother up the most was a call to the United States to talk to me. Stella would hold the phone to my grandmother's ear as I would chatter, and then she would say to her, "Did you hear Alia? Did you hear her?" She told me that she would then see a tear fall, one my grandmother could not wipe away on her own. When I told Suha this detail later, I saw the same pain I had felt flicker across her face.

I went on to write my master's project about Syrian Jews. While many Syrians tried to convince themselves that what had happened to the Syrian Jews was just a consequence of unfortunate geopolitics (some feeling bad about it, others not really), to me it felt like an utter failure to protect Syrian society as a whole. That an ancient Syrian community could be amputated from the Syrian body politic because it was *inconvenient* always felt like a frightening precedent. In 2005, I had feared what that could portend, even though at the time, the Syrian ambassador in the United States had been reaching out to the Syrian Jewish community, and their property in Syria was still protected by the government.

As I met with Syrian Jewish families, they'd show me their pictures from Syria. Many were printed on the same 3.5-by-4.5-inch grainy matte paper with the rounded—not square—edges, like the pictures I had of my baptism.

At our first meeting, Nanette gave me a beautiful picture of Stella in Damascus—same size, same paper, same curved corners. She was leaning on the balcony of her old Damascene house, overlooking its internal garden. She was surrounded by pink roses, her naturally wavy and feathered locks cut to her shoulders. Light reflected off the surrounding stucco walls, casting a glow like the one that used to surround all my memories of Damascus before I became reacquainted with it as an adult.

Now in Suha's house, looking at Marianne's portrait and hearing how Syrian Armenians might have options in Armenia, I had to wonder how real and viable Syria's ethnic and religious mosaic was, and what could possibly be put back together once the dust cleared.

ࢣ

FOUR MONTHS LATER, I was in Yerevan, hoping to uncover some truths about Syria.

Armenians have been in Syria since at least the eleventh century. In fact, religiously inspired Armenians—Armenia was one of the world's first Christian countries—had been traveling and settling in the area long before that, especially near Greater Syria's sites of Christian pilgrimage. Many of these Armenians had long been Arabicized, but they maintained their religious customs. Of course, in the early twentieth century, as the Ottoman Empire sought to exterminate them, they fled to Syria and their numbers swelled.

Those who survived began to pick up the pieces of their lives in Syria. Refugee camps for Armenians in Aleppo would later become bustling Armenian neighborhoods as tents became cement dwellings and the camps evolved from limbo to permanency. Many Armenians stayed, made Syria their home, and became Syrian. The community numbered an estimated 150,000 at its peak in the 1990s. They resuscitated, rebuilt, and preserved in Aleppo their language, churches, and schools. Others left for Lebanon, Europe, South America, or the United States, forming the many communities that today make up the Armenian diaspora. But they all passed through Syria first, and in the collective Armenian imagination, Aleppo, in particular, is a place of refuge and rebirth.

Syrian Armenians had always been part of our family history—starting when Marta and Abdeljawwad took in Teta Marie in our ancestral village.

Then, in Baltimore, Syrian Armenians belonged to our cobbled-together Middle Eastern community. I had assumed that Yerevan would be automatically familiar. From my window seat on my flight there, I had immediately recognized the incredible Mt. Ararat, an Armenian symbol.

On landing, however, I found that nothing felt familiar at all. This Armenia was in the rugged Caucasus, and there was not an olive tree or a palm tree in sight. The very light was different—the sky was not flawlessly blue, but grayer as the sun dodged in and out of the clouds—and the architecture was also nothing like that in Syria, Lebanon, or Turkey. Whereas in those countries a hint of the Mediterranean was never difficult to find, the buildings often white and ringed in balconies, Yerevan seemed to specialize in various types of gray and pink stone. Only the churches seemed similar, with the same pointed domes that Armenian places of worship had elsewhere in the Middle East.

But then again, the Armenians I had known all my life weren't exactly from what Armenians call "Eastern Armenia." Rather, their origins were in "Western Armenia," a homeland not a part of today's Armenia, but part of Turkey. The magnificent summit of Mt. Ararat has split the two Armenias' destinies throughout history. While Western Armenia ceased to exist except in memory, its culture was preserved in the Arab world. Eastern Armenia became a Soviet state in 1922 and regained its independence in 1991. Both in ancient and modern times, Eastern Armenia has been in the spheres of Iran and Russia. Accordingly, even the language spoken in Yerevan differs significantly from the one carried into exile by those who fled the genocide. Often impoverished, Eastern Armenia has long depended on remittances from the wealthy diaspora (mostly Western Armenians, including the community in Syria), especially during the war with Azerbaijan. But in recent years, increasing numbers of Syrian Armenians had begun to visit Armenia during the summer, and in June 2012, many had come on vacation as usual.

In July, however, a few months before my September visit, Aleppo—where most of Syria's Armenian community lived—erupted in violent battle between the regime and armed rebels. Syrian families vacationing in Yerevan kept putting off their return home until things "cooled down" in Aleppo. Instead, things only deteriorated. Already about 6,000 Syrians had sought refuge in Armenia, and more were arriving each week, even as a few trickled back, unable to afford Yerevan or unwilling to stay away from houses and businesses they left behind unguarded in Syria.

The evidence of their presence was visible—and audible. When Syrian Armenians didn't want to be understood, they would switch to Arabic. There were new restaurants opening up serving Armenian-influenced Aleppan cuisine and plenty of cars with license plates from Aleppo. With the road to the airport in Aleppo perilous, many had instead driven from Syria to Turkey to Georgia and finally to Armenia, and Armenia had waived taxes and fees that are usually levied on cars in order to ease the costs for Syrians either taking temporary refuge in Armenia or permanently moving there. In fact, in 2005, Armenia had amended its laws to make it easier for ethnic Armenians in the diaspora to claim citizenship. While some Syrian Armenians did, few were trying to relocate to Armenia permanently. But with Syria in the throes of conflict, the applications were steadily increasing.

There were Armenians who spoke with nationalist zeal and excitement about the possible "repatriation" of Syrian Armenians as a wonderful thing for Armenia, which greatly needed an invigorating influx of people, ideas, and money. But that celebration was initially difficult to hear, not just for me, but for many of the newly arriving and traumatized Syrian Armenians. Many were still reeling, and many of them had yet to give up on Syria. Several Syrian Armenians had even opened a school in Yerevan that I visited in its first days. With Xeroxed copies of Syrian textbooks, it taught the curriculum of Syrian schools, so that when they returned to Syria as they expected to, their children wouldn't have fallen behind.

༄

WHILE OTHER SYRIANS I met in Yerevan remained bewildered, still layering their summer vacation clothes for warmth as fall approached and only just beginning to realize that they wouldn't be resuming their lives in Syria anytime soon, Anto had seen the writing on the wall a full year before. His new life in Yerevan was already up and running, as was his new restaurant. A friend's uncle, he kept me well fed, and over a meal I asked him how he got his head start.

"My business was in Idlib, where I saw what was coming," he explained, "And my neighbors told me to go."

Before coming to Yerevan, he had run a restaurant and inn in northwestern Syria that had been a family business since 1938. His grandfather had built the restaurant high in the hills above the city of Idlib as a spring and summer escape for Syrians living in the region below, including people from Aleppo, where Anto lived in the off-season. People came for the fresh air, their delectable food, and the impromptu musical sets that Anto and his father and grandfather had provided. But in April 2011, when Anto would have usually opened the restaurant up for the spring, he had kept it shuttered instead. Syrians were staying close to home, hoping that by ignoring what was brewing in other parts of the country, it might just go away. With summer, fruit had ripened as usual but had rotted uneaten on the trees. Both the restaurant and the inn had remained idle and empty.

If people thought things would calm down, Anto had known they were wrong. Idlib and the surrounding area became strongholds for opposition fighters, including religious extremists. Thus, religion and ethnicity became a congenital liability: the wrong belief or background, at the wrong moment, was potentially fatal. Guilt became collective; one individual could be traded for another of the same sect or community in escalating cycles of brutality and vengeance. Anto could not avoid a certain vulgar calculus: as a Syrian Armenian Christian in a country where sectarianism was looming, he was marked.

"A local friend told me," he recounted, 'You're like an Arab in Tel Aviv!'"

To the more conservative people in the hills, Anto was already an affront because the restaurant served alcohol and allowed the genders to mix. Moreover, he was neither Muslim nor Arab—despite being Syrian—and that made him fair game as a scapegoat for a regime that claimed to be supported by minorities. It also made him an easy target for kidnappers, who were taking advantage of the chaos, hoping to net a pretty ransom without the risk of angering a much more numerous or powerful community. For those who, in their fervor, believed that a better Syria required everyone to be the same, there was little room for him. The warnings from his neighbors became explicit: it was time for him to go—echoing what Anto's father (who, like his father before him, had been born in Syria) used to tell him, repeating what had been passed down through four generations: "Like we came from Turkey, we may also one day leave from Syria."

The relative who had left Turkey had been Anto's great-grandfather Abkar. The local puppeteer in Urfa, Abkar had been beloved by Armenians and Turks alike. In 1915, the latter warned him that something was coming and that he should make a run for it. So he packed his puppets, dug up his gold, and stole away quickly, under darkness, on foot with his wife and six children. They had walked to Aleppo.

Almost a hundred years later, with his own neighbors' warnings in his ears, Anto had known to listen. He began to quietly liquidate whatever he could, at a fraction of market value. For his security, he never announced when he was coming from Aleppo, not wanting to gamble on the hope that people might come back to their senses. Early one morning in October 2011, a month after his neighbors warned him he would not be safe, one of the locals who spotted him at the inn joked, "Why didn't you tell us you were coming? We were going to kidnap you." Anto laughed it off but he had in fact come for the last time. Silently he had bid goodbye to the trees, the hills, the ground itself. He had nodded to the statue of the Madonna and to the little room he had built so Muslim workers or guests could pray. He had paused at the chair where he used to sit with his water pipe, and gazed at the spot where, as a boy and as a man, he had watched his father and grandfather sing to the rapt diners.

"Abu Artin [the business's name] was history; it was real and it can't be erased," he told me defiantly. "It was there before Bashar, before Hafez, before all the presidents."

On that last day and before returning to Aleppo, he'd left the keys to the business with Mohammed, a local who had worked for his family for years and who had held Anto's father's hand in the hospital when he had died. When Anto kissed him farewell, Mohammed whispered in his ear, "Don't come back, *mu'alem*," calling him "teacher," as a sign of respect.

A week later, Mohammed told Anto over the phone that the door to the inn had been broken. Everything had been stolen by neighbors, and displaced Syrians had moved into the empty rooms. Anto cursed the thieves but didn't begrudge the squatters; they needed a place to sleep.

He began thinking about moving to Armenia. Anto had first visited the country for a music festival in 1993, when he was twenty-five years old and performing with a Syrian Armenian dance troupe. Back then, Armenia was newly independent and already at war with neighboring Azerbaijan. Its border with Turkey was closed. Landlocked, Georgia and Iran on Armenia's other shared borders were the country's only lifeline to the rest of the world. There were also shortages of food, and the Armenian diaspora, including the wealthy community in Syria, had to bolster its economy with remittances.

Without enough electricity, Anto had passed his nights in the fledgling state entirely by candlelight.

"Of course most Syrian Armenians ignored Armenian nationalist calls to 'come back' to Armenia," he told me, shaking his head at how fortunes had changed. "Our lives in Aleppo were beautiful."

I asked him what he had thought, at the time, about how, just before his first trip to Armenia, the Jews had left Syria—also courted by nationalists from a would-be homeland. The excision was not unnoticed, he told me. But they all thought, back then, that the contradiction of being Jewish and Syrian was a special case, thanks to geopolitics. There were, they thought then, no other such contradictions.

When Anto told his mother in early 2012 that he was leaving Syria and moving to Armenia, she was aghast. "The mafia will kidnap you," she said. "And you and your wife will get divorced."

She was convinced, like many others in the Armenian community in Aleppo, that what was happening in other parts of Syria would not—could not—reach them there. But what Anto had already lost in Idlib convinced him otherwise. He decided to sell his house in the city, causing the community to gossip. Why would he do such a desperate thing? He told them he had debts to pay, letting people speculate about which way he had failed as a man and as a provider.

With Aleppo oblivious to what was coming, he got a price for the house that suggested nothing of a country at war. He took the money and in February 2012 came to scout out a life in Yerevan. Since 1993, diaspora money had poured in, and there were glitzy new hotels, offices, shops, and streets in the city center. Anto had continued to come frequently to Armenia, where he had pursued his musical ambitions, recording and producing records. He knew Yerevan well enough, and he planned to open a restaurant.

But then he began to have second thoughts. He loved Syria, and Aleppo was his city. Maybe it really would all be over as quickly as it had started. He only found his resolve again at the thought of his young children, and knew he couldn't stake their future in a place he felt sure was imploding. By May, he had moved his family to Yerevan.

Slowly, he gained customers, and business had picked up over the summer, with vacationing Syrian Armenians and other Western Armenians in town. In June, when Syrians began arriving from Aleppo, they chastised him, telling him the troubles would all be resolved—even before their vacations ended. When, in July, the battle for Aleppo itself began, and fighting engulfed the city, eventually leaving much of Aleppo in ruins, he hated that he had been right. Many Syrians extended their stays in Armenia, saying they would wait out the rough period in Yerevan. That fall, many still continued to tell me that it would all be over in weeks.

Anto had mounted a large flat-screen TV in the restaurant and set the satellite dish to channels from Syria. That's where, in August, he had watched as the historic souks of Aleppo burned.

How did he feel now? I asked him during one of our many conversations.

"I cannot cry now," he said. "I have no time. I have to feed my family. I have to survive in this new country. If my situation gets better, and I can relax, I will cry."

Taking a sip of coffee, he added, "I miss the past." But he planned to keep moving forward; rolling grape leaves, skewering kabobs, and keeping jovial for the business.

Besides, he wasn't sure anymore which were the events to be marked and the places to be mourned—Urfa? Idlib? Aleppo?

છુરૈ

WHILE I WAS in Armenia, I felt like Mt. Ararat was everywhere I turned, dominating the skyline in Yerevan and beyond. As beautiful as it was, even I found it painful, a constant reminder of the longing for Western Armenia and of what had been lost in genocide. No longer a part of any Armenia, it was an open wound, and yet, at the same time, it was the symbol of being Armenian.

One night, I joined a group of Armenian North Americans for dinner. They were traveling together on a promise they had sworn to the year before: if their friend, a member of the group, survived cancer, they would all make this pilgrimage to the reduced remains of their ancestral homeland. They had come from Los Angeles and Montreal, all descendants of genocide survivors, all people who had passed through Syria. Although they were Western Armenians, we were engaging in the very Eastern Armenian appreciation of mulberry vodka and their local guide's extreme appreciation for drinking a shot every few minutes, with any toast serving an acceptable pretext. We often had to stand as we said "Cheers."

By the end of that night, after having toasted survival (national and individual) and fraternity (ethnic and platonic), the group clinked their shot glasses and said, "For Syria." They then looked my way to make sure I heard. Not quite in unison, but in beautiful slurred speech, they repeated, "For Syria."

After nearly a month in Armenia, I understood that the toast was more than just a welcoming gesture to me. As one Armenian politician in Yerevan had told me—upon finding out that I was Syrian American—"You gave them life again." Many other Eastern Armenians, learning I was Syrian, had also thanked me, as a proxy for thanking Syria.

At dinner, I couldn't help but be choked up by this simple toast: "For Syria." The solidarity was moving. But what really gripped me was how, one hundred years ago, Syria had offered a decimated people refuge and home and life. Now, Syria offered safety to no one. This included the many ethnically Armenian Syrians, who were more fortunate than other Syrians, able to wait out the violence in Armenia. But unlike other Syrians, they had landed in a place that wished them to stay and was actively courting them.

I began to wonder about all the possible futures: Would Armenians go back to Syria? Would they become a bridge between a new Syria and the Caucasus? Would their presence and history in Syria—which once seemed innate (as did the Jews, as do the Christians)—recede? Would those who left be replaced with newcomers to Syria? There were already foreign fighters seeking fame, fortune, redemption, meaning—whatever—in our country. Would their children become the new Syrians?

Were waves of expulsion, migration, refuge, and exile just the natural course of things—no tragedy greater or less than another? Was permanence only ever illusory?

17

POWER

Tartus, March 2013

A S SYRIA ENTERED ITS THIRD YEAR OF DISINTEGRATION IN March 2013, I went to Tartus, a small port city on the country's Mediterranean coast. March—the month the Dara'a demonstrations had begun in 2011—had become a natural pause in time to contemplate the year that had just passed. In 2012, international pressure had seemed to be at an all-time high, but an end to the conflict did not appear to be in sight; casualties were nearing 100,000. The opposition abroad had continued to prove ineffective. Syria had traded fire with Turkey and Israel, but without great escalation. Much of Aleppo had been damaged (including its UNESCO World Heritage Sites).

Although rebel fighters had been able to hold onto different pockets of territory across the country, they had not been able to push further into regime-controlled land. Nor was the regime able to retake areas it had lost. Backers of the fighters and of the regime stepped up their support. Gulf countries (as well as Turkey and the United States) were funding, arming, or training rebel groups, and the regime continued to receive arms from Iran; Iran's Lebanese proxy, Hezbollah, sent fighters into Syria to reinforce regime forces.

In the chaos, there had been a loss of personal safety—which hadn't been the case before 2011. Gangs now kidnapped people and held them for large ransoms. The regime looked the other way, and families found themselves liquidating everything to get their loved ones back. My family feared I was an easy target—people perceived expatriate Syrians to be rich. So I had rented a small apartment in Beirut and kept my comings and goings to Syria irregular.

I had last been to Tartus in 2004, with my parents, and had found it then a languid town by the sea. Its potential as a tourist destination had not been developed. The most I could say about Tartus until I returned in 2013 was that at a seaside restaurant there, I had eaten the most delicious grilled fish I'd ever tasted. But since Syria had begun to come apart in 2011, Tartus had been booming. Many internally displaced Syrians fleeing other parts of the country (Aleppo, Homs, Idlib, Qamishli, Raqqa) had come to Tartus for its relative safety and normalcy. It was fairly well protected from the varying degrees of hell being experienced elsewhere.

After all, the Assad family came from nearby Qardaha, a village located above Latakia, a city fifty miles north of Tartus along the Mediterranean. Many were speculating that Bashar al-Assad was keeping the coastal regions and their hills secure should he need to beat a retreat from Damascus. Others suggested the region might serve as a possible location for a future Alawite state should Syria end up in pieces.

A friend of my mother's, Sami, had invited me to visit him in Tartus. Both Sami and his wife, Sarab, had been Lamya's university classmates. They had broken up partway through their courtship, but then my mother had gotten them to dance together at a party at Salma's house, and they soon reconciled. After thirty-five years of happy marriage, Sarab had died the previous August from cancer.

Sami was from Damascus but had settled in Sarab's hometown after they returned from Germany, where they did their medical specializations. It was easier to set up their practices in a smaller community, her family was there, and he loved the sea—he was a windsurfer. Both of their daughters—doctors themselves—were in the United States now, but his son, Laith, who worked at a bank, still lived with him.

I caught a ride from Lebanon on a clear day with Sami's friends—it was easier to get to Tartus from Beirut than from Damascus. I had never entered Syria from the coastal border; the drive toward Tartus was a straight shot up the coast, with the sea always on the left and into the west. Sometimes, however, cars would have to detour to avoid getting caught in the crossfire when Syria's conflict would spill over into Lebanon, and tensions would flare up between Lebanese Sunnis and Alawites who lived around Tripoli. But our path that morning was clear. As we made our way toward Syria, I chatted with my companion in the back seat, a doctor who had lived in the United States. He had had the opportunity to stay there, but chose a life in Syria instead.

I asked him if he wished he had not come back. "No regrets," he smiled at me without hesitation. "I love my country."

Seeing the border crossing ahead of us, I began to tense up. The Lebanese control was not what I worried about: they had no problem with people leaving Lebanon, but the lines of Syrians trying to get in were packed. A small country with limited resources and a highly dysfunctional government, Lebanon was becoming increasingly burdened by all the fleeing Syrians and was trying to make it harder for them to enter, especially if they appeared to be poor.

At passport control, there were few women. One came running to me straightaway when she saw me. Wearing a long, dusty robe and carrying her belongings in bundles, she begged me to help her fill out the paperwork required by the Lebanese to enter; she was illiterate. My other traveling companion, an important businessman, immediately began to shoo her away until I explained what she needed. He then snatched the entrance form from the woman and did it for her, telling me to go finish my own paperwork. Later he explained that he wanted me in and out of there before word got out that I was an American and the news could beat us to the Syrian side.

We got back into the car and crossed into Syria—the men told me we wouldn't have to get out. Instead, the runner they always bribed to smooth their entry met us. He took our documents and disappeared inside Syrian border control. We waited in silence, until he came out with a look of consternation and apology all at once. There was a bit of a problem with my American passport—even though it was accompanied by a Syrian ID card (which should have guaranteed automatic entry). The businessman said he would handle it and told me to remain in the car while he did. When he finally reappeared, he signaled the driver to quickly start the car. We sped away, and he handed me my passport, saying, "Bury that in your belongings and only use the Syrian one." I'd have to keep it handy, as there would be many checkpoints ahead.

I settled back into my seat, but recoiling from the smell of open sewage, I began to roll up my window when I suddenly stopped. We were approaching groves of citrus trees. The air would soon be perfumed with orange blossoms, a scent Syrians bottle in *mazahar* (orange blossom water) and then use for sweets, drinks, and even on the skin. It reminded me that my parents and I had also been here in March, nearly a decade before.

At Tartus's entrance, a huge statue of Hafez al-Assad greeted us. Periodically I would wonder what he would have thought of what was going on. Many who had hated him and found him ruthless nonetheless believed he must be rolling over in his grave at his son's handling of the situation. More and more buildings eventually came into view, with posters of Bashar al-Assad adorning them. These were different from the ones in Damascus, though. Here he was dressed mostly in military fatigues, pictured with the leader of Hezbollah and a number of other men. They were *shaheed*, martyrs—that is, Syrians who had died in the Syrian Army. There were also several women on the streets, wearing all black with white scarves around their necks. They were the mothers of the *shaheed*; once they were anointed with loss, this was their public uniform.

Sami was waiting for me when we arrived. On the gate outside his house, the church announcement of Sarab's passing remained posted, frayed and faded by the sun and rain. Only a few months gone, her presence still strongly lingered throughout their home, as if she might appear again at any moment. In death, she had become true to her name—a *sarab*, or "mirage."

❧

THAT AFTERNOON, SAMI and Laith took me by car back to the same seaside restaurant we had once visited with Sarab and my parents.

As the road lowered us to the level of the coast, it narrowed. Tall wetland grasses brushed against our vehicle as we navigated our way. Any spare patches of soil between the buildings were being used to cultivate vegetables. Between the Mediterranean and us were the pastel-colored beachfront chalets that used to be full of beachgoers and fun-seekers in the summer months. They were now, at the beginning of spring, already crammed with those internally displaced Syrians who had fled the violence in their home provinces. Several hundreds of thousands had reportedly found shelter here. The locals claimed they were immediately identifiable to them—they were generally more conservatively dressed, with cars bearing license plates from other parts of the country.

We sat at a table with a view of the water. There was so much I wanted to ask Sami—though he was a doctor, he'd been one of the few friends of Lamya's who would speak about Syrian politics while still inside Syria. He had even published his proposal for constitutional reforms online. He was staunchly secular, refusing to publicly extol Hezbollah (a traditional Assad ally) for its victories against Israel, even as other Syrians praised the Shiite party, overlooking the reality that it was a religion-based organization. He was no longer willing to accept any party or ideology that was fundamentally antidemocratic—and that was all the parties in the region, as far as he was concerned.

But any real conversation would have to wait until we were safely out of earshot. At lunch, we talked about the food, about dieting, about anything inoffensive. While we ate freshly caught fish—both fried and grilled—we watched displaced families as they gathered at the shore. Women in the full black *abaya* watched as excited children—who didn't have a school to be in—ran barefoot through the sand.

"They must be from Aleppo. It's not yet warm enough to swim," said Laith, pointing to little boys wading in the water as it rocked against the sand. Watching them as they jumped, splashed, and laughed in the sea, he added, "Let them enjoy it while they can."

That afternoon, Laith took me to see the sights of Tartus. We visited the old city, known as Al Saha, built around the military garrison of the Crusaders. The museum, though closed, was housed in a twelfth-century Crusader church, which had been built over a Byzantine church. The building was later used as a mosque, and then as barracks by the Ottomans. We also went to Al Khandaq, the area where the original residents of Tartus had lived.

These treasures were rundown. The bigger attractions appeared to be the unfinished area where a port was being developed, where cafés, restaurants, and bars were opening. We had a coffee there. Out in the water we could see the island of Arwad. Natural beauty, history, archaeology, great food—I was again struck by Tartus's easy potential as tourist destination.

Though home to Sunnis and Christians as well as Alawites, the coastal region and its peaks had become an Alawite stronghold. The Alawites had escaped past religious persecution here. They had also once been the lowest socioeconomic rung of society, exploited and abused. When Hafez al-Assad had seized power, the fortune of many—though hardly all—of the sect's members had improved. If the regime was so committed to improving the Alawites' lot, I thought, it could have long ago developed these coastal towns into major tourist and vacation resorts. Instead, Hafez al-Assad had brought many of his co-religionists to Damascus when he had seized power and housed them in rings around the city to bolster his own security.

I continued to think the same thing the next day, when we went for a drive up into the hills to see the incredible vistas. It would be a day of simple and easy pleasures. Before leaving downtown Tartus, we picked up Sami's friend and his wife, who were both from the area. We began to climb away from the Mediterranean and into the hills on a winding road. With posters of dead soldiers left below us and in the dreamy landscape of rolling hills above the sparkling Mediterranean Sea, I briefly forgot Syria's troubles. But then I started to notice that at each point where the road widened, groups of men and boys were amassing. My companions explained: they were waiting for the corpses of Alawite soldiers—conscripts in the Syrian Army—to arrive from below. They would accompany them back to their home villages higher up. A funeral procession was building, one motorcycle or open-cabbed truck at a time, each with several passengers. They were joined by the mothers, now newly dressed in black clothes and white scarves.

Those gathering had affixed large posters of the men and boys to their cars. The photos showed the fallen still alive, posing in uniform or with a gun. Many were very young, the tickle of mustaches below their noses not-withstanding. A photo of Assad, sporting aviator sunglasses and military fatigues, hovered above their images, assuming a posture of determination and leadership—his finger pointing to something on the horizon that we couldn't see. Was it a goal, a future, a death? Many of these soldiers had died in places far away from where they had grown up in these hills. We contin-ued our ascent.

Though not exclusively Alawite by any count, this was clearly Alawite territory. The few road signs here directed travelers to the tomb of Saleh al-Ali, the Alawite leader who had opposed French rule in the 1920s—the same man my great-grandfather Abdeljawwad had gifted with a horse and a sword, supposedly to help support the resistance against the French.

A statue of Ali graced the entrance to the village of Sheikh Badr, which sat along the ever-climbing road to an Independence Day site of pilgrimage for Alawites and government officials. Cast in stone, Ali appeared victorious, a rifle raised high into the air—could that have been the gun Abdeljawwad had given him? I joked to myself. Still, he looked cartoonish, his head and limbs out of proportion. (Somehow there are a lot of bad statues in Syria, even though there are many talented sculptors.)

The hills were verdant and gently terraced, yet for a region that was supposed to be protected and privileged, it was still remarkably underdeveloped. The road was just maintained well enough to be functional. Weren't forty years of Assad rule supposed to have made Alawites the best off in Syria? Weren't they facing impending retaliatory massacre for having thrown in their lot with the sons of these hills?

I asked out loud if the Alawites had been swindled. "There never was a real Alawite plan to rule," Sami replied. "But many of the networks where Hafez al-Assad cultivated loyalty were Alawite, especially as he was rejected by conservative Sunnis." Something about the legend of Saleh al-Ali seemed to speak to how the myth of Alawite privilege never quite corresponded to the reality. As one historian told me, "Ali was a petty nationalist inflated into gigantic proportions by Syria's first president, Shukri al-Quwatli." His goal was to give the Alawites "an alternate hero after the government hung cult leader Suleiman al-Murshed," who had led an Alawite revolt against the newly independent state in 1946. As we passed the statue, one of our traveling companions, from a village atop another hill, shrugged, saying, "He used to steal chickens from my great-grandfather."

Farther up the twisting road, each turn offering a more stunning view, we pulled over to take in a dramatic vista, joining several others in quiet reverie. With one's back to the line of coffins coming up the road, it seemed like the violence raging in Syria might as well have been in a different country. A patchwork of different shades of green—pine, olive, cypress, grass—and their different textures lit up each time the sun ventured from behind the clouds. Children were subdued, couples held hands, young men smoked cigarettes.

Several thoughts ran through my head. Of course, people here wanted to protect their home's tranquility. Yet was it ever at risk? The original demonstrators never had ambitions here. So who had it put it in the crosshairs? What would it cost these hills once the inevitable calls for vengeance and retribution pierced this bubble? What had it cost Syria for this area to avoid the fate of the rest of the country? Was it too late to alter this zero-sum formula by which Syria was being destroyed and reimagined?

The breeze carried with it the scent of burning trash—the lack of effective government waste removal was yet another hint that this was hardly some lavish enclave of wealthy oligarchs. As the air was already several degrees colder than it had been at sea level and the smell offensive, we hurried our departure.

Descending back to Tartus, the road—generally wide enough for a lane of traffic in each direction with room for passing—was overtaken by the funeral convoy we had left behind earlier. The vehicles on our side pulled over to give way. I could see the women's faces contorted with pain as they walked next to a van carrying the coffins. Young men revved their motorcycles while keeping the slow pace, and boys standing on the backs of the bikes occasionally broke a smile before remembering the solemnity of the occasion.

I thought of the Mustache, the dissident who I had met the spring before, who also happened to be Alawite. He had finally just been smuggled to safety in Beirut. (The regime had begun to prevent him from leaving the country in 2012. Several times they had turned him back from the airport or the border crossing to Lebanon. He came to be under virtual house arrest, and it was easier for the regime to keep him there after it broke his leg.) The Mustache had once explained to me that for a member of his sect, "defecting" could carry greater costs than it did for other Syrians. "A Sunni can escape to Turkey or to his home village; if he's an Alawite, the regime will kill him and his family, or his own village will do it," he said. "He's dead either way."

Once the last of the convoy passed, we resumed our drive, only to have to stop again when we came upon an armed checkpoint. Cars were already queuing up, drivers obligingly rolling down their windows to present the ID cards of all the men (and the women, if asked) and popping their trunks for inspection. Some of the men who guarded these checkpoints worked for the regular army, while others belonged to local pro-regime militias. Some wore combat boots; others were in sneakers, loafers, or even flip-flops. Several of their guns had an extra ammunitions magazine attached by duct tape. Most had managed to find a pair of camouflaged pants, and many wore what appeared to be newly minted black baseball caps emblazoned with a Syrian flag, suggesting "Team Syria" had just won a pennant somewhere.

❧

LATER THAT NIGHT over dinner, Sami shared his parents' photos with me and told me many of the family stories. His father had been a handsome air force pilot (Laith had inherited his looks) who in 1948 had downed an Israeli plane. When Sami's father was courting his mother, a schoolteacher, he had flown his one-propeller plane over the schoolyard to get her attention. It was so loud she would have to stop teaching until he passed. He would later become one of Syria's first civilian pilots, flying for Syrian Airlines.

He was also a member of the Syrian Social Nationalist Party, and his fortunes (and that of his wife and children) had taken a disastrous turn in 1956, when he was arrested and imprisoned for his suspected role in a conspiracy to overthrow then president Shukri al-Quwatli (who had also been president in the 1940s). Sami was only six at the time, and his father was sentenced to seven years in military prison in Damascus.

Once his father was taken, the government continued to harass his family. One morning in 1958, after Syria had joined with Egypt in the United Arab Republic, or UAR, he quickly realized as soon as he awoke that something was amiss; his mother, in her wine-colored velvet *robe de chambre*, was crying almost hysterically. Sami had slept through a government raid of the apartment. All the closets and drawers in the house had been opened and emptied; across the floor were strewn letters, papers, and books. His mother was inconsolable and refused to leave the house for weeks. Finally her mother convinced her to at least take a stroll at the fairgrounds, for the sake of the children. While they were there, two men approached her.

Only years later did Sami understand the details. One of those men was in fact the head of the UAR *mukhabarat* and had also been in their house the morning of the raid. His men had barged in on them that day tipped off by an informant working at a restaurant across the street; he had claimed that communications equipment was hidden in their house. Although the agents found nothing of the sort, they had confiscated one singular piece of paper. That day at the fairgrounds, the intelligence head had told Sami's mother that with that paper, she had insulted the leader of the nation, and only because she had children would he restrain himself from teaching her a lesson.

What was on the paper? The lyrics of a popular song about an "Abu Samra," reworded to mock "Abu Zahra," a supposedly derogatory nickname for Nasser (the head of the UAR). Sami's mother had written the lyrics down to entertain her husband while he was in jail.

"Abu Samra, Abu Zahra," Sami shook his head, as he told me the story. "The same things go on today."

After four years in prison, Nasser decided to send Sami's father and other political prisoners into exile in Cairo. There they were kept under surveillance, neutered—and even paid a monthly stipend by the government of the

UAR. When the UAR collapsed the following year, Sami's father went to Lebanon to lay low, sending his family back to Damascus. He kept out of politics. But then the Syrian Social Nationalist Party unsuccessfully attempted a coup in Lebanon. The Lebanese crackdown was thorough, and Sami's father had again gone into hiding.

The family was ultimately reunited in 1962 in Amman; the Jordanians had given Sami's father asylum. Only after the 1967 war with Israel were they allowed to finally return to Syria. With no income—because no one would give Sami's father a job—they lived in poverty. They struggled to survive until the new minister of defense, Hafez al-Assad, allowed Sami's father to work again for the national air carrier. Assad, after all, had come from the air force, and he respected Sami's father's talents as a pilot.

At school, Sami had joined the sanctioned Orthodox Youth Movement and was secretly a part of his father's party, more out of emotional attachment than out of actual conviction.

"I was trying out God and politics," he said. By the end of university, he had decided to quit them both.

As far as he could tell, the party had fascist elements. Like the Ba'athists and the communists, the party's ideology included a vision for how society itself should be organized. "There's no room for the 'other,'" Sami told me. He wanted the freedom to disagree.

For Sami, none of the Syrian parties were actually democratic. Throughout the region, he saw parties that might participate in an electoral process, but without any commitment to it beyond serving as a means to an end, one that was ultimately totalitarian in vision. He didn't think it meant that any of them—from his father to Hafez al-Assad—didn't love Syria. He believed they all had noble visions on some level—but used ignoble means to carry them out. This was the problem that had haunted Syria for decades, Sami said. The noble visions had receded while the means had become regular. There could be no power sharing, because the only way power ever was transferred was by seizing it. The nature of power in Syria necessitated wiping out the "other."

I thought then of Salma's beloved neighbor, Um Ragheed. Her husband—the one involved in the coup to bring back Nasser after the UAR came apart—had died a few years before. He had left politics behind completely and become a poet. But he had never been part of Syria again.

With a zero-sum way of looking at power, I wondered how much longer Tartus would survive. While there may not have been the sounds of gunfire, shelling, or bombardments, it was clear Tartus was living in a bubble. Its residents had to know that a thousand pins—of revenge, reckoning, and reality—would one day burst it.

Sami hadn't been to Damascus in a few years. He had last gone when Sarab was in the hospital there for an operation. He now had questions for me. Had I gotten what I wanted from coming to Syria? I told him that, no, things for the country had not gone the way I would have hoped. But I was happy to have finished Salma's house and to have moved into it. To have met those who had known her. And to have had a chance to ask about her and learn about her.

"She had an interesting personality, almost masculine," Sami observed. "She had that thick husky voice."

I asked him to tell me more.

"She was living in the past. She was really into her family, into the whole 'House of al-Mir' mythology."

"For all that was worth," I added, thinking of how she had been loved so much more by her husband and children than by her siblings.

"But—don't get upset with me—" Sami continued, "I felt that she was not happy in life."

"How so?" I asked.

"This wasn't the life she wanted. I think she thought she should be something other than what she had. But I didn't really know her."

"You're not at all wrong," I said. "Everything I have heard seems to back that up."

"I'll tell you," he laughed, "that cigarette never left her hand."

18

DISPLACED

Atmeh, Syria, April 2013

THERE ARE COUNTRIES THAT ONE CAN IMMEDIATELY RECOGNIZE from the sky because the borders are so natural—formed by deep mountain ranges, mighty rivers, or vast oceans. Italy, for example, is easy: it mostly floats in the Mediterranean Sea, visibly separated from other landmasses. Then there are those borders that are much less organic, having been arbitrarily drawn.

The border between Syria and Turkey's Hatay Province is one of those. Flying to Hatay in April 2013, I couldn't see how Syria would naturally end here; historically, it never had.

Through successive regimes, Syria has never renounced its claim to what it calls Iskenderun, and Syrian maps continued to show it as a part of Syria. After Bashar al-Assad came to power and relations between Turkey and Syria improved, families divided by the border were allowed to visit each other during both Muslim and Christian holidays. In February 2011, the two countries were about to build a "Friendship Dam" together, and it appeared that perhaps Assad was relinquishing Syria's claim to the land. But with the rapid deterioration between Erdogan and Assad (thus between Turkey and Syria), the project was never actualized, and Syrian state media began to again demand the territory's return.

Now, thousands of Syrians were escaping the violence at home, and many were crossing over daily into Hatay, with an ease that might suggest that the border, at the very least, was not natural at all.

Refugees have never been unfamiliar to Syrians. In the past century alone, Syria took in fleeing Armenians, Palestinians, and Iraqis. As a condition, it afflicted those people's privileged classes as much as their poorest. Wealth could mitigate its indignities, almost hiding it from view. But many suffered from it openly, and the refugee camp became the most visible symbol of this terrible circumstance.

I doubt that many Syrians imagined that such a fate would ever befall them. One of the supposed tradeoffs from living under authoritarian regimes was stability. And yet, by spring 2013, *registered* Syrian refugees numbered over 1 million. The actual number of Syrians who had left their homes and crossed a border was likely much larger. They had fled mostly to the neighboring countries of Lebanon, Jordan, Turkey, and Iraq. I had come to Reyhanli, a small Turkish border town where many of the Turkish inhabitants were originally Syrian, to cross back into Syria, to rebel-held territory. There in Atmeh, a Syrian American foundation was running a camp for those Syrians who had been *internally displaced.*

The Maram Foundation had been started by Yakzan Shishakly, the thirty-five-year-old grandson of one of Syria's first presidents, Adib Shishakly. Salma had liked him because he was also from Hama and because she believed he had *shakhsiyeh.* I wondered now as I prepared to meet Yakzan if he would have it too. I knew very little about him—other than who his grandfather was and that his older brother Adib was a visible member of the opposition.

By the time I arrived from the airport in Antakya, the sun had already begun to set, and Yakzan was back in his office, which was on the Turkish side of the border, after a full day in the camp. From the looks of things, that didn't mean his day had ended. I arrived to what I imagine was a daily scene: Yakzan sitting behind his desk, almost holding court. People were coming in and out with woes, requests, and complaints.

When he rose, I had to admit he had the large physical presence that suggests natural leadership. At six feet four inches, he stood above everyone else there. He could have been a professional athlete. And with a full head of dark, wavy hair, and those light eyes so coveted by Syrians, he could have been an actor. His cargo pants and construction boots—which contrasted with the slacks and loafers (or flip-flops) of the other Syrian and Turkish men—gave him an air of masculinity that seemed much more Texan than Mediterranean. But Yakzan, who was soft spoken, did not particularly seem to like this part of the job—that is, the constant flow of people coming to him because they wanted something. Until Syria began to fall apart, Yakzan had been a content owner of an air-conditioning installation and repair business in Houston, Texas.

Yakzan had left Syria for Texas in 1997 at the age of nineteen, even though he had lived well in Syria, in the toniest of neighborhoods in Damascus. If his lineage sometimes afforded him favor, it also meant that the regime had watched his family closely, lest their historical legacy threaten its grip on the country. They were generally unharmed, though, under certain conditions: basically, stay away from politics, and don't open your mouth. Yakzan's father had long chosen to accede. He used to tell his children, "If we leave the country because of those people, who is going to stay?"

In Texas, Yakzan had been unburdened by his name and expectations. He waited tables at T.G.I. Friday's, putting the money toward English classes. He enrolled in a local community college and earned a degree in air-conditioning installation and repair, a sensible choice in a place as hot as Houston. Eventually, he started his own business, assembling a fleet of seven trucks and vans branded with his "U.S. Refrigeration" decal and the motto "Live Above the Weather."

"So how did you end up here?" I asked him when we met.

He laughed. "I don't know."

I think that was in part true—there was a bit of a bewildered air about him. Still, he was able to describe the sequence of events that had preceded that very moment.

After Syrians began protesting in March 2011, Yakzan had helped organize weekly protests in Houston against the regime's crackdown. From there, he joined efforts to organize Syrian Americans across the United States. Meanwhile, however, more and more Syrians were leaving their homes, and a humanitarian crisis was developing. So, exasperated with what he saw as global indifference, and eager to do more, Yakzan had journeyed in September 2012 to the Turkish side of the border, where he distributed aid gathered in the United States to the refugees. It was there, while looking across to the Syrian side, that he unexpectedly first saw families among the olive trees: hundreds of men, women, and children were living there. Tauntingly close to Turkey, yet refused entry, and with the clashes in their homeland at their backs, they had taken refuge under the silvery leaves of a hilltop grove.

Yakzan snuck across the border to Syria to speak to them. They had already been there a month, they said, having brought what they could carry with them, and aside from a few makeshift tents, they were living in the open. Because they were still in their own country and therefore not "refugees"—who, by definition, cross national borders—these people were in a no-man's land in terms of international aid. Yakzan asked them what they needed. Tents and water tanks, they said, so he crossed back into Turkey, purchased the supplies with his own money, then stole across the border into Syria again to deliver them. For two weeks, Yakzan did what he could for them, then returned to Texas. By then he had decided to start an organization to aid these IDPs, or internally displaced persons.

Back in Houston, Yakzan worked with other Syrian Americans to register and organize a foundation, which he named Maram after a Syrian refugee girl he had met at a rehab center in Turkey. She had become paralyzed as a result of a shell fragment striking her. Her tenacity—she tried repeatedly to move her legs, to no avail—and her unwavering hope that she would eventually walk again inspired him. The next step was to find a responsible liaison at the Syria-Turkey border to manage Maram's activities on the ground. So in October 2012, Yakzan booked a flight to Turkey to find such a person and told family and friends in Texas, "I'll be back in two weeks."

Once he arrived in Turkey, one thing led to another, and soon he was operating out of office space borrowed from another nongovernmental organization. With the rush of refugees, Reyhanli had become a hub of activity. Many expat Syrians had arrived, sensing they had a positive role to play in this moment of crisis, one that many hoped would give way to the era when they'd rebuild Syria, once the fighting ended. He spent his days working with other groups that provided aid, coordinating supplies sent in from donors around the world. Tents, tins of food, medicine, portable bathrooms, school supplies—they all poured in and were channeled to the ever-swelling masses of Syrian IDPs. And the camp was getting bigger by the day. People fleeing some of Syria's most besieged cities—Idlib, Homs, Hama, Aleppo—arrived, and Yakzan struggled to meet their needs. By December, there were several thousand IDPs in the camp. Winter had brought with it new needs. What was adequate shelter in summer and fall would fail them in the cold; better tents—and now blankets, too—had to be acquired and distributed. The camp city also needed more bathrooms and showers, a kitchen, a school, and a clinic.

Meanwhile, in Houston, Yakzan's air-conditioning business began to fail in his absence. Yakzan had slipped into the role of director of what became known as the Olive Tree Camp, and administrative duties were handled through Maram. Almost five months went by before Yakzan finally returned for a few days to Houston, in February 2013, to attend fundraisers for the foundation. By then, Olive Tree was growing so quickly that it had already become a sprawling encampment of almost 25,000 people living in nearly 4,000 tents over a few square miles. By the time we met, Yakzan's air-conditioning business was defunct. He had rented an apartment in Reyhanli and a large office for Maram. He had hired five people. Yet he still asked me quite earnestly at our first meeting, "Should I move here permanently?"

"Looks like you have," I said, noting the irony of his name: it was more poetic than it was common and means "he who is awake or aware."

I would think about his name later when it all began to come undone. For all the dedicated volunteers who flocked to stem the suffering, there were as many, if not more, warlords, traffickers, extremist recruiters, and other opportunists who would prey on the misery of Syrians for their own purposes. The struggle had long begun for who would inherit the revolution. Accusations and rumors would also taint Yakzan—that he was corrupt or cooperating with armed factions. His kindest critics would say that despite his best intentions, he simply didn't know how to navigate the morass Syria had become.

But on that first night, we spoke about needs and hope, and the rewards of serving, talking well after most of the office staff had left. We grabbed a quick dinner at a snack shack run by Turks of Syrian origin, and then he took me to my hotel. Many of the young men who worked there were Syrian. While one could assume they were likely anti-regime and not reporting back to it on comings and goings, I didn't want to take any chances. With Yakzan by my side, I was able to avoid showing any ID to check in, which the law generally requires. When they asked my name, I instead used my sister's first name and my mother's maiden name.

୧୦୨

THE NEXT MORNING I walked to Maram's offices with Raghad, a Maram employee who was living full time in the hotel. She had left Syria the summer before, long fed up with the corruption and what she felt was the superficial nature of bourgeois Damascene society. Through family connections she had made it to Moscow; from there, she had hoped to find a way to Canada, where she also had family, to study for a master's degree.

Then she saw a video of a crying orphan in the Atmeh camp. She had worked for years with the Office of the United Nations High Commissioner for Refugees (UNHCR) in Damascus on behalf of refugees in Syria. They had come mostly from Iraq, but some were from Iran, Somalia, Sudan, Ethiopia, or Afghanistan. She felt she couldn't turn her back on Syrians who now found themselves in need of the very skills she had used on behalf of other populations.

She heard about Yakzan through a cousin, and when she looked for him on Facebook, she saw that he was already friends with both of her brothers. She contacted him and said she wanted to work for him, but asked him not to tell her family she was coming—she didn't want them to fear for her. In Moscow, she sold some of her gold jewelry to buy a ticket to get to Turkey. Once in Istanbul, she sold what gold she still had, and she had now been working at Maram—just for housing and pocket money—since December 2012. She began as the office manager, then helped start the school for the children, before setting up and managing the women's center.

We arrived at the offices as the rest of the staff was gathering for breakfast together, which also doubled as a morning meeting to discuss the day ahead. Raghad would catch a ride with Yakzan into the camp, and I'd go with them.

We set out toward the nearby Syrian border. A tacit agreement with the Turkish soldiers allowed Maram staff to pass daily. Driving down a dirt road, we made our way to the camp and parked outside. Its entry was in theory controlled, so that arms supposedly couldn't get in. Stepping out of the car, near the camp's entrance, I felt the earth give. All it would take would be an extended rain to render everything a slippery, muddy disaster. I was grateful to be there on a sunny day. White tents, weathered and muddied to various degrees, stretched out before us. Several children walked around with trays, loaded up with various items for sale, such as smokes, chocolates, pencils, and Kleenex. They yelled out what they were hawking and their prices. Adults queued at various larger tents that served as clinics and schools.

We walked past a canteen for tea and coffee, a makeshift butcher's shop (a diesel-operated generator keeping meat minimally refrigerated), and a camp bakery. With no industrial oven, the bakers had used mud to build *tanour*, earthen ovens like those my great-great-grandmother Marta had built to feed the hungry a century before, when she had had her gates torn down. A kitchen paid for by Syrians in the diaspora employed four cooks and provided food for an estimated 55 to 60 percent of the camp's population. Not all availed themselves of it, as many were still able to provide for themselves. They had come for safety, not charity.

Yakzan was quickly swarmed by camp residents who wanted or needed something: medicine, a new tent, more food. Others wanted him to resolve disputes among the factions that had arisen, most often along geographical lines, but sometimes within families. Some called out to him by name; others yelled out, "*Ya, mukhtar!*" (Hey, Mayor!) I noticed that among those who were gathering, some of the teenagers were armed, and they brandished their Kalashnikov-ordained manhood proudly. People were staring at me intently. My clothes clearly marked me as an outsider, and I was the only woman anywhere with an uncovered head (I had wrapped my hair into a bun). I was being assessed: Who was I? Did I have the power to make anything better?

Raghad and I left Yakzan to go to the women's center. As we passed through a maze of tents, several of the residents invited me in for tea or coffee; a few of the children ran after me. When I spoke to them in Arabic, however, they stopped in their tracks, confused, before giggling and tagging along. Raghad beamed as we arrived at the women's center. "This is my baby," she told me.

The large tent that served as the women's center offered several classes geared toward teaching skills that might help them earn some income. There were classes in literacy, knitting, crocheting, and hair cutting and styling (in one corner there were even a few hairdryers). So as to avoid alienating the more conservative families and arousing their suspicion, Raghad also offered Quran (religion) classes. Even though Raghad wore a hijab, there were often complaints that she wasn't modest enough. Her sleeves were always long, but there were those who objected to her jeans. They would have preferred that she wear a coat at least to her knees.

The women were much younger than me, though they looked much older. Many had been widowed already. They came mostly from rural areas around Idlib, Hama, and, to a lesser extent, Homs. Sometimes entire villages had relocated together. They all wanted to go back home, though many—Raghad estimated 40 percent—had their houses or farms destroyed by regime shelling. Of those who were not widows, many had husbands who were unable to earn an income because of the conflict in Syria.

At the center, the women were eager to show me what they had made. It was also important for many of them to tell me what their houses and lives had been like before. Several pulled out old mobile phones and showed me pictures they had of what had been. But they were also very curious about me. How was I Syrian? How old was I? (I universally shocked them with my answer.) Was I married? Did I have children? Didn't I want to be married? Didn't I want to have children? Where in Syria was my family from?

Each asked me my name, and I had to remember to use my sister's instead of my own. I kept any details that might identify me as ambiguous as possible; I'd soon be back in Damascus and didn't want my relatives to face any repercussions. The regime considered these people—and any who gave them comfort—to be enemies of the state. Informants likely had made their way here as well.

They unanimously wanted to know how long I'd be staying. I was ashamed of how short my stay would be. It was hard to explain the purpose of my visit. As the day came to an end, one of the beautiful and much-too-young widows (much too young to have been a wife, really) handed me a flower she had crocheted from purple yarn. "Keep it with you and remember me," she said. Several women accompanied me back toward the camp's entrance, but not without trying to coax me into their tents for tea. Those with children ran to fetch them so I could meet them before I left. I was sickened—not so much by the squalid conditions as by how I had heard other Syrians talk about those who had fled: "They deserve it," some had said. "They shouldn't have let armed groups into their villages"; or, "They shouldn't have protested."

❧

THERE WAS SOMETHING familiar in the horrid realities of camp existence: it all reminded me of what had been wreaked upon the Palestinians since 1948. But I kept finding myself thinking about how, at least in Israel's dispossession of Palestine, the aggressor had been a foreign people, not a neighbor, or a government tasked with protecting them. A competing nationalism drove the Israelis to do what they did—misguided, illegal, and unjust, sure—but the upheaval done to Syria's people had been done for one man to hold onto power. Surely one family's greed should have been easier to confront than Zionism.

But I could also see how Syrian society could maybe one day be pieced together along new lines that we hadn't previously imagined. Friendships and relationships were being built among folks who would never have met each other before, because their lives would not have taken them beyond their own villages. It was also bringing them into contact with Syrians from the diaspora of different classes. The status quo in Syria had depended so much on keeping people afraid of each other, of telling each that the other would devour him or her if given the opportunity.

When I got back to the office, I spoke at length with one of the women who worked there. She had given up her graduate studies in Europe to come work for Maram, and she wouldn't be able to return to Syria because of it. We swapped frustrations. Mine were about what I had just seen, how people were increasingly speaking in sectarian terms, and how others were surrendering their logic and their independent thought to deny what was happening.

She was worried most about the increasing presence of religious extremists—in the camp and in Syria. "You're Muslim?" she asked.

I usually demurred from this question; I never wanted it to have any relevance. But knowing that my being "Christian" might counter the prevalent idea that Christians were uniformly pro-regime, I answered, "I'm secular. I come from a Christian family."

"My husband is Sunni," she said. "But I am not," she added, her voice beginning to tremble.

What religion she was hadn't really occurred to me. She wore no outward signs of religiosity—no hijab or religious bling like a cross, or a golden page of the Quran.

Lowering her voice as if sharing a dirty secret, she said, "I'm Alawite."

I could only nod in silent understanding, as if she'd just told me she had a grave illness.

"No one knows," she sighed, "not even Yakzan."

19

GONE

Damascus, May 2013

A s I packed my things on my last weekend in Salma's house and looked at what my father had left behind, I tried not to dwell on how much he wanted to return and how unlikely it would be—if the doctors were correct—that he could.

In the bedroom, I dusted the windowsills and shook out the quilts on each bed. It didn't take a long absence in dry Damascus for the specks of dirt and pollution to work their way onto these surfaces, especially with the windows, doors, and shutters still original to Salma's day. But with my departure and my father's illness, none of us knew how long this new separation would last. Suha would still be right across the hall and would continue to turn the lights on and off, as she had done whenever I was gone, to make it look like someone lived here. She had also stocked Salma's front balcony with plants and would keep them watered for the same reason. But the house deserved more, and I encouraged her to make an atelier out of what had once been her and my mother's bedroom.

In the kitchen, Suha used the empty cabinets to stock extra lentils, rice, cooking oil, and water, in case food became scarce. She had also loaded the freezer with the spring's *mouneh*. I had bequeathed my leftovers.

Across the hall, Suha was expecting me for coffee, and I went—although it was hard to leave Salma's house before the time came, even for a moment. As it became clear that I would be leaving Syria, I had chastised myself repeatedly for taking my ability to be in the country for granted. Aleppo had already been ravaged—what if the same fate befell Damascus? But I had known each time I had coffee with Suha to relish that ritual with her. I could only hope my own nieces would love me as much as I loved her.

By my standards, Suha's pot of Arabic coffee was the best in the family. But every single time she made it, she'd be distracted or turn her back on the kettle and it would overflow—without fail. A demitasse or two was always lost to the top of the stove. This time, I stood sentinel, determined to commit to memory what it was she did that made it so perfect. Once the water boiled, she lowered the flame and stirred in the sugar, then the coffee. As we waited for the brew to boil again, thinking there was time, I drifted away from the kettle and started opening her cabinets, searching for what goodies she might have prepared while I had been gone. She made her own vinegar, and when I found the latest batch, I unscrewed the top and carefully smelled it.

Behind me, I heard Suha yelp in frustration, and of course, turned around in time to see the brown coffee spill over the top and onto the white porcelain of the stove, leaving the same kind of scattered destiny we usually looked for in our cups.

She laughed, "You wanted to know the secret!"

※

THAT NIGHT, I went to Good Friday Mass with Majed and Tala. Even though Easter is much more significant than Christmas in the Eastern Christian calendar, Majed's wife and two other daughters decided not to risk it. But I somehow felt I owed it to my father to go, to see for him in case he couldn't return.

Only during the forty days of Lent in the United States would my parents, who had always been fairly secular, find themselves longing for Syrian rituals. They would take us to Mass on Good Friday—essentially a funeral for Jesus in the Orthodox tradition—which, in the early years, Baltimore's Arab Christians celebrated in the rented basement cafeteria of a Catholic school. On those occasions, I often caught my parents wiping away a tear. The melancholic dirges with Arabic lyrics made them remember their childhoods when they had attended the same services in Syria with their now long gone parents. As with so many other things, their nostalgia had become my own.

For safety reasons, Friday's Mass was being held at dusk instead of midnight. The streets surrounding the church had been closed off, and we parked as close as possible before walking the rest of the way. As we approached the cathedral grounds, we could hear its music from quite a distance. I had last been here nearly a year before, when on my father's orders I had given cash to its affiliated orphanages. Immediately noticeable were the armed men the regime had sent. They were there ostensibly to protect the Christians, but it made me and others nervous.

The regime had spent the past two years insinuating that minorities were in danger and that only Bashar al-Assad could protect them in a sea of intolerant Sunnis. These armed men reinforced that claim of protection, and if the Christians were attacked that night, it would only provide more evidence for the regime's assertion that Sunni extremists were intent on doing minorities harm. Now that the regime had opened the door to sectarianism, and religious extremist fighters had predictably entered the Syrian fray, such an attack wouldn't even necessarily have to be staged by the regime to bolster its version of events.

I thought with sadness again of how all this had started—with Syrians simply asking to be included in their own governing—and looked up at the sky and hoped nothing would explode. Others seemed far less preoccupied. Even though we were at what was supposed to be a funeral Mass, teenagers, dressed more for a party, posed for group selfies in the churchyard. The church itself was overflowing with the more devout. For the young people, it was as if finally—despite the siege mentality and all the precautions—tonight, there was an opportunity of seeing and being seen.

I had moved to Syria two years before, on the day after Easter; the holiday, itself a celebration of spring and renewal, had become a natural moment for me to pause and evaluate the year that had just passed, to think about where we were now compared to where we had been and where we thought we were going. Everyone came up short in this reckoning, except for those who had suffered the most and shown humbling resilience. For many, Syria's unraveling had crept up on them, like the boiling of frogs—and the water had yet to even reach its most scalding temperatures.

After the Mass and back at my uncle's house, we carefully unwrapped and shared a Cadbury chocolate bunny that I had brought from Beirut. We waged battle with our dyed eggs, where we each picked one and knocked them together to see which would be the last to crack.

The sounds coming from the sky were those we were accustomed to and which accompanied our lives daily, mostly exchanges of gunfire that sounded more like the finale of a fireworks show, no less startling even if they had become common. But then came a loud boom. We looked at each other, as if making sure we were still all seated together around the dining-room table.

"That was a mortar," said Majed's eldest daughter, breaking the silence.

"No, it was a bomb," my uncle declared, setting off a lively debate.

"Baba," Tala interrupted, with confident authority. "If it were a bomb, we would have felt the vibrations," she said, reaching over to tear off the chocolate bunny's remaining ear.

❦

ON MY LAST morning in Damascus, I awoke at dawn, having slept in what had been my paternal grandparents' bed, which my grandfather had exquisitely made nearly a century before from walnut wood. My cousins had wanted me to spend that night with them, and not alone at Salma's house.

I rolled over and looked through my phone. All over social media was news that the Israelis had just bombed a military installation on the other side of Mt. Qasiyoun, which embraces Damascus and which we could see from the balcony. I had apparently slept through it, although a few nights before I had awoken when Syrian jets had raced by to hit rebels near what had been the commercial airport.

My car would soon be arriving—drivers wanted to leave as early as possible so that they would be sure to make it back from Beirut while there was still light. Checkpoints had made moving about Damascus less fluid than it had been, and border controls had become much tighter on both the Syrian and Lebanese sides.

Everyone had risen with me, and Randa made us coffee and laid out some Easter pastries. Together we sat on the third-floor balcony and sipped the deep black cardamom-scented brew as the sun rose.

I wondered what Majed and Randa would do if they had to leave Syria. But devising a "Plan B" in a country that had seemed stable, in a life that had seemed stable, was still too strange for them to consider the matter. Many older Syrians had resigned themselves to the indignities of a life circumscribed under totalitarian rule in exchange for well-deserved years of relaxation and the chance to see the weddings of their children and grandchildren. They never imagined that anything else was part of the bargain.

I looked out across the way at the other households still sleeping. I looked beneath us at the warehouse that was the regulated-price fruit and vegetable market, yet to start bustling for the day. I looked directly below at the peasant farmers, who had already come to the city to sell their fresh sheep and goat milk, yogurt, and cheese out of large buckets just outside of the official market. I hoped not to forget these views, and wished I had never taken them for granted.

A few beeps of a car horn below meant my ride had arrived. I would soon be on my way to Beirut, and a few days later I would be returning to the United States to be with my family as my father began intensive treatment and surgery. I had also taken a job that would let me be close by in New York City. The fact I was going to work for the new Al Jazeera America channel, part of the regime-despised Qatar-based news network, convinced my relatives that I wouldn't be welcome again in Syria as long as this regime stayed in power.

We didn't talk about that, however, as we loaded my bag into the car. As I got into the back seat, the first of the car's passengers to be picked up, my family all insisted that once I had crossed safely into Lebanon I was to let them know. But all I wanted was someone to tell me that I would be coming back.

When the driver started the engine, I turned around and looked out the rear window to see if anyone would tell me to stay. Instead, I saw Majed smiling in his shiny tracksuit. He would be off to take his walk in the public garden nearby. From the balcony above, my cousins in their PJs waved at me before heading back in and stealing whatever sleep might still be possible. I only turned back around when I could no longer see anyone.

As I drove away, all the distracting packing and goodbyes done, the realization that my time was really up sank in. All I could think about were the shutters on Salma's house. I had meant to restore them to their original emerald green, her favorite color, the way they had been in the late 1940s when she was a bride and the house was new, and when the country, too, had been new and hopeful.

EPILOGUE: BOUND

Saarbrücken, Germany, March 2016

ON SATURDAY, MARCH 19, 2016, I MADE MY WAY WEST FROM Heidelberg, Germany, toward the country's border with France. Spring had arrived earlier in Germany than in New York, where I was based. The drive took me through lush valleys and hills where the flowers had already bloomed.

I was driving away from Frankfurt, where my flight was scheduled to depart early the next day, because there was a family I had finally found and needed to meet.

Over the past few years, Syrians escaping the hell of their country had begun seeking safety far beyond their immediate borders. Lebanon, Jordan, Turkey, Iraq, Egypt, and North Africa had collectively already taken in an estimated 4.8 million refugees. But if these countries were safer places to be, they did not provide an opportunity for a *life*. Instead, these host countries were limbos where Syrians for the most part were unable to work, study, and earn a livelihood. Such activities were greatly curtailed, if not outright prohibited. They began to look west.

Dispensing with the waits, queues, and requirements of Western embassies and organizations, and handicapped by having a Syrian passport, or no passport (travel documents had become an important determinant of global privilege), an estimated half a million Syrians had taken to the sea in 2015 alone.

If those who had been condemned to the tent didn't have the means to leave the region, many of these Syrians did—even if it still meant an illegal and terribly dangerous journey via rubber dinghy, bus, train, ferry, taxi, and/or by foot. Many of these refugees came from Syria's working middle class—they were teachers, bakers, construction workers, farmers, shop owners, university students, computer scientists, architects, interpreters, nurses and engineers. Not all would make it alive; in 2015 alone, at least 3,500 people drowned at sea trying to reach Europe. Most had their sights set on Germany—the country that had essentially opened a door to them, agreeing to take them in as well as to let them transit from there on to other countries.

In the fall of 2015, I had made the journey, as a journalist, with many of these Syrians. As they clung to the few belongings they had chosen to bring with them, I was constantly reminded of how different their leaving Syria was from my parents' own departure; only the vagaries of fortune separated us. When I'd see a pregnant woman making this arduous journey, I'd think of my mother who left pregnant with me and wondered what would happen to this child.

In Syria, and again on what has been dubbed the refugee trail, Syrians told me that it was inconceivable to them that the likes of what was happening to their home—in terms of brutality, loss, and displacement—had ever been seen before in contemporary human history. They despaired as to how their country could ever again emerge, let alone prosper. They wondered how they could all live together after everything that had transpired between them. Ironically, we had these conversations even as we journeyed through the states that had emerged from the disintegration of Yugoslavia, whose residents had also once wondered how everything had so quickly come apart. And even as the refugees were completely focused on reaching the European Union—itself created in the wake of bitter conflict, after erstwhile enemies decided that they had more to gain by confronting and reconciling with the past (not just forgetting it) and forging the future together.

Similarly, as the xenophobic discussion about the refugees reached a fever pitch in Europe, it seemed that many Europeans themselves had forgotten their own past of devastation and migration. With this in mind, I was speeding now toward the French border to meet head-on my own family's history and begin to reconcile with it.

I reached the small city of Saarbrücken by early afternoon. As soon as I parked, I sent a message that I'd be arriving in minutes. Then I took a deep breath.

I walked along a uniform wall of buildings, their entrances flush against their facades. Ahead of me, I saw a little girl peeking out from one door, waving and smiling at me. A man with a silver beard and thinning hair stood behind her.

I'd never met him before but knew immediately who he was. At fifty, Shadi was only fifteen years younger than his father was when I last saw him in Salma's house, thirteen years ago. The resemblance was uncanny; he looked much like Hassan.

༄

HASSAN AND HILAL had barely moved out of the Tahaan and into their new home when everything fell apart for them.

That same year, in 2010, Shadi had eloped with the woman whom he had long loved. He chose to live with her in secret, setting up house in an apartment in Harasta. Shadi's relationship with Hassan was already so strained that it wasn't difficult to keep the truth from his father. Shadi soon had a baby girl, but Hassan didn't know about her, either. The reason Shadi had hidden what should have been happy milestones in his life was that his wife was an Alawite woman, and Hassan hated Alawites.

When Hassan eventually discovered the truth about his son's marriage and found out that Hilal—who regularly visited Shadi and took him storage containers filled with home cooking—knew about it, Hassan divorced her on the spot and kicked her out of their home. He then sold the new house—that he had purchased in part with my parents' money—rented his own apartment, and bought his daughter, who worked in Dubai, a house in Harasta, telling Hilal to go live there. He refused to meet his only grandchild, a beautiful little girl named Zahra, Arabic for "flower."

By the end of 2010, as we were renovating Salma's house, Hassan, who provided money to Hilal in Harasta, nonetheless refused to reconcile. When the ladies' group from Ain al-Kirish would meet, she'd lament her fate to them. They, however, would tell her she should never have taken "that money from Lamya." But Hilal protested as she always had: it was their right under Syrian law. She would also meekly add that by living in the house, they had protected it for my parents in their absence.

Right before the uprising began in March 2011, Shadi's wife left him and Zahra, who was still just a baby. The next year, the Syrian Army moved into Harasta. One morning, the army told the residents of Shadi and Hilal's neighborhood that they had to leave their houses, which were now in a military zone; they gave them only a few hours to gather some belongings and go. Shadi managed to rent an apartment for all of them in central Damascus. Six months later, the army allowed Shadi and his neighbors to return to their homes for one day, from 6 a.m. to 8 a.m. They were not allowed to enter with cars and could only take what they could carry.

They returned to find all the glass in their building and the surrounding buildings shattered. The exteriors were pockmarked by bullets and cratered by mortars. The houses had been robbed bare. The clothes had been snatched from their closets, furniture taken from their rooms, and electrical wires excavated from the walls and stripped of their copper. Shadi had been forced to leave behind several expensive paintings. Though the neighborhood had been under the exclusive control of the Syrian Army, the government told the residents that it had been the rebels who had pillaged them.

Shortly thereafter, Hassan fell ill; fearing time might run out, Shadi tried to reconcile with his father, but Hassan refused. When both his condition and the situation in Syria deteriorated further, Shadi insisted they all move to Dubai to join his sister. Too sick to refuse, Hassan traveled with them, and they were finally all together—albeit in two apartments in the same building. (Hassan and Hilal were not in the same one.) Shadi took his daughter without telling his ex-wife, who moved in circles he believed were not only pro-regime but also active in militias that supported the regime. After one year in Dubai, Hassan died. It was February 2014; several Arabic news sites carried obituaries.

A neighbor back in Damascus then informed Shadi that all their houses in Harasta had been reduced to rubble in the fighting between the Syrian Army and its enemies. Unable to find work in Dubai, Shadi decided to take Zahra and go to Turkey—he wanted to get to Europe. Hilal stayed behind in Dubai with her daughter.

In Turkey, it took him one month to find a smuggler who would arrange their passage to Europe. This was before the borders were open and the path was as well traveled as it would become in 2015, when Hilal, too, would make the journey. Finally, with approximately forty other people, in October 2014, Shadi and Zahra were jammed into a small wooden fishing boat. They would spend seventeen hours in the Aegean Sea before arriving exhausted in Rhodes, Greece. Shadi had held Zahra the entire time.

By March 2016, Shadi and Zahra had had their permit to remain in Germany for exactly one year. The journey had cost them 21,000 euro.

❧

As I walked up to Shadi and his daughter, he, too, began to smile and quickly extended his hand to me. We shook hands and touched our cheeks on both sides.

Fifteen hours before, I had resigned myself to the conclusion that this meeting would not happen. When I had found out that Hassan's family had made it to Germany, I had reached out through my upstairs neighbor Fatima to ask if they would meet with me. I would soon be in Germany again, to visit the refugees I was following, six months into their lives in Europe. (Fatima's son had long become an American and was a doctor practicing in Chicago. He had convinced his parents to leave the Tahaan a full year before me.) She soon relayed the request, telling them I was writing about Salma.

At first, Hilal readily agreed. But then she almost immediately retracted. Her daughter—who was moving to Canada, having married a Canadian of Lebanese origin—was adamant that I wasn't welcome. The way Fatima explained it to me, Hilal had said that her family had "nothing good to say about Salma, especially after what she did to us." They didn't want to speak about her if they only had ill things to say.

Fatima then told me that Hilal had newly claimed that in the 1970s, Salma had demanded rent from them that had already been paid. That didn't ring true for either of us, though I said I would look into it. Fatima added that Hassan used to make up all kinds of stories to convince Hilal that they were right not to give the house back to Lamya.

Hearing the dejection in my voice, Fatima had said she would try again. I wasn't hopeful. I imagined that Hassan's family also blamed my mother for all the misfortune that had befallen them after their departure from the house. After all, the Tahaan still mercifully stood, while their homes in Harasta had been destroyed, with no compensation forthcoming. Salma's apartment had remained empty after I had left in May 2013—until late 2015, when Lamya rented it to Suha's sister-in-law.

Fatima asked me what I wanted her to tell them. I said what I wanted them to know was that I was writing about Salma and the house, a house that my grandmother, my mother, they, and now I had lived in. Its history included all of us, and they had been in it for forty years. Even if it was at the expense of my family, I didn't want to erase their lives from it.

I heard nothing for a long time. Fatima tried to console me; she kept telling me she had lived everything with them, being tight neighbors in the Tahaan, and that she could tell me whatever I wanted to know. But I wanted something different for those of us who had shared our house in the Tahaan, as much as I did for the whole country.

From the moment I had arrived in Europe two weeks prior, I had intensified my campaign. Finally, on Friday night, just as it seemed that time had run out, I received a message from Fatima. She had continued to entreat them on my behalf, and it had paid off. Shadi shared his number with me and gave me an address.

I called him right away and asked if I could see him the next day. He was incredibly kind and apologized if I had felt unwelcome. He told me he would be happily waiting for me, along with Hilal and Zahra.

Now in Saarbrücken, he led me inside to a modest and impersonal apartment on the ground floor. It smelled of tobacco. We sat in the small family room, which had a TV against the wall, a small sofa, a few chairs, and ashtrays on the coffee table. He met my gaze straight on. Dreading any awkward silences, I immediately handed him something I had bought from a bakery—it wasn't quite a cake, nor was it really bread. I then started apologizing for being late—there had been an accident on the highway.

The door opened and an older woman came in with grocery bags; it was Hilal. I rose to greet her.

"You might not recognize me," she said. "I took off the hijab."

I'm not sure I would have recognized her anyway. In 2003, when I visited her in Salma's house, I had spent much more time studying Hassan's face. The reference image I had of Hilal was a photograph of her looking beautiful at my parents' engagement party in 1972. In that picture, she stood taller than my mother, her long, thick hair gathered at the top of her head and left cascading. Her hair was now shorn, and she was bent. She looked at me only in fleeting glances.

Why, I asked, had she removed the veil?

"I never liked it," she said. "I only put it on because of pressure from our ladies' group back in Ain al-Kirish."

She motioned us to sit back down, joining me and Shadi around their coffee table.

Right away she asked me, "How's your mother? Your father?"

I told them everyone was well. Indeed, my father's doctor had managed his illness aggressively, and three years after that terrible diagnosis, he was still with us.

I asked them about their journeys to Europe.

From Athens, Shadi and Zahra had traveled by airplane with false documents. The smugglers advised against him, an older man, traveling with a little girl. So Shadi had let the smuggler's wife take Zahra to Poland before promising to deliver her to Shadi's aunt in Berlin. Shadi only managed to board a flight days later and on his third try. He told me that the days between handing Zahra over to the woman and picking her up in Germany had been the hardest of his life.

Hilal told me that from Turkey, it had taken her months to work up the courage to cross the waters, as she didn't know how to swim and was terrified of drowning.

"I used to talk to the sea," she said. "But to enter it, never!"

What finally convinced her was the fact that she could no longer bear the separation from her granddaughter.

Like Hassan, she, too, was from Dara'a, and much of their family from that besieged town had made it to Germany. At least they were now all together. By the time Hilal had come, it only cost about 3,000 euros to make the journey from Turkey to northern Europe, and she had been able to travel across borders by land, unimpeded for the most part.

When Shadi got up to go to the kitchen and roll a new cigarette, I was left alone with Hilal. She looked at me, and I smiled, hoping it might dispel what I sensed was her suspicion or discomfort. Again she asked me how my parents were, and again I said they were fine—these sentences in Arabic are almost ritualistic and often fill the spaces of conversation.

"I was at your parents' engagement party," she said finally.

"I know," I said excitedly. "Tell me how it was?"

She said it had been one of the few times she had gone out all dressed up with her hair done. She described the dress she had borrowed from her sister as if she had worn it yesterday. The smile then disappeared from her face. "When Abu Shadi [Hassan] found out I had gone to this party while he was in Germany, he got very upset. 'Who said you could go?'" she recounted.

She had explained to him that Lamya had insisted, telling me, as an aside, that she really liked my mother, who had her father's kindness and sweetness. But apparently Hassan was unmoved. "He continued to yell at me for having gone for the next five years," she said.

Since she had opened the door, I asked her about her marriage to Hassan and if she had been happy in the Tahaan. Hilal told me she had taken pleasure in her children—Hassan never wanted kids, she said—and the friends she made in Ain al-Kirish. But the marriage had been difficult and unhappy. "For the first twenty-five years, he was drunk every night," she said. "Shadi saw it all, ask him." But she also told me that she had remained in love with Hassan for a long time.

"Your grandmother liked him a lot, too," Hilal said. "She helped him a lot. This is a fact," she said, telling me about how, for example, Salma had lowered the rent when he couldn't afford it. Hilal also told me about the kindness Salma had shown her specifically. When she had first moved to the building, it was Salma who had introduced her to the various women of the Tahaan. When Salma used to invite her and Shadi to dinner weekly to watch the show Hassan worked on, Hilal told me, Salma would lay out nice dishes and flatware.

Returning to Hassan, Hilal spoke about how he used to bring revelers to their house late at night and rouse Hilal from sleep to prepare food and drinks—I'd heard this from the building residents as well. He'd never allow her to join them, insisting she hand them prepared trays from behind the door. After she'd returned to bed, they'd take seats around the dining-room table Salma had left Hassan and feast.

"Why didn't you ever say no?" I asked.

She paused, thinking it over. "I guess he trained me to not say no," she said.

When Shadi returned, I asked him to describe his father. He answered, "He was honorable."

Truth be told, I hadn't expected that response. "Can you explain?" I said.

"He never took money from the government. They wanted him to write nice poems about Hafez but he refused."

"Was he a good father?" I asked.

"He was not present," he said lucidly and unapologetically. "But he provided. We never wanted for anything. The money was always there."

I couldn't help thinking to myself that part of that money didn't really belong to Hassan, but I hadn't come to make demands—though Shadi would later tell me that when Fatima had first contacted them on my behalf, they were afraid that was my purpose. That was why they had refused to see me initially.

I spent several more hours there with them. We talked about Syria, the regime, the war, the wasted generations, the staggering loss of life, the leveling of millennia-old patrimony, and what might still yet come.

Telling me about his childhood in the Tahaan, Shadi insisted I write down that before our dead-end street in Ain al-Kirish was opened up to the newly paved Revolution Street in the late 1970s, the Tahaan boys would play soccer against those from the neighboring building. And, gesturing to my notebook to make sure I jotted the following, Shadi made clear that it was an undisputed fact that the Tahaan team always won.

"Akeed!" I cheered for our building, "of course." I could visualize it so perfectly, like all the stories Hilal and Shadi told me about the building and the neighborhood. I was grateful for the missing years they had filled in.

Eventually I could no longer put off leaving. As I rose to go, we promised to stay in touch. Next time I was in Germany, they insisted I stay with them.

I walked back out into the cooler evening air—the first smoke-free breath I had drawn in hours—with much to think about, digest, and process.

I don't know if I would have been able to sit across from Hassan in the same way, knowing how much pain he had caused my grandmother. But although Hassan's refusal to leave Salma's house had been a significant impediment to our returning to Syria, the life his actions had denied us had been replaced with the one that allowed me to be in Germany as an American tourist whose being Syrian was just an exotic curiosity to Germans. Such circumstances couldn't be more different from those of Hassan's family, whom I had left behind in an apartment I imagined would never feel to them like home. As Shadi put it, "No matter what I do, I will always be a stranger here."

I quickened my pace back to the car, struck by how all these years Shadi and I—strangers to each other—had been bound by a single home, each of our fates determined by the moments when the other possessed it.

Now that neither of us called it home, even if the mourning of our exile from it could be measured and compared, would it matter? Now that someone else lived there, would any of our shadows linger longer than the others'? How many more years would the building still stand, and how many more bitter oranges would Salma's tree—which Hassan had named "Suha"—still yield? Who would remember it was Salma's house, and how the neighbors were once so well known to one another? Who would remember the Syria that was, and who would be there to greet its new dawn and dream it a better future?

ACKNOWLEDGMENTS (*SHUKRAN!*)

I AM FOREVER INDEBTED TO MY RELATIVES AND THE MANY SYRIANS who shared their lives with me as well as their memories of those who have long passed. Without them, I could have never pieced together the narrative of my family over a century. Nor could I have included the deeply personal experiences of other Syrians as well. Though I cannot name them by their real names for now, they are what made this book possible—*alf shukr* for trusting me with your stories.

I am especially grateful to my mother, her sister, and her brother, who spent long hours telling the same stories several times over. I asked them painful questions, especially of my *khalo*, and we shared many tears as we recreated their mother's terrible demise. Similarly, to my father, thank you for always making the time to revisit the past even as the present made so many unfair demands of you. To his brother who insists on speaking to me in formal classical Arabic, *shukran jazeelan ya 'azizi*. And a *Shami merci kteer* to his daughters.

I am thankful to my grandmother's remaining siblings and siblings-in-law and their children, as well as many of my second cousins from Egypt to Syria to Lebanon to the United States who helped me put this narrative together. I want to especially thank Team Cape Cod—my great-uncle's widow and her children, who participated in an epic six-year group email where we shared memories, rumors, and scraps of information, debating their accuracy and theorizing on the motivations, intents, and feelings of the long dead. It was a séance held virtually across many cities.

From our building, I extend my appreciation to the el-Maarry family in Cairo and my mother's cousins on her father's side who were also neighbors. I am so grateful to Fatima and her son Amjad not just for being wonderful neighbors but also for the essential memories they shared as well as the interviews and meetings they facilitated. The most important, of course, was the one with the family who lived in my grandmother's apartment for forty years. A special thank you to them for welcoming me in Germany and their openness to the project and to me.

The following people contributed important memories, verifications, information, dates, documents, figures, tidbits, photos, and insights: Ghaith Alabdallah, Doaa Mehdi, S. Wehbeh, Yakzan Shishakly, Rabee Khouzam, Pamela Shehadi, Wissam Smayra, Dalia Hashad, Daalia Refaat, Avideh Moussavian, Renée and Nadim Boustany, Sona Tatoyan, Harout Ekmanian, Vahe and Nora Yacoubian, Bashar Azmeh, Hala Kahal, Tarek Butayhi, Lamya Farra, Ayham Bakhos (and his parents), Dominique Tohme, Hassan Abbas, Rose and Suzy Kanbar, Mirvat Haddad, Samar Haddad, Fadi Hallisso, Anas Joudeh, Lina Sergie, Sarab al-Jijakli, Mohammed Heraiba, Omar Dahi, Jihad Yazigi, Sami Moubayed, Yonca Verdioğlu, Ahmet Şık, Can Atalay, Sinan Ulgen, Esin Arsan, Efe Karasabun, Dina Shehata, Karim Abou Youssef, Shaden Khallaf, Obaida El-Dandarawy, Raja Alabdallah, Ibtissam and Zuhair Farah, Issam Cheikh, Naela Attar, Lisa Goldman, Lisa De Bode, Mickey Lee Bukowski, Scratch Rogers.

Thank you to Alan Chin for leading me to Dr. Alexander Flint, expert in neurocritical care and stroke, who was greatly helpful in walking me through the science and medicine of what happened to my grandmother.

For questions relating to music and help augmenting sound files, an audible thanks to Kareem Roustom, Kinan Azmeh, Bruce Wallace, and to Sousan Hammad and Nick Fitzhugh for connecting me with Tom Paul. To Kinan especially, your music was often my soundtrack as I wrote, capturing too well how our collective hearts have broken.

A poetic *shukran* to Fady Joudah for translation help.

And to poetess Keayr Braxton, thank you for putting your discerning eyes on early, unpolished drafts.

My work is indebted to the following scholars who eagerly let me interview them or ask incessant questions about small historical details, who read sections for accuracy, and who offered valuable tips and leads: Michael Provence, James Gelvin, Nadya Sbaiti, Bassam Haddad, Kevin Martin, Max Weiss, Khaled Malas, James Reilly, Yezid Sayegh, Abdullah Al-Arian, Abdul-Karim Rafeq, Yektan Turkyilmaz, Nader Atassi, Chris Gratien, Lorenzo Trombetta, Donatella Della Ratta, Emile Hokayem, and map gurus Zach Foster and Nicholas Danforth.

Thank you to my research assistants Michael Pizzi and Abeer Souhel Jamal, especially Michael who sometimes amazed me with what he could track down and without whom I might have lost my sanity. And thanks to Martin Nibali for the website, where the extended bibliography also lives.

The wonderful MacDowell Colony blessed me with a Calderwood grant, a breathtaking place to work for five weeks, and a wonderful community of colleagues who were so giving and critical to the juncture I was in with the book. Similarly, I could not have done this without the financial support of the Nation Institute and the Puffin Foundation. To the Dallas Institute of Humanities and Culture, your generous endorsement of this work has been a humbling validation and an extension of solidarity that is profound.

At Nation Books, *grazie mille* Alessandra Bastagli—editor, but also champion, tough love coach, translator, believer, and *amica*. To Katherine Haigler and Shena Redmond who guided these words through the production process and to Katherine H. Streckfus who fixed every last one of them, you are an incredible team, and I salute you. To Mike Morgenfeld, map maker, to Chris Nolan, legal reader, and to Chris Juby, publicist, my gratitude. To all the dedicated sales reps and booksellers large and small who have supported this and my previous books, your work is much appreciated.

Thank you Anna Ghosh for ushering my move to Nation Books.

Several friends hosted me in their beautiful homes when I had to travel but also work long days, especially in the most difficult last months. So, *gracias* Moises Saman and Cale Salih in Spain; *merci* Simon Blakey in France; cheers Bert Fink, in England, and *grazie ancora* Gwynne Master and Leonardo O'Grady.

Samuel G. Freedman remains one of the best professors I have ever had, and I've been to school now three times. He also looked at early drafts. For this and more, here's to many Sicilian bottles in the future all together.

To Dave Eggers, who never stops believing and opening doors—you are a legend. Thank you.

Though he is no longer with us, I am deeply beholden to Anthony Shadid. He was a mentor, friend, and the best example of how to report on, write about, and represent this place that he and I both loved. He is so sorely missed, and I mourn his loss every day.

This kind of work is impossible without the cheerleaders who stop you from jumping off the ledge repeatedly and who, when all else fails, buy you a drink. So to the following folks, I've got the next round: Mom, Dad, my brilliant siblings; the Brooklyn crew—Keayr, Niki Hall, Farah Malik, Hosanna Marshall; the sister journalists—Jina Moore, Rawya Rageh, Leila Fadel, Rania Abouzeid, Hannah Allam, Vivian Salama, Jamie Tarabay, Maria Abi-Habib, Rym Momtaz; longtime cheer squad Jennifer Gaver, Maya Kulycky, and Alisa Newman. Shirley Temples to my nieces and nephew, whose hugs and nose rubbies make the world and its worries almost disappear.

To Peter van Agtmael, who read drafts, listened to the minutiae, encouraged me daily, soothed my fears, made many a dinner, fixed pictures and took some too, and waited patiently for me to finish this work, thank you for your comprehension, your belief, your challenges, your thoughts, and your love.

Lastly, to Syria and the generations before, which gave us life, beauty, and this profound pain, thank you for making us your children. And may you find it possible to forgive us.

A NOTE ON SOURCES

WHILE THIS BOOK IS THE MULTIGENERATIONAL STORY OF ONE FAMILY, the personal lives recounted here were lived against very real historical contexts. To make sense of these eras, I relied heavily on the work of scholars who have carefully excavated a myriad of sources. I also spoke at length with several of them, who gave generously of their time. They include Drs. Michael Provence, James Gelvin, James Reilly, Nadya Sbaiti, Bassam Haddad, Kevin Martin, Max Weiss, and Yezid Sayegh and doctoral candidates Khaled Malas, Zach Foster, and Nader Atassi.

In the United States, my research assistant Michael Pizzi diligently hunted down several sources in both Arabic and English in order to confirm old recollections and even "facts" often taken for granted. My Syria-based research assistant, lawyer Abeer Souhel Jamal, pulled the relevant Syrian property laws and municipal records and visited the national archives, the Assad library, and the Damascus Center for Statistics to verify and/or ascertain decades-old information.

In addition, I was greatly assisted by the map and photo archives found at the websites Syrian History (www.syrianhistory.com) and The Afternoon Map (www.midafternoonmap.com) and the Facebook pages "The Past of Syria," "Syrian History" (different from the website), "Syrian Art Treasures," and "The Damascene Women's Club, Founded by Nazid al Abed." I have also spent countless hours listening to episodes of The Ottoman History Podcast—an absolute gem.

I have listed below a very selected bibliography of works that were essential in crafting this book, particularly in earlier pre-2011 eras. I've grouped them thematically; though some have a scope greater than the era I've placed them in, for the sake of space, they have not been repeated. Finally, this list is by no means exhaustive of the sources consulted; please see www.aliamalek.com for a complete bibliography.

The Ottoman Empire Through the Mandate Years

Al-Darb Al-Tawil. Unpublished memoir.

Fawaz, Leila Tarazi. *A Land of Aching Hearts: The Middle East in the Great War.* Cambridge, MA: Harvard University Press, 2014.

Frankel, Jonathan. *The Damascus Affair: Ritual Murder, Politics, and the Jews in 1840.* Cambridge: Cambridge University Press, 1997.

Gelvin, James L. *Divided Loyalties: Nationalism and Mass Politics in Syria at the Close of Empire.* Berkeley: University of California Press, 1999.

———. "The 'Politics of Notables' Forty Years After." *Middle East Studies Association Bulletin* 40, no. 1 (2006): 19–29.

Haddad, Robert M. *Syrian Christians in a Muslim Society: An Interpretation.* Princeton, NJ: Princeton University Press, 1971.

Heritage and Art of Suqaylabiyah, www.ghaith-a.com.

Hourani, Albert. "Ottoman Reform and the Politics of Notables." Pp. 41–68 in W. R. Polk and R. L. Chambers, eds., *Beginnings of Modernization in the Middle East.* Chicago: University of Chicago Press, 1968.

Khoury, Philip. *Syria and the French Mandate: The Politics of Arab Nationalism 1920–45.* Princeton, NJ: Princeton University Press, 1987.

Levy, Avigdor. *Jews, Turks, Ottomans: A Shared History, 15th–20th Century.* Syracuse, NY: Syracuse University Press, 2002.

Lewy, Guenter. *Armenian Massacres in Ottoman Turkey: A Disputed Genocide.* Utah Series in Turkish and Islamic Studies. Salt Lake City: University of Utah Press, 2005.

Marcom, Micheline Aharonian. *Three Apples Fell from Heaven.* New York: Riverhead Books, 2002.

Masters, Bruce. *Christians and Jews in the Ottoman Arab World: The Roots of Sectarianism.* Cambridge: Cambridge University Press, 2004.

———. *The Arabs of the Ottoman Empire, 1516–1918: A Social and Cultural History.* Cambridge: Cambridge University Press, 2013.

Meouchy, N., and P. Sluglett. *British and French Mandates in Comparative Perspectives.* Leiden: Brill, 2004.

Moubayed, Sami. *Steel & Silk: Men & Women Who Have Shaped Syria, 1900–2000.* Seattle: Cune Press, 2005.

"Partant Pour La Syrie (French, 'Departing for Syria')." In Susie Dent, ed., *Brewer's Dictionary of Phrase and Fable.* London: Chambers Harrap, 2012.

Provence, Michael. *Great Syrian Revolt*. Austin: University of Texas Press, 2005.

———. "Ottoman and French Mandate Land Registers for the Region of Damascus." *Middle East Studies Association Bulletin* 39, no. 1 (2005): 32–43.

Qundraq, Adib. *As-Suqlabiyah: History and Memory*. Damascus: Ekrema, 2001.

Rafeq, Abdul-Karim, Peter Sluglett, and Stefan Weber. *Syria and Bilad Al-Sham Under Ottoman Rule*. Leiden: Brill, 2010.

Reilly, James A. *A Small Town in Syria: Ottoman Hama in the Eighteenth and Nineteenth Centuries*. Oxford: Peter Lang Press, 2002.

Shehadeh, Lamia Rustum. "The Name of Syria in Ancient and Modern Usage." In Adel Beshara, ed., *The Origins of Syrian Nationhood: Histories, Pioneers and Identity*. London: Routledge, 2011.

Shields, Sarah. *Fezzes in the River: Identity Politics and European Diplomacy in the Middle East on the Eve of World War II*. Oxford: Oxford University Press, 2011.

Smeaton, Winifred I. G. *The Ghassanids*. Dissertation, University of Chicago, 1940.

Tauber, Eliezer. *The Formation of Modern Syria and Iraq*. Ilford, UK: Frank Cass, 1995.

Thompson, Elizabeth. *Colonial Citizens: Republican Rights, Paternal Privilege, and Gender in French Syria and Lebanon*. New York: Columbia University Press, 2000.

Wilson, Mary Christina. "Mandate Rule." Pp. 754–757 in Thomas Benjamin, ed., *Encyclopedia of Western Colonialism Since 1450*, vol. 2. Detroit: Macmillan Reference, 2007.

Yilmaz, Gulay. "Becoming a Devshirme: The Training of Conscripted Children in the Ottoman Empire." Pp. 119–134 in Gwyn Campbell, Suzanne Miers, and Joseph C. Miller, eds., *Children in Slavery Through the Ages*. Athens: Ohio University Press, 2009.

Watenpaugh, Keith D. *Being Modern in the Middle East: Revolution, Nationalism, Colonialism, and the Arab Middle Class*. Princeton, NJ: Princeton University Press, 2006.

Zachs, Fruma, and Sharon Halevi. *Gendering Culture in Greater Syria*. London: I. B. Tauris, 2015.

Zürcher, Erik Jan. "The Ottoman Conscription System in Theory and Practice, 1844–1918." *International Review of Social History* 43, no. 3 (1998): 437–449.

From Independence to Assad (Including the UAR)

Batatu, Hanna. *The Old Social Classes and the Revolutionary Movements of Iraq: A Study of Iraq's Old Landed and Commercial Classes and of Its Communists, Ba'thists, and Free Officers*. Princeton, NJ: Princeton University Press, 1978.

———. *Syria's Peasantry, the Descendants of Its Lesser Rural Notables, and Their Politics.* Princeton, NJ: Princeton University Press, 2012.

Ben-Hanan, Eli. *Our Man in Damascus: Elie Cohn.* Tel-Aviv: ADM, 1967.

Keilany, Ziad. "Land Reform in Syria." *Middle Eastern Studies* 16, no. 3 (1980): 209–224.

Krókowska, K. "The Fall of Democracy in Syria." *Perceptions* 16, no. 2 (2011): 81–98.

Lundgren Jörum, Emma. *Beyond Syria's Borders.* London: I. B. Tauris, 2014.

Mansfield, Peter. *Nasser's Egypt.* Baltimore: Penguin, 1965.

Martin, Kevin. "Presenting the 'True Face of Syria' to the World: Urban Disorder and Civilizational Anxieties at the First Damascus International Exposition." *International Journal of Middle East Studies* 42 (2010): 391–411.

Mufti, Malik. *Sovereign Creations: Pan-Arabism and Political Order in Syria and Iraq.* Ithaca, NY: Cornell University Press, 1996.

Rabinovich, Itamar. *Syria Under the Ba'th: 1963–66, The Army-Party Symbiosis.* Jerusalem: Israel Universities Press, and New Brunswick, NJ: Transaction Books, 1972.

Rathmell, Andrew. "Brotherly Enemies: The Rise and Fall of the Syrian-Egyptian Intelligence Axis, 1954–1967." *Intelligence and National Security* 13, no. 1 (1998): 230–253.

Vatikiotis, P. J. "Nasser's Second Revolution." *SAIS Review* 6, no. 3 (1962): 3.

Assad Years

Corrao, Francesca Maria, ed. *Le rivoluzioni arabe: La transizione mediterranea.* Milan: Mondadori Education, 2011.

Della Ratta, Donatella. *La fiction siriana: Mercato e political della television nell'era degli Asad.* Le monografie di Arab Media Report, no. 2. Rome: Arab Media Report, 2014.

Haddad, Bassam. *Business Networks in Syria: The Political Economy of Authoritarian Resilience.* Palo Alto, CA: Stanford University Press, 2011.

Halasa, Malu, Zaher Omareen, and Nawara Mahfoud, eds. *Syria Speaks: Art and Culture from the Frontline.* London: Saqi Books, 2014.

Heydemann, Steven. *Authoritarianism in Syria.* Ithaca, NY: Cornell University Press, 1999.

Hinnebusch, Raymond A. *Syria: Revolution from Above.* London: Routledge, 2001.

Lefevre, Raphael. *Ashes of Hama: The Muslim Brotherhood in Syria.* Oxford: Oxford University Press, 2013.

Perthes, Volker. "The Syrian Economy in the 1980s." *Middle East Journal* 46, no. 1 (1992): 37–58.

Rosiny, Stephan. "Power Sharing in Syria: Lessons from Lebanon's Taif Experience." *Middle East Policy* 20, no. 3 (2013): 41–55.

Seale, Patrick, and Maureen McConville. *Asad of Syria*. Berkeley: University of California Press, 1989.

Trombetta, Lorenzo. *Siria: Dagli ottoman agli Asad. E oltre*. Milan: Mondadori Education, 2013.

Van Dam, Nikolaos. *The Struggle for Power in Syria: Politics and Society Under Asad and the Ba'th Party*. London: I. B. Tauris, 2011.

Wedeen, Lisa. *Ambiguities of Domination: Politics, Rhetoric, and Symbols in Contemporary Syria*. Chicago: University of Chicago Press, 1999.

Yassin-Kassab, Robin, and Leila Al-Shami. *Burning Country: Syrians in Revolution and War*. London: Pluto Press, 2016.

Ziadeh, Radwan. *Power and Policy in Syria: Intelligence Services, Foreign Relations and Democracy in the Modern Middle East*. Library of Modern Middle East Studies. London: I. B. Tauris, 2012.

Zisser, Eyal. *Commanding Syria: Bashar al-Asad and the First Years in Power*. London: I. B. Tauris, 2007.

Damascus and the Archaeology of Syria

Al-Jabi, Zaki. "A Guide to Damascus." Damascus: Damascus Police Department, 1949.

Burns, Ross. *Damascus: A History*. London: Routledge, 2007.

———. *Monuments of Syria: A Guide*. London: I. B. Tauris, 2009.

Darke, Diana. *Syria*. Chalfont St. Peter, UK: Bradt Travel Guides, 2010.

De Miranda, Adriana. *Water Architecture in the Lands of Syria*. Rome: L'Erma di Bretschneider, 2007.

Harrison, Peter. *Castles of God*. Woodbridge, UK: Boydell Press, 2004.

Salamandra, Christa. *New Old Damascus: Authenticity and Distinction in Urban Syria*. Bloomington: Indiana University Press, 2004.

Samara, Yussof. *Damascus, Past and Present*. Damascus: Al Incha, n.d.

Syrian/Arab Jews

Aciman, André. *Out of Egypt: A Memoir*. New York: Farrar Straus and Giroux, 1994.

Lagnado, Lucette. *The Man in the White Sharkskin Suit: My Family's Exodus from Old Cairo to the New World*. New York: Ecco, 2007.

Shohat, Ella. "Dislocated Identities: Reflections of an Arab-Jew." *Movement Research: Performance Journal*, no. 5 (Fall-Winter 1992).

―――. "Rupture and Return: Zionist Discourse and the Study of Arab Jews." *Social Text* 21, no. 2 (2003): 49–74.

Sutton, Joseph. *Magic Carpet: Aleppo in Flatbush. The Story of a Unique Ethnic Jewish Community*. New York: Thayer-Jacoby, 1979.

Zenner, Walter P. *A Global Community: The Jews from Aleppo, Syria*. Detroit: Wayne State University Press, 2000.

ALIA MALEK is a journalist and civil rights lawyer. Born in Baltimore to Syrian immigrant parents, she began her legal career as a trial attorney at the US Department of Justice's Civil Rights Division. After working in the legal field in the United States, Lebanon, and the West Bank, Malek, who has degrees from Johns Hopkins and Georgetown universities, earned her master's degree in journalism from Columbia University. In April 2011 she moved to Damascus, Syria, and wrote anonymously for several outlets from inside the country as it began to disintegrate. In November 2013, she was honored with the Marie Colvin Award for her reporting from Syria. She returned to the United States in May 2013 for the launch of Al Jazeera America, where she was senior writer until October 2015. After her departure, she was a Puffin Foundation Writing Fellow at the Nation Institute and in residence at the MacDowell Colony. In 2016, she received the Hiett Prize in the Humanities. Malek is the author of *A Country Called Amreeka: US History Re-Told Through Arab American Lives* and editor of *Patriot Acts: Narratives of Post 9/11 Injustices*. With collaborators the Magnum Foundation and Al Liquindoi, Malek edited *EUROPA: An Illustrated Introduction to Europe for Migrants and Refugees*. Her reporting has appeared in the *New York Times*, *Foreign Policy*, the *Nation*, the *Christian Science Monitor*, *Jadaliyya*, *McSweeney's*, *Guernica*, and other publications.

The Nation Institute

NATION
BOOKS

Founded in 2000, **Nation Books** has become a leading voice in American independent publishing. The imprint's mission is to tell stories that inform and empower just as they inspire or entertain readers. We publish award-winning and bestselling journalists, thought leaders, whistleblowers, and truthtellers, and we are also committed to seeking out a new generation of emerging writers, particularly voices from underrepresented communities and writers from diverse backgrounds. As a publisher with a focused list, we work closely with all our authors to ensure that their books have broad and lasting impact. With each of our books we aim to constructively affect and amplify cultural and political discourse and to engender positive social change.

Nation Books is a project of The Nation Institute, a nonprofit media center established to extend the reach of democratic ideals and strengthen the independent press. The Nation Institute is home to a dynamic range of programs: the award-winning Investigative Fund, which supports groundbreaking investigative journalism; the widely read and syndicated website TomDispatch; journalism fellowships that support and cultivate over twenty-five emerging and high-profile reporters each year; and the Victor S. Navasky Internship Program.

For more information on Nation Books and The Nation Institute, please visit:

www.nationbooks.org
www.nationinstitute.org
www.facebook.com/nationbooks.ny
Twitter: @nationbooks